8

ANIMAL LAND

Makoto Raiku

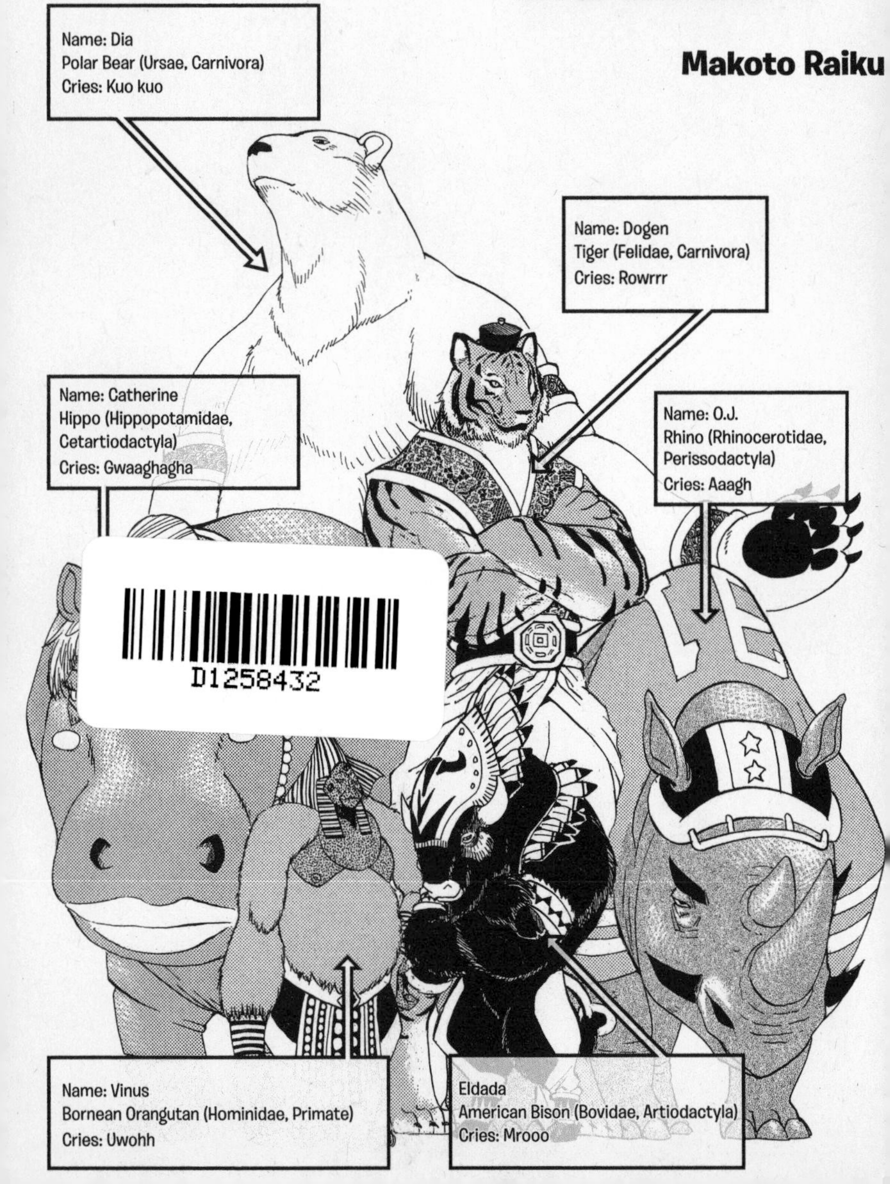

Name: Dia
Polar Bear (Ursae, Carnivora)
Cries: Kuo kuo
Name: Dogen
Tiger (Felidae, Carnivora)
Cries: Rowrrr
Name: Catherine
Hippo (Hippopotamidae, Cetartiodactyla)
Cries: Gwaaghagha
Name: O.J.
Rhino (Rhinocerotidae, Perissodactyla)
Cries: Aaagh
Name: Vinus
Bornean Orangutan (Hominidae, Primate)
Cries: Uwohh
Eldada
American Bison (Bovidae, Artiodactyla)
Cries: Mrooo

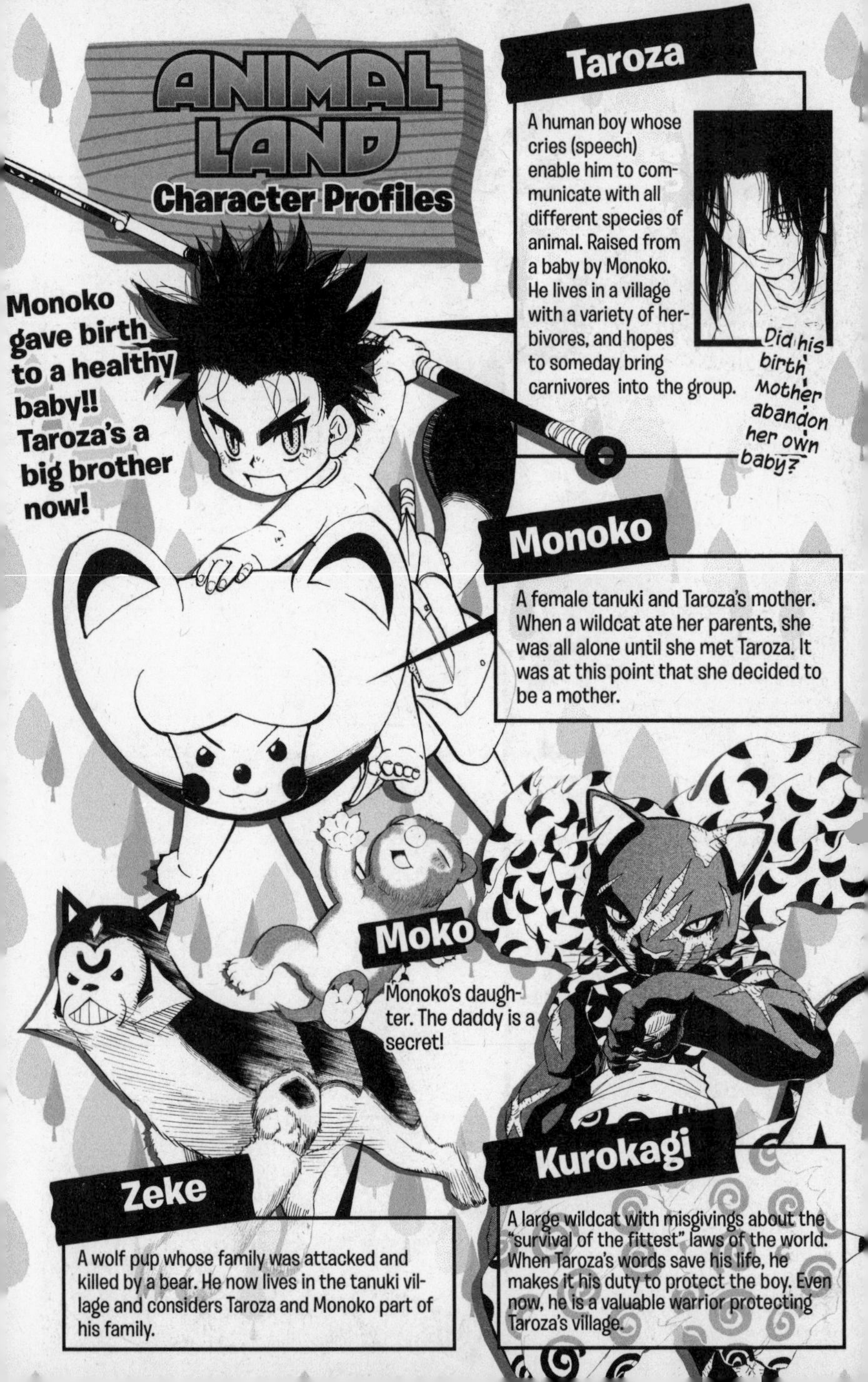
ANIMAL LAND
Character Profiles
Taroza
A human boy whose cries (speech) enable him to communicate with all different species of animal. Raised from a baby by Monoko. He lives in a village with a variety of herbivores, and hopes to someday bring carnivores into the group.
Did his birth mother abandon her own baby?
Monoko gave birth to a healthy baby!! Taroza's a big brother now!
Monoko
A female tanuki and Taroza's mother. When a wildcat ate her parents, she was all alone until she met Taroza. It was at this point that she decided to be a mother.
Moko
Monoko's daughter. The daddy is a secret!
Kurokagi
A large wildcat with misgivings about the "survival of the fittest" laws of the world. When Taroza's words save his life, he makes it his duty to protect the boy. Even now, he is a valuable warrior protecting Taroza's village.
Zeke
A wolf pup whose family was attacked and killed by a bear. He now lives in the tanuki village and considers Taroza and Monoko part of his family.

Jyu

A boy who wanders Animal Land with his carnivorous companion, Olivia. He believes animals are meant to kill one another, and hates Taroza's ideal of every animal living together in peace.

Giller

He seems to be hanging around the Tower of Babel, but his identity is a mystery... He leads an army of his creepy chimeras in an attack on Gene Grail, and steals Quo's notebook from Riemu.

Capri

A human girl raised by a pride of lions. A carnivorous girl who thought all herbivores were "prey" until she met and befriended Taroza and his group. Now she won't eat herbivores who are her friends!

Chimera

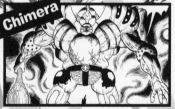

Mysterious monsters under Giller's control.

Riemu

A girl raised by gorillas, she has lived in Taroza's village ever since her paradise home of Gene Grail was attacked by Giller and her gorilla family was slaughtered. She owns a notebook left behind by Quo.

In the previous volume...

Giller stole Quo's notebook from Riemu, but unbeknownst to him, there was actually another secret notebook! In that book, Quo had written down the means to help all animals live together in peace, meant for the eyes of five children: Taroza, Riemu, Capri, Jyu, and Giller. But Riemu is afraid, because the notebook Giller stole contains the secrets of forbidden biotechnology. It says that the chimeras were one of the animals that Quo created in the course of his research... What kind of world was Quo envisioning?

Quo

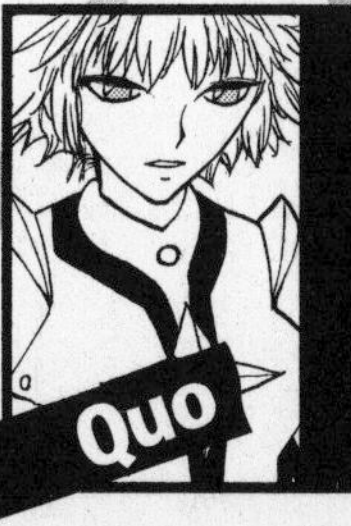

A human who lived before Taroza and the other children. He wrote down his method to bring all animals together in peace in a notebook. For some reason, he jotted down the names of the five kids with the description of "the miracle children"...

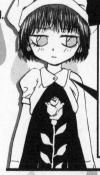

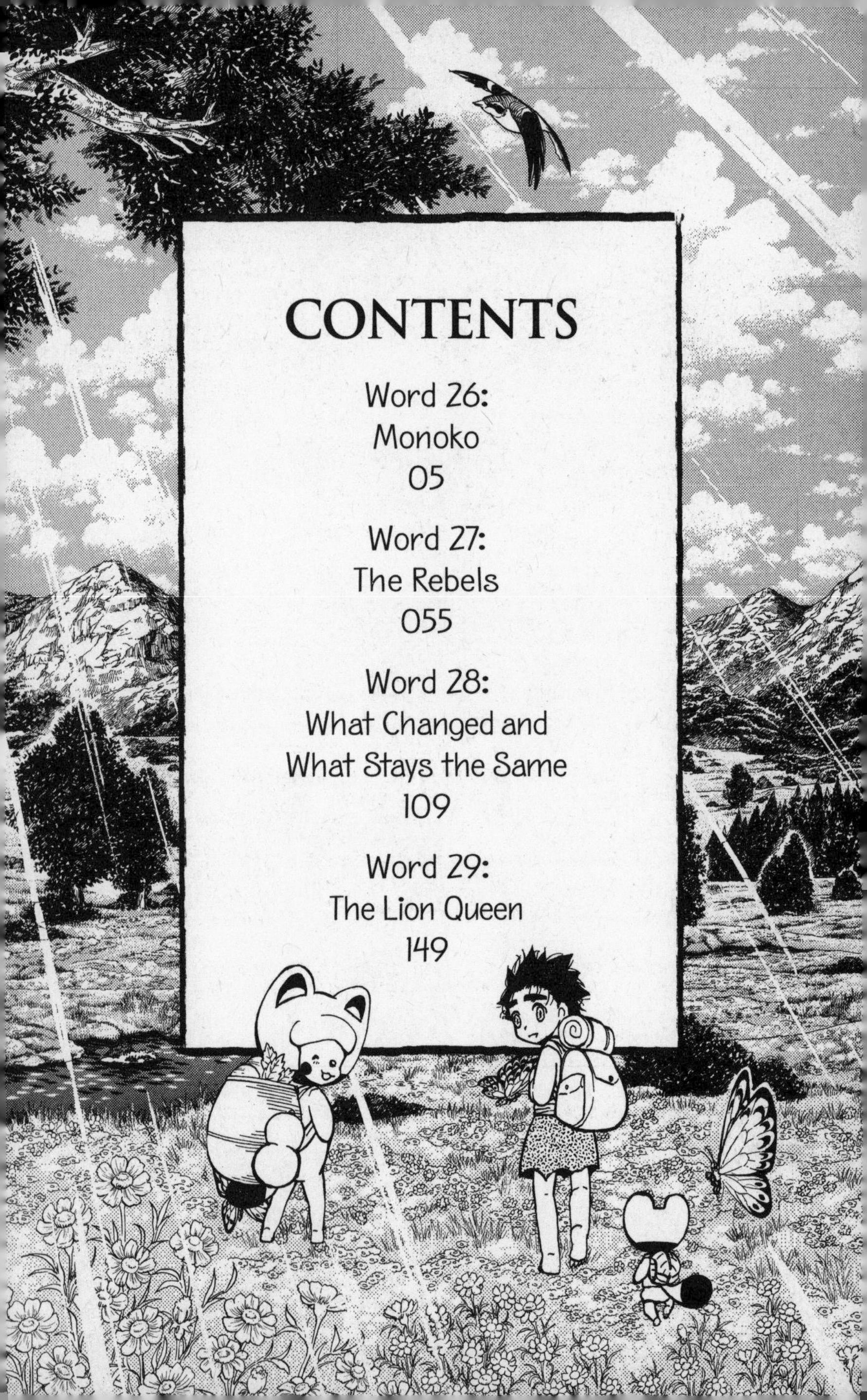

CONTENTS

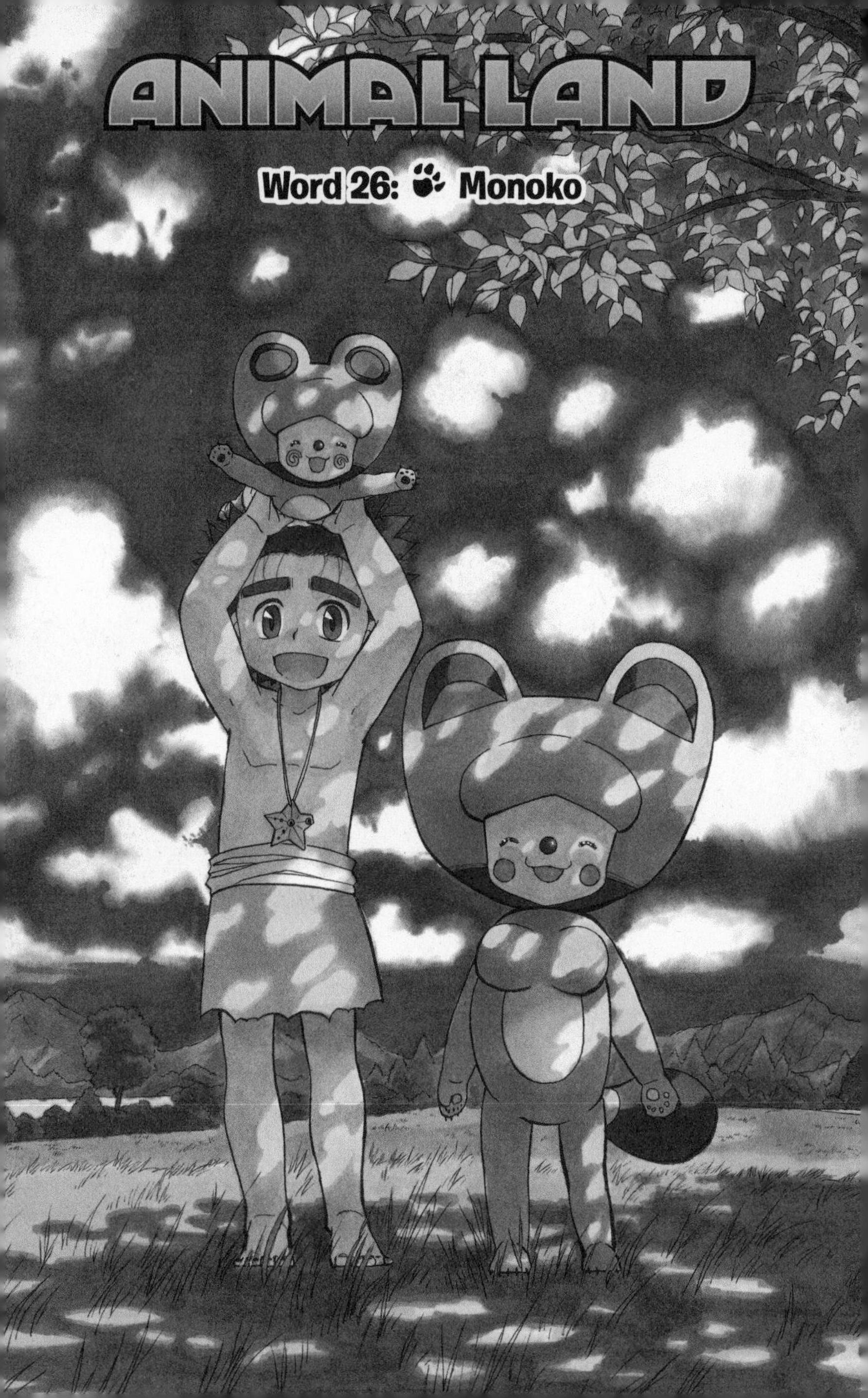
ANIMAL LAND
Word 26: Monoko

ANIMAL
LAND

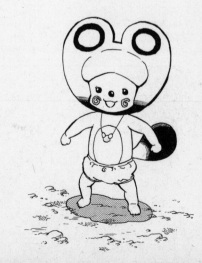

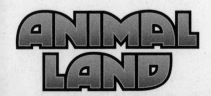

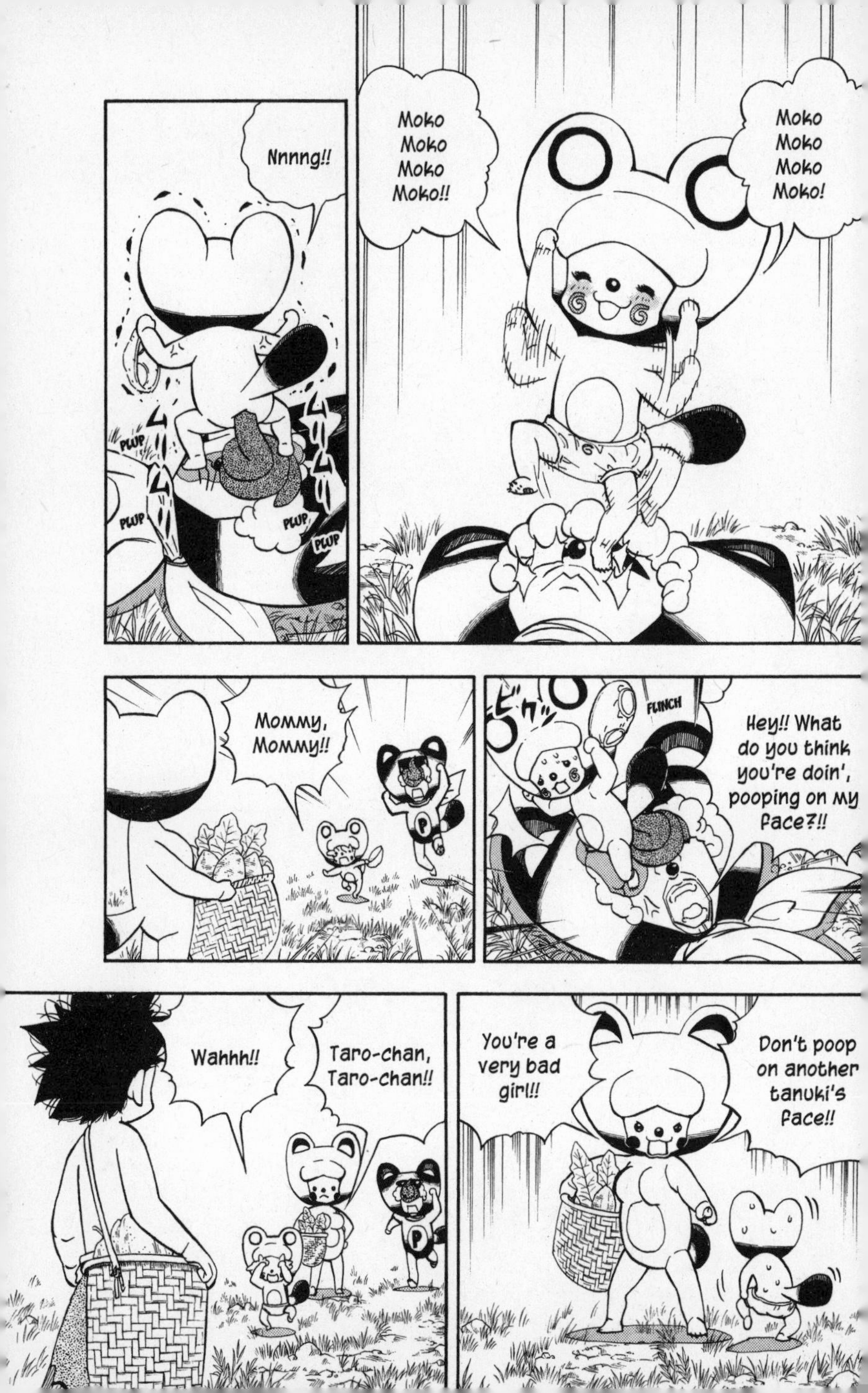
Moko Moko Moko Moko!
Moko Moko Moko Moko!!
Nnnng!!
PLUP
PLUP
PLUP
PLUP
FLINCH
Hey!! What do you think you're doin', pooping on my face?!!
Mommy, Mommy!!
Don't poop on another tanuki's face!!
You're a very bad girl!!
Taro-chan, Taro-chan!!
Wahhh!!

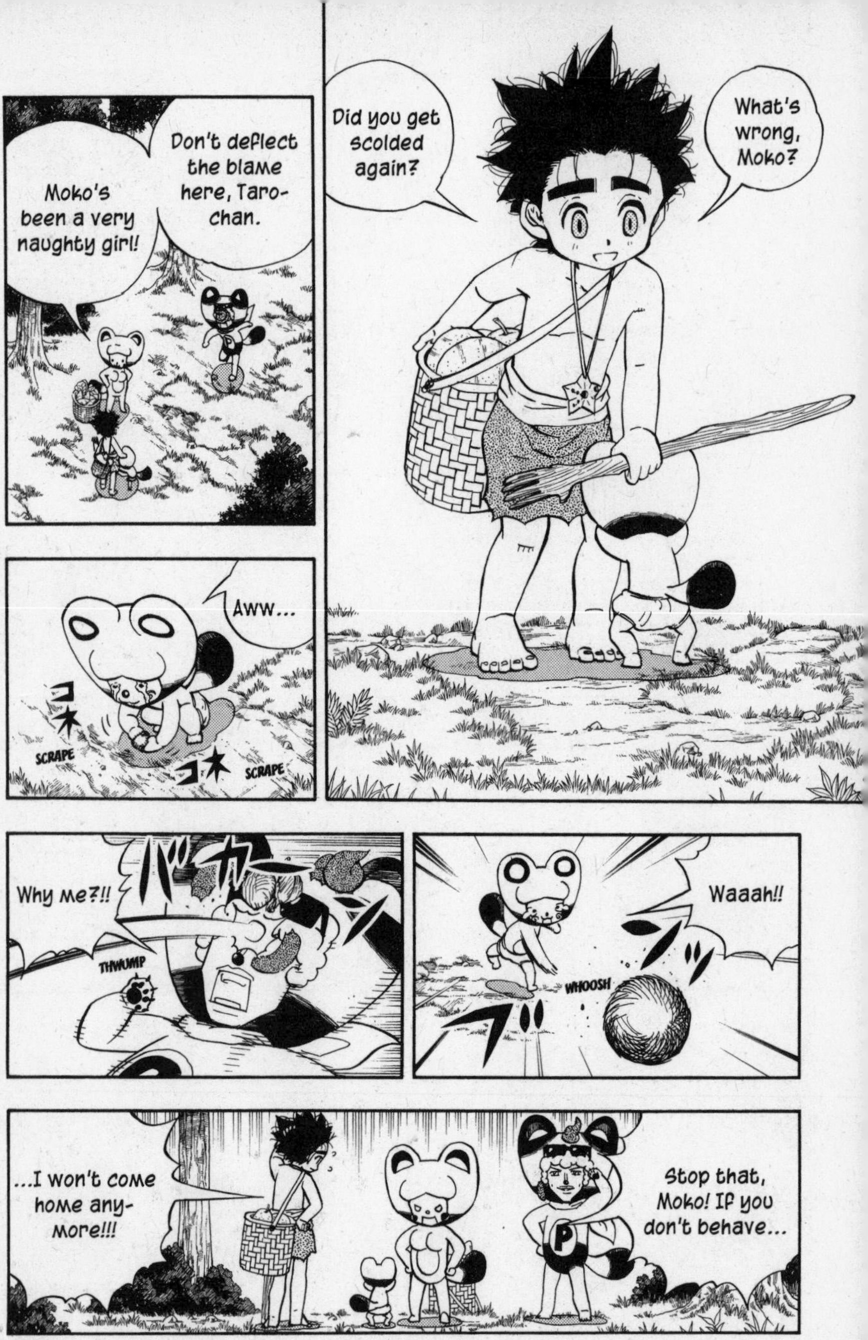
What's wrong, Moko?
Did you get scolded again?
Don't deflect the blame here, Taro-chan.
Moko's been a very naughty girl!
Aww...
SCRAPE
SCRAPE
Waaah!!
WHOOSH
Why me?!!
THWUMP
Stop that, Moko! If you don't behave...
...I won't come home any-more!!!

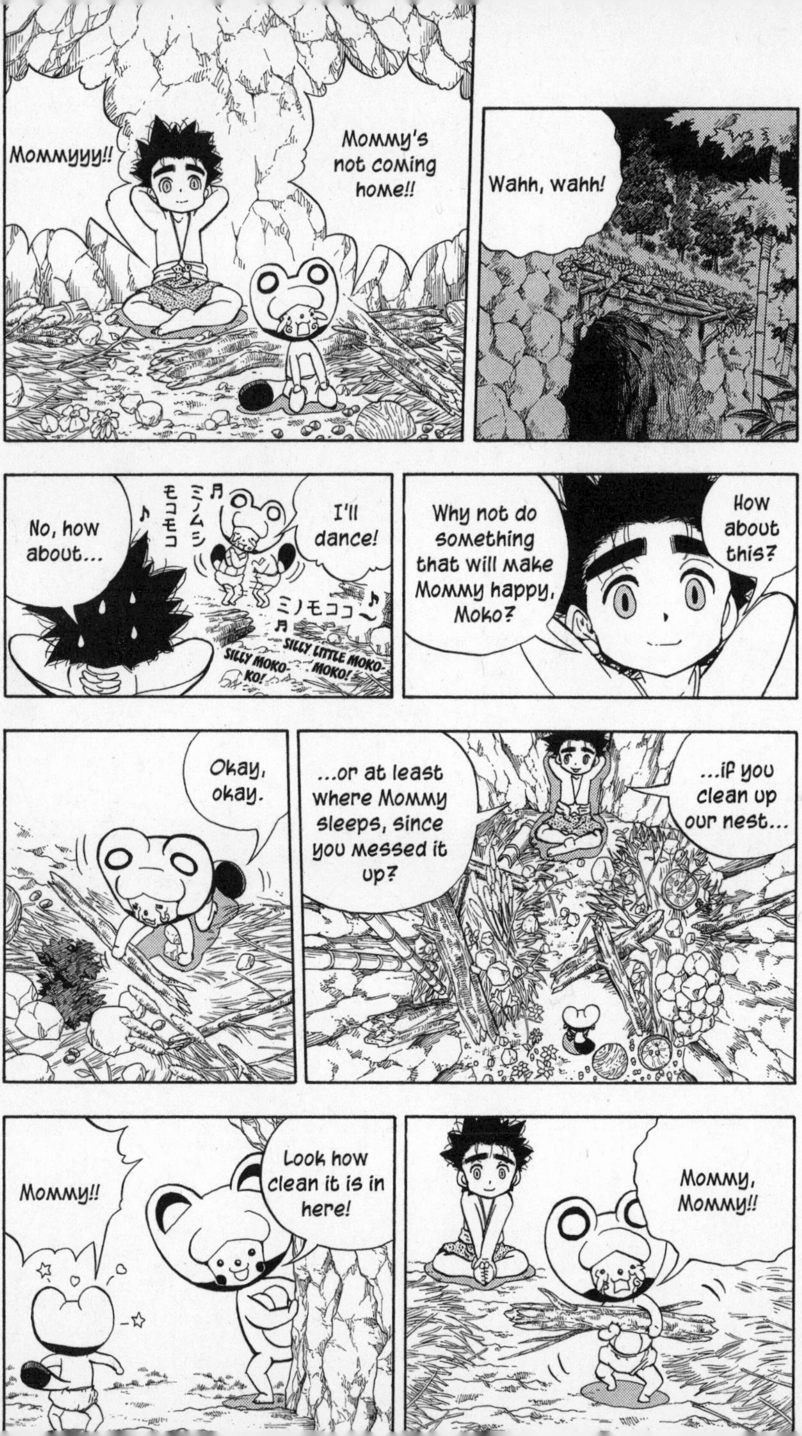
Wahh, wahh!
Mommy's not coming home!!
Mommyyy!!
How about this?
Why not do something that will make Mommy happy, Moko?
I'll dance!
ミノムシ モコモコ ♪
ミノモココ ♪
SILLY LITTLE MOKO-MOKO!
SILLY MOKO-KO!
No, how about...
...if you clean up our nest...
...or at least where Mommy sleeps, since you messed it up?
Okay, okay.
Mommy, Mommy!!
Look how clean it is in here!
Mommy!!

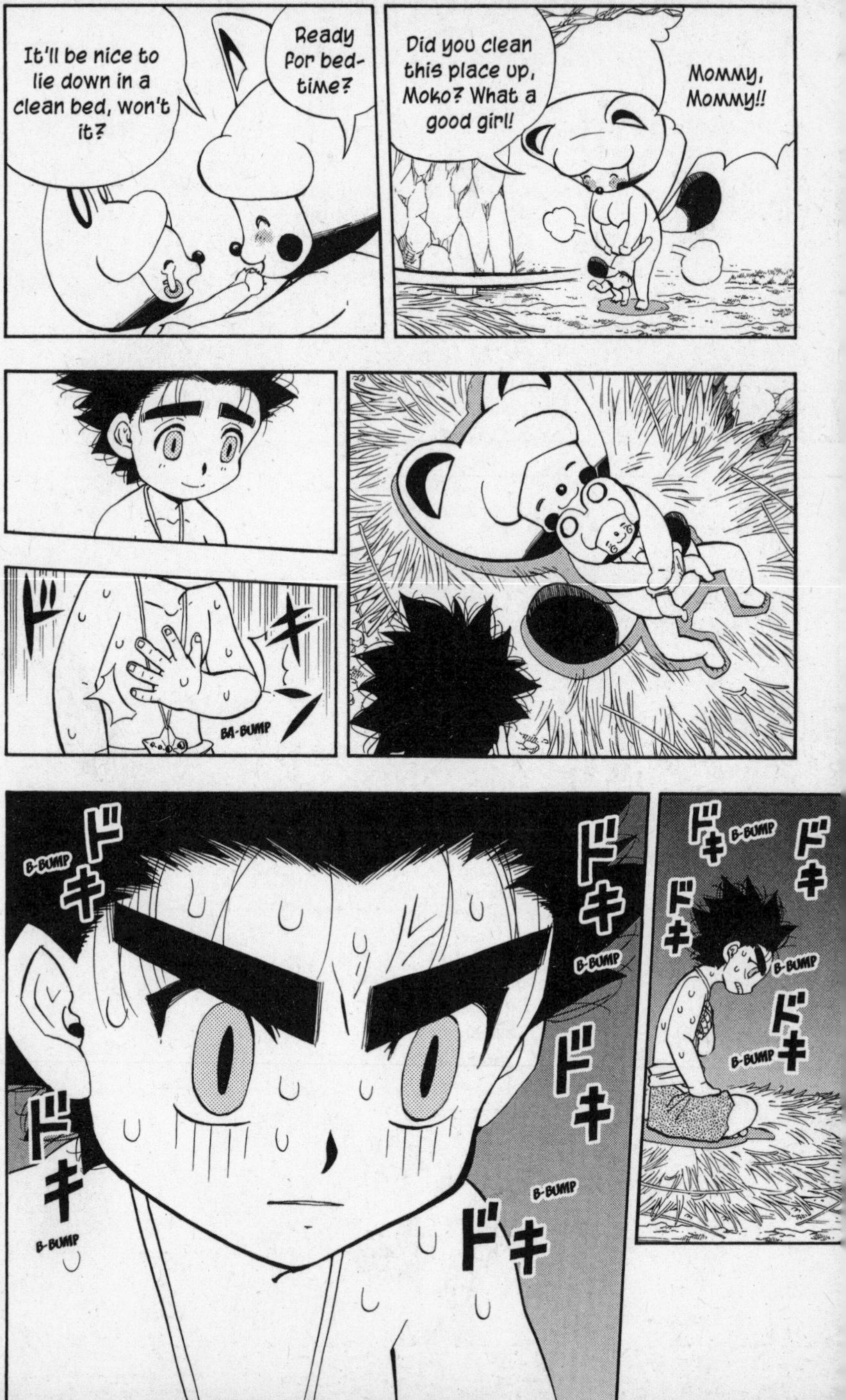
Mommy, Mommy!!
Did you clean this place up, Moko? What a good girl!
Ready for bed-time?
It'll be nice to lie down in a clean bed, won't it?
ドキ
BA-BUMP
ドキ
B-BUMP
ドキ
B-BUMP
ドキ
B-BUMP
ドキ
B-BUMP
ドキ
B-BUMP
ドキ
B-BUMP
ドキ
B-BUMP
ドキ
B-BUMP

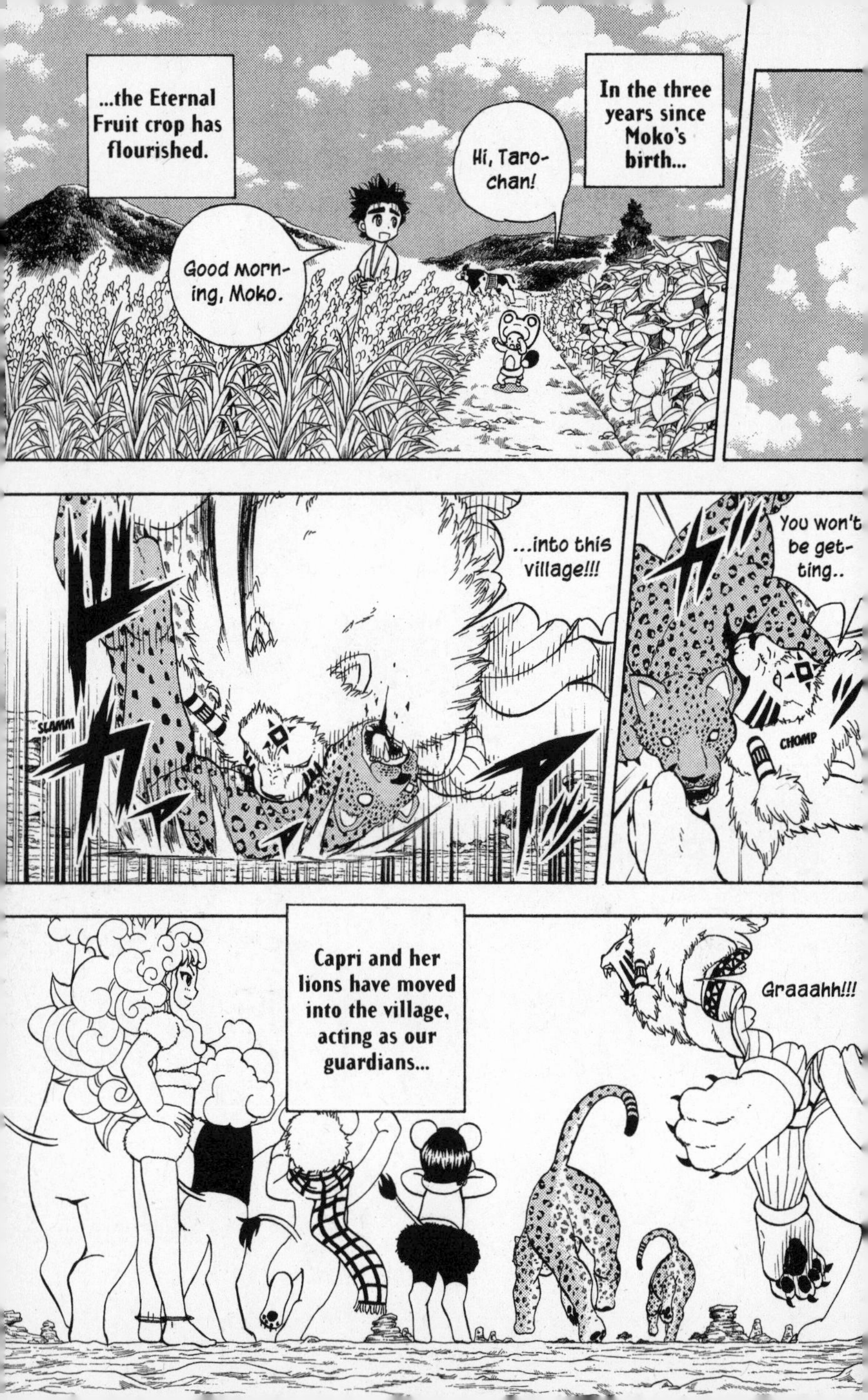
In the three years since Moko's birth...
Hi, Taro-chan!
...the Eternal Fruit crop has flourished.
Good Morning, Moko.
You won't be getting..
CHOMP
...into this village!!!
SLAMM
Graaahh!!!
Capri and her lions have moved into the village, acting as our guardians...

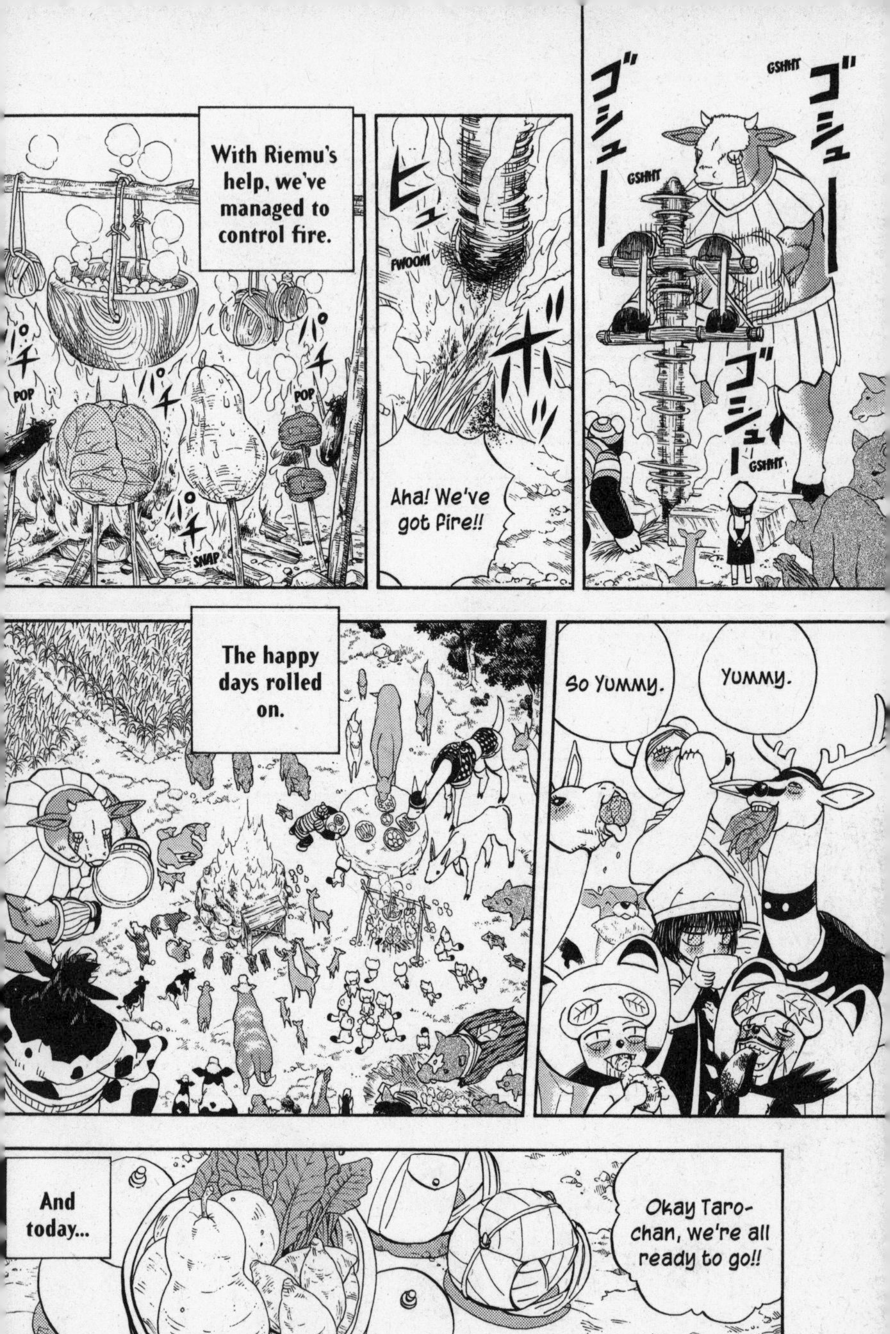
ゴシュー
GSHHT
ゴシュー
GSHHT
GSHHT
ゴシュー
ヒュ
FWOOM
ボッ
Aha! We've got fire!!
With Riemu's help, we've managed to control fire.
パチ
POP
パチ
POP
パチ
SNAP
Yummy.
So yummy.
The happy days rolled on.
Okay Taro-chan, we're all ready to go!!
And today...

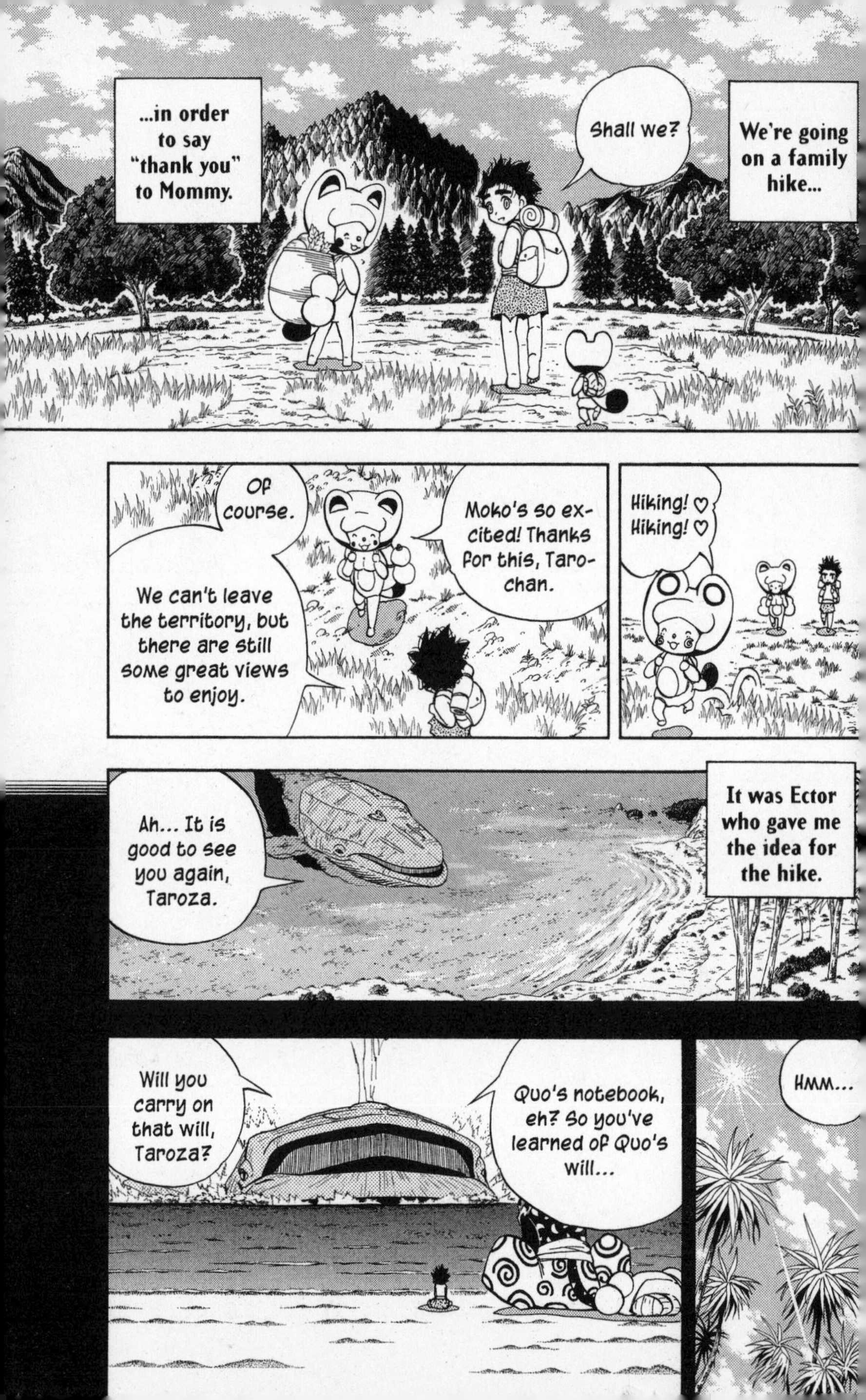
We're going on a family hike...
Shall we?
...in order to say "thank you" to Mommy.
Hiking! ♡ Hiking! ♡
Moko's so excited! Thanks for this, Taro-chan.
Of course.
We can't leave the territory, but there are still some great views to enjoy.
It was Ector who gave me the idea for the hike.
Ah... It is good to see you again, Taroza.
HMM...
Quo's notebook, eh? So you've learned of Quo's will...
Will you carry on that will, Taroza?

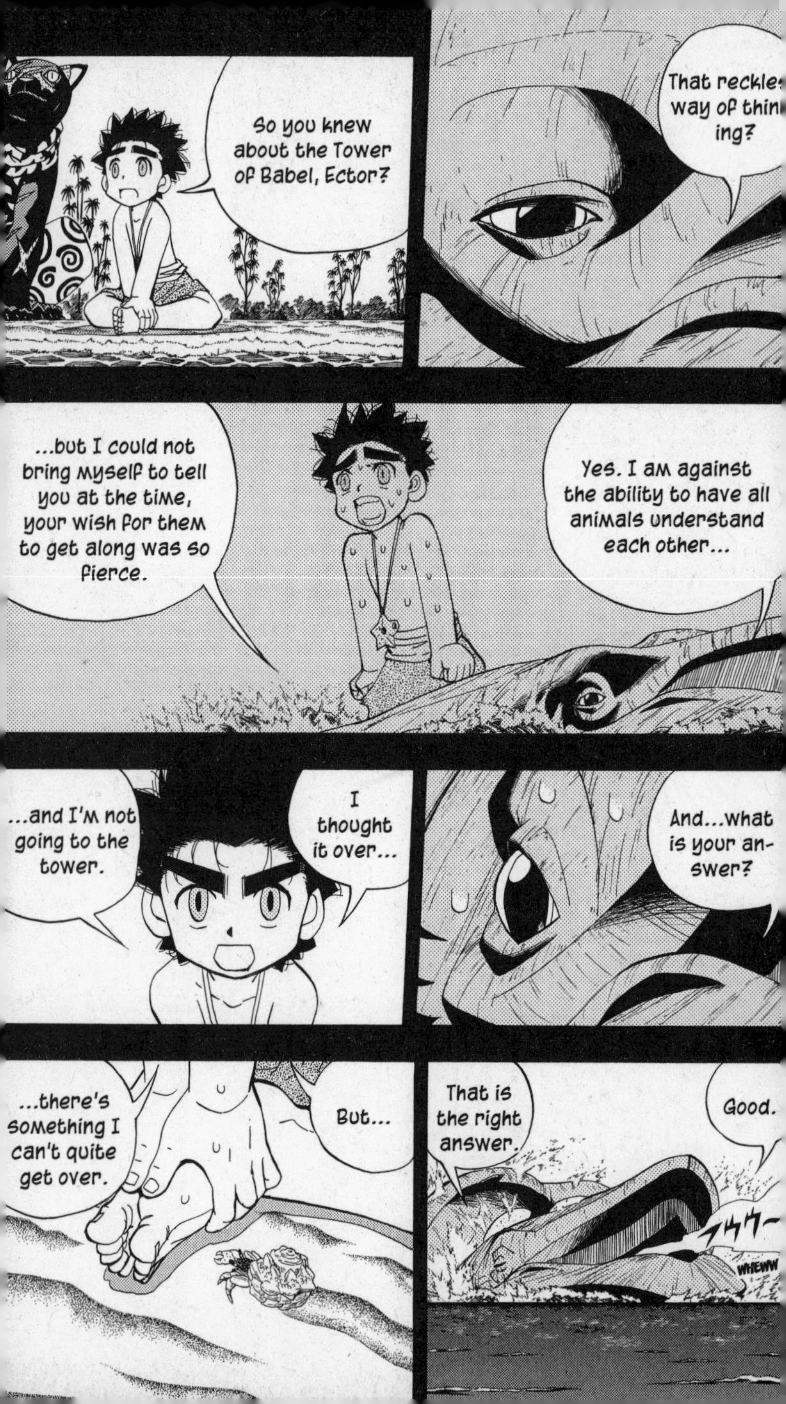
That reckle way of thin ing?
So you knew about the Tower of Babel, Ector?
Yes. I am against the ability to have all animals understand each other...
...but I could not bring myself to tell you at the time, your wish for them to get along was so fierce.
And...what is your answer?
I thought it over...
...and I'm not going to the tower.
Good.
That is the right answer.
WHEWW
But...
...there's something I can't quite get over.

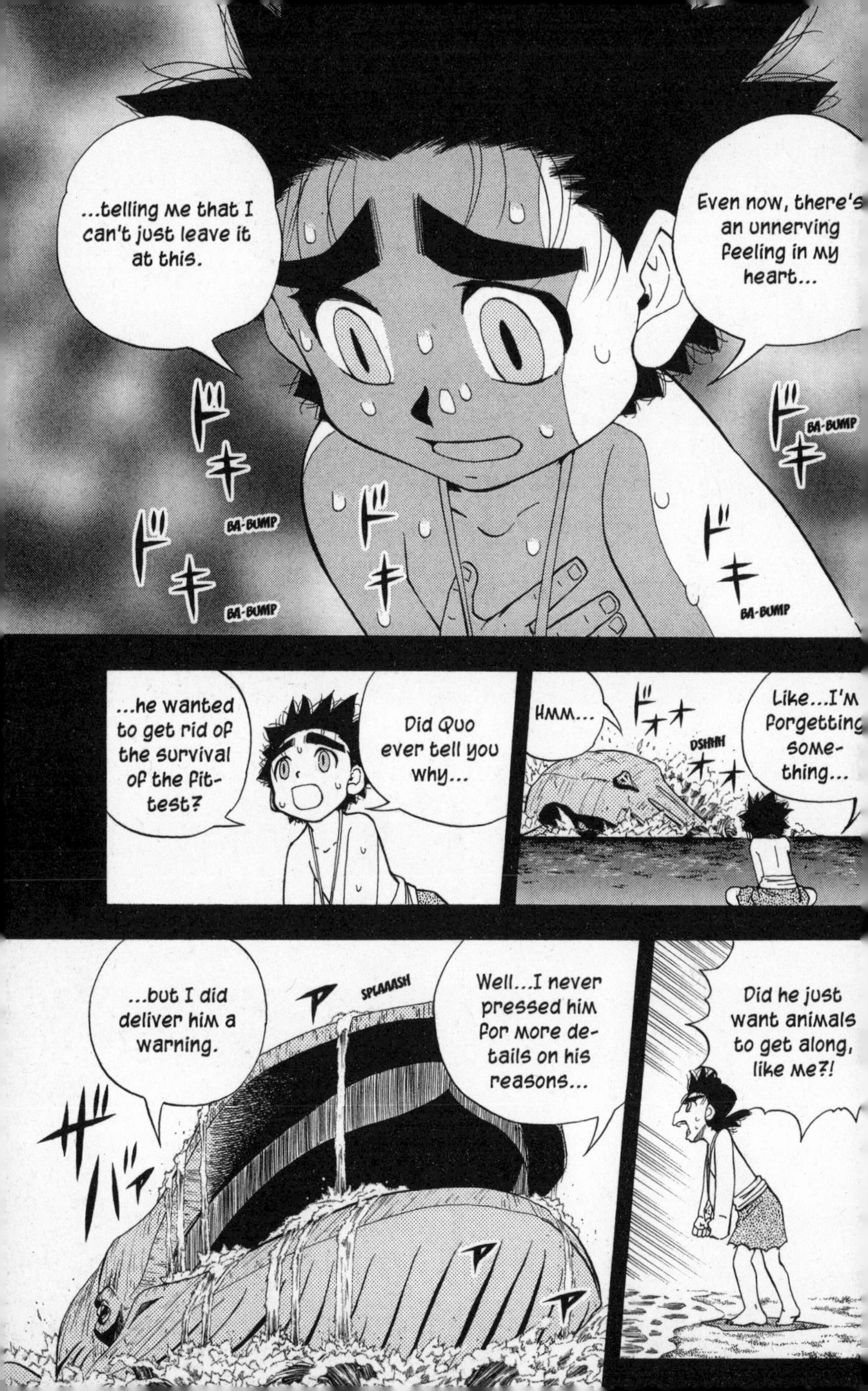
Even now, there's an unnerving feeling in my heart...
...telling me that I can't just leave it at this.
BA-BUMP
BA-BUMP
BA-BUMP
BA-BUMP
Like...I'm forgetting some-thing...
DSHHH
HMM...
Did Quo ever tell you why...
...he wanted to get rid of the survival of the fit-test?
Did he just want animals to get along, like me?!
Well...I never pressed him for more de-tails on his reasons...
SPLAAASH
...but I did deliver him a warning.

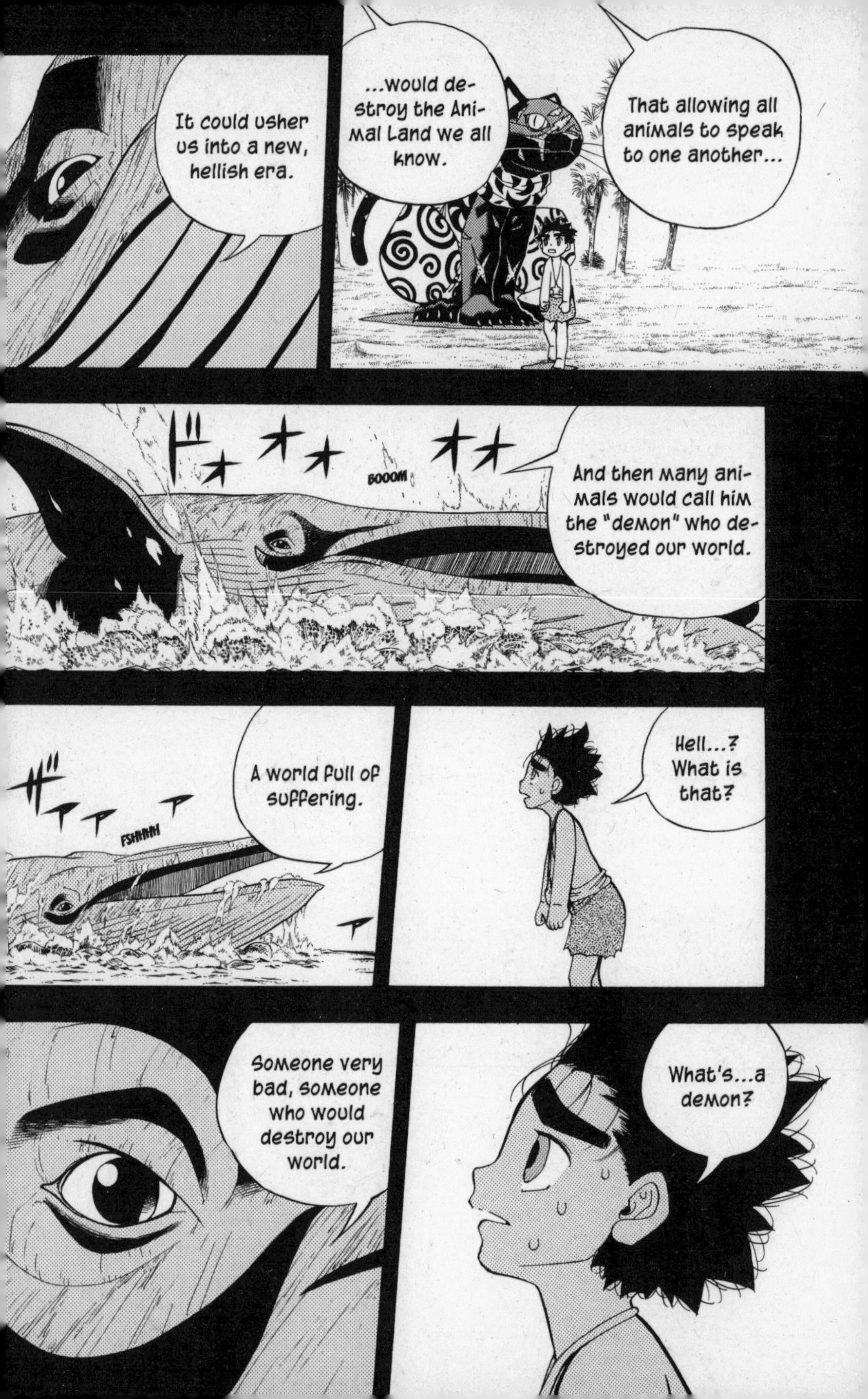
That allowing all animals to speak to one another...
...would destroy the Animal Land we all know.
It could usher us into a new, hellish era.
And then many animals would call him the "demon" who destroyed our world.
BOOOM
Hell...? What is that?
A world full of suffering.
FSHHHH
What's...a demon?
Someone very bad, someone who would destroy our world.

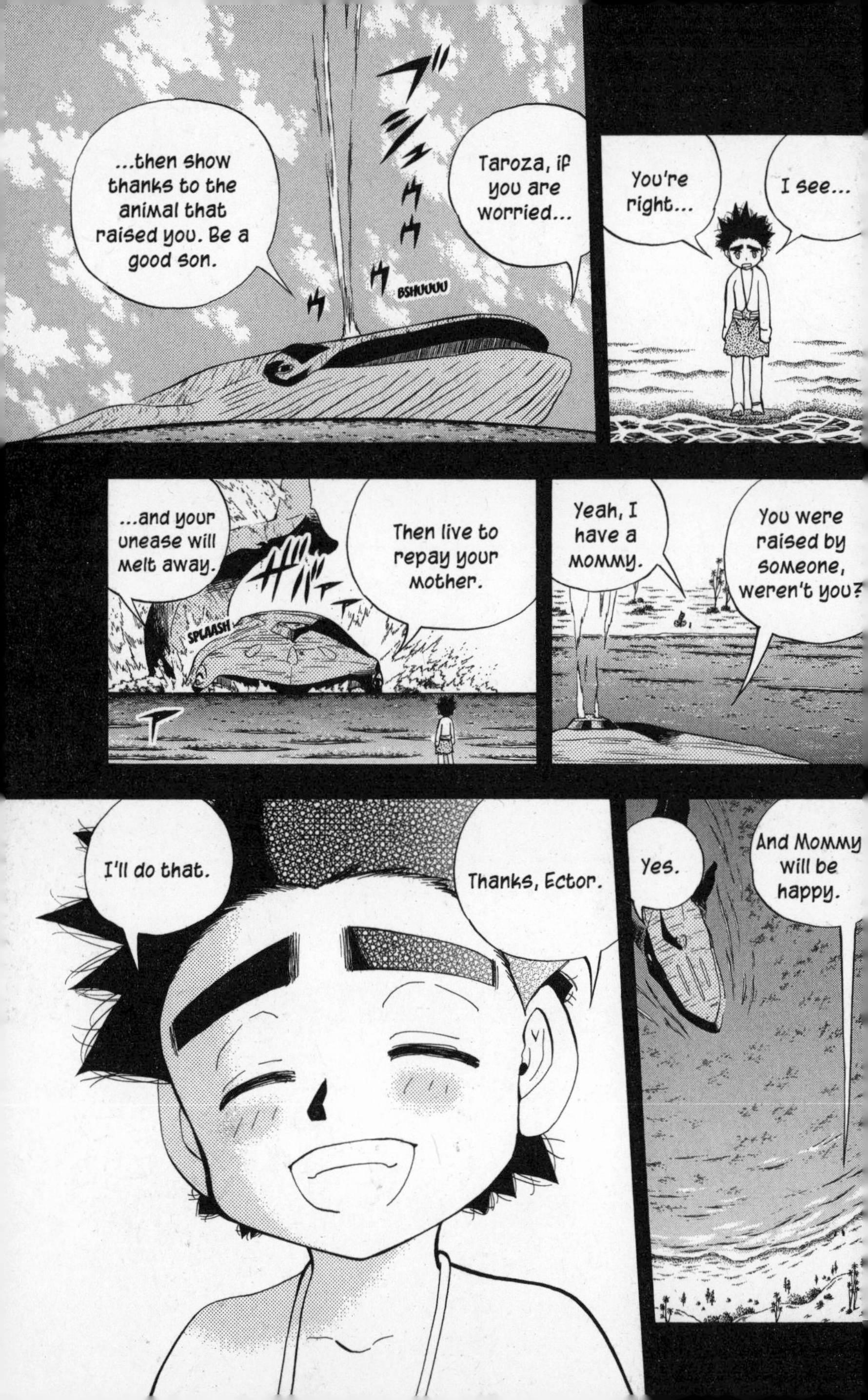
I see...
You're right...
Taroza, if you are worried...
...then show thanks to the animal that raised you. Be a good son.
BSHUUUU
You were raised by someone, weren't you?
Yeah, I have a mommy.
Then live to repay your mother.
...and your unease will melt away.
SPLAASH
And Mommy will be happy.
Yes.
Thanks, Ector.
I'll do that.

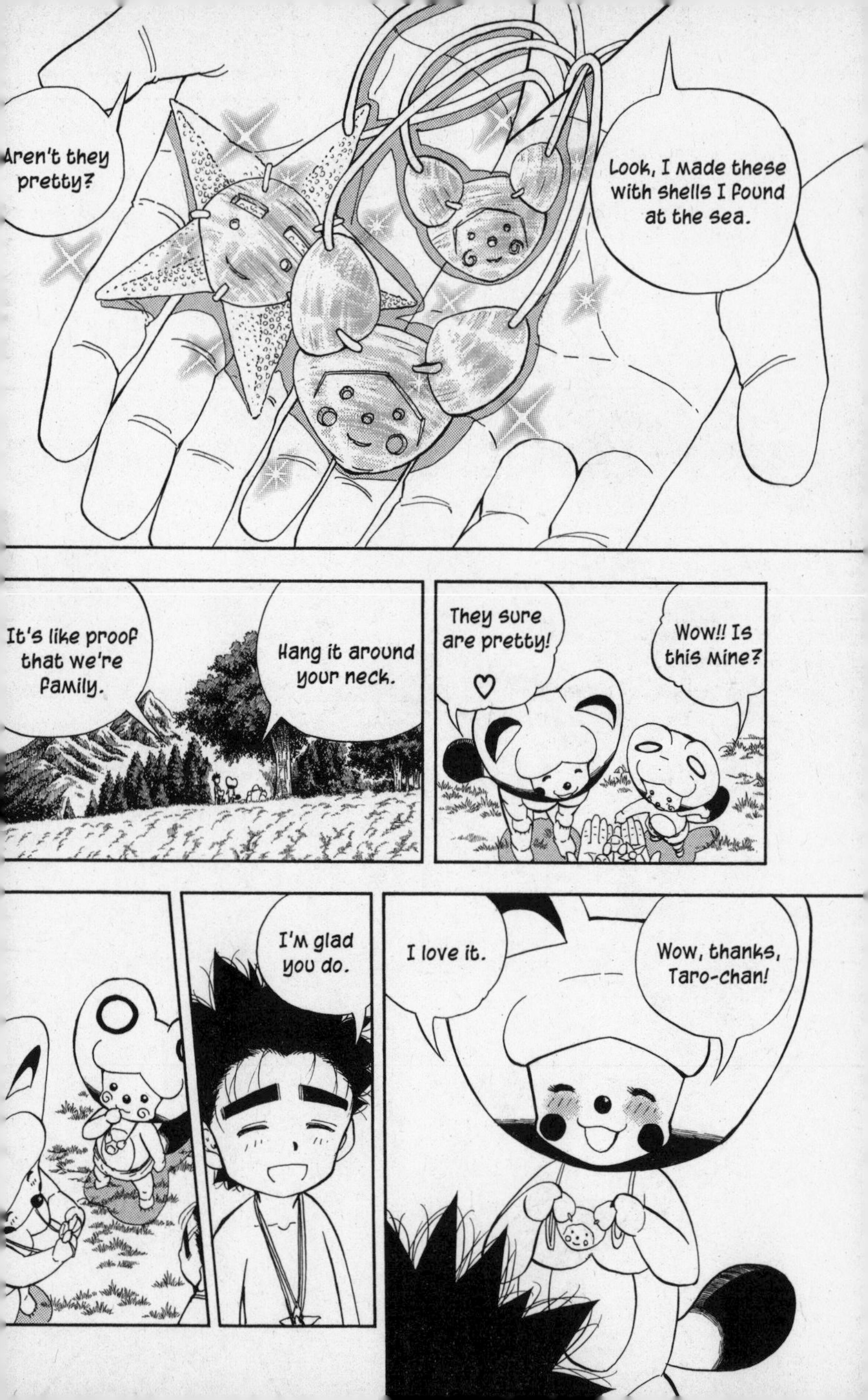
Look, I made these with shells I found at the sea.
Aren't they pretty?
Wow!! Is this mine?
They sure are pretty!
Hang it around your neck.
It's like proof that we're family.
Wow, thanks, Taro-chan!
I love it.
I'm glad you do.

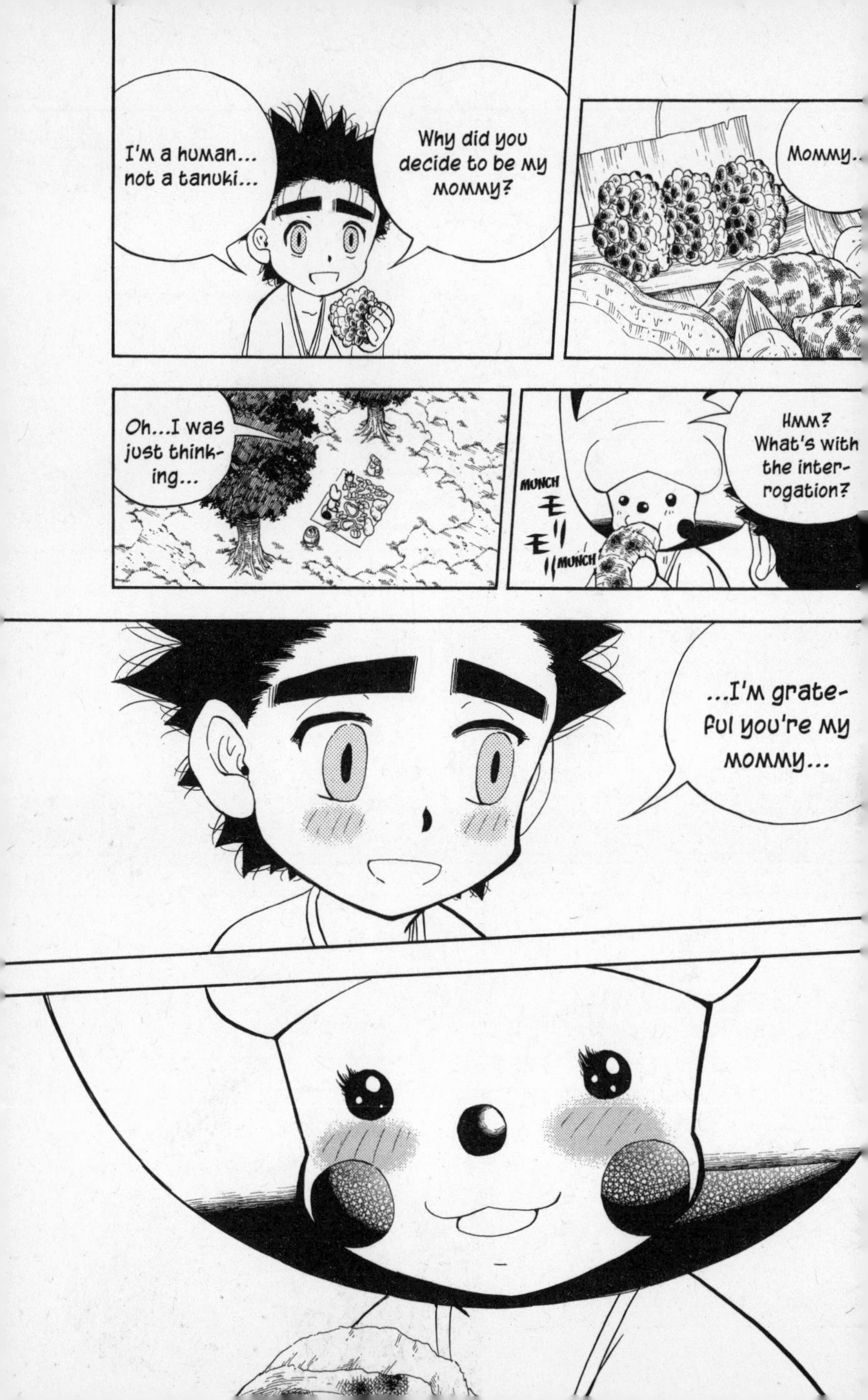
Mommy...
Why did you decide to be my mommy?
I'm a human... not a tanuki...
Hmm? What's with the inter-rogation?
MUNCH
MUNCH
Oh...I was just think-ing...
...I'm grate-ful you're my mommy...

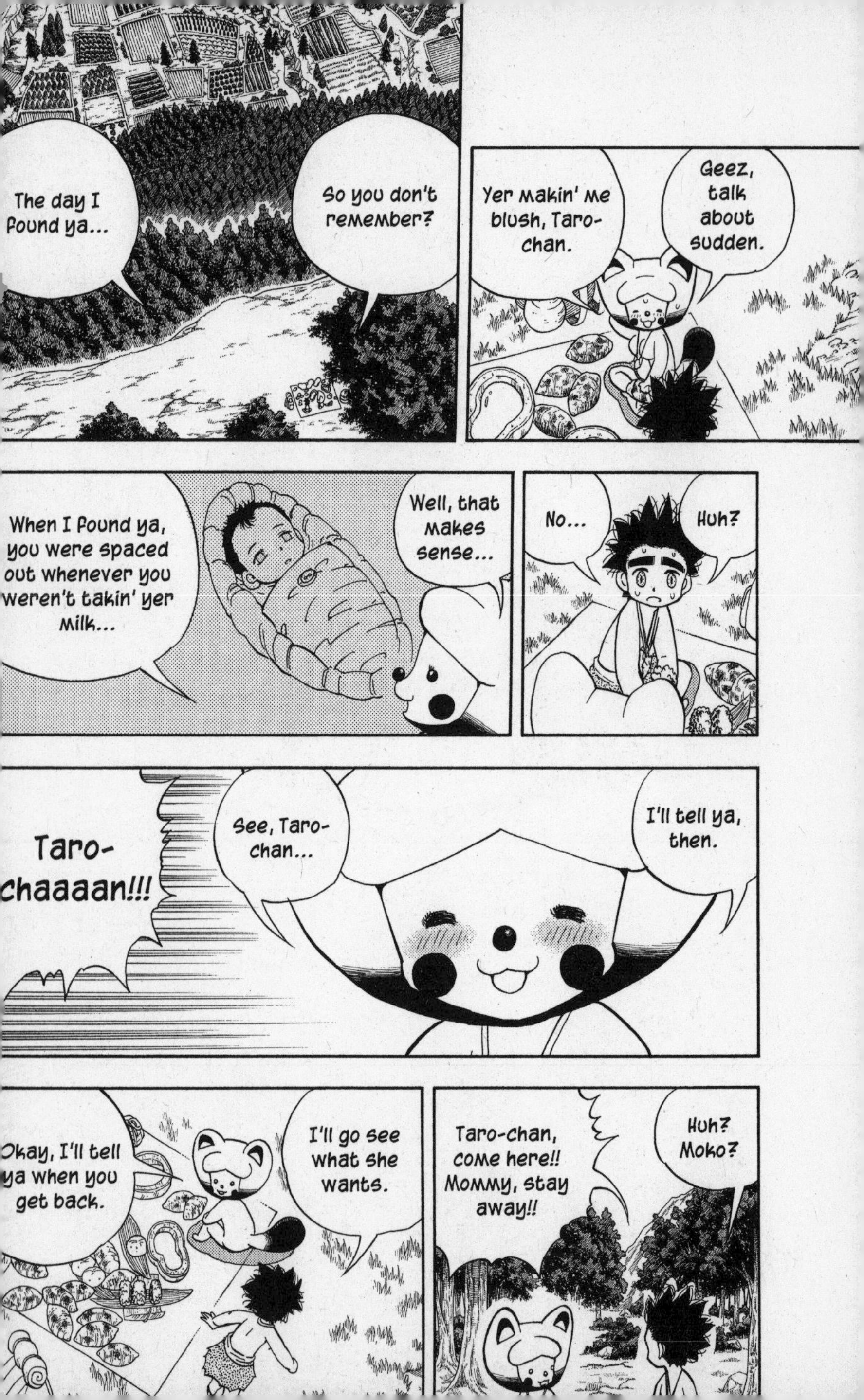
Geez, talk about sudden.
Yer makin' me blush, Taro-chan.
So you don't remember?
The day I found ya...
Huh?
No...
Well, that makes sense...
When I found ya, you were spaced out whenever you weren't takin' yer milk...
I'll tell ya, then.
See, Taro-chan...
Taro-chaaaan!!!
Huh? Moko?
Taro-chan, come here!! Mommy, stay away!!
I'll go see what she wants.
Okay, I'll tell ya when you get back.

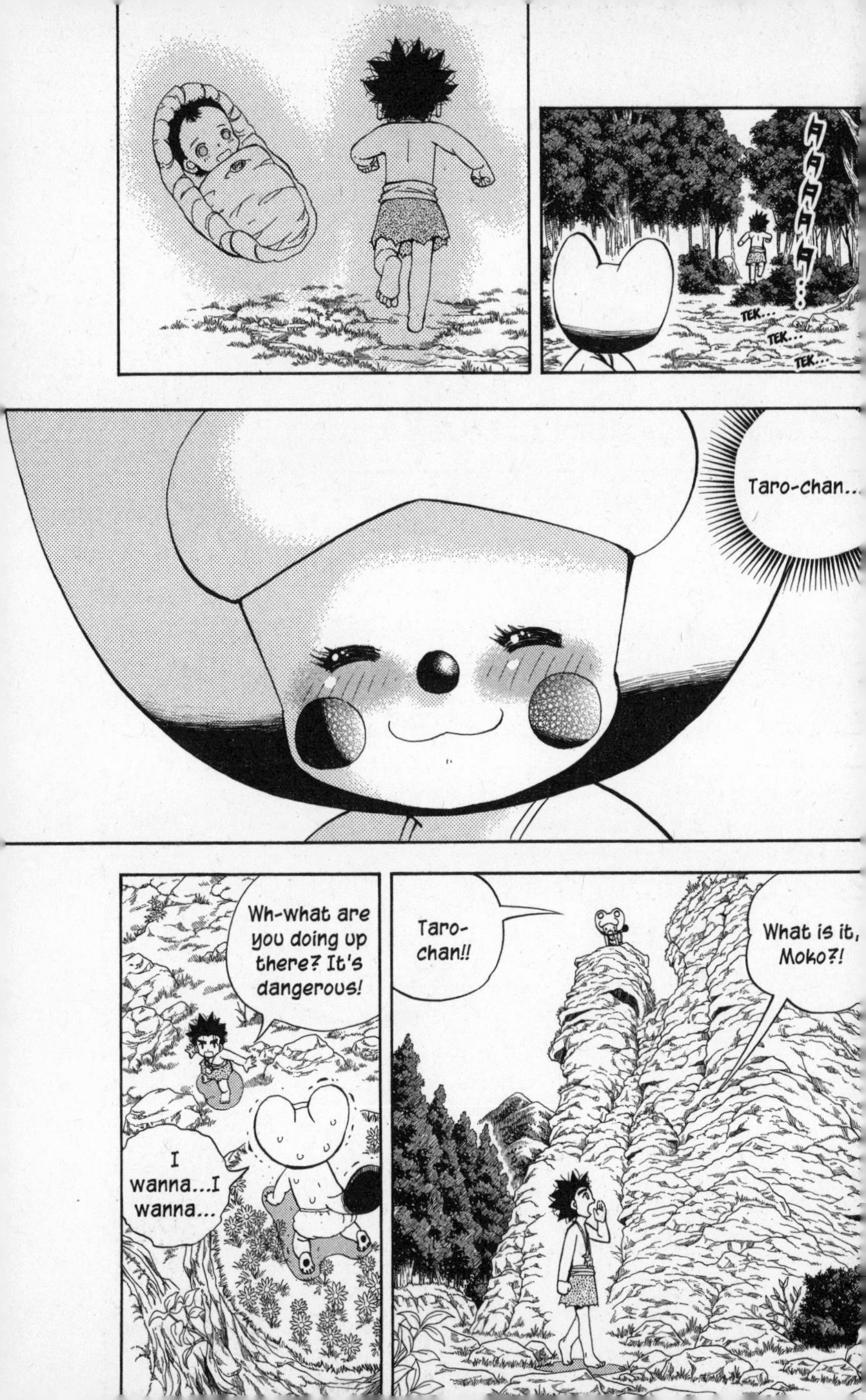

タタタタタ…
TEK...
TEK...
TEK...
Taro-chan...
What is it, Moko?!
Taro-chan!!
Wh-what are you doing up there? It's dangerous!
I wanna...I wanna...

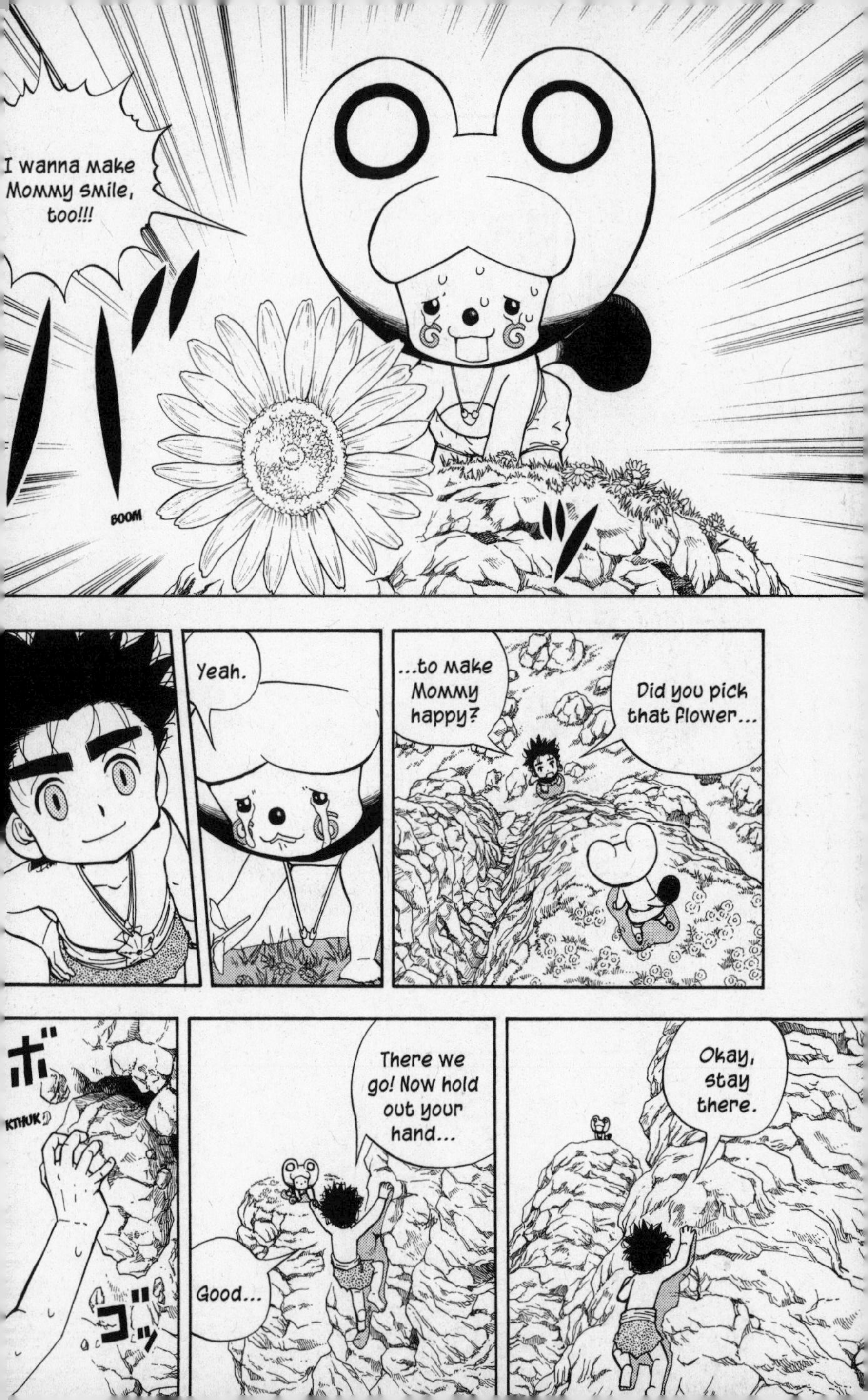
I wanna make Mommy smile, too!!!
BOOM
Did you pick that flower...
...to make Mommy happy?
Yeah.
Okay, stay there.
There we go! Now hold out your hand...
Good...
ボ
KTHUK
ゴッ

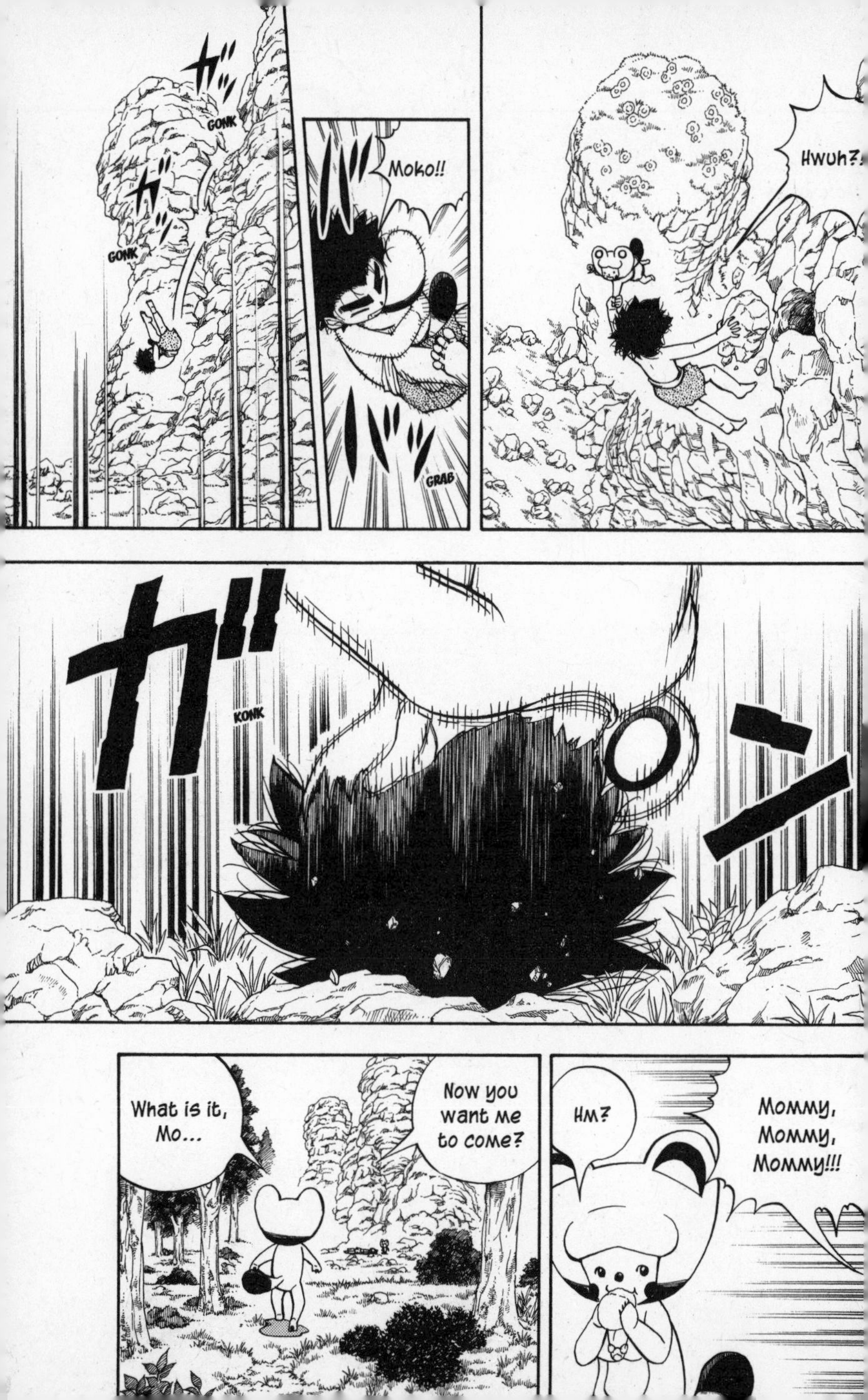

Hwuh?!
Moko!!
GRAB
GONK
GONK
KONK
Mommy, Mommy, Mommy!!!
Hm?
Now you want me to come?
What is it, Mo...

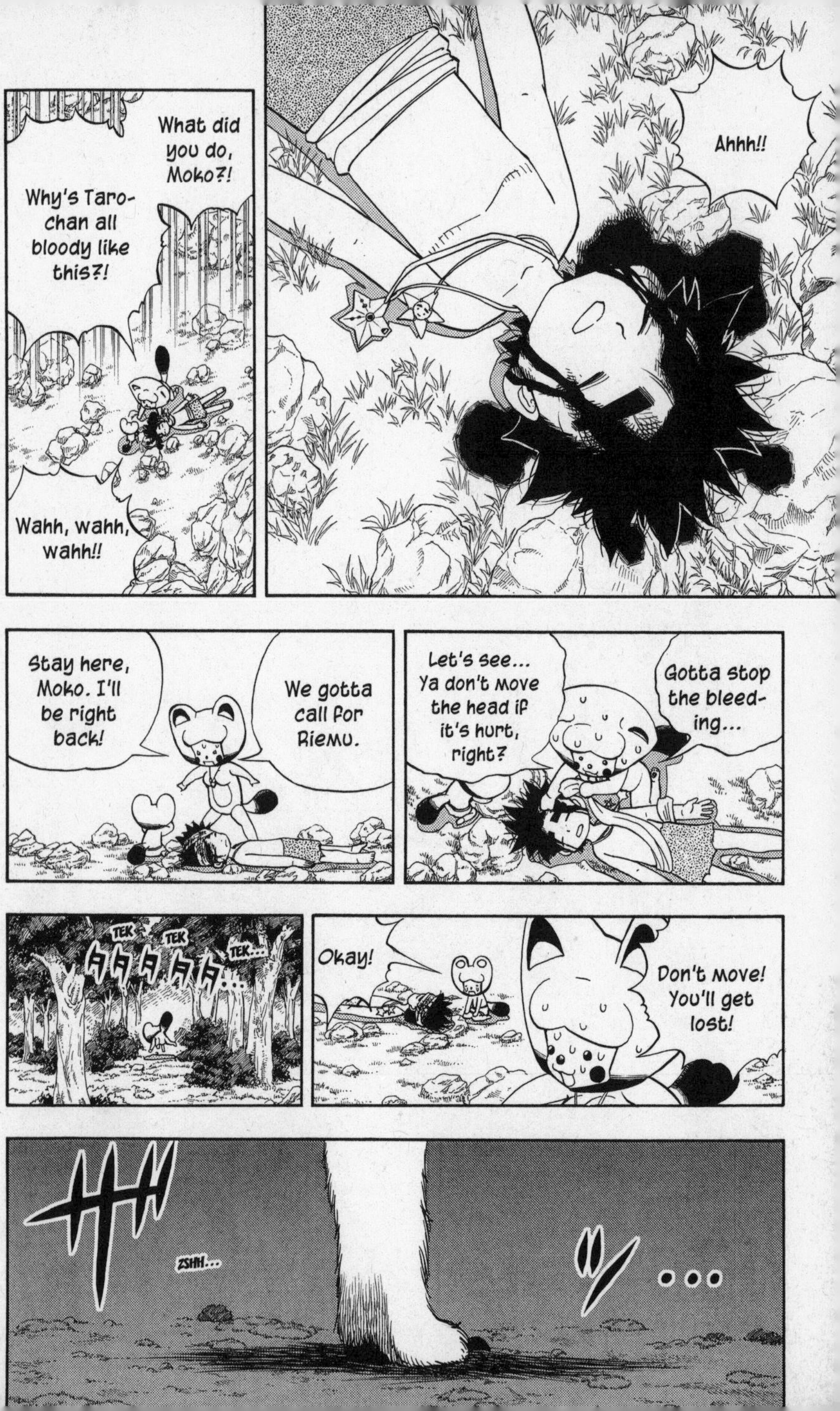

Ahhh!!
What did you do, Moko?!
Why's Taro-chan all bloody like this?!
Wahh, wahh, wahh!!
Gotta stop the bleed-ing...
Let's see... Ya don't move the head if it's hurt, right?
We gotta call for Riemu.
Stay here, Moko. I'll be right back!
Don't move! You'll get lost!
Okay!
TEK
TEK
TEK...
ZSHH...

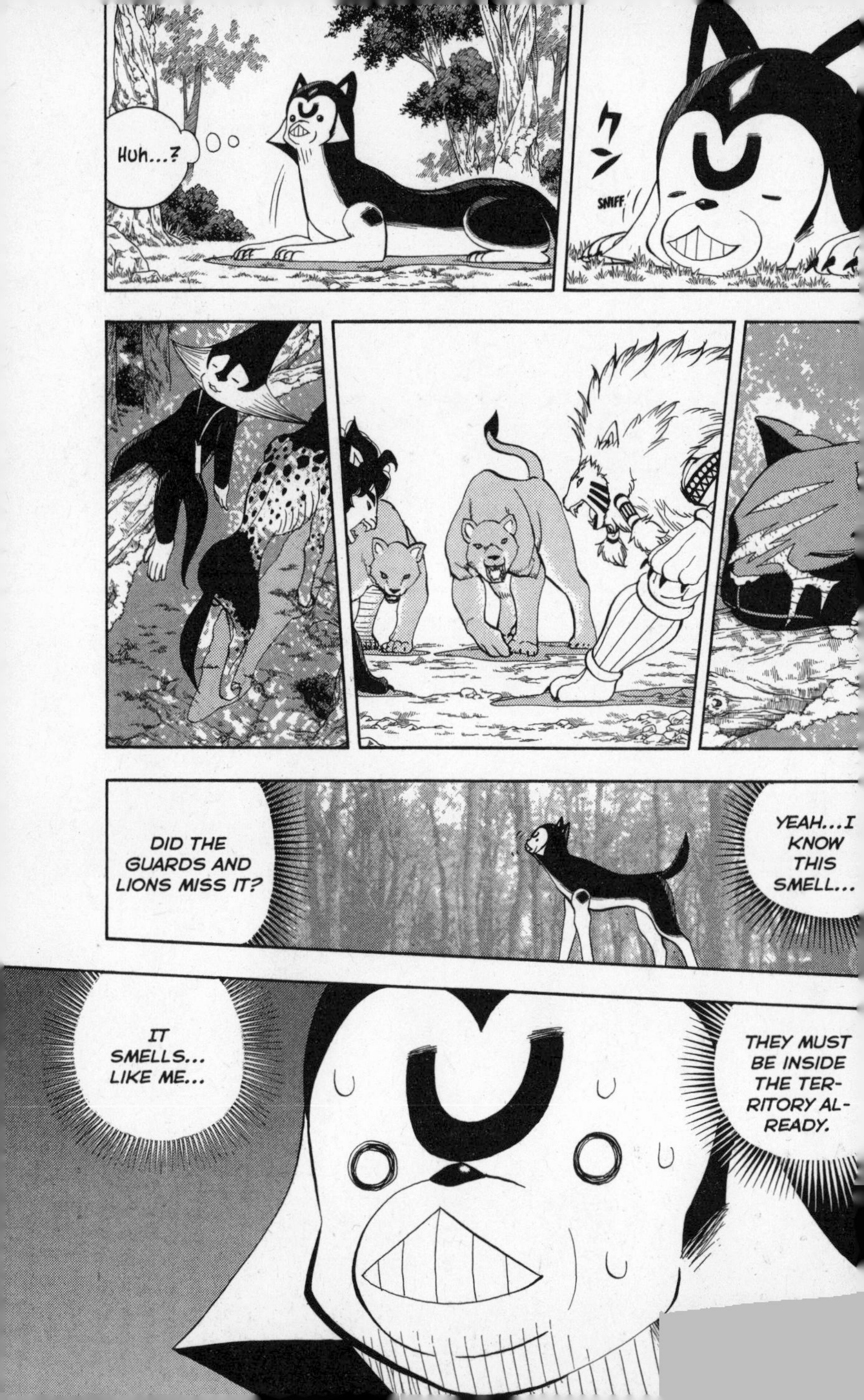

クン
SNIFF
HUH...?
YEAH...I KNOW THIS SMELL...
DID THE GUARDS AND LIONS MISS IT?
THEY MUST BE INSIDE THE TER-RITORY AL-READY.
IT SMELLS... LIKE ME...

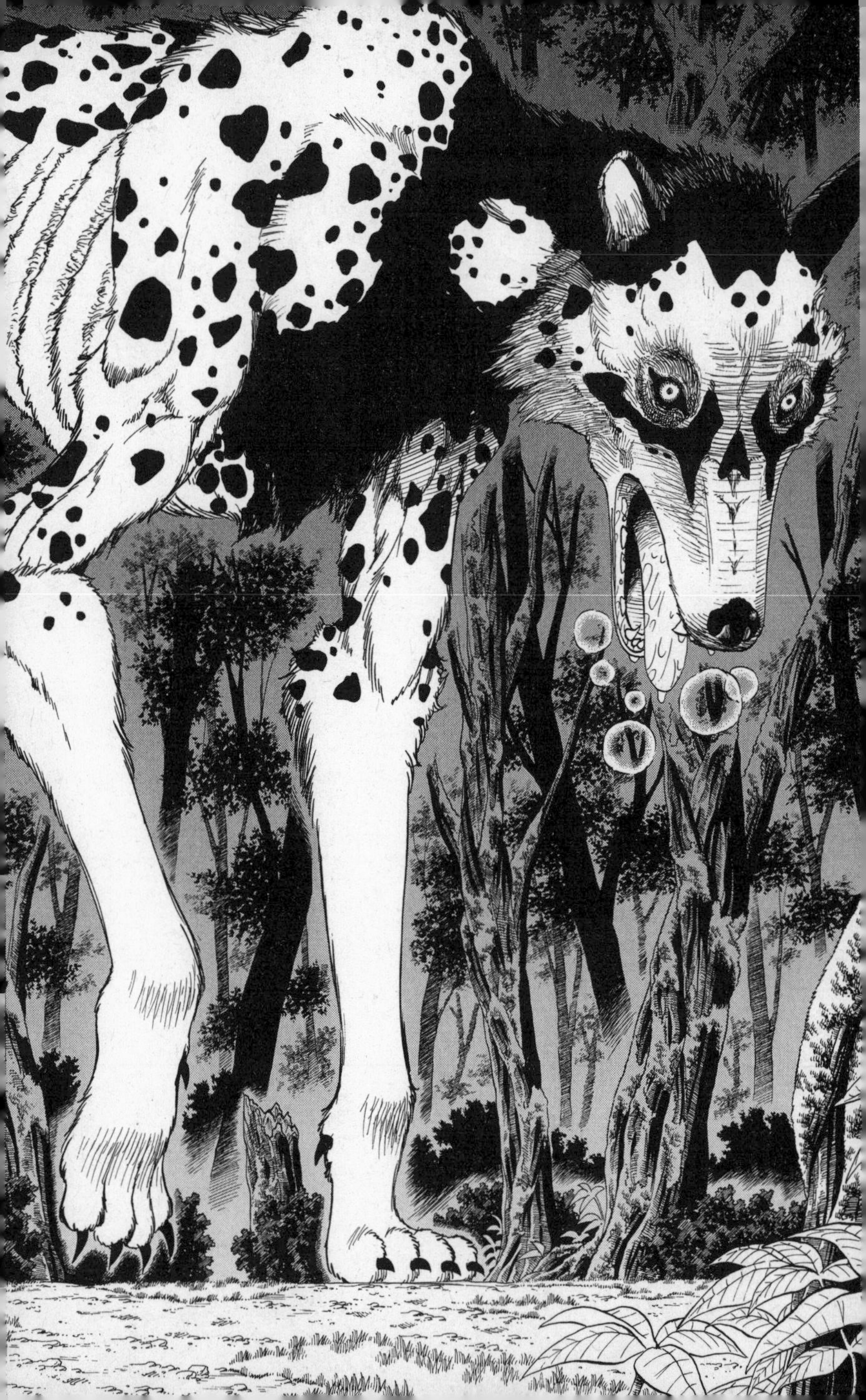

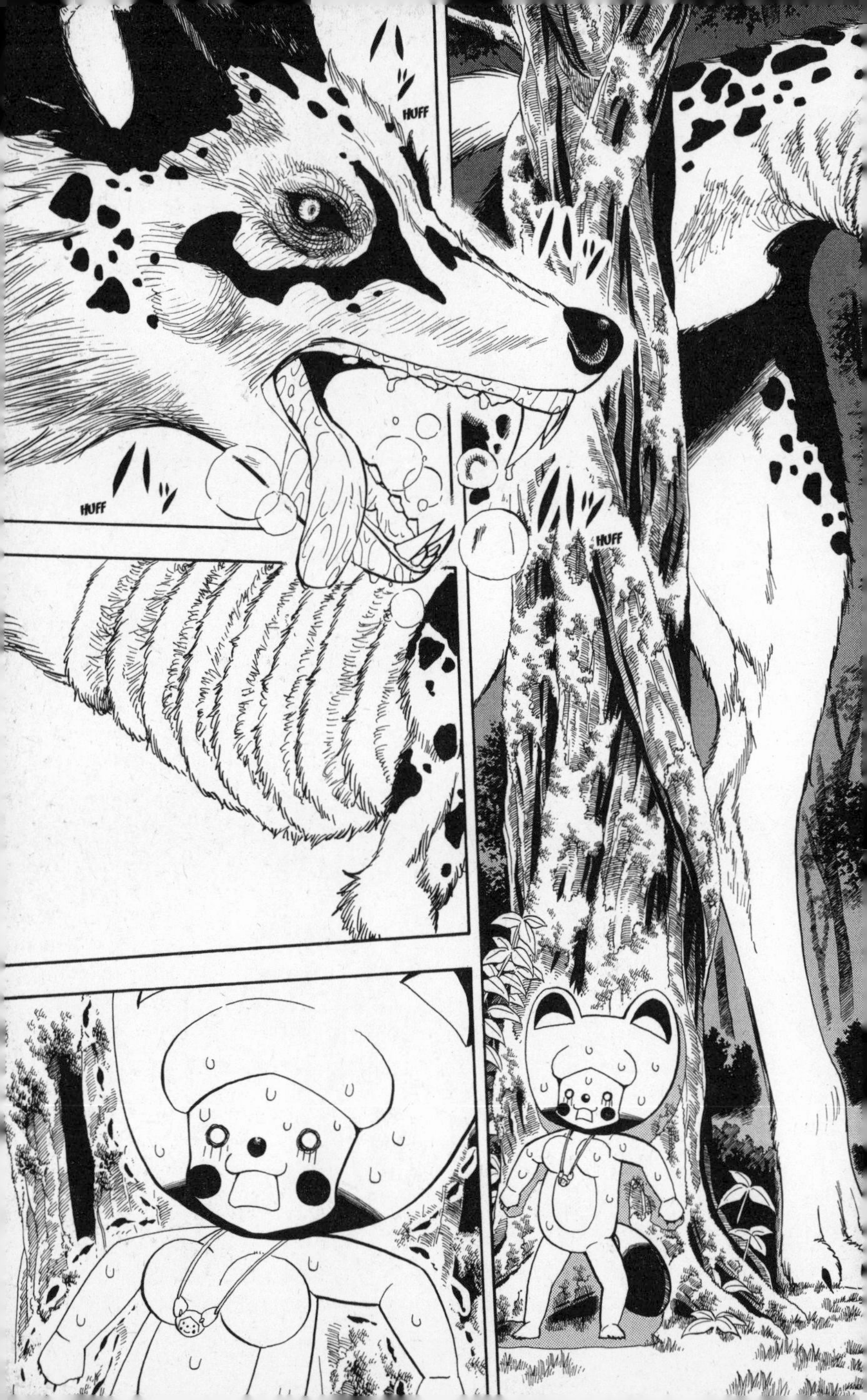
HUFF
HUFF
HUFF

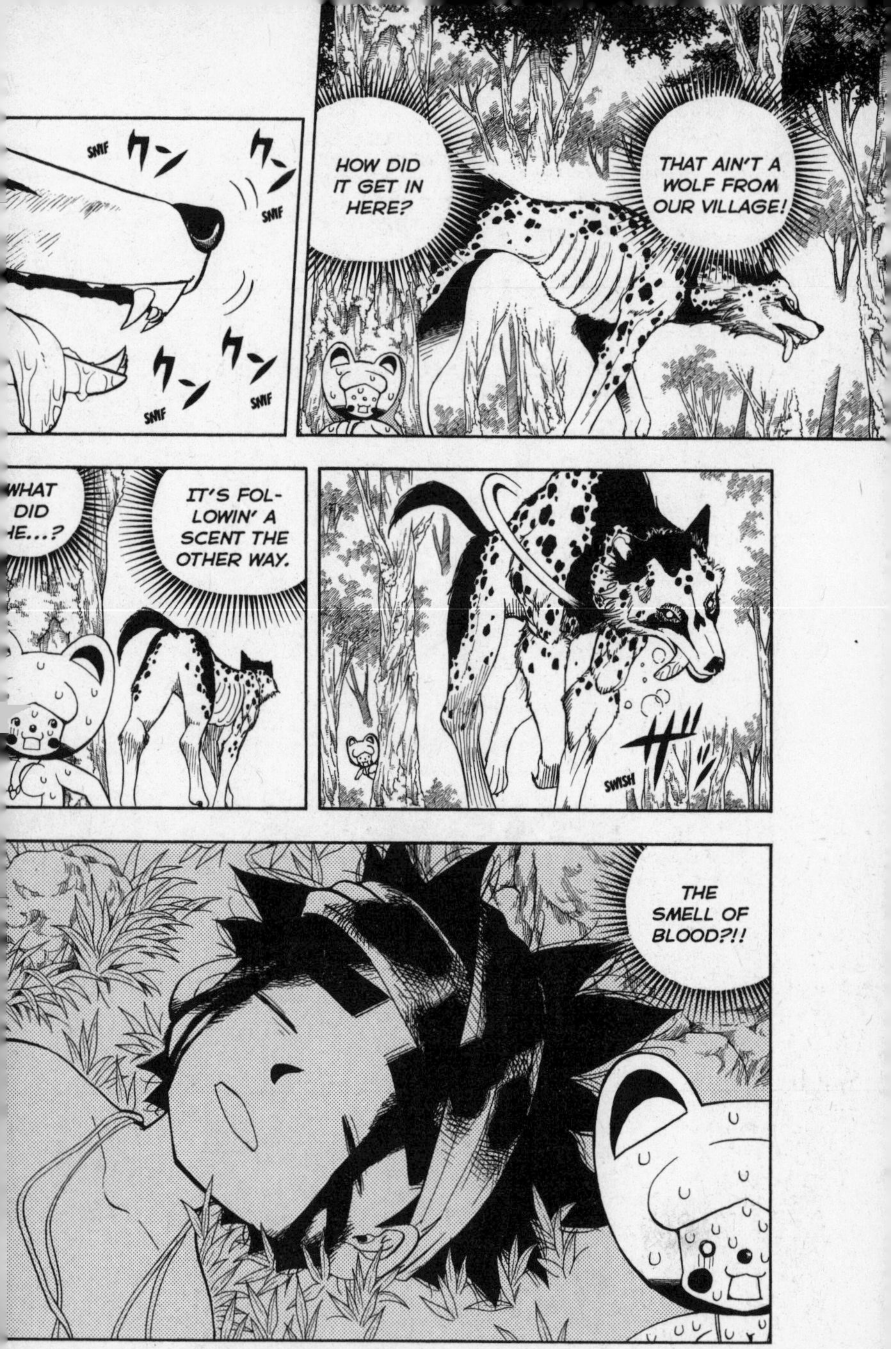
THAT AIN'T A WOLF FROM OUR VILLAGE!
HOW DID IT GET IN HERE?
クン
SNIF
クン
SNIF
クン
クン
SNIF
SNIF
SWISH
IT'S FOL-LOWIN' A SCENT THE OTHER WAY.
WHAT DID HE...?
THE SMELL OF BLOOD?!!

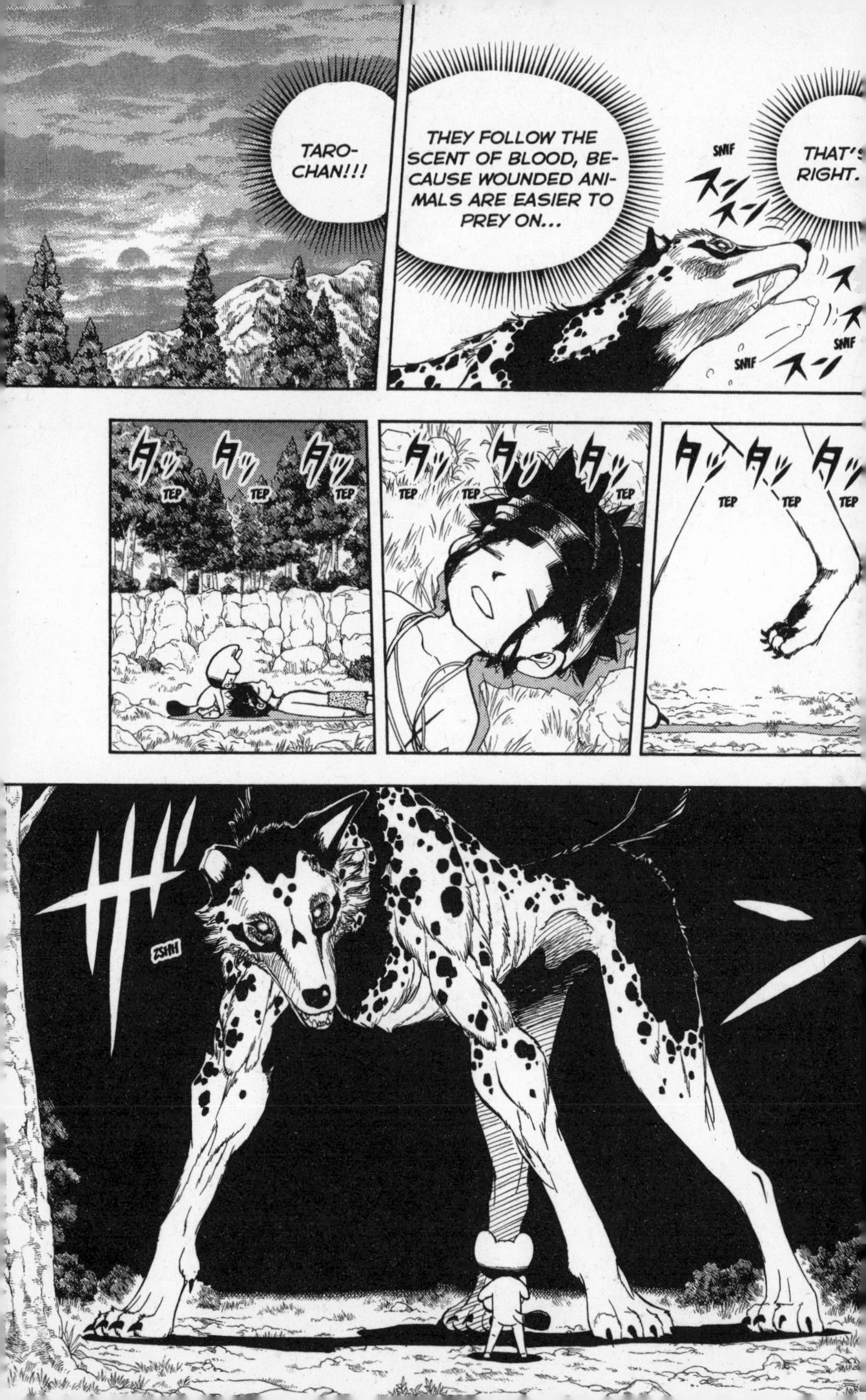
SNIF
スン
スン
THAT'S RIGHT.
スン
スン
SNIF
SNIF
スン
THEY FOLLOW THE SCENT OF BLOOD, BECAUSE WOUNDED ANIMALS ARE EASIER TO PREY ON...
TARO-CHAN!!!
タッ TEP
タッ TEP
タッ TEP
タッ TEP
タッ TEP
タッ TEP
タッ TEP
タッ TEP
タッ TEP
ザッ
ZSHH

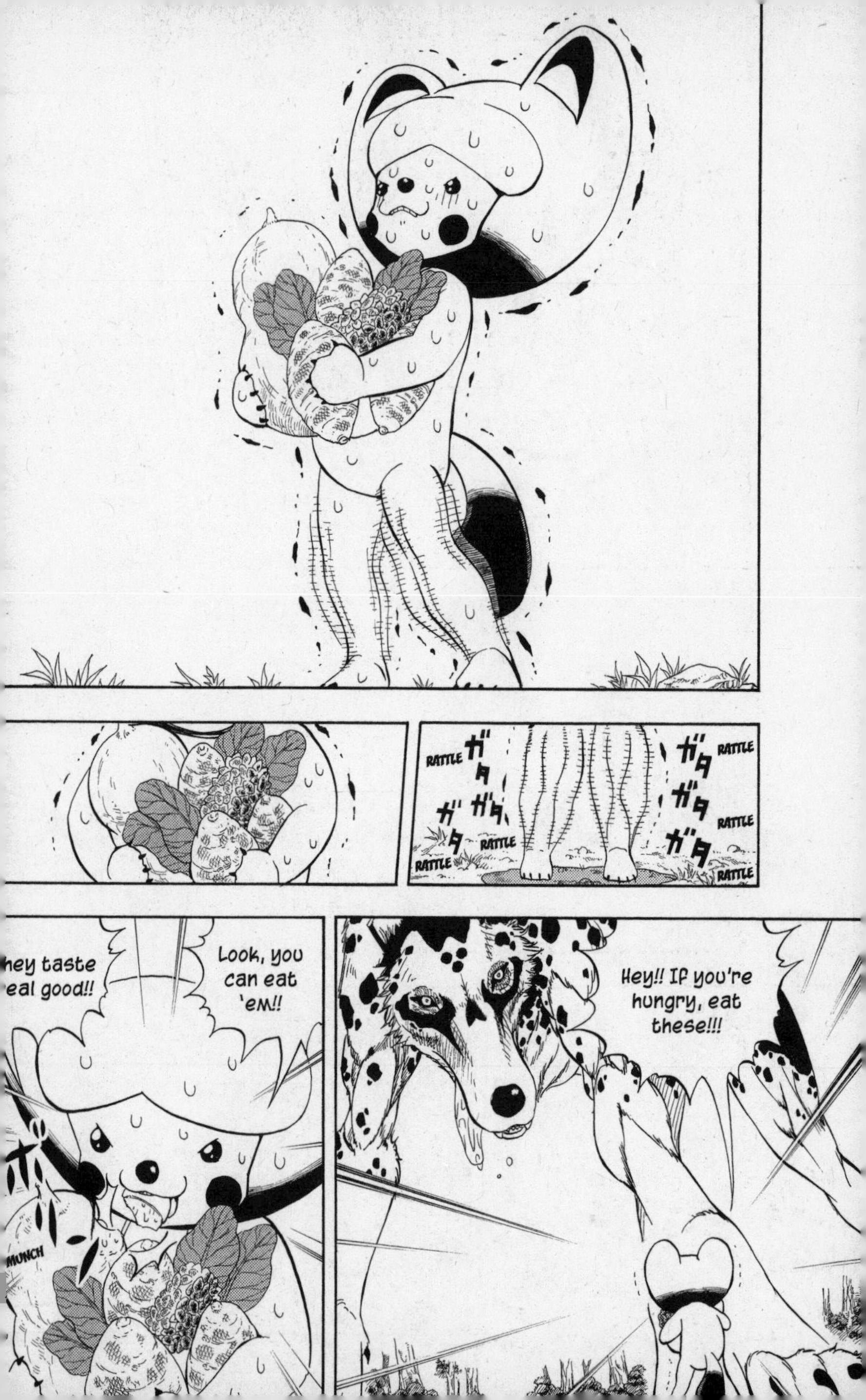
ガタ RATTLE
ガタ RATTLE
ガタ RATTLE
RATTLE ガタ
ガタ
ガタ RATTLE
RATTLE
Hey!! If you're hungry, eat these!!!
Look, you can eat 'em!!
hey taste eal good!!
MUNCH

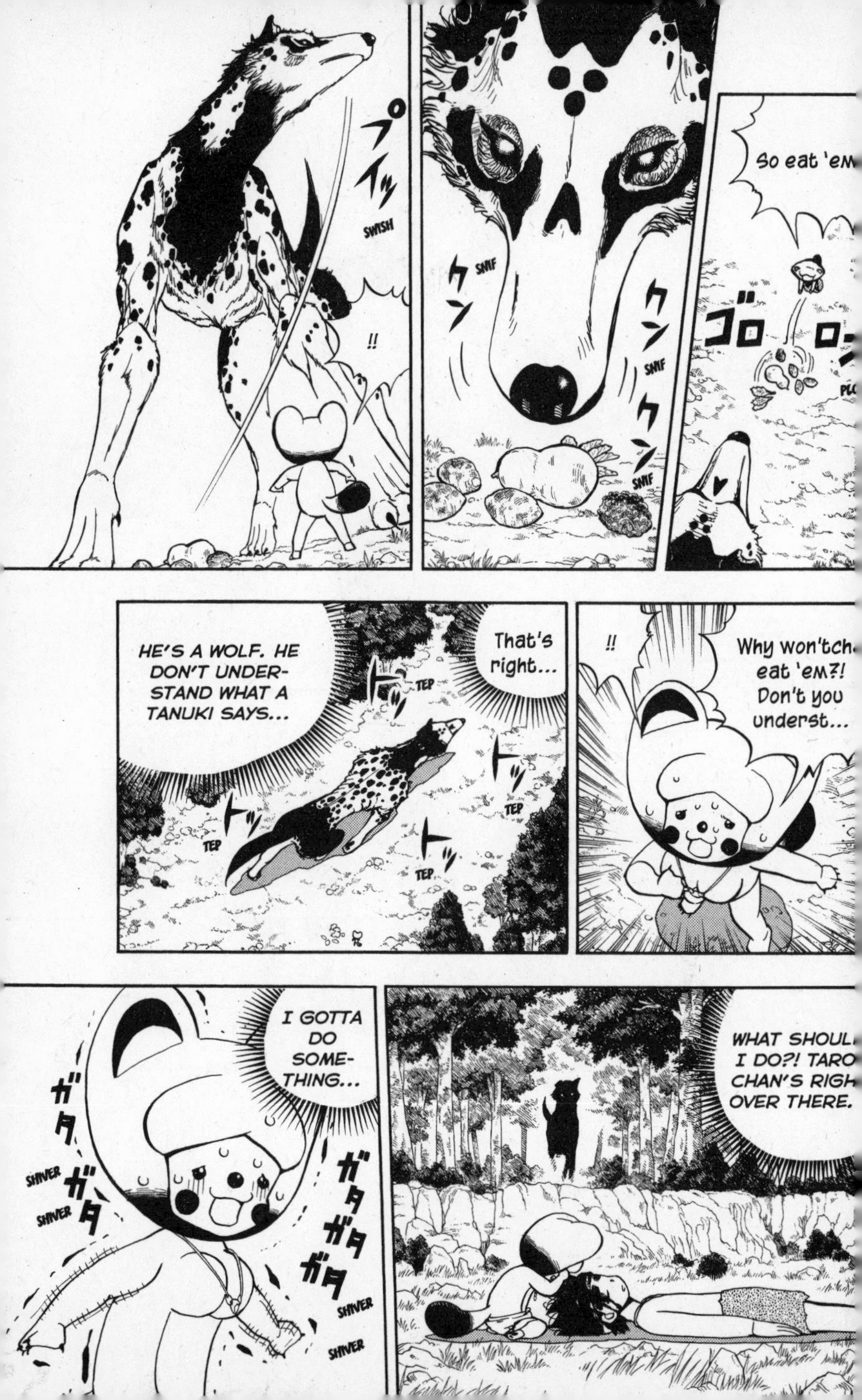
So eat 'em
ゴロ ロッ
PLO
SNIF
クン
SNIF
クンクン
SNIF
プイッ
SWISH
!!
!!
Why won'tch eat 'em?! Don't you underst...
That's right...
HE'S A WOLF. HE DON'T UNDERSTAND WHAT A TANUKI SAYS...
トッ
TEP
トッ
TEP
トッ
TEP
トッ
TEP
WHAT SHOUL I DO?! TARO CHAN'S RIGH OVER THERE.
I GOTTA DO SOMETHING...
ガタ
ガタ
SHIVER
SHIVER
ガタガタ
ガタ
SHIVER
SHIVER

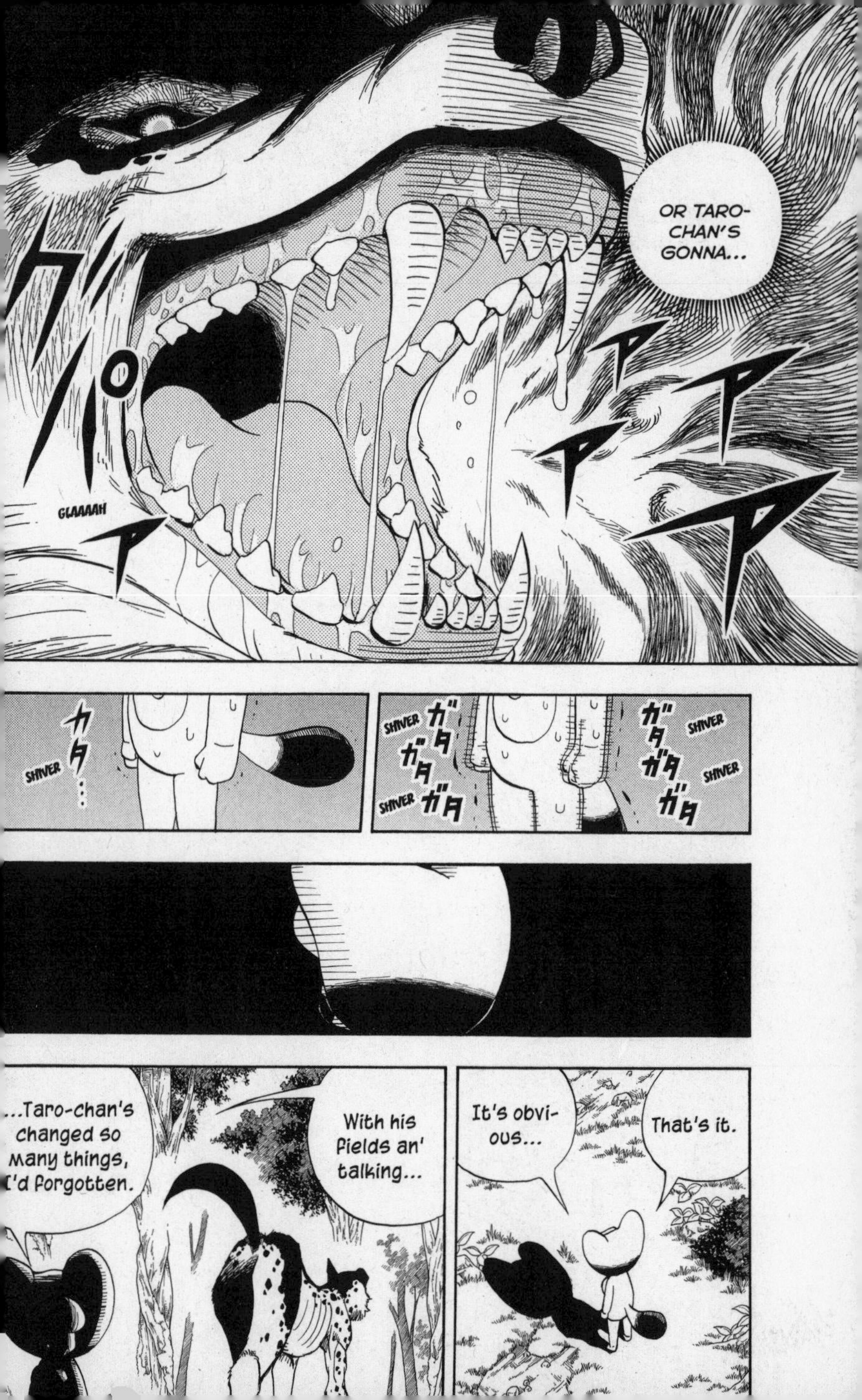
OR TARO-CHAN'S GONNA...
GLAAAAH
SHIVER
SHIVER
SHIVER
SHIVER
SHIVER
SHIVER
That's it.
It's obvi-ous...
With his fields an' talking...
...Taro-chan's changed so many things, I'd forgotten.

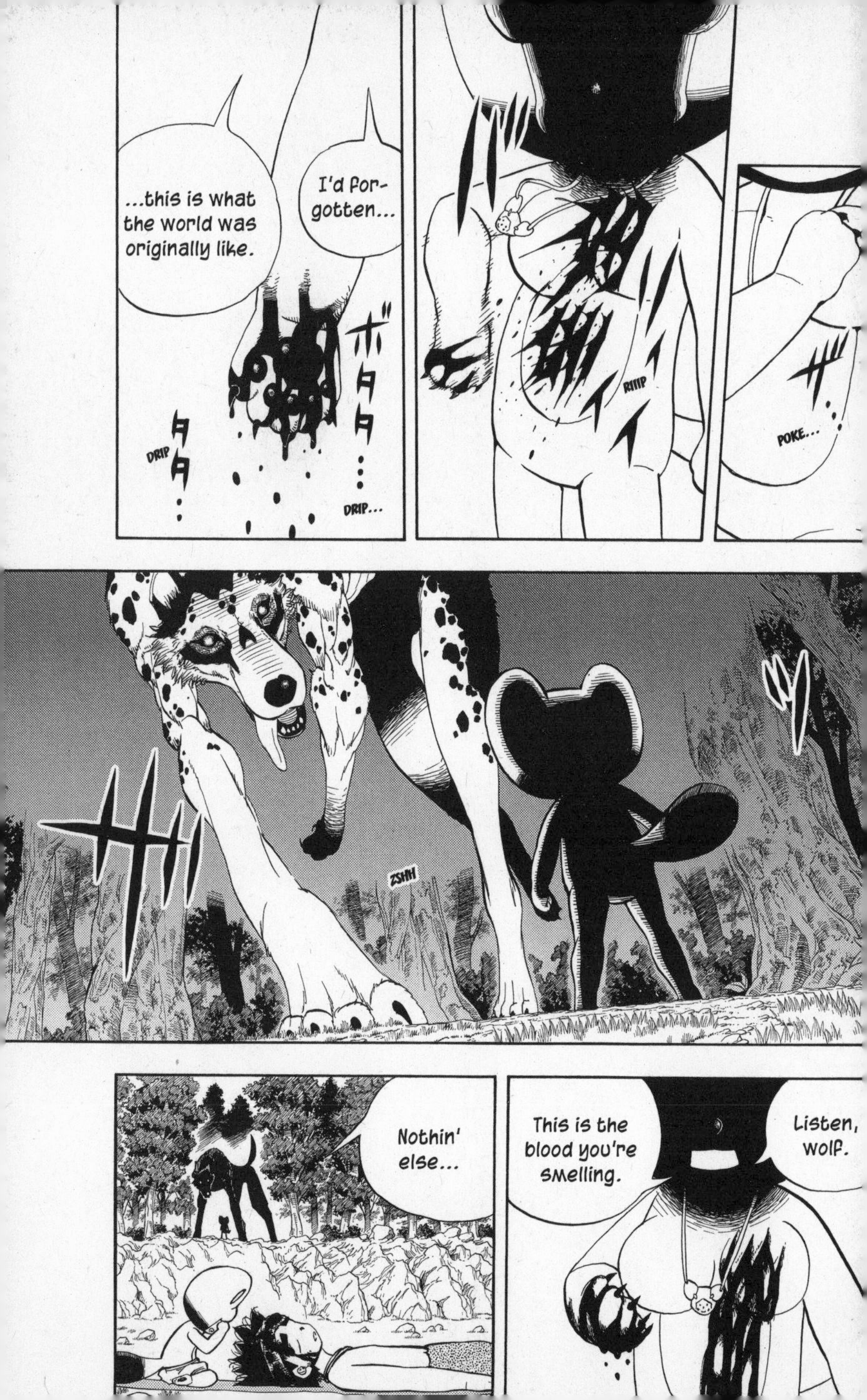
POKE...
RIIIP
I'd for-gotten...
...this is what the world was originally like.
DRIP...
DRIP
ZSHH
Listen, wolf.
This is the blood you're smelling.
Nothin' else...

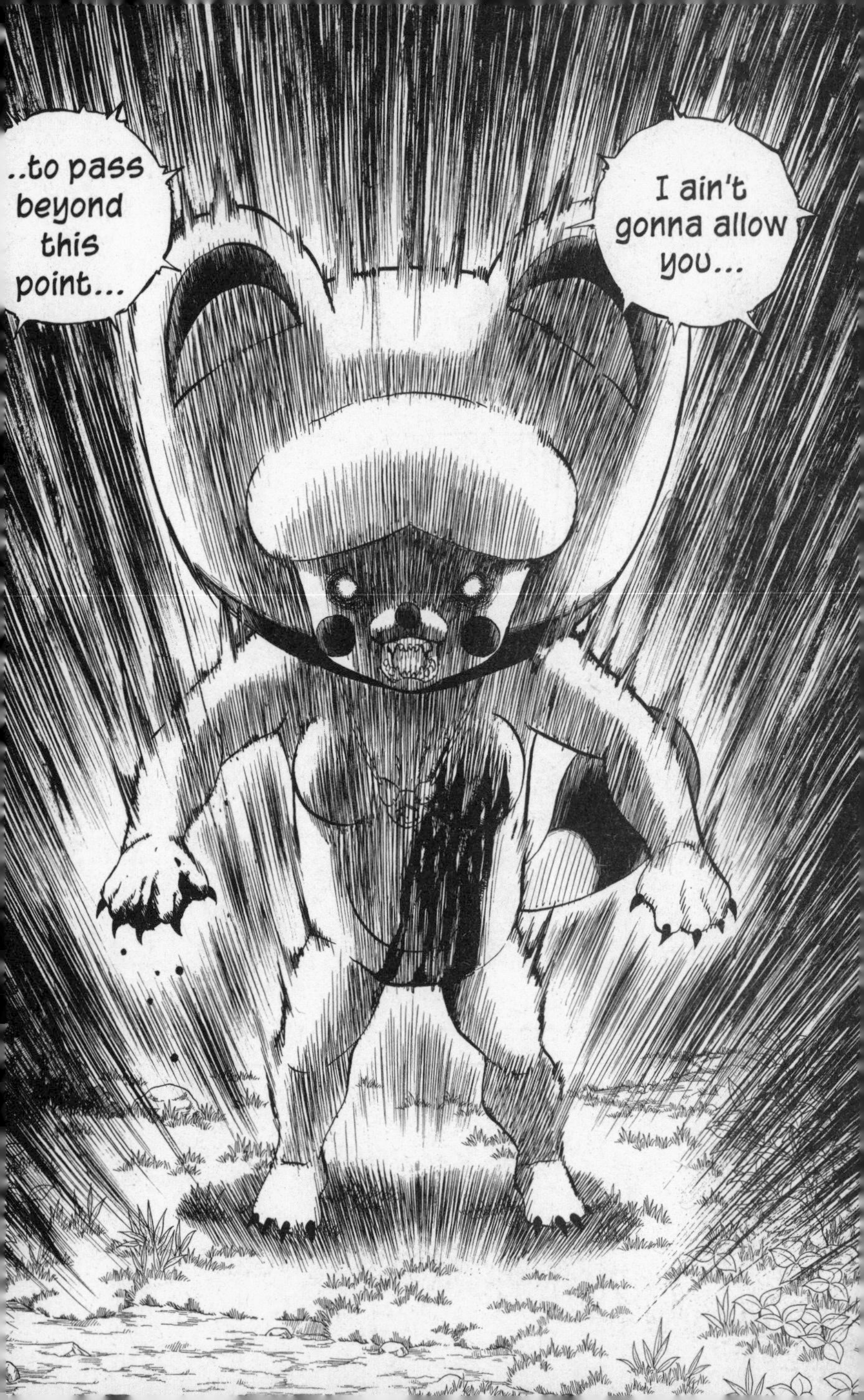
I ain't gonna allow you...
..to pass beyond this point...

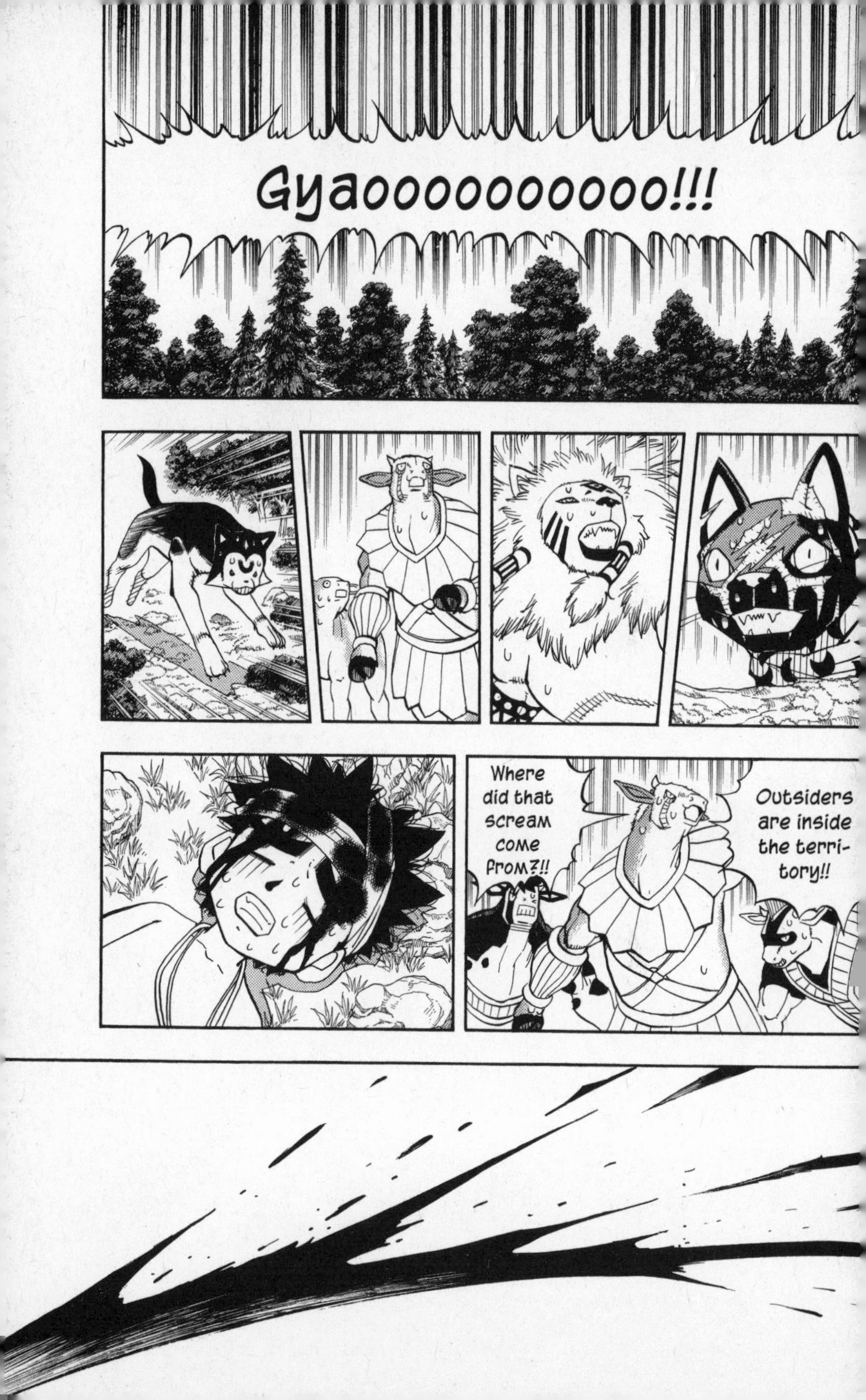
Gyaoooooooooo!!!
Outsiders are inside the terri-tory!!
Where did that scream come from?!!

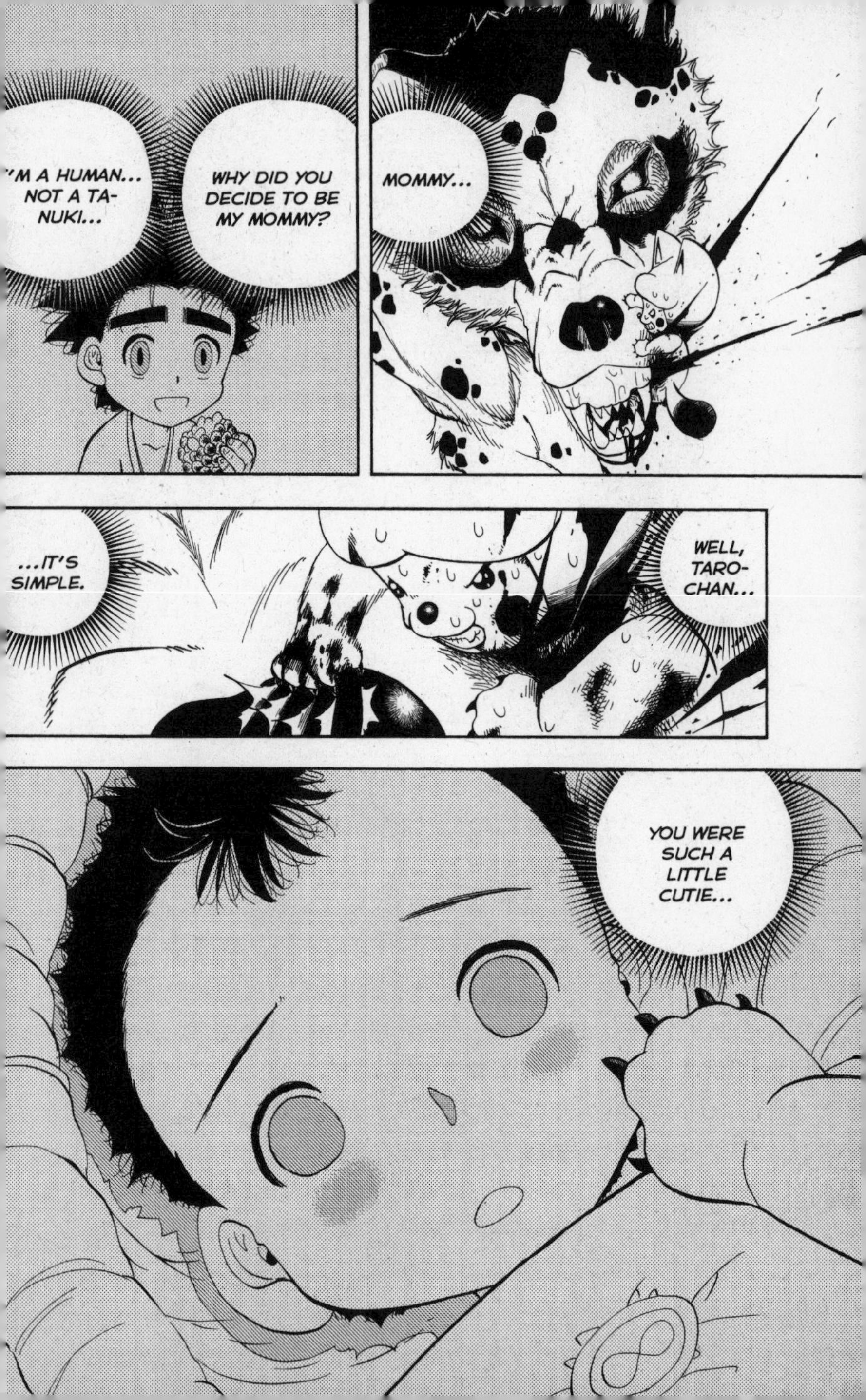
MOMMY...
WHY DID YOU DECIDE TO BE MY MOMMY?
'M A HUMAN... NOT A TA-NUKI...
WELL, TARO-CHAN...
...IT'S SIMPLE.
YOU WERE SUCH A LITTLE CUTIE...

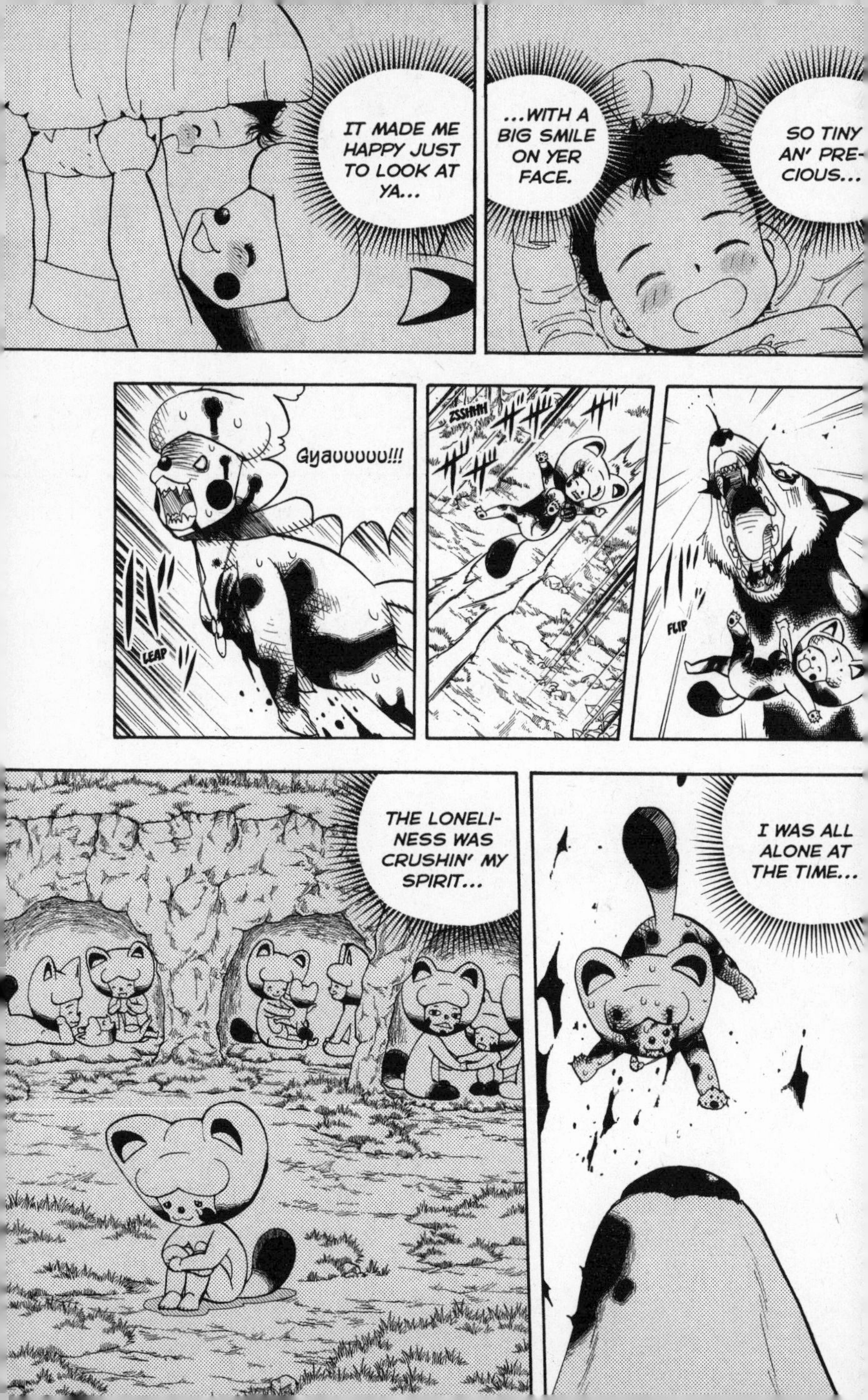
SO TINY AN' PRECIOUS...
...WITH A BIG SMILE ON YER FACE.
IT MADE ME HAPPY JUST TO LOOK AT YA...
FLIP
ZSSHHH
Gyauuuuu!!!
LEAP
I WAS ALL ALONE AT THE TIME...
THE LONELINESS WAS CRUSHIN' MY SPIRIT...

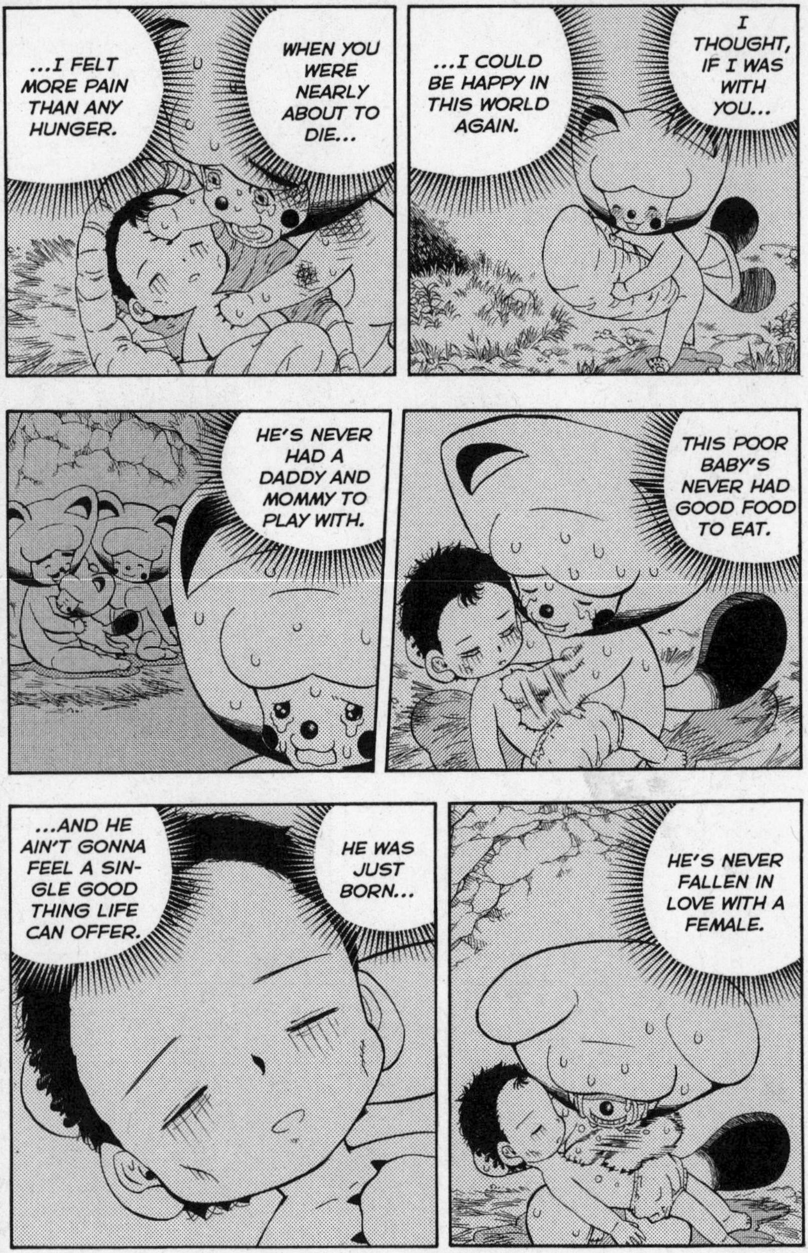
I THOUGHT, IF I WAS WITH YOU...
...I COULD BE HAPPY IN THIS WORLD AGAIN.
WHEN YOU WERE NEARLY ABOUT TO DIE...
...I FELT MORE PAIN THAN ANY HUNGER.
THIS POOR BABY'S NEVER HAD GOOD FOOD TO EAT.
HE'S NEVER HAD A DADDY AND MOMMY TO PLAY WITH.
HE'S NEVER FALLEN IN LOVE WITH A FEMALE.
HE WAS JUST BORN...
...AND HE AIN'T GONNA FEEL A SIN-GLE GOOD THING LIFE CAN OFFER.

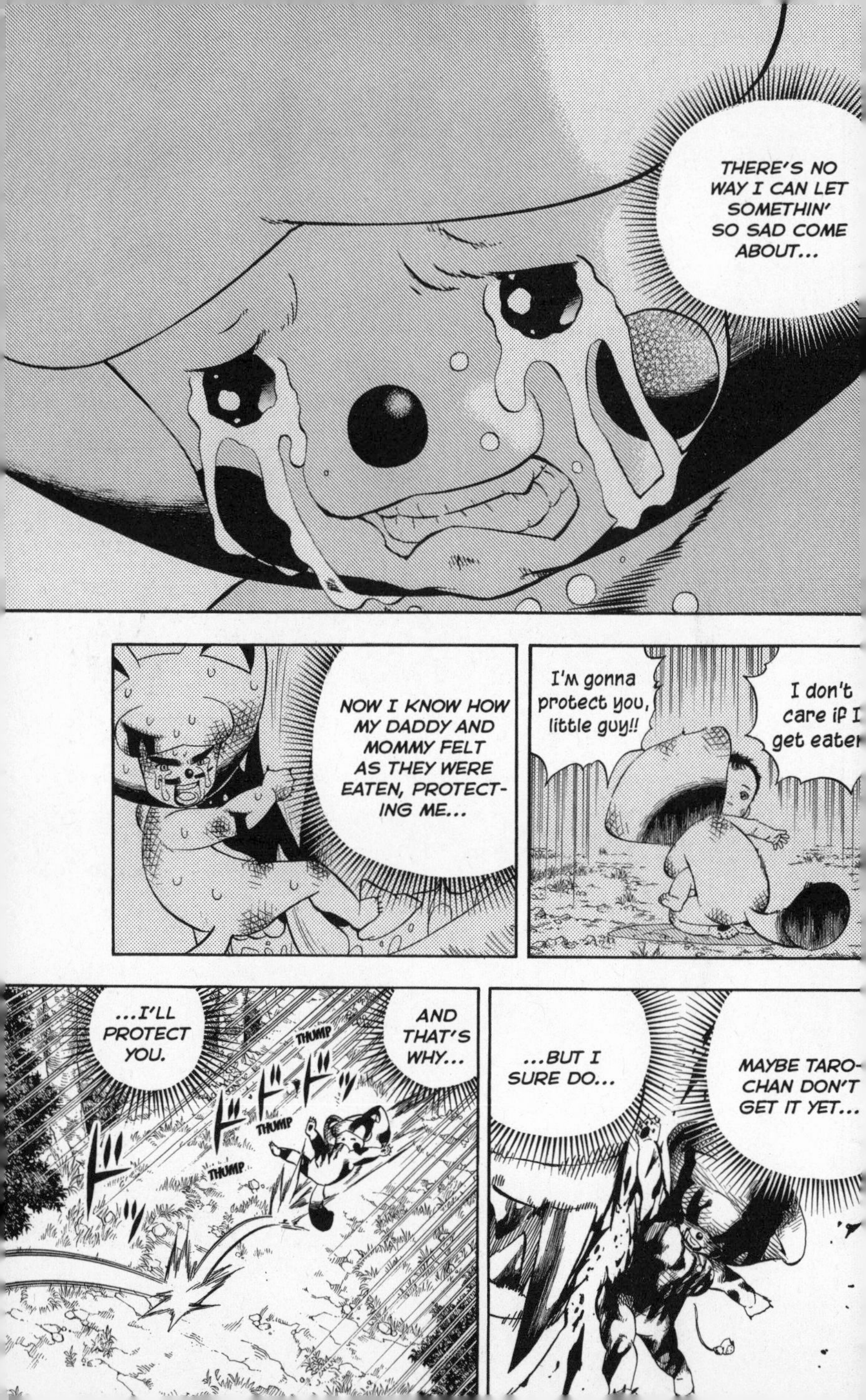
THERE'S NO WAY I CAN LET SOMETHIN' SO SAD COME ABOUT...
I don't care if I get eate
I'm gonna protect you, little guy!!
NOW I KNOW HOW MY DADDY AND MOMMY FELT AS THEY WERE EATEN, PROTECTING ME...
MAYBE TARO-CHAN DON'T GET IT YET...
...BUT I SURE DO...
AND THAT'S WHY...
...I'LL PROTECT YOU.
THUMP
THUMP
THUMP

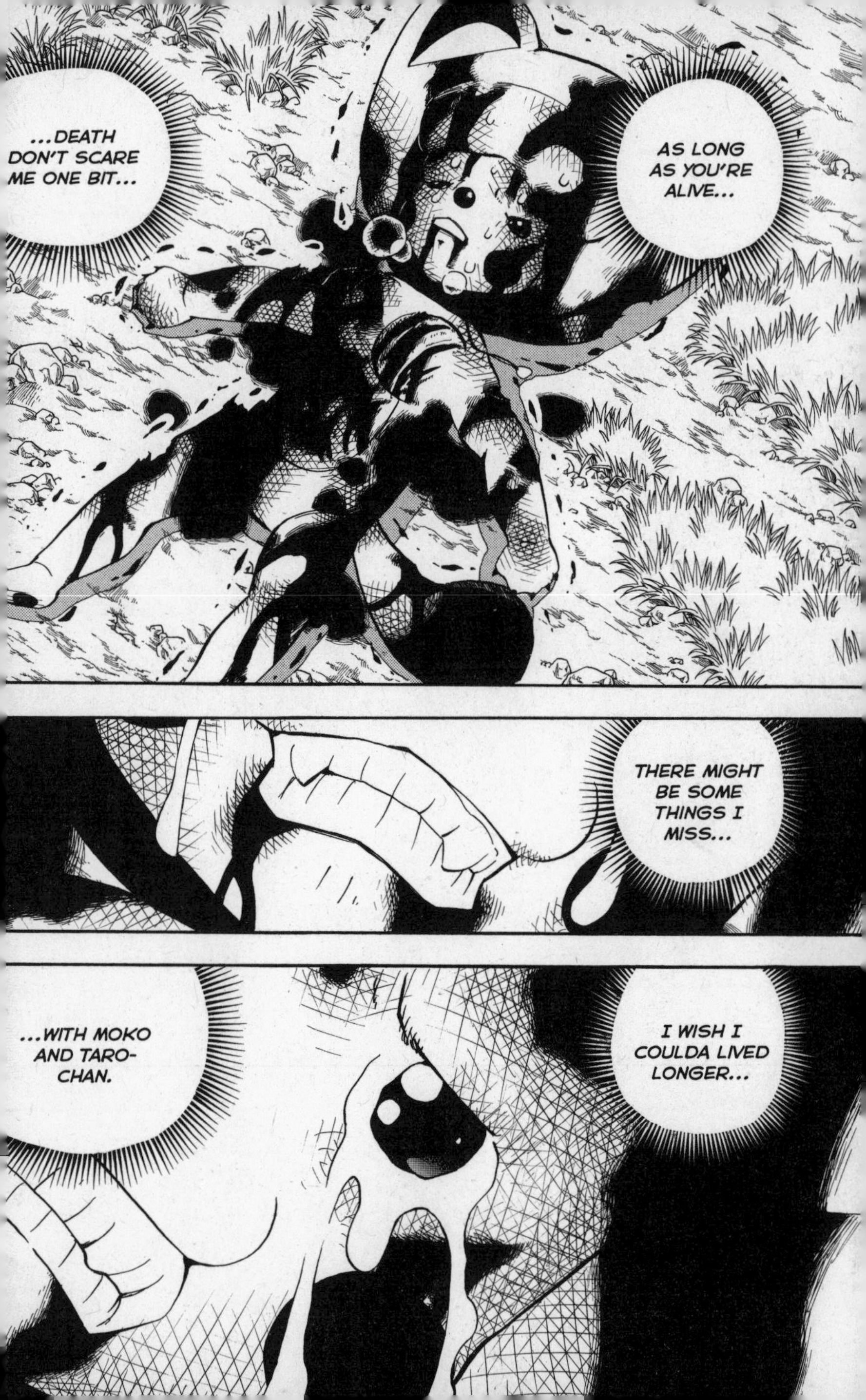
AS LONG AS YOU'RE ALIVE...
...DEATH DON'T SCARE ME ONE BIT...
THERE MIGHT BE SOME THINGS I MISS...
I WISH I COULDA LIVED LONGER...
...WITH MOKO AND TARO-CHAN.

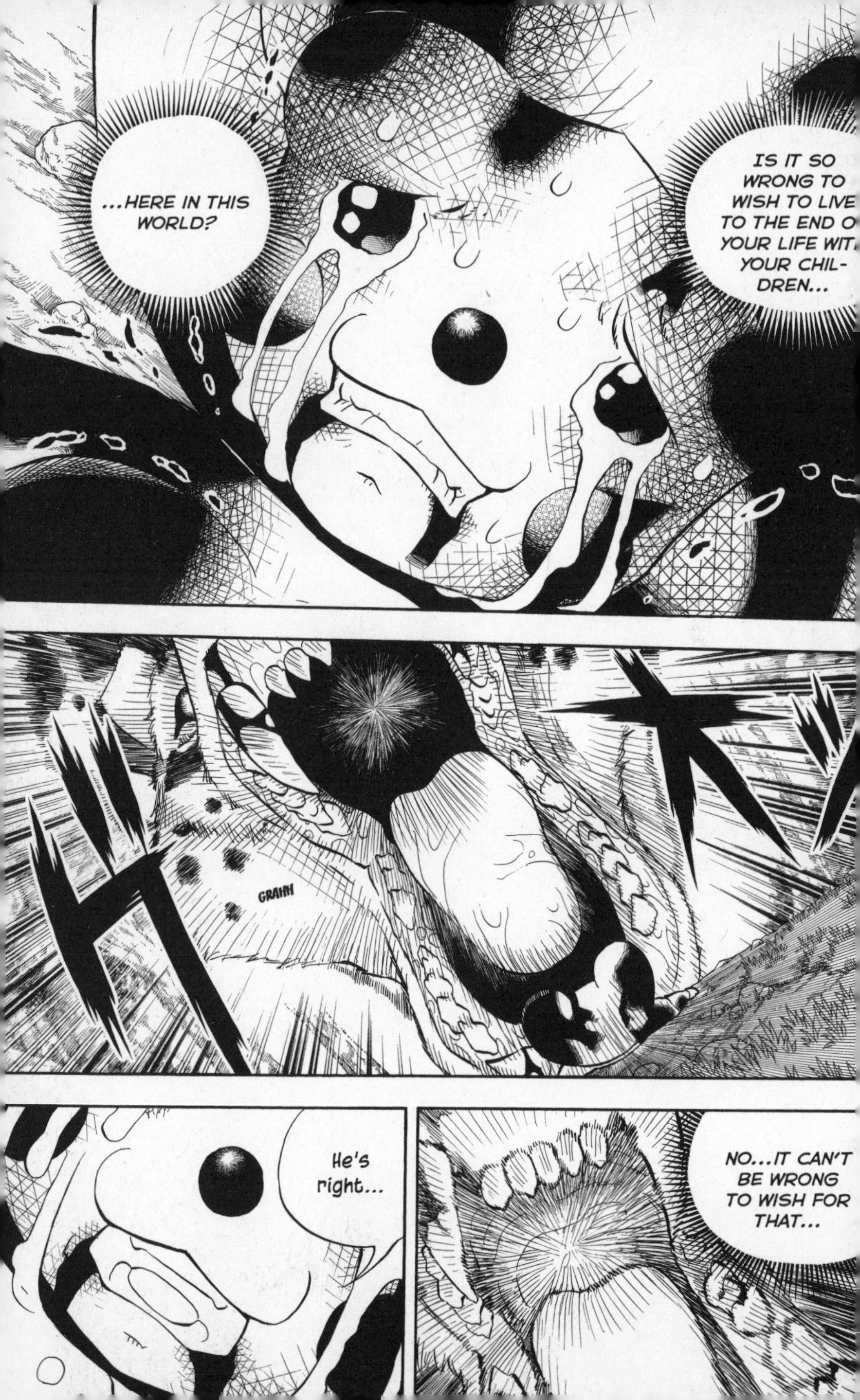
IS IT SO WRONG TO WISH TO LIVE TO THE END O YOUR LIFE WIT YOUR CHIL-DREN...
...HERE IN THIS WORLD?
GRAHH
NO...IT CAN'T BE WRONG TO WISH FOR THAT...
He's right...

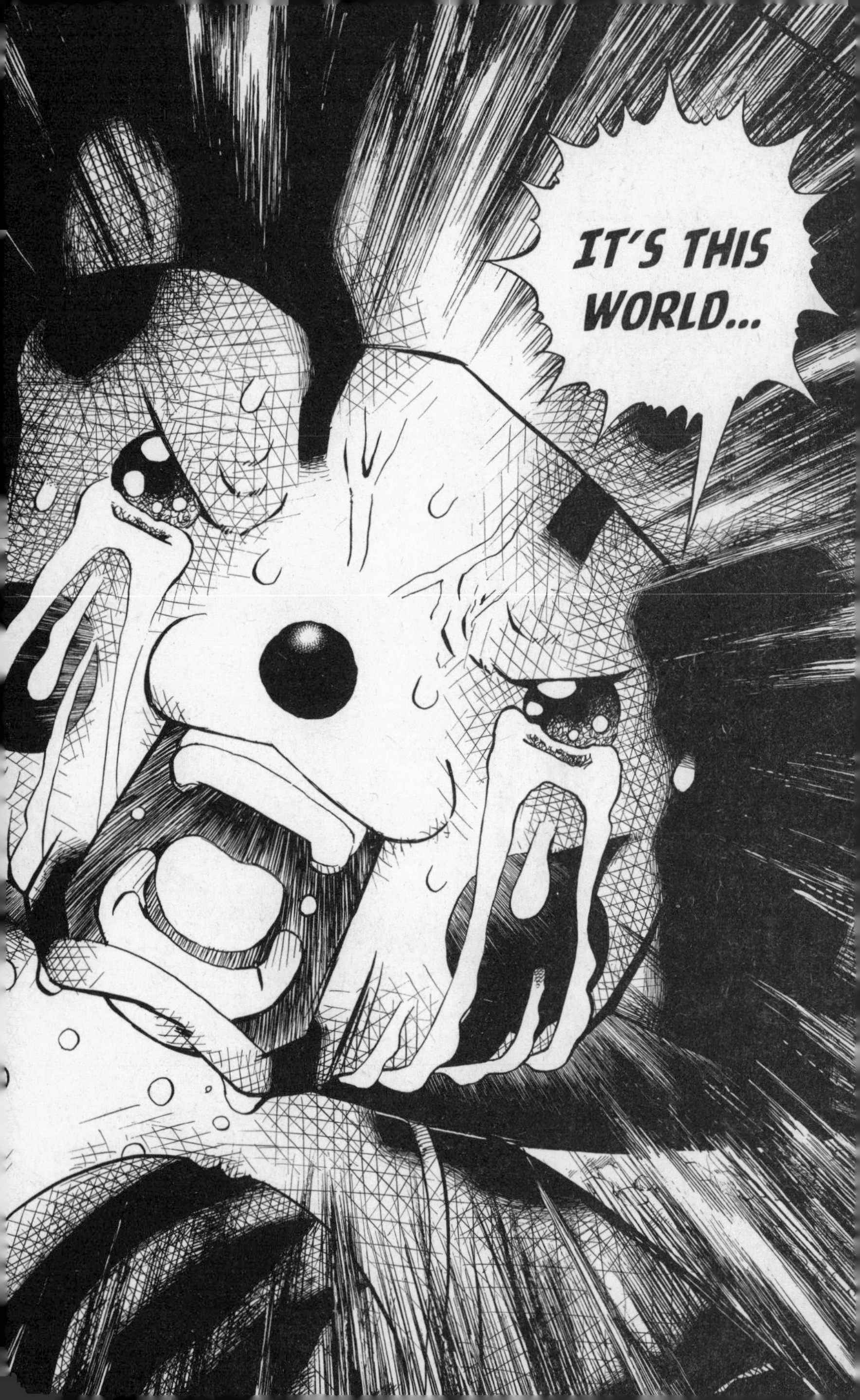
IT'S THIS WORLD...

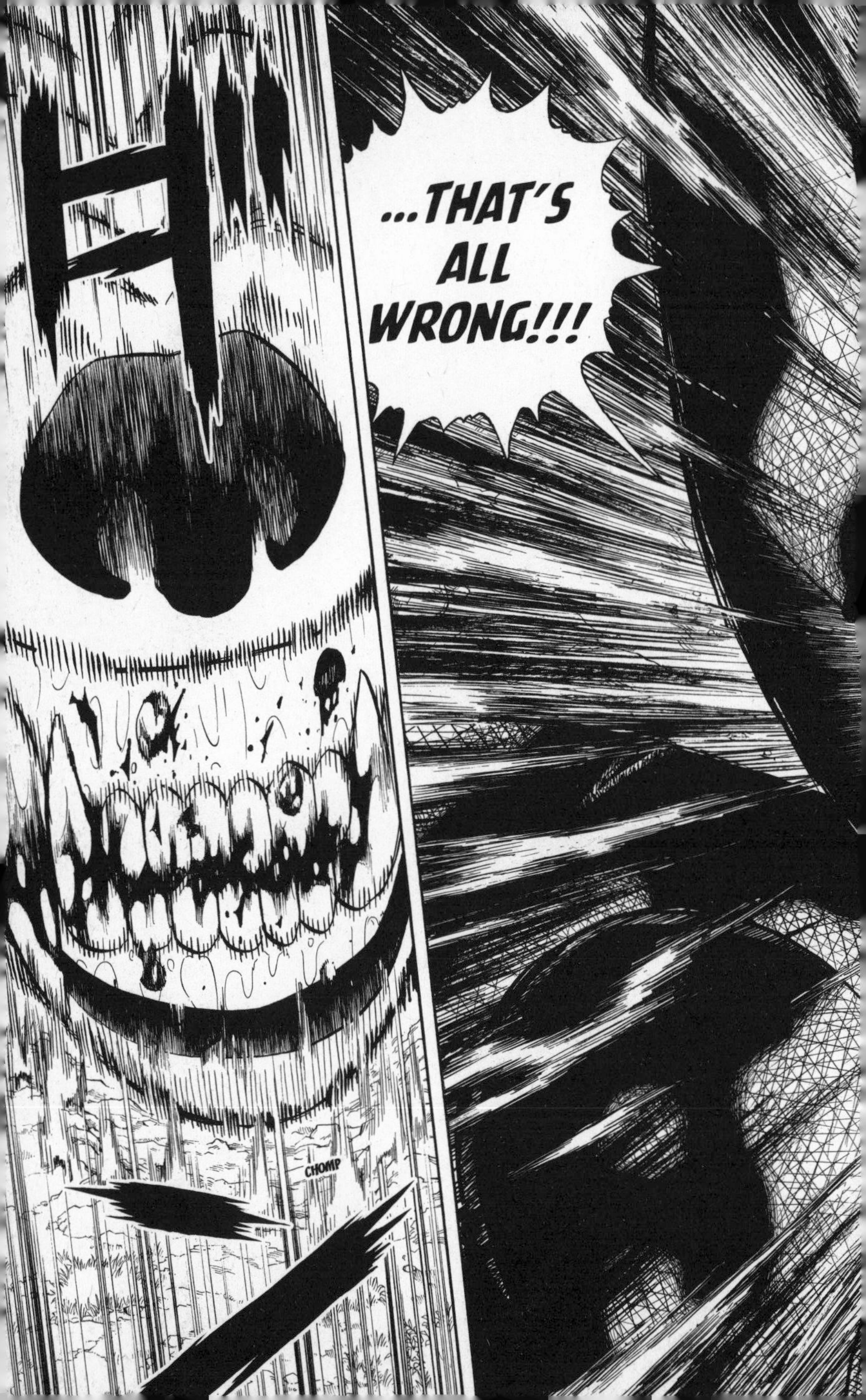
...THAT'S ALL WRONG!!!
CHOMP

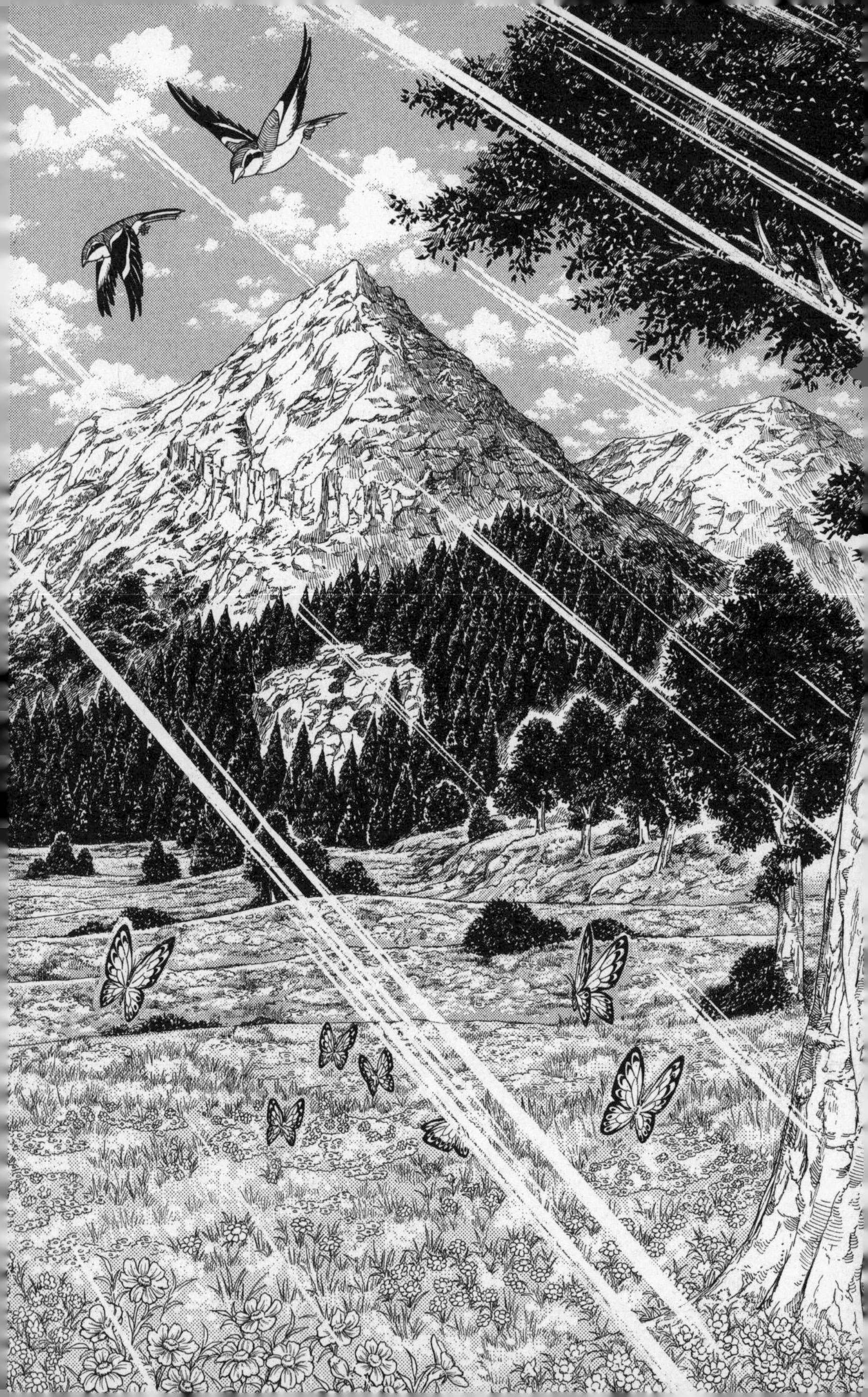

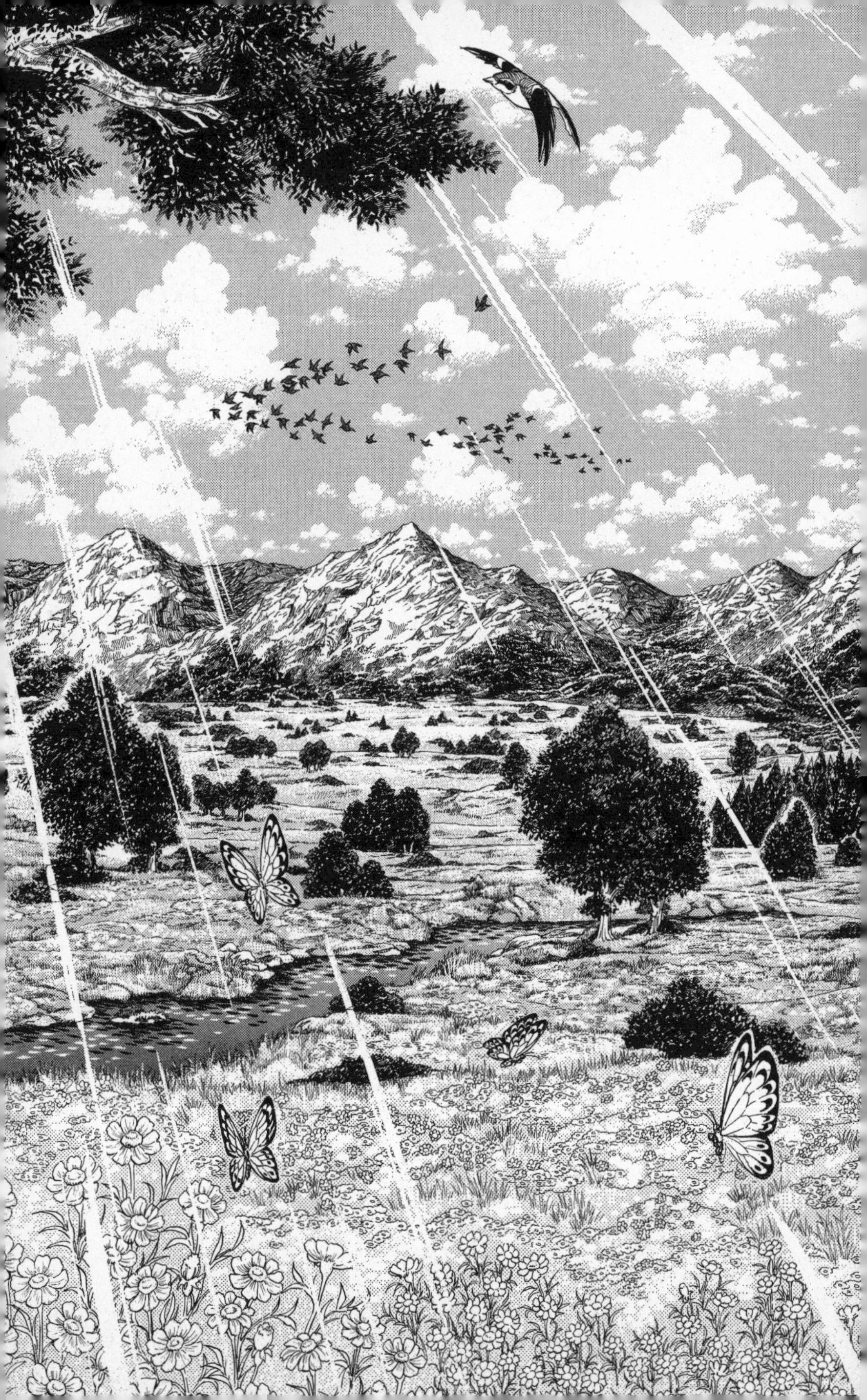

This is all I could find...

I'M SORRY, TAROZA...

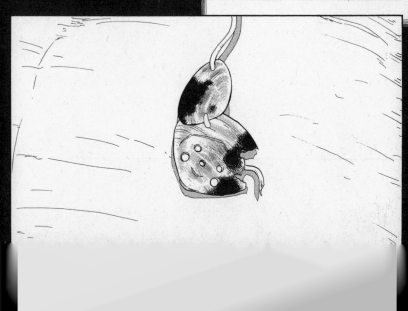

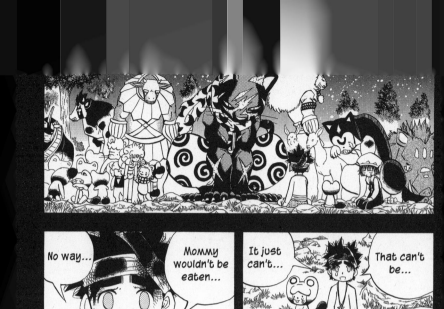

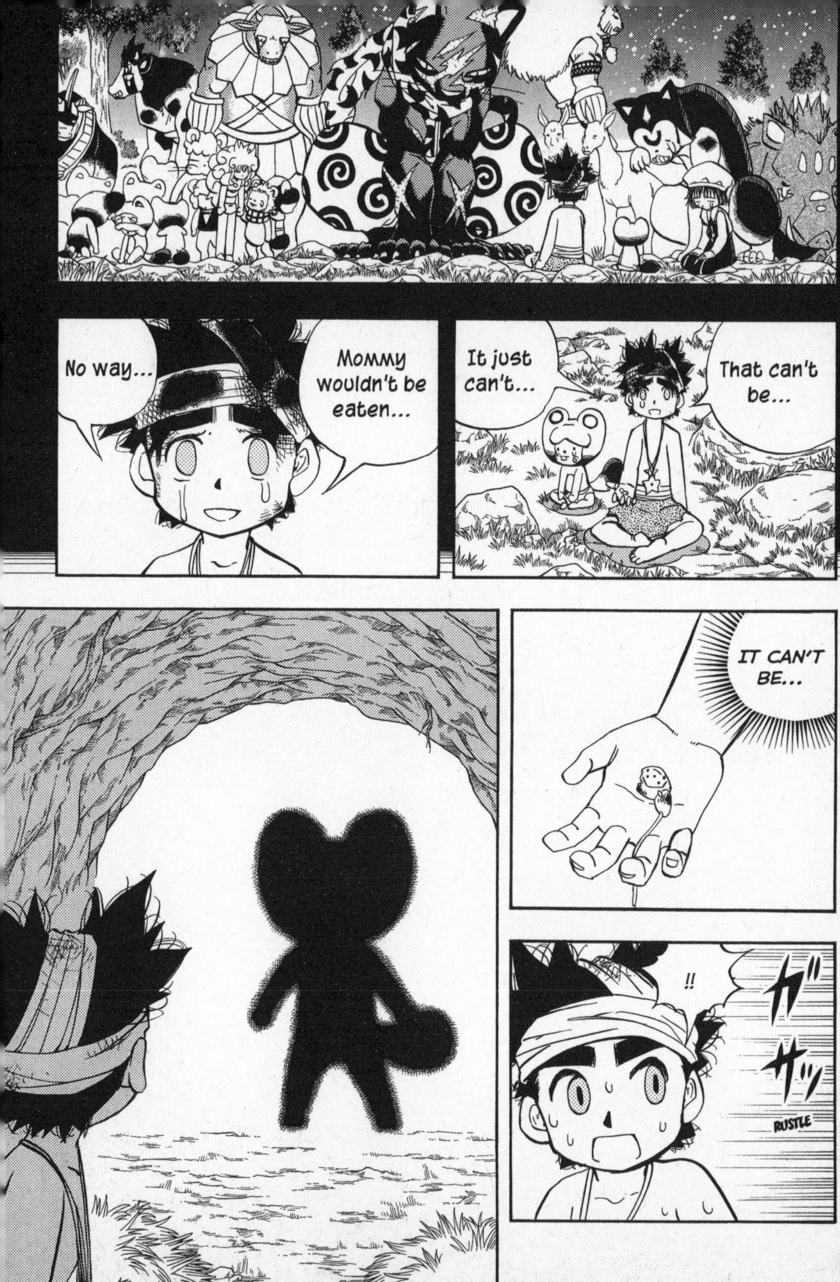
That can't be...
It just can't...
Mommy wouldn't be eaten...
No way...
IT CAN'T BE...
!!
ガサッ
RUSTLE

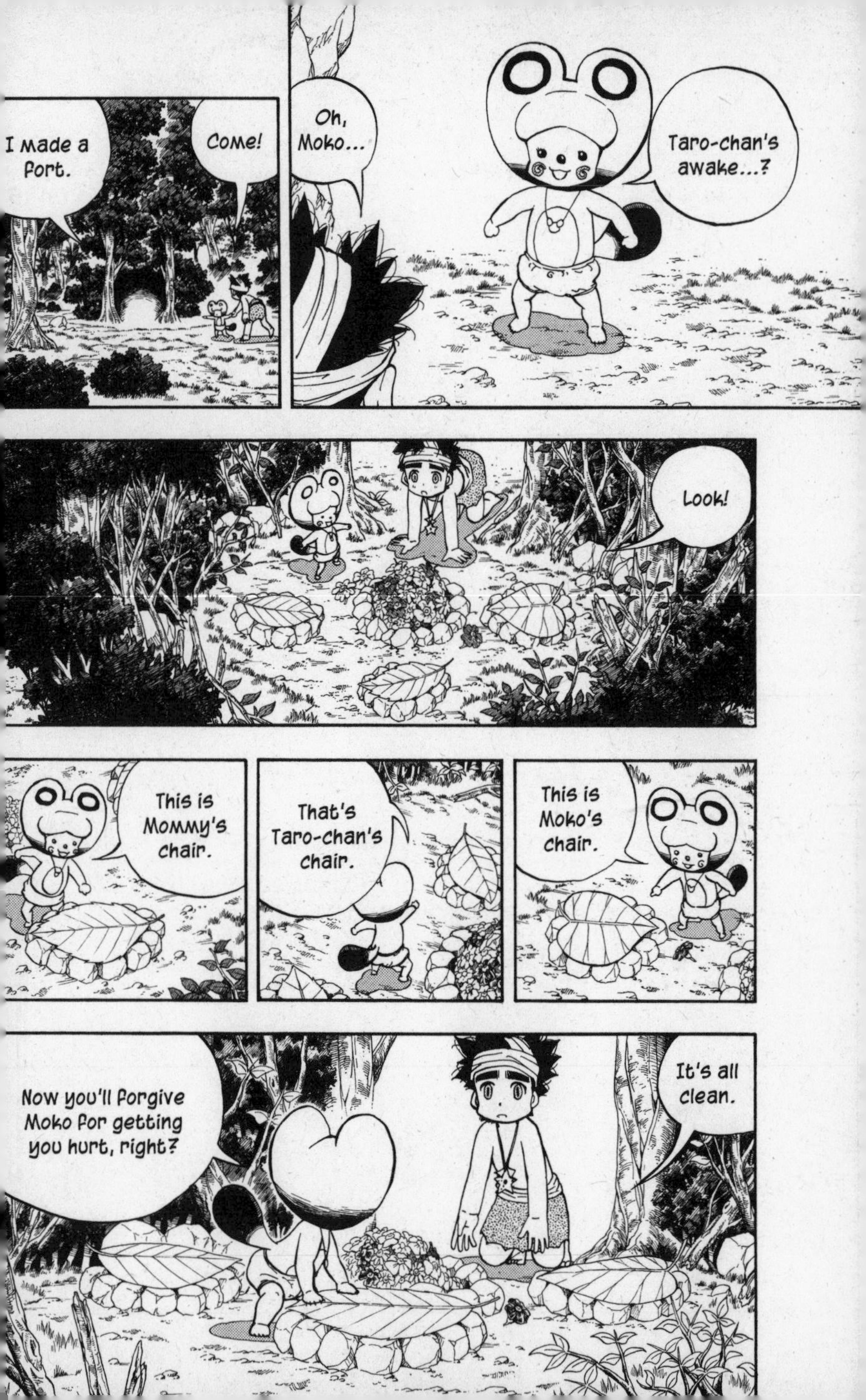
Taro-chan's awake...?
Oh, Moko...
Come!
I made a fort.
Look!
This is Moko's chair.
That's Taro-chan's chair.
This is Mommy's chair.
It's all clean.
Now you'll forgive Moko for getting you hurt, right?

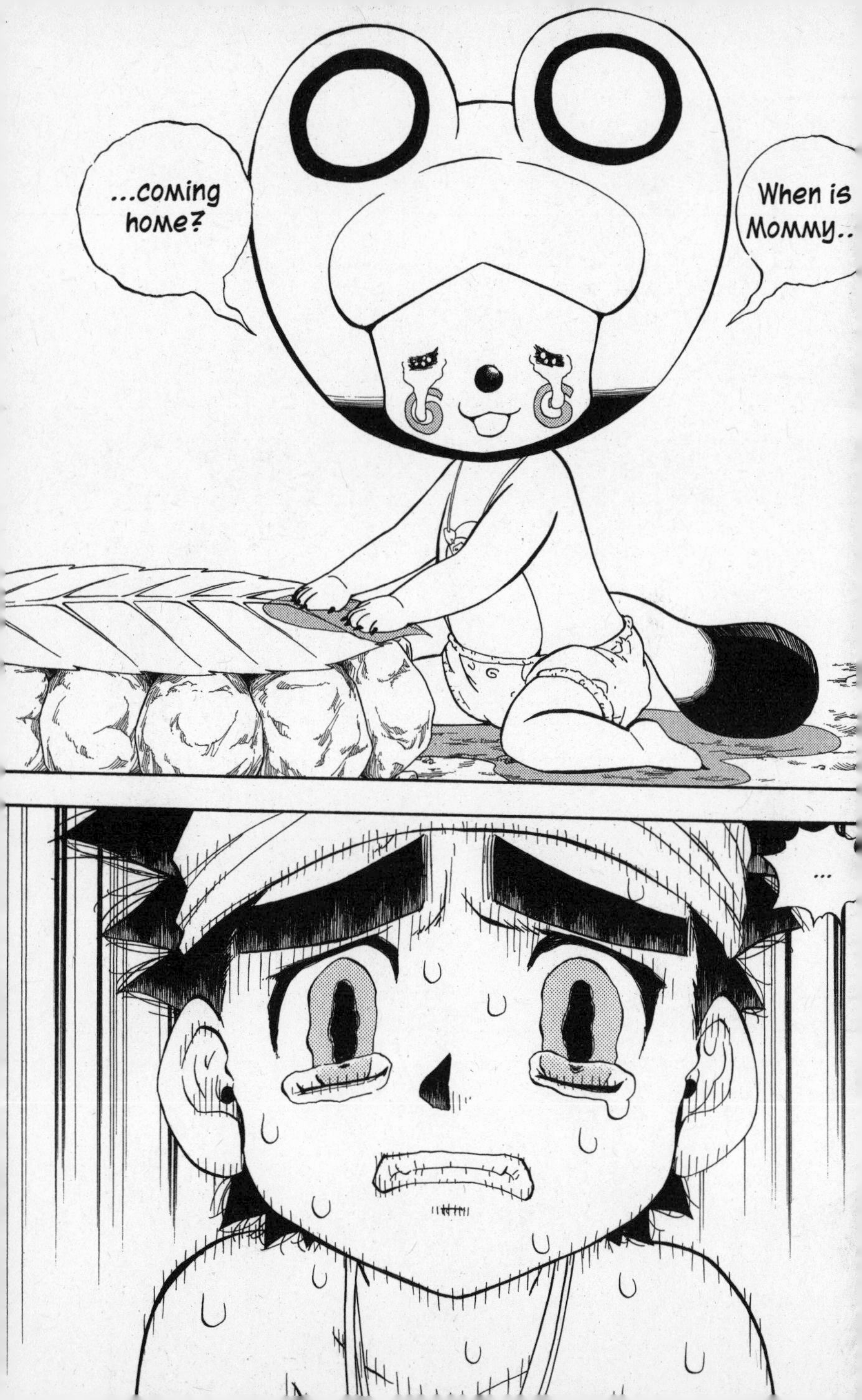
When is Mommy..
...coming home?
...

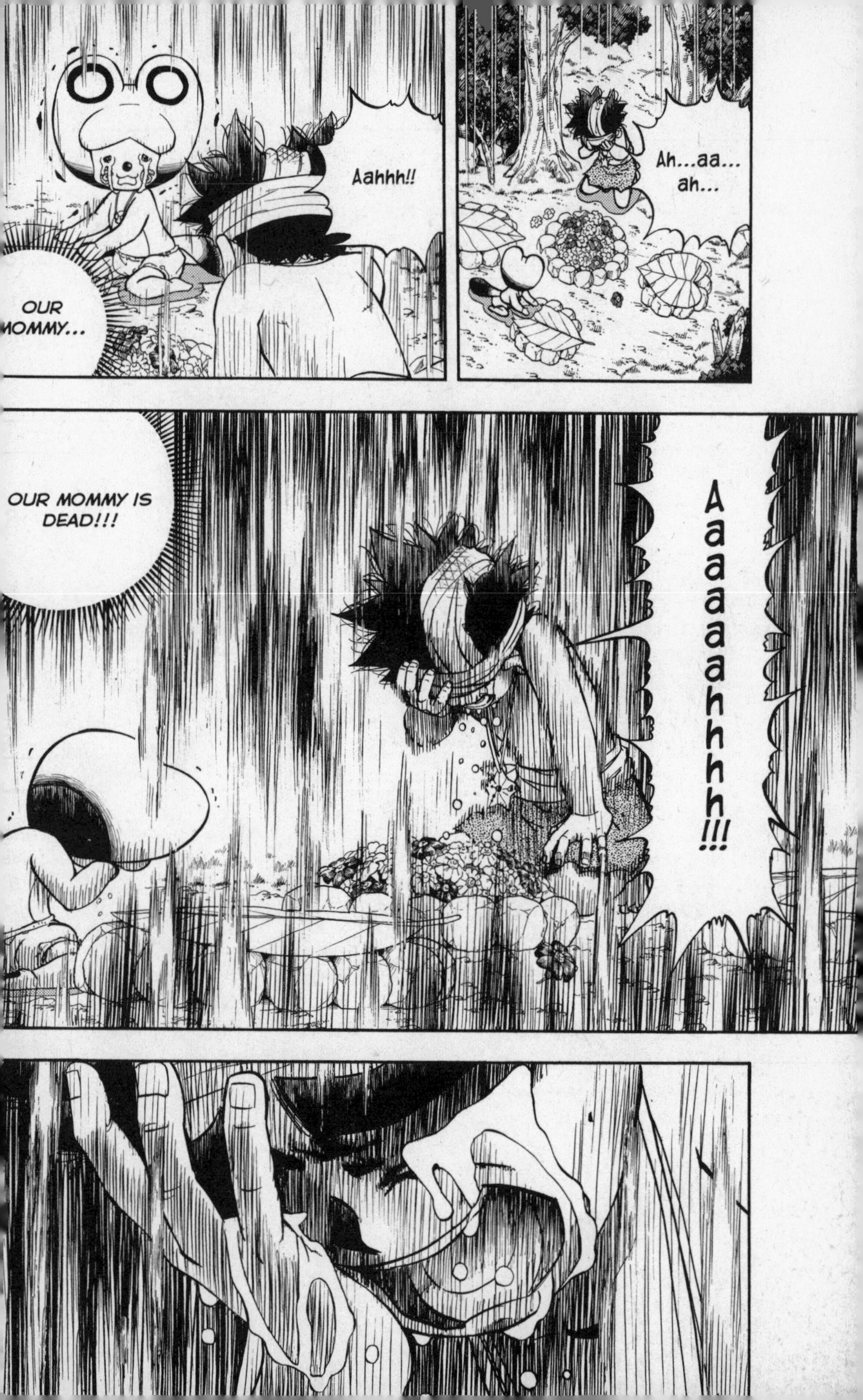
Ah...aa...
ah...
Aahhh!!
OUR MOMMY...
Aaaaaahhhh!!!
OUR MOMMY IS DEAD!!!

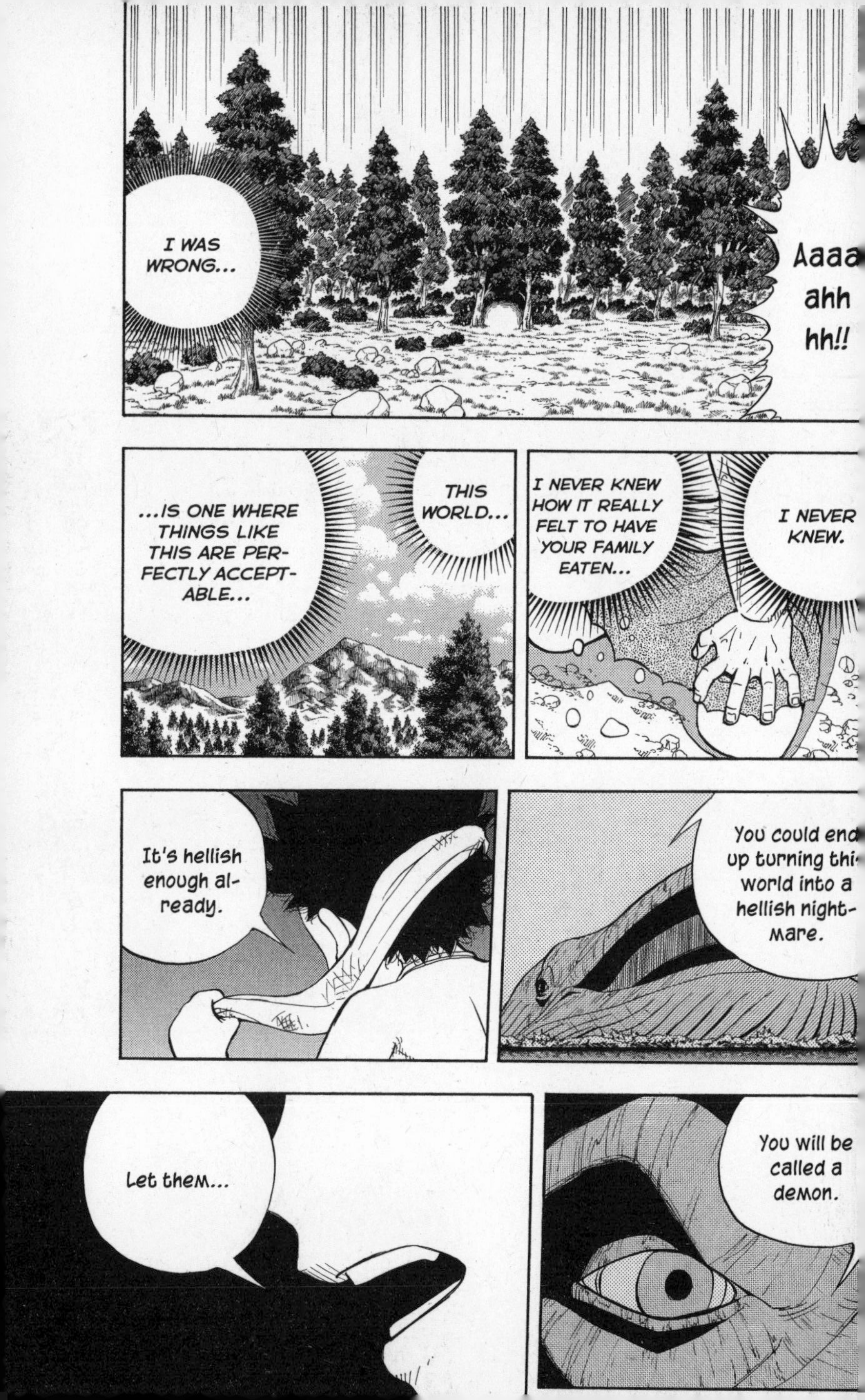
Aaaaahhhh!!
I WAS WRONG...
I NEVER KNEW.
I NEVER KNEW HOW IT REALLY FELT TO HAVE YOUR FAMILY EATEN...
THIS WORLD...
...IS ONE WHERE THINGS LIKE THIS ARE PERFECTLY ACCEPTABLE...
You could end up turning thi world into a hellish nightmare.
It's hellish enough already.
You will be called a demon.
Let them...

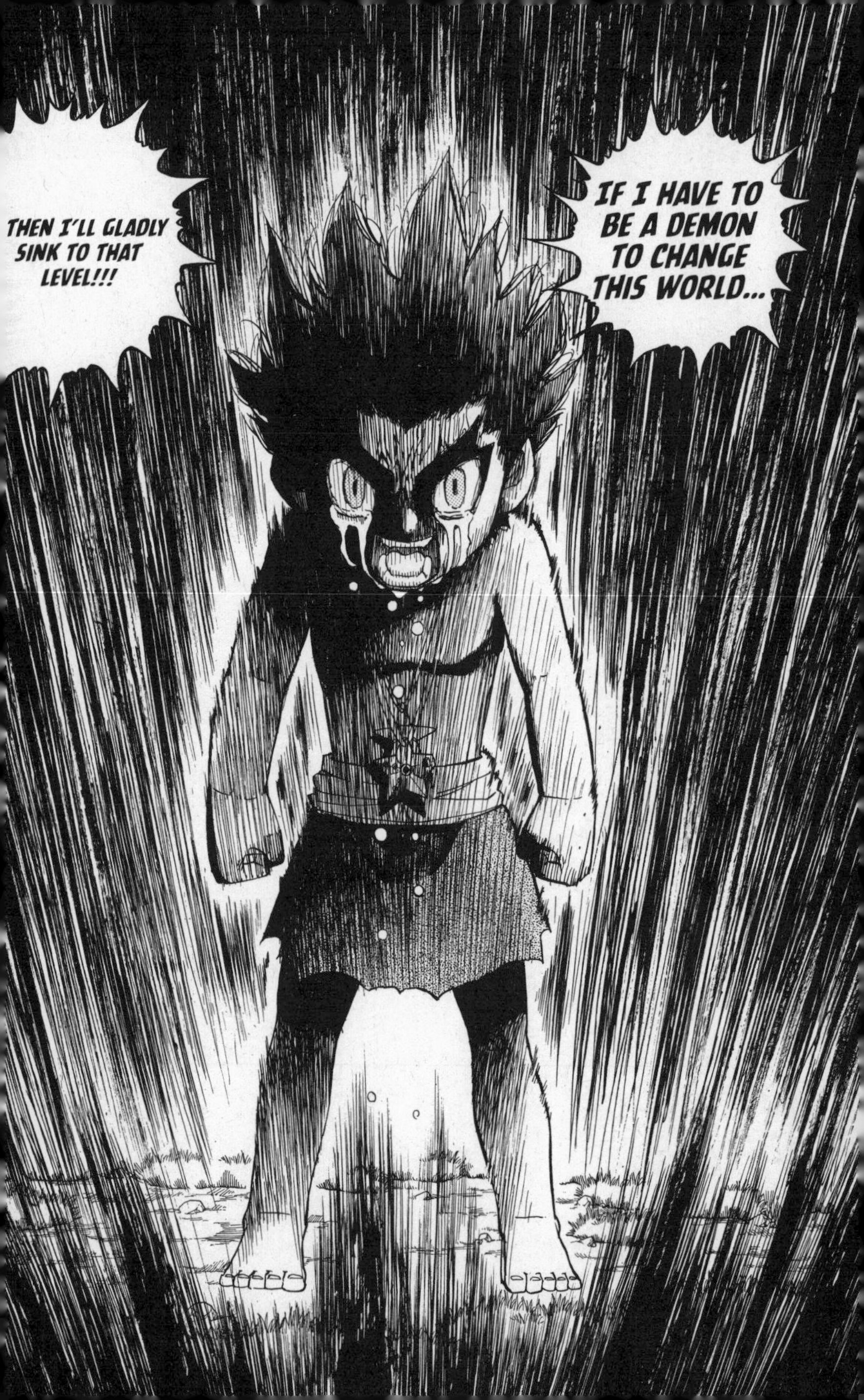
IF I HAVE TO BE A DEMON TO CHANGE THIS WORLD...
THEN I'LL GLADLY SINK TO THAT LEVEL!!!

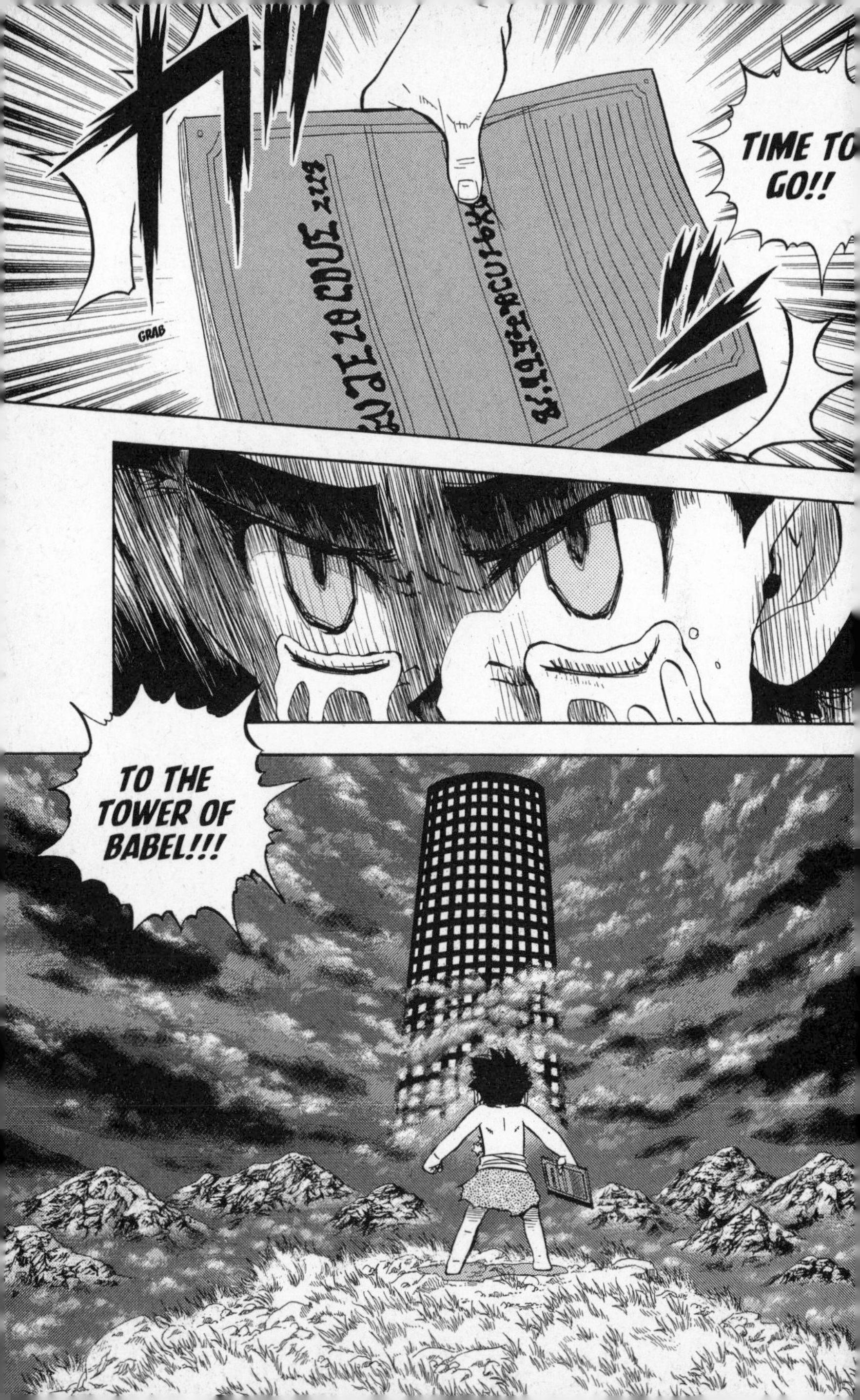
TIME TO GO!!
GRAB
TO THE TOWER OF BABEL!!!

Five years later...

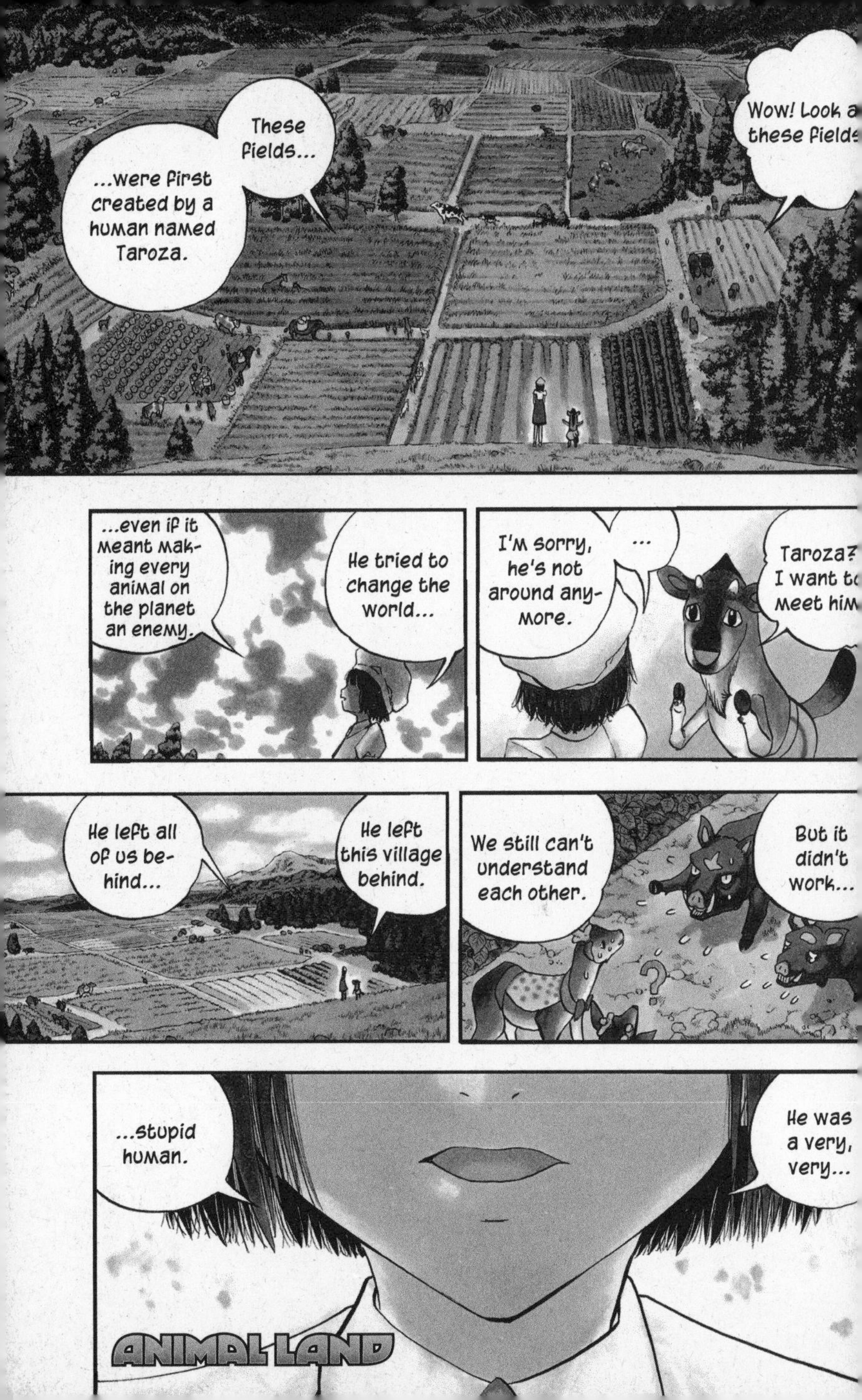

Wow! Look a these field
These fields...
...were first created by a human named Taroza.
Taroza? I want t meet him
...
I'm sorry, he's not around any-more.
He tried to change the world...
...even if it meant mak-ing every animal on the planet an enemy.
But it didn't work...
We still can't understand each other.
He left this village behind.
He left all of us be-hind...
He was a very, very...
...stupid human.
ANIMAL LAND

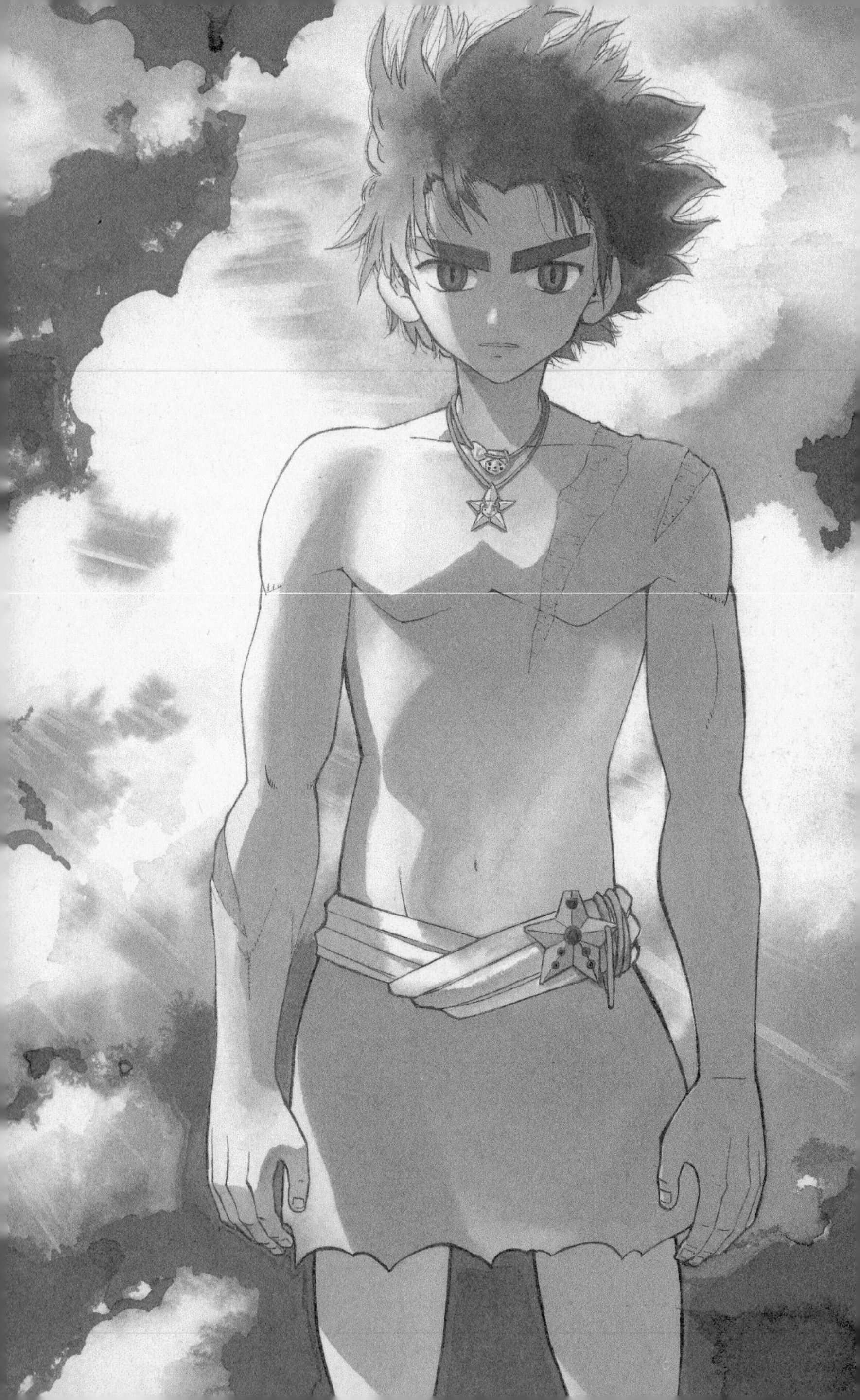

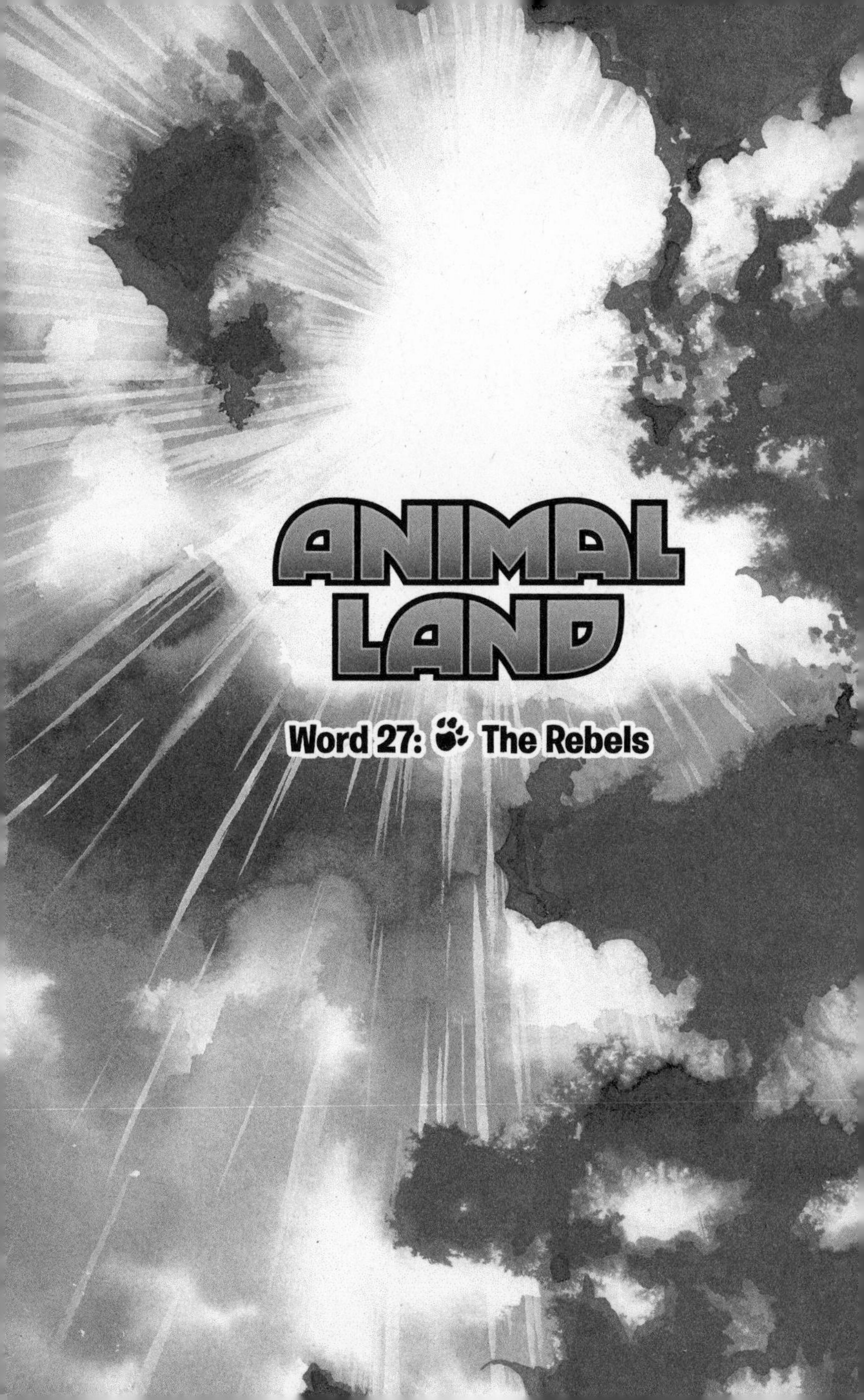
ANIMAL LAND
Word 27: The Rebels

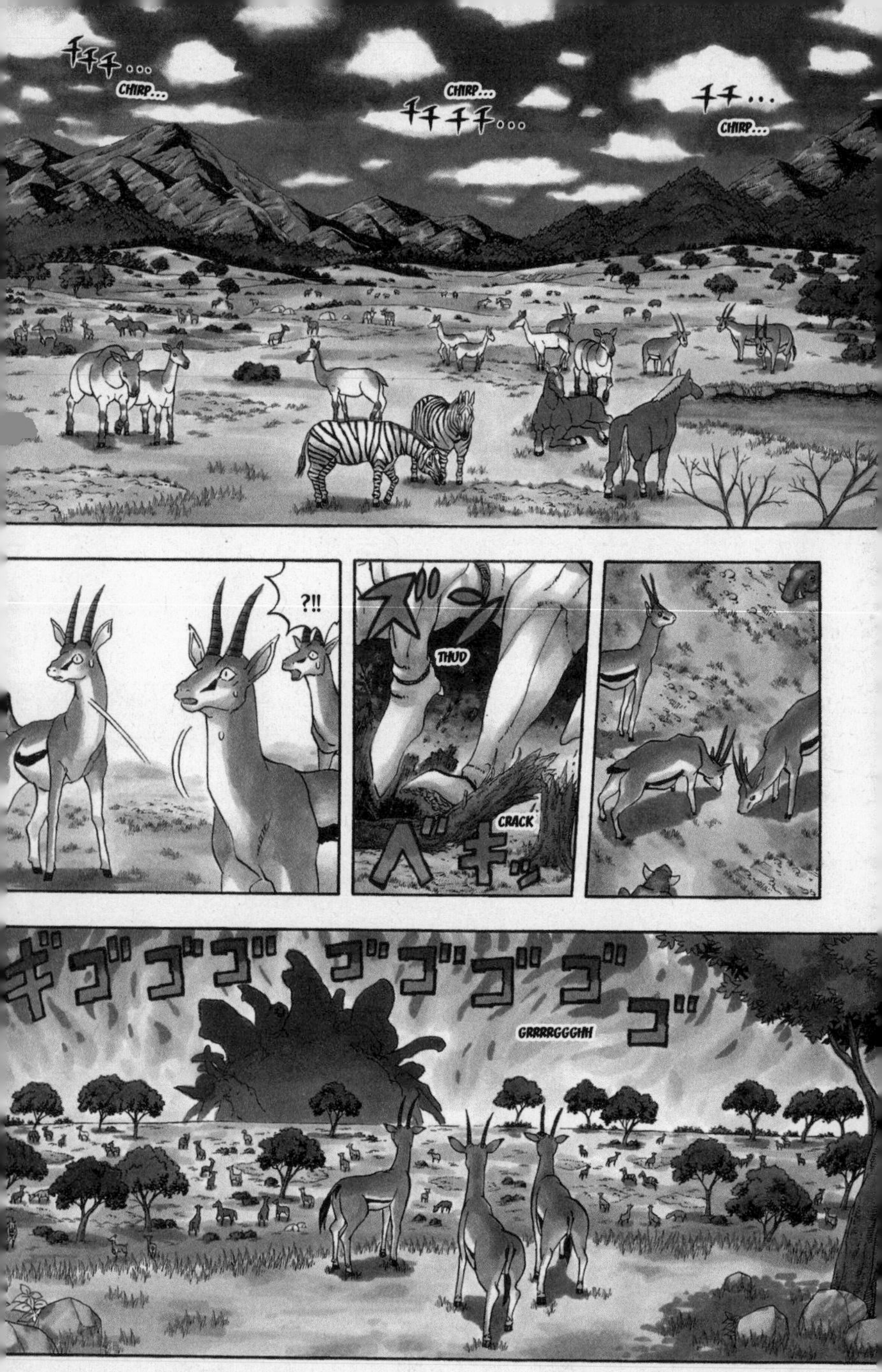
チチ…
CHIRP…
CHIRP…
チチチチ…
チチチ…
CHIRP…
ズ
THUD
ベキッ
CRACK
?!!
ギゴゴゴゴゴゴゴ
GRRRRGGGHH

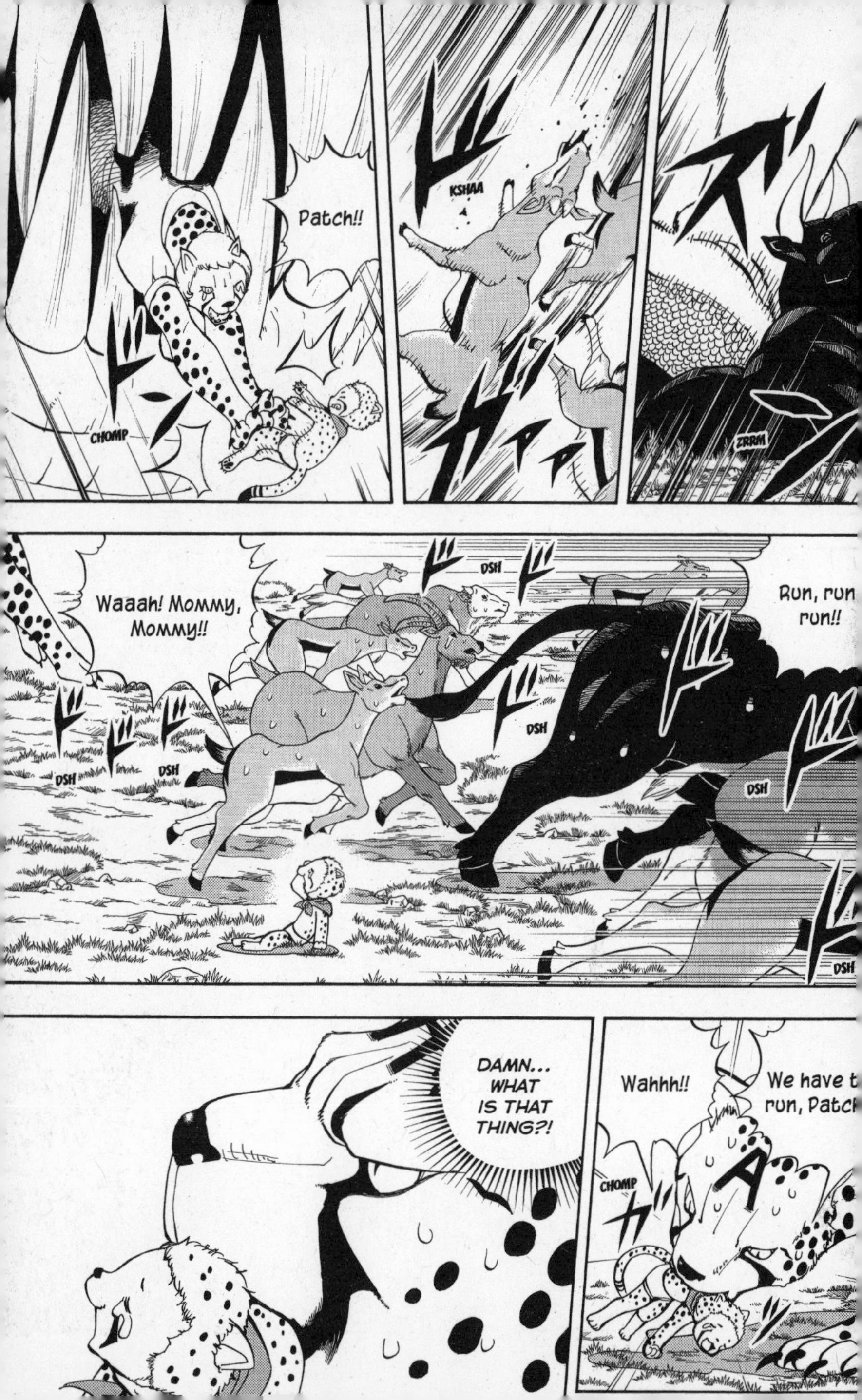
ZRRM
KSHAA
Patch!!
CHOMP
Run, run run!!
DSH
DSH
DSH
DSH
Waaah! Mommy, Mommy!!
DSH
DSH
We have t run, Patc
Wahhh!!
CHOMP
DAMN... WHAT IS THAT THING?!

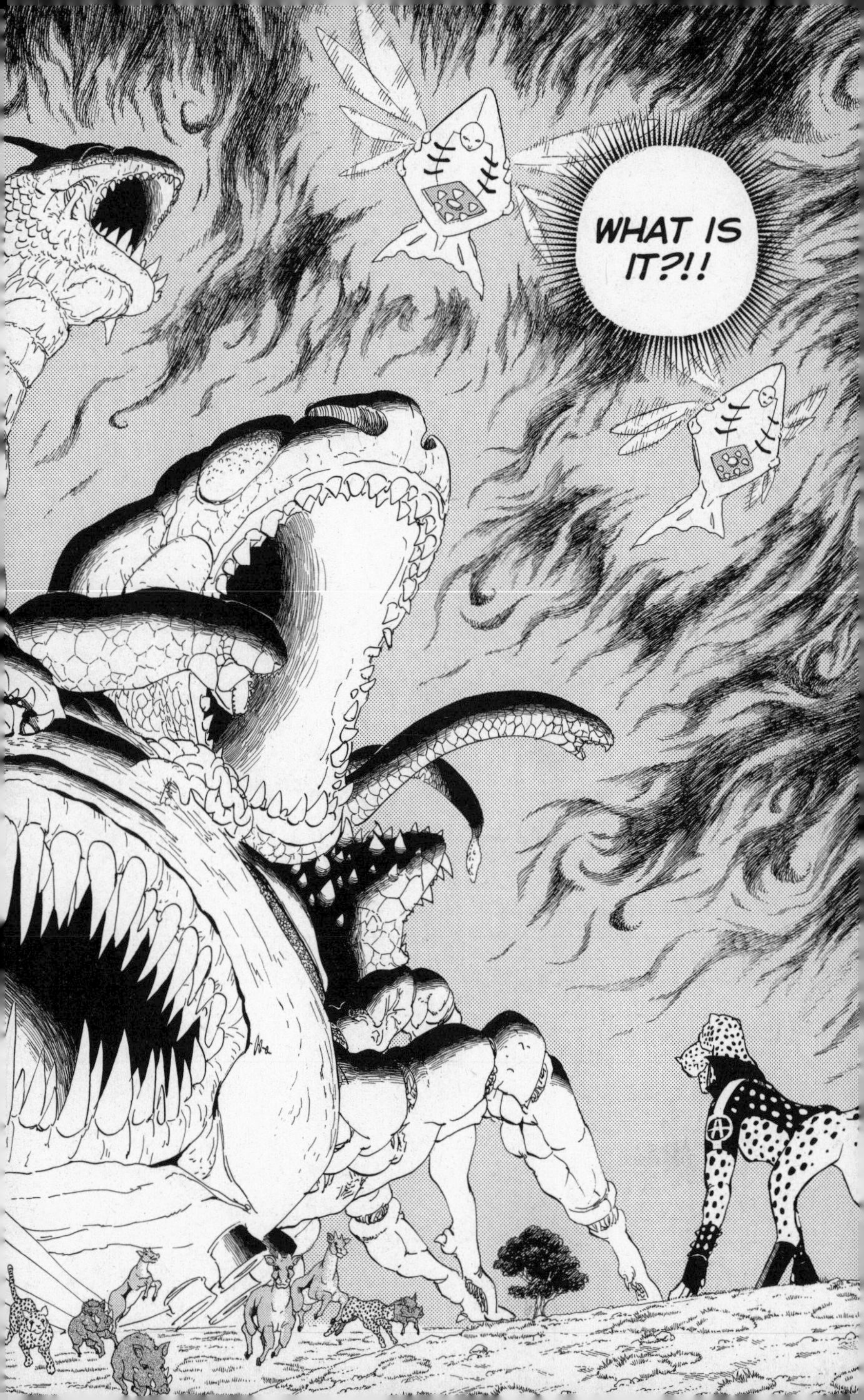
WHAT IS IT?!!

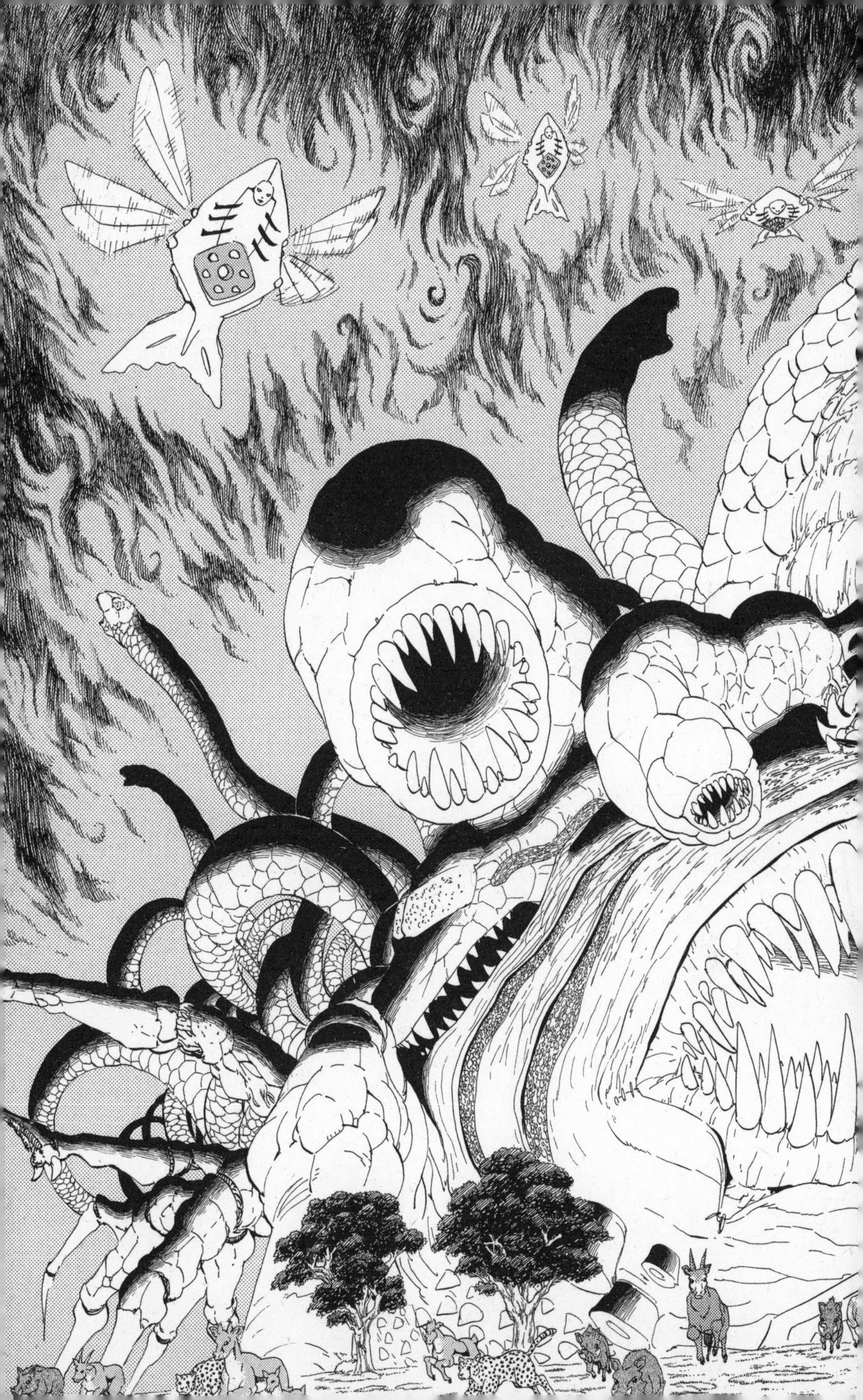

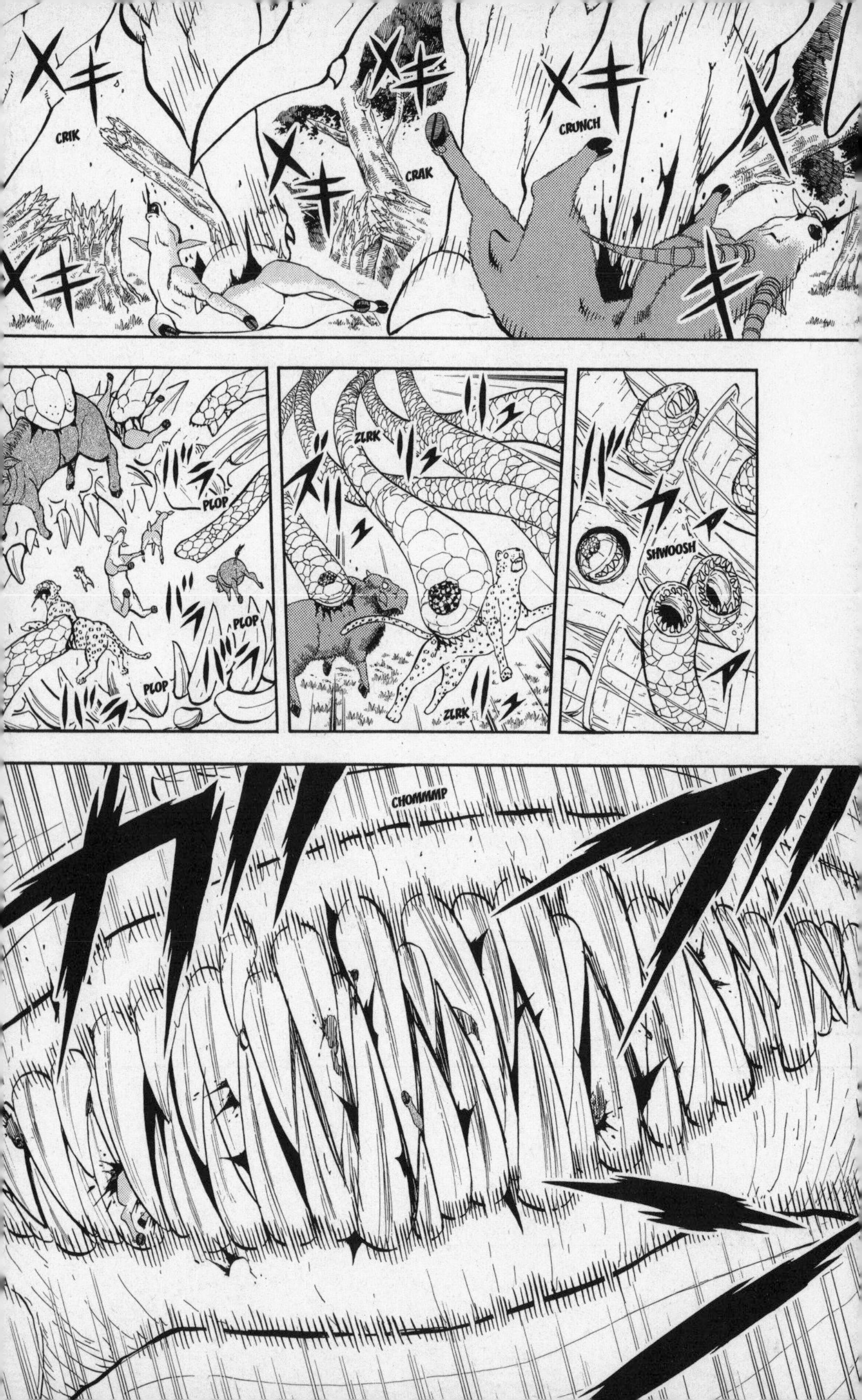
CRUNCH
CRAK
CRIK
SHWOOSH
ZLRK
ZLRK
PLOP
PLOP
PLOP
CHOMMMP

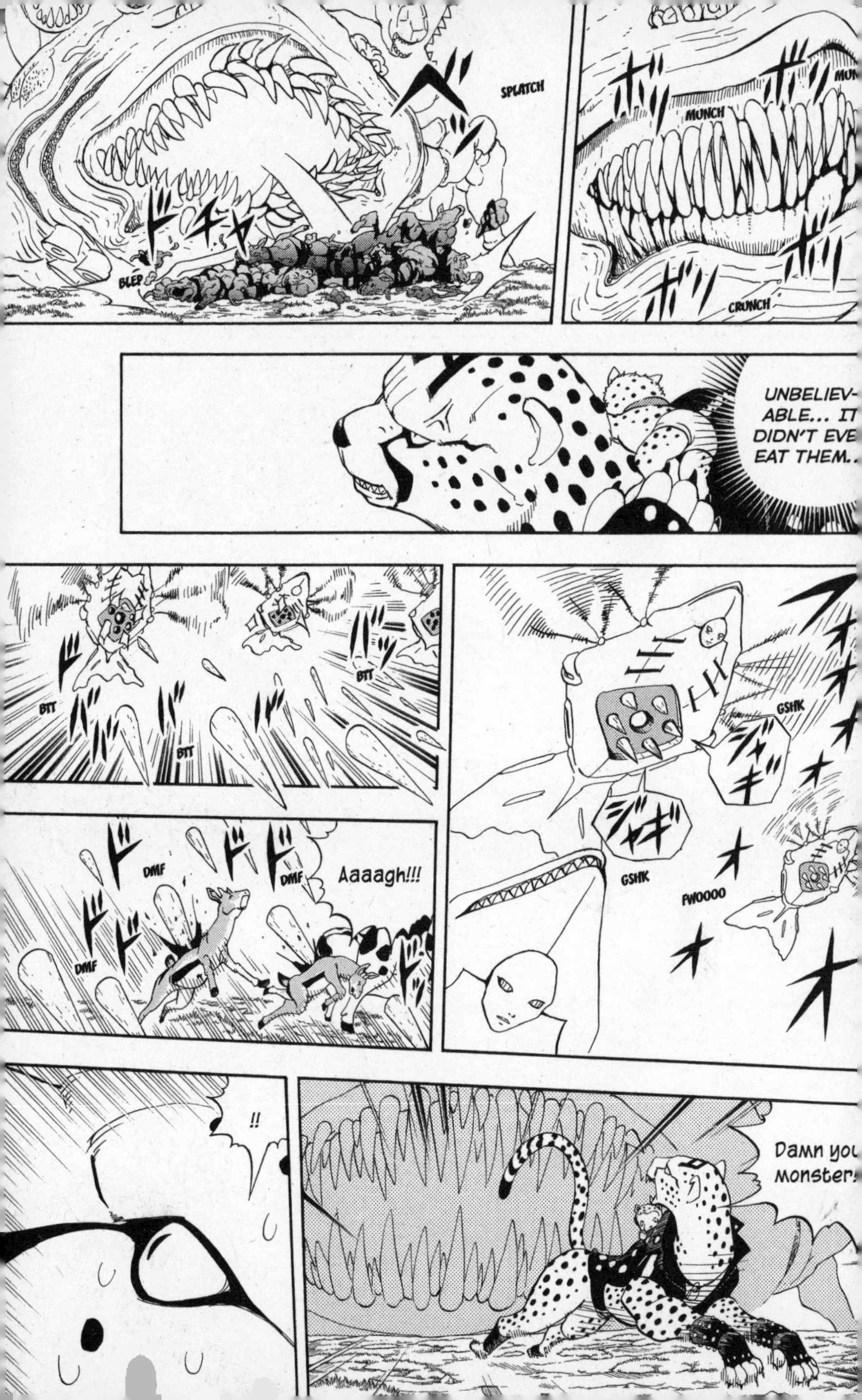
MUNCH
MUN
CRUNCH
SPLATCH
BLEP
UNBELIEV-
ABLE... IT
DIDN'T EVE
EAT THEM..
GSHK
GSHK
FWOOOO
BTT
BTT
BTT
DMF
Aaaagh!!!
DMF
DMF
Damn you
monster!
!!

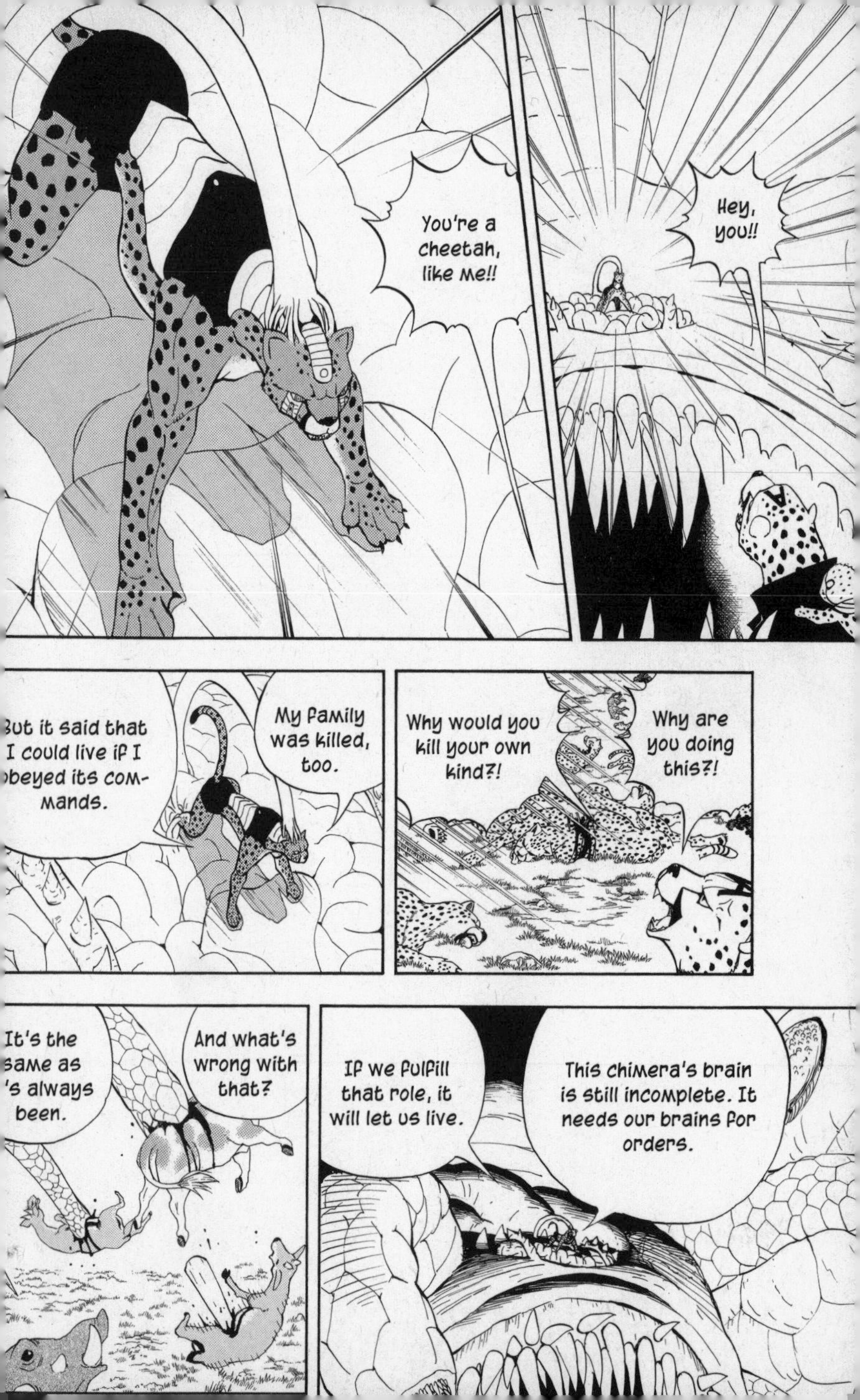
Hey, you!!
You're a cheetah, like me!!
Why are you doing this?!
Why would you kill your own kind?!
My family was killed, too.
ut it said that I could live if I beyed its com-mands.
This chimera's brain is still incomplete. It needs our brains for orders.
If we fulfill that role, it will let us live.
And what's wrong with that?
It's the ame as 's always been.

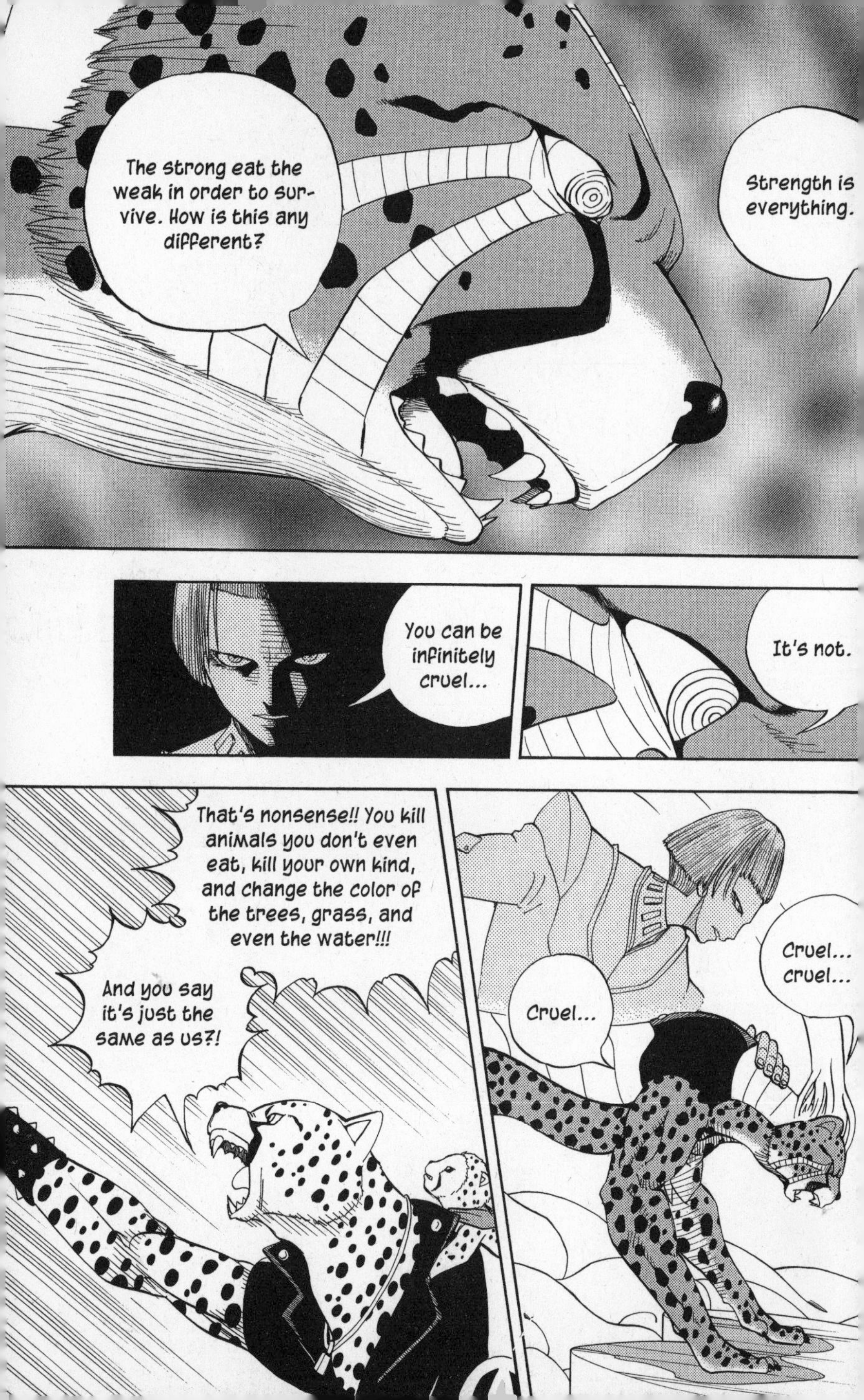
Strength is everything.
The strong eat the weak in order to survive. How is this any different?
It's not.
You can be infinitely cruel...
Cruel... cruel...
Cruel...
That's nonsense!! You kill animals you don't even eat, kill your own kind, and change the color of the trees, grass, and even the water!!!
And you say it's just the same as us?!

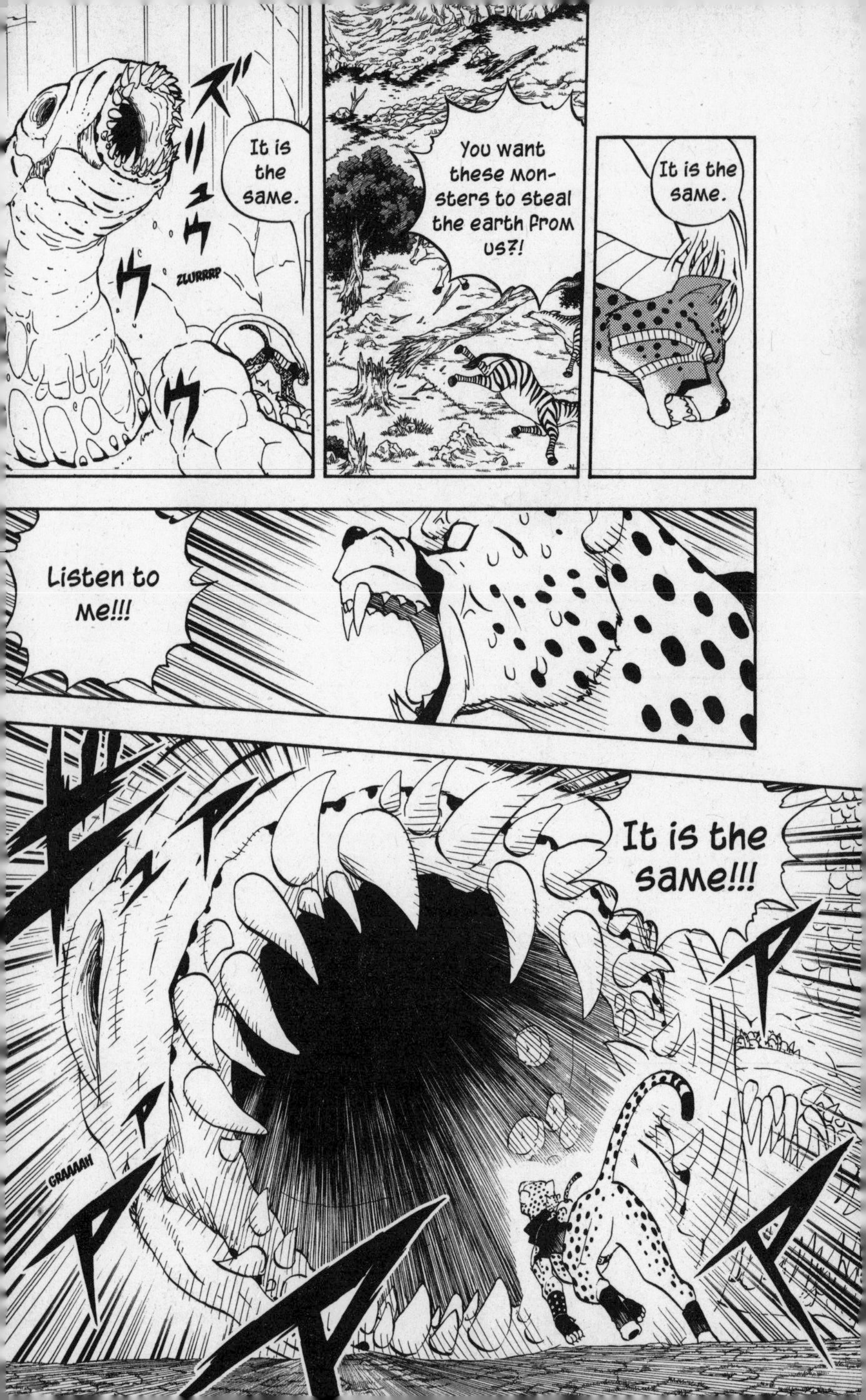
It is the same.
You want these mon-sters to steal the earth from us?!
It is the same.
ZLURRRP
Listen to me!!!
It is the same!!!
GRAAAAH

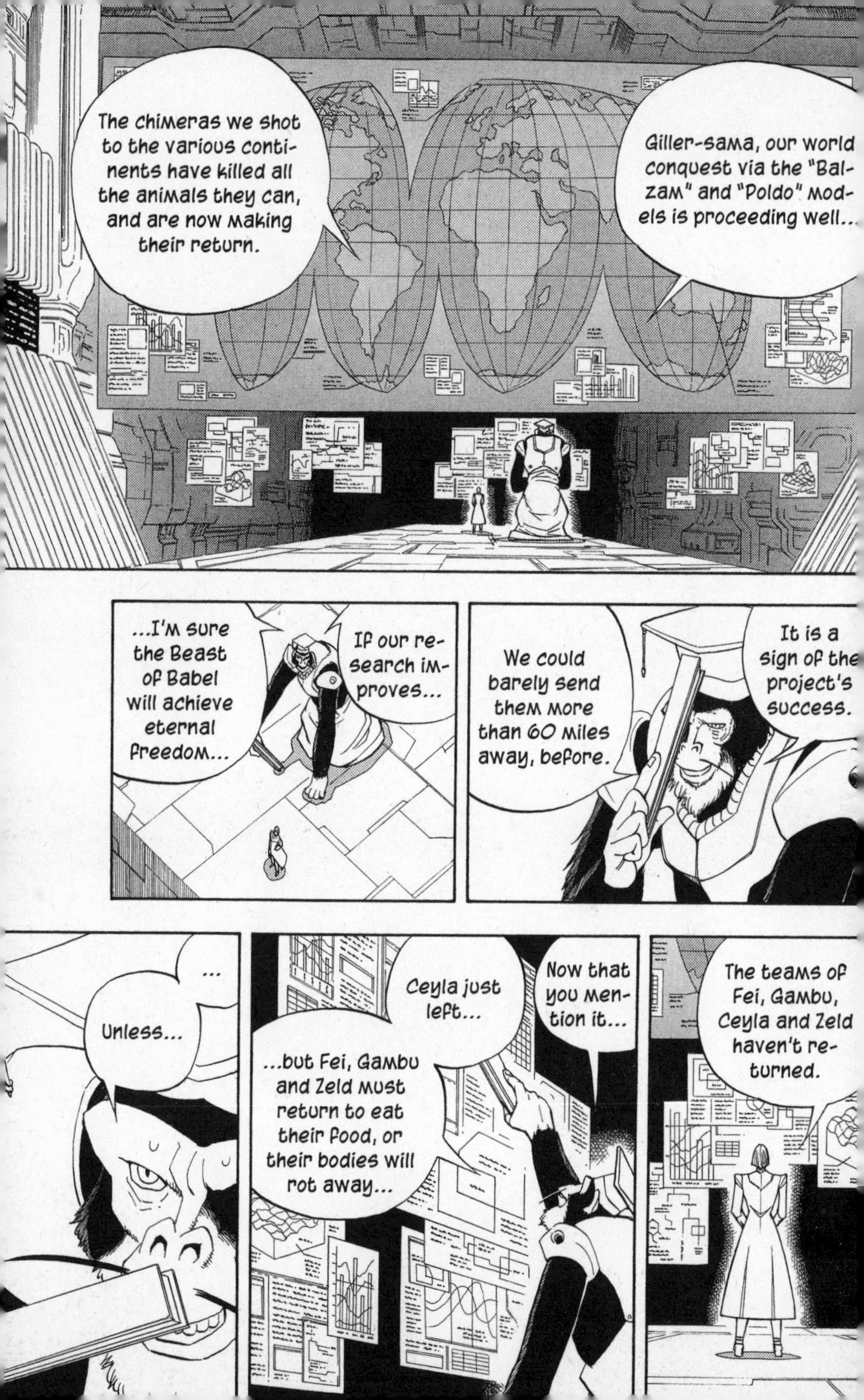
Giller-sama, our world conquest via the "Balzam" and "Poldo" models is proceeding well...
The chimeras we shot to the various continents have killed all the animals they can, and are now making their return.
It is a sign of the project's success.
We could barely send them more than 60 miles away, before.
If our research improves...
...I'm sure the Beast of Babel will achieve eternal freedom...
The teams of Fei, Gambu, Ceyla and Zeld haven't returned.
Now that you mention it...
Ceyla just left...
...but Fei, Gambu and Zeld must return to eat their food, or their bodies will rot away...
...
Unless...

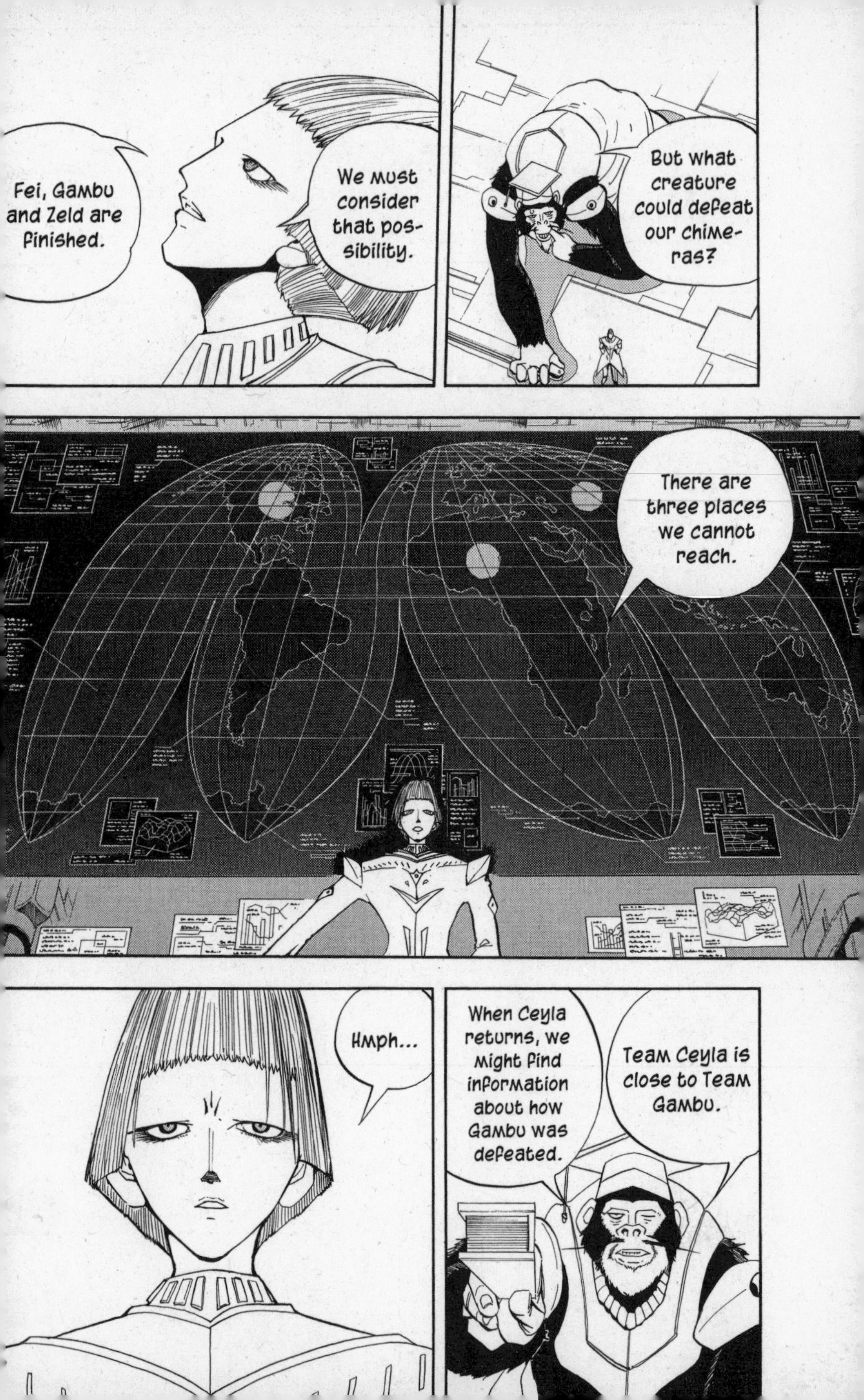
But what creature could defeat our chimeras?
We must consider that possibility.
Fei, Gambu and Zeld are finished.
There are three places we cannot reach.
Team Ceyla is close to Team Gambu.
When Ceyla returns, we might find information about how Gambu was defeated.
Hmph...

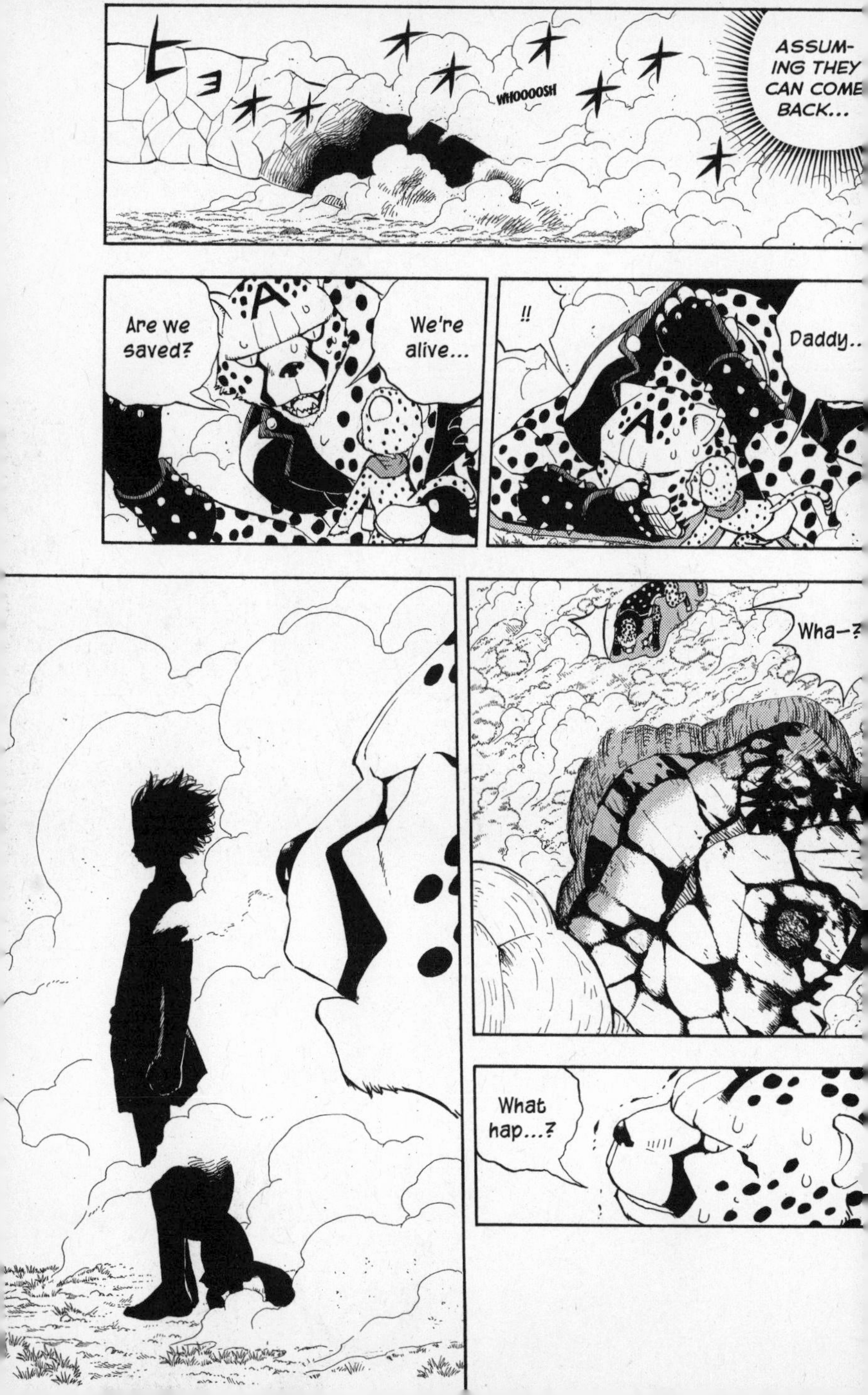
ASSUMING THEY CAN COME BACK...
WHOOOOSH
ヒョ
Daddy...
!!
We're alive...
Are we saved?
Wha—?
What hap...?

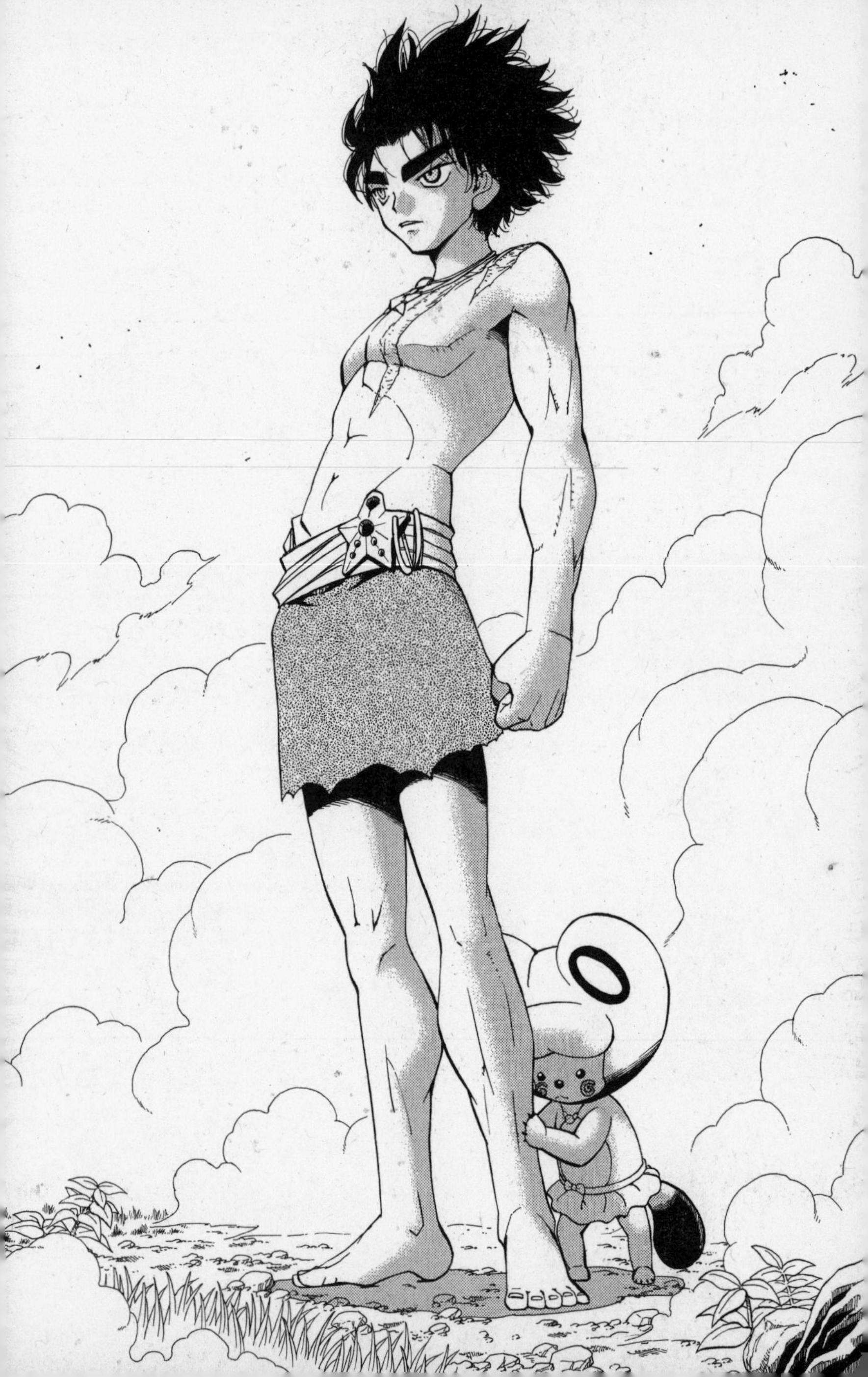

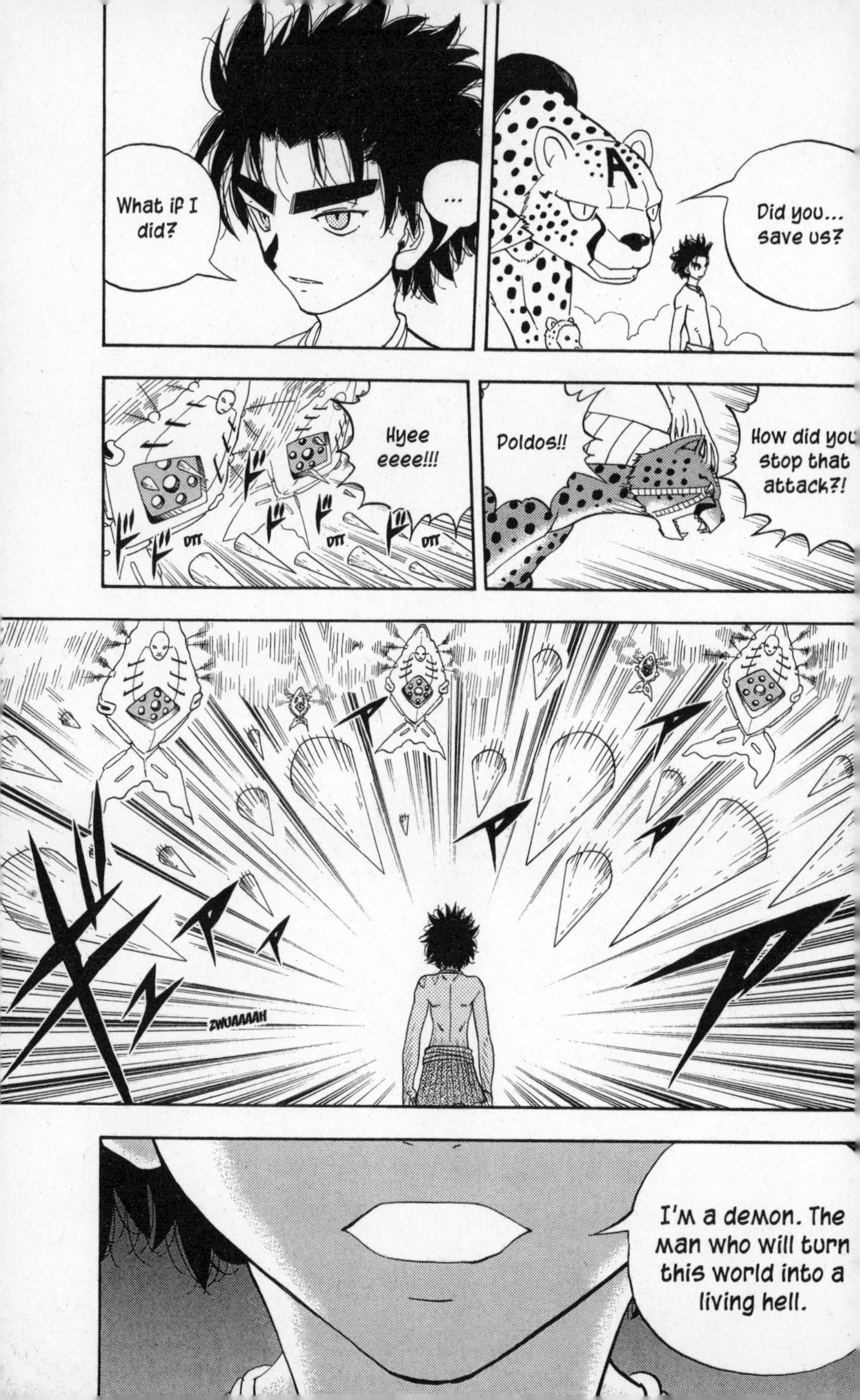
Did you... save us?
...
What if I did?
How did you stop that attack?!
Poldos!!
Hyee eeee!!!
DTT
DTT
DTT
ZWUAAAAH
I'm a demon. The man who will turn this world into a living hell.

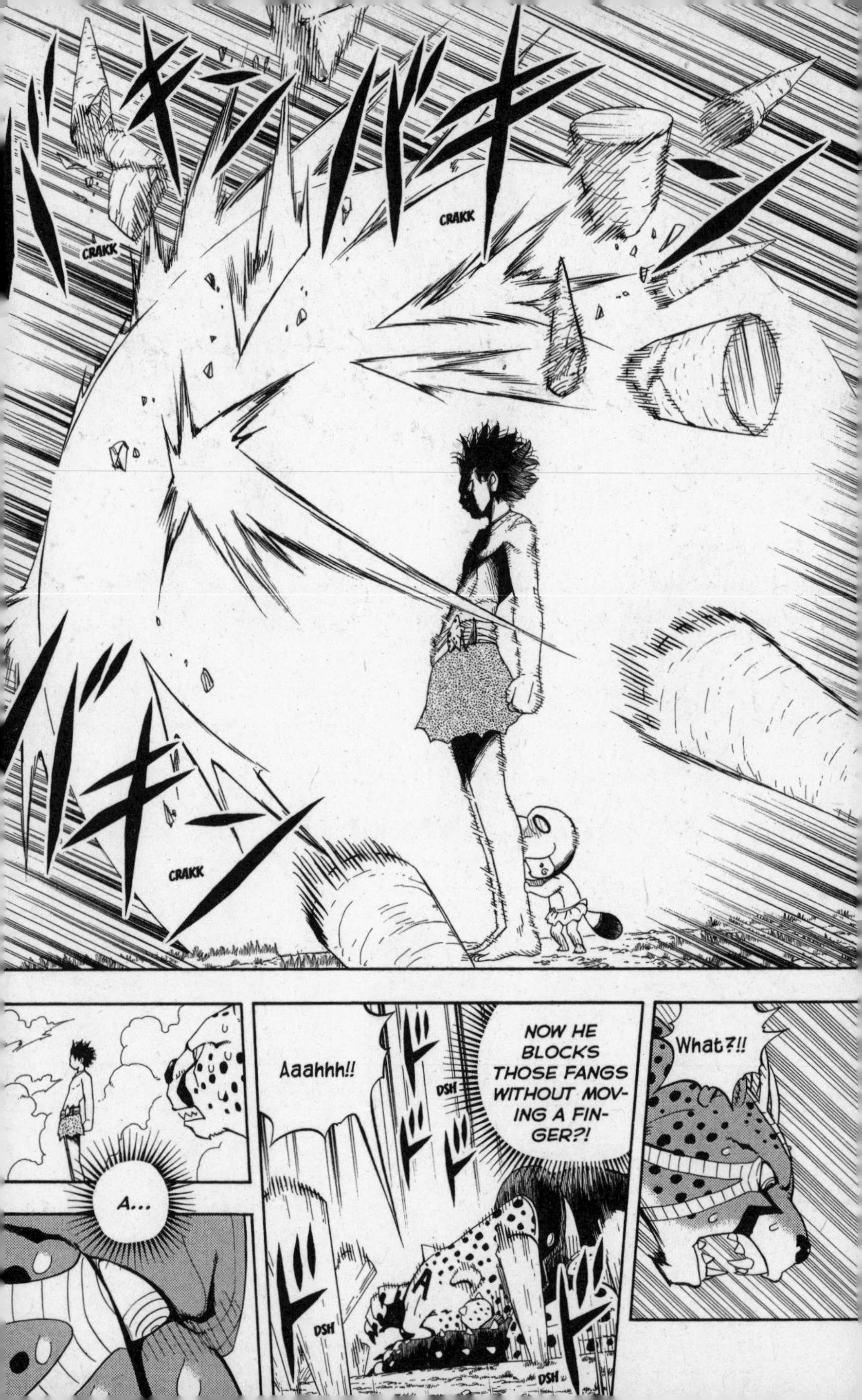
CRAKK
CRAKK
CRAKK
What?!!
NOW HE BLOCKS THOSE FANGS WITHOUT MOV-ING A FIN-GER?!
Aaahhh!!
DSH
DSH
DSH
A...

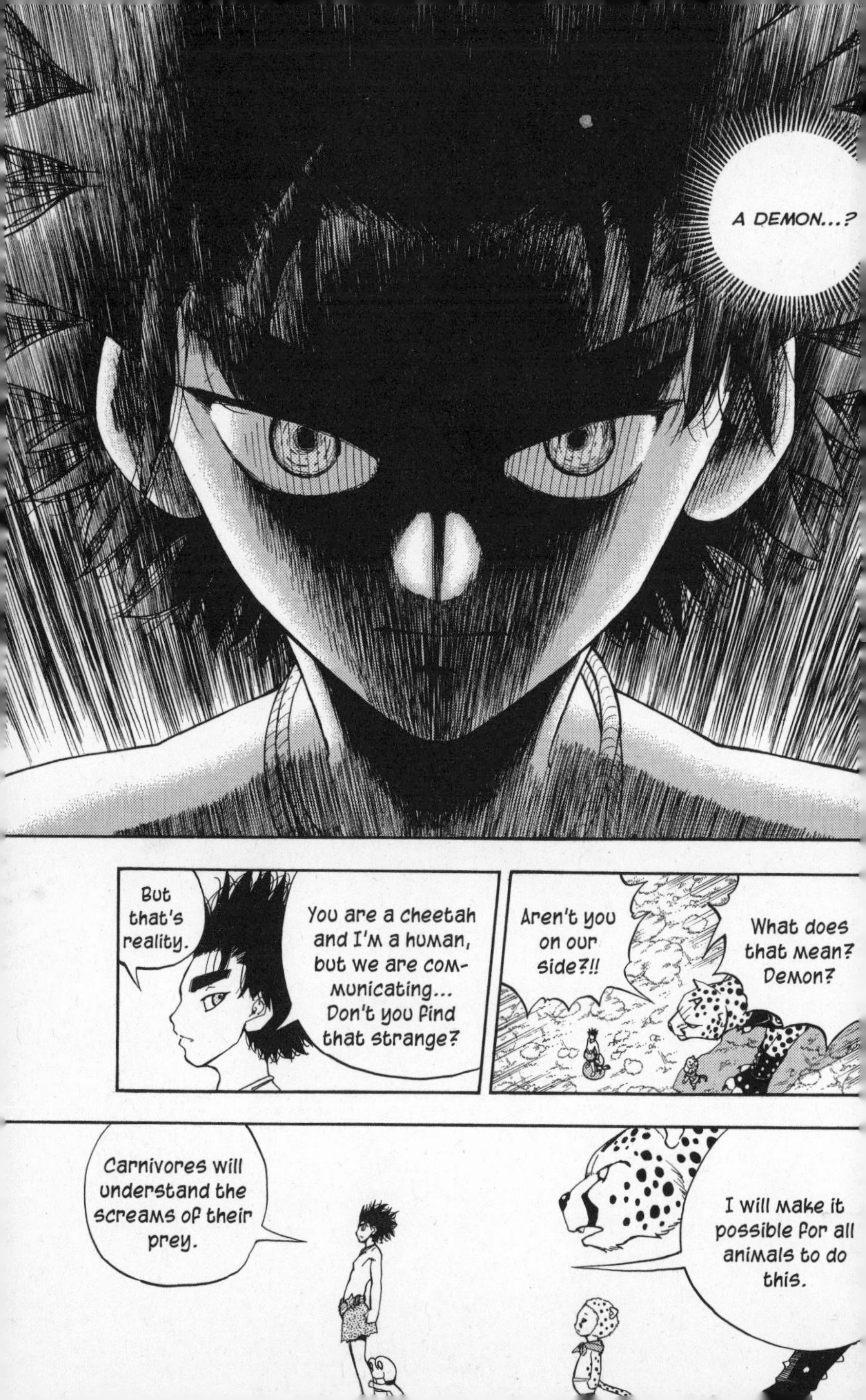
A DEMON...?
What does that mean? Demon?
Aren't you on our side?!!
You are a cheetah and I'm a human, but we are com-municating... Don't you find that strange?
But that's reality.
I will make it possible for all animals to do this.
Carnivores will understand the screams of their prey.

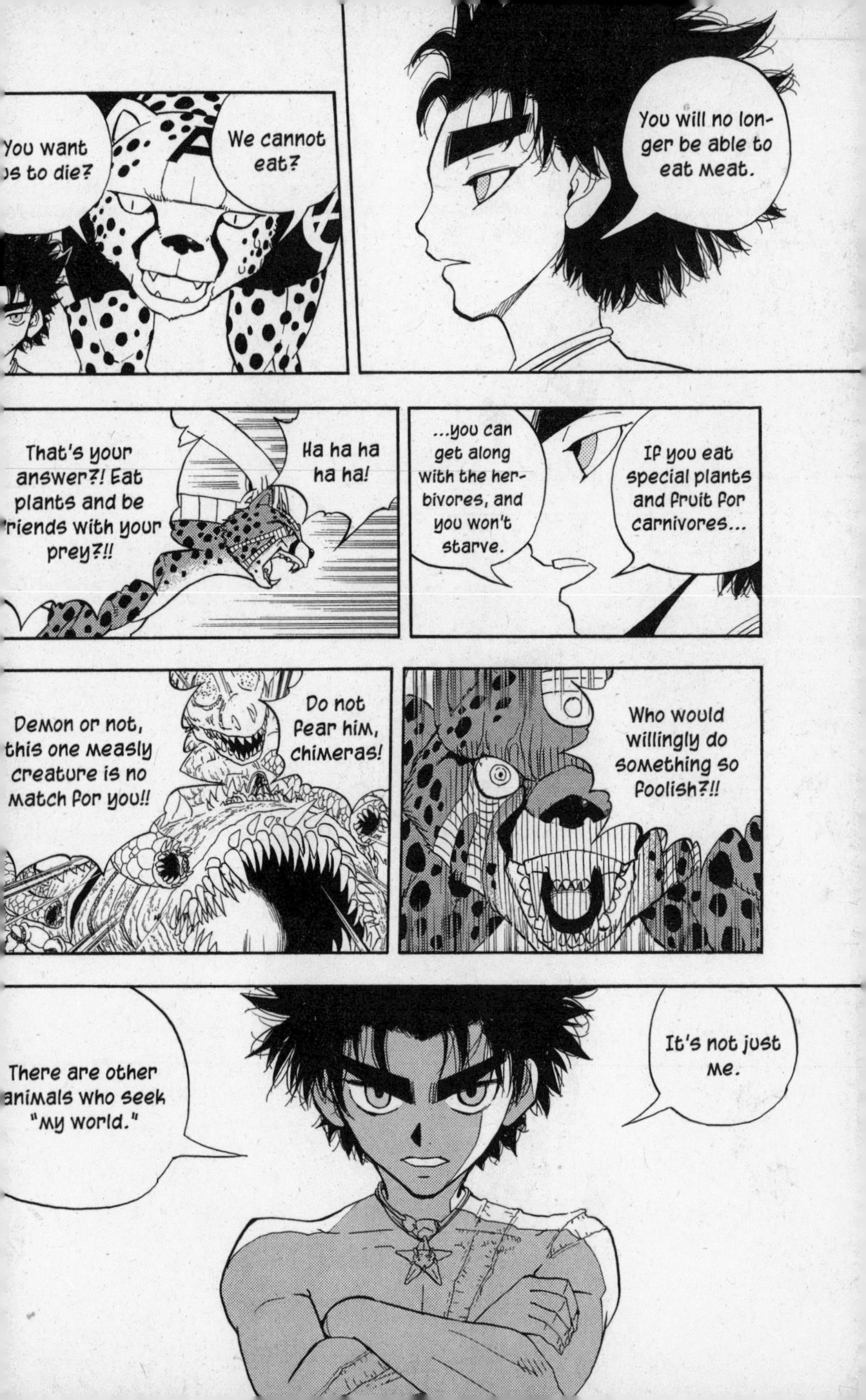
You will no longer be able to eat meat.
We cannot eat?
You want s to die?
If you eat special plants and fruit for carnivores...
...you can get along with the herbivores, and you won't starve.
Ha ha ha ha ha!
That's your answer?! Eat plants and be riends with your prey?!!
Who would willingly do something so foolish?!!
Do not fear him, Chimeras!
Demon or not, this one measly creature is no match for you!!
It's not just me.
There are other animals who seek "my world."

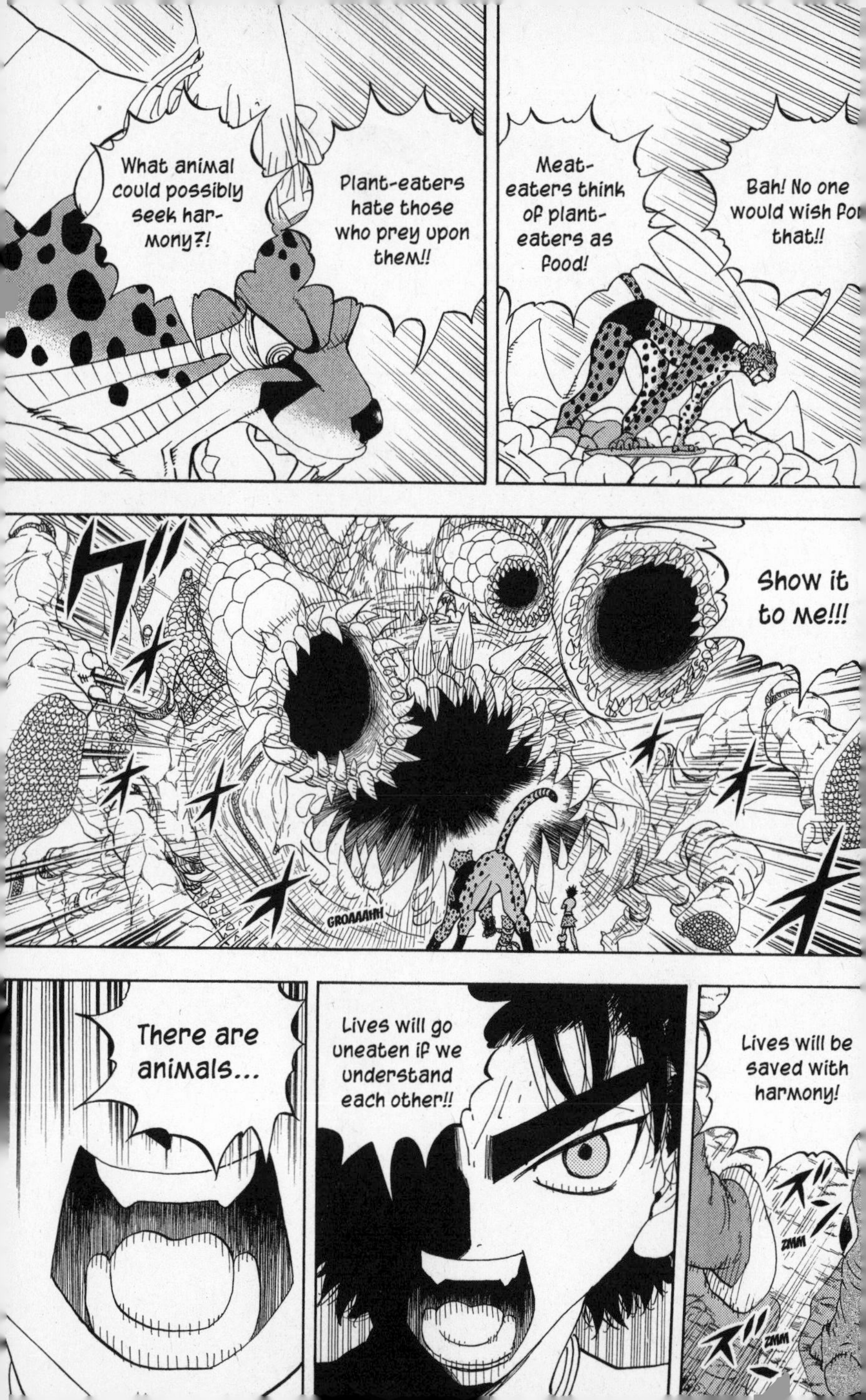

Bah! No one would wish fo that!!
Meat-eaters think of plant-eaters as food!
Plant-eaters hate those who prey upon them!!
What animal could possibly seek harmony?!
Show it to me!!!
GROAAAHH
Lives will be saved with harmony!
ZMM
ZMM
Lives will go uneaten if we understand each other!!
There are animals...

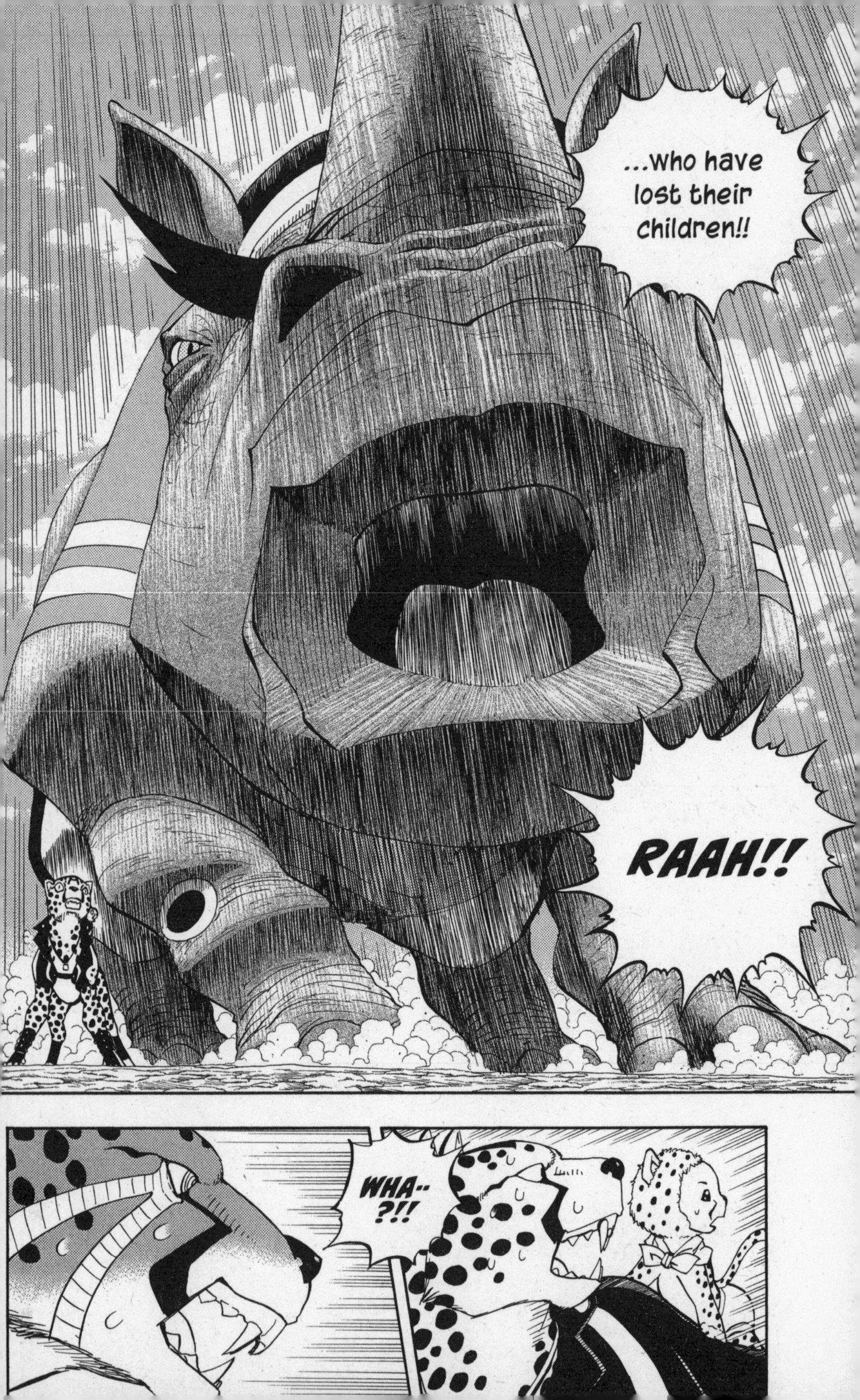
...who have lost their children!!
RAAH!!
WHA-- ?!!

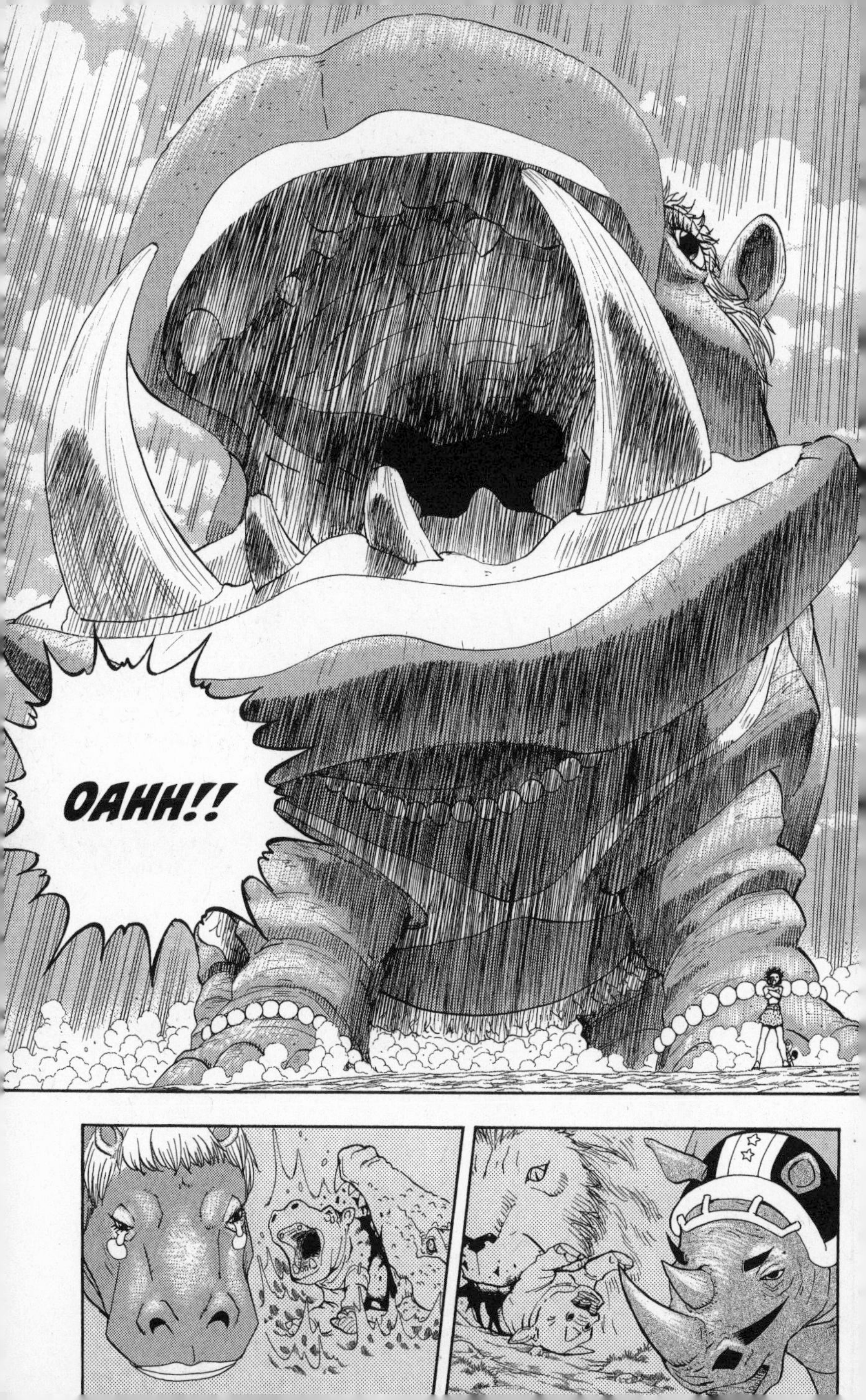
OAHH!!

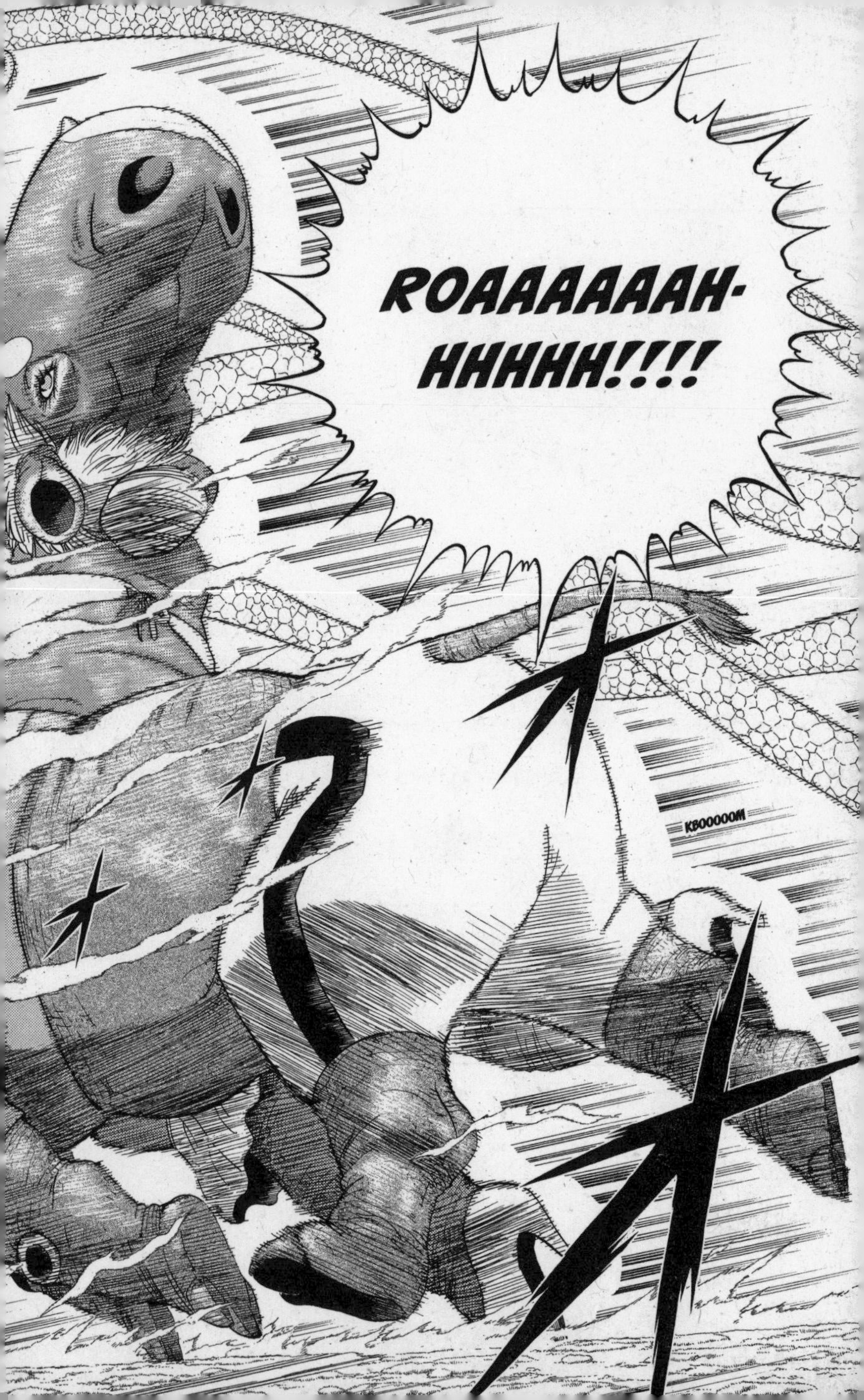
ROAAAAAAH-HHHHH!!!!
KBOOOOOM

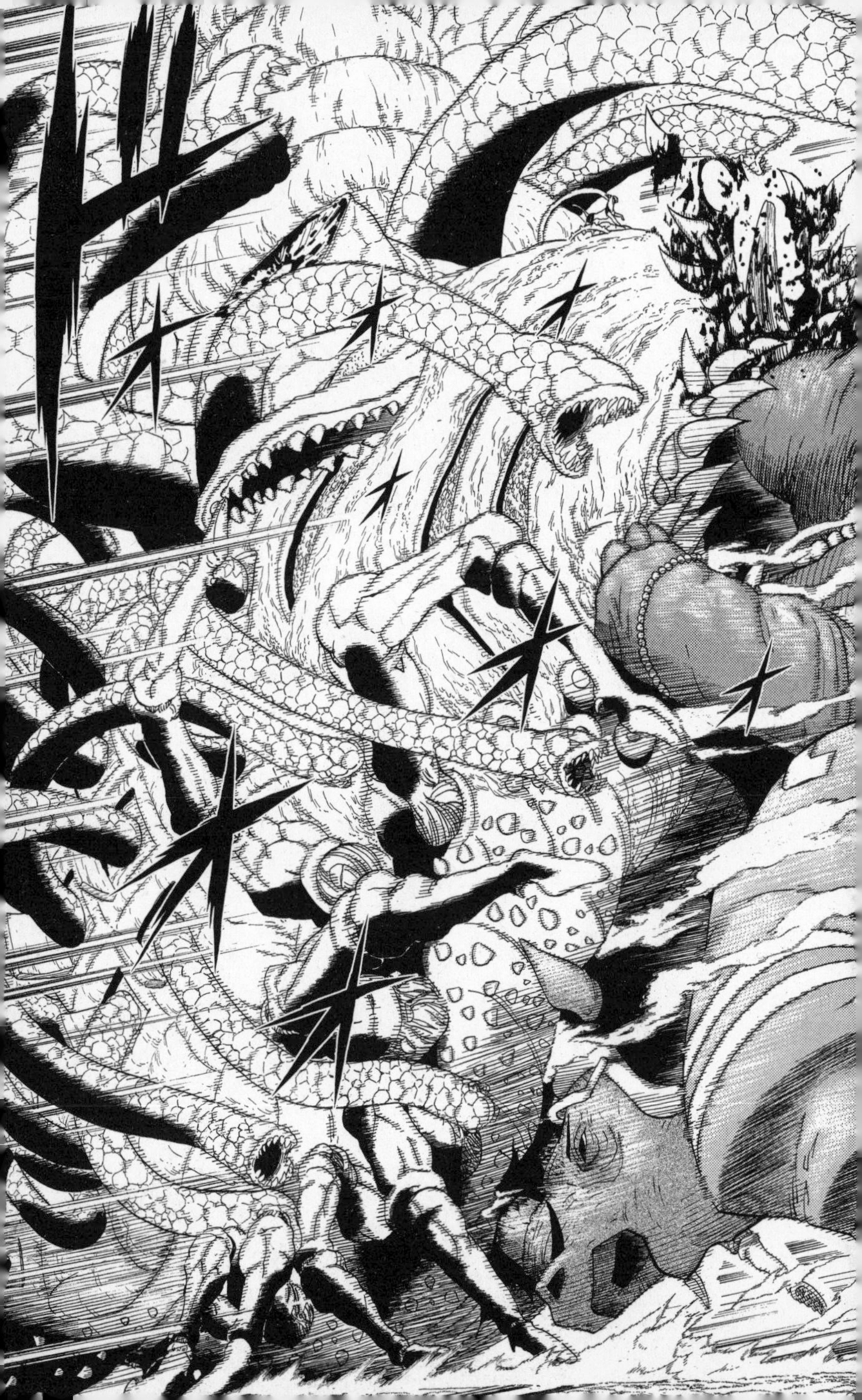

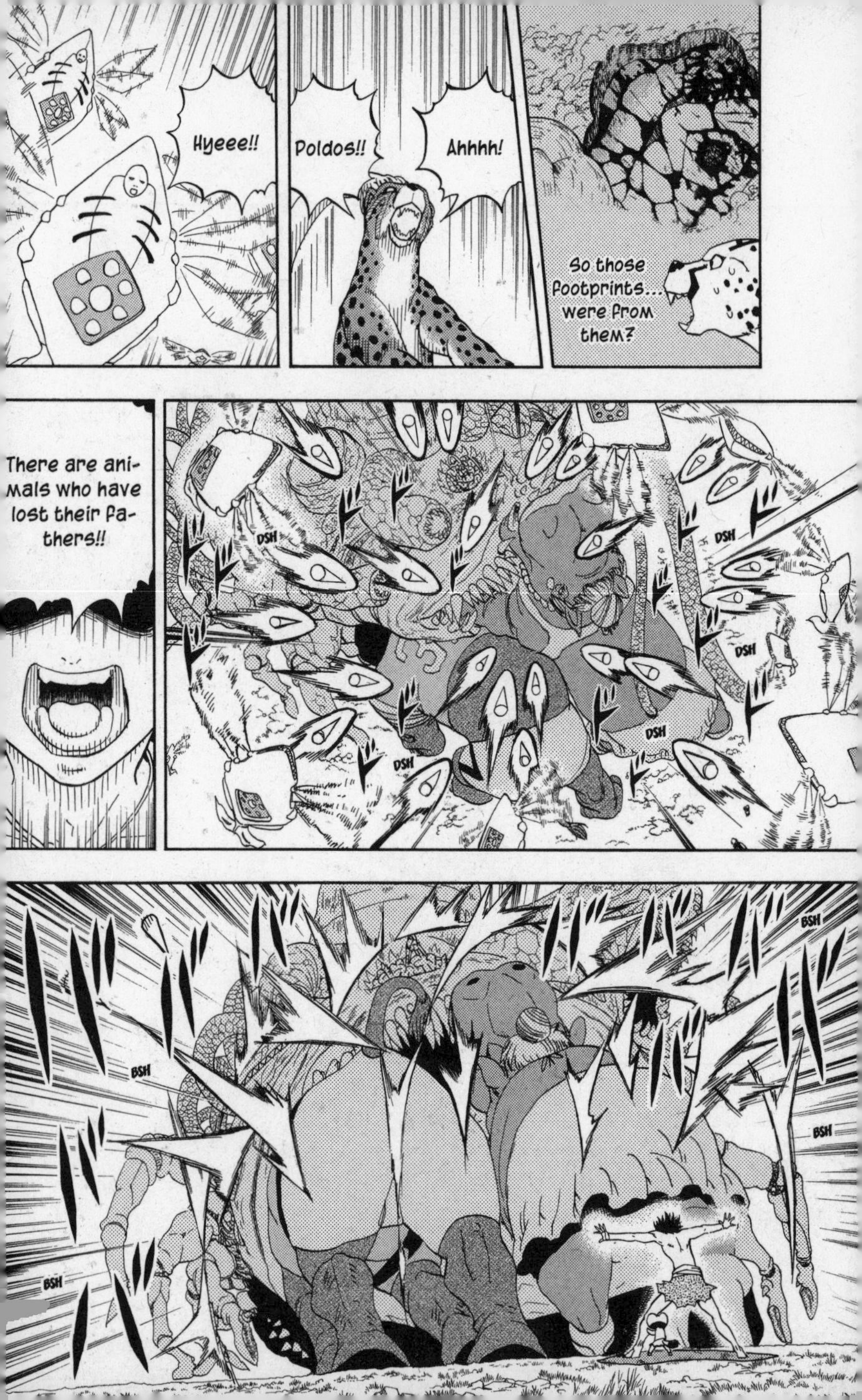
So those footprints... were from them?
Ahhhh!
Poldos!!
Hyeee!!
DSH
DSH
DSH
DSH
DSH
There are animals who have lost their fathers!!
BSH
BSH
BSH
BSH

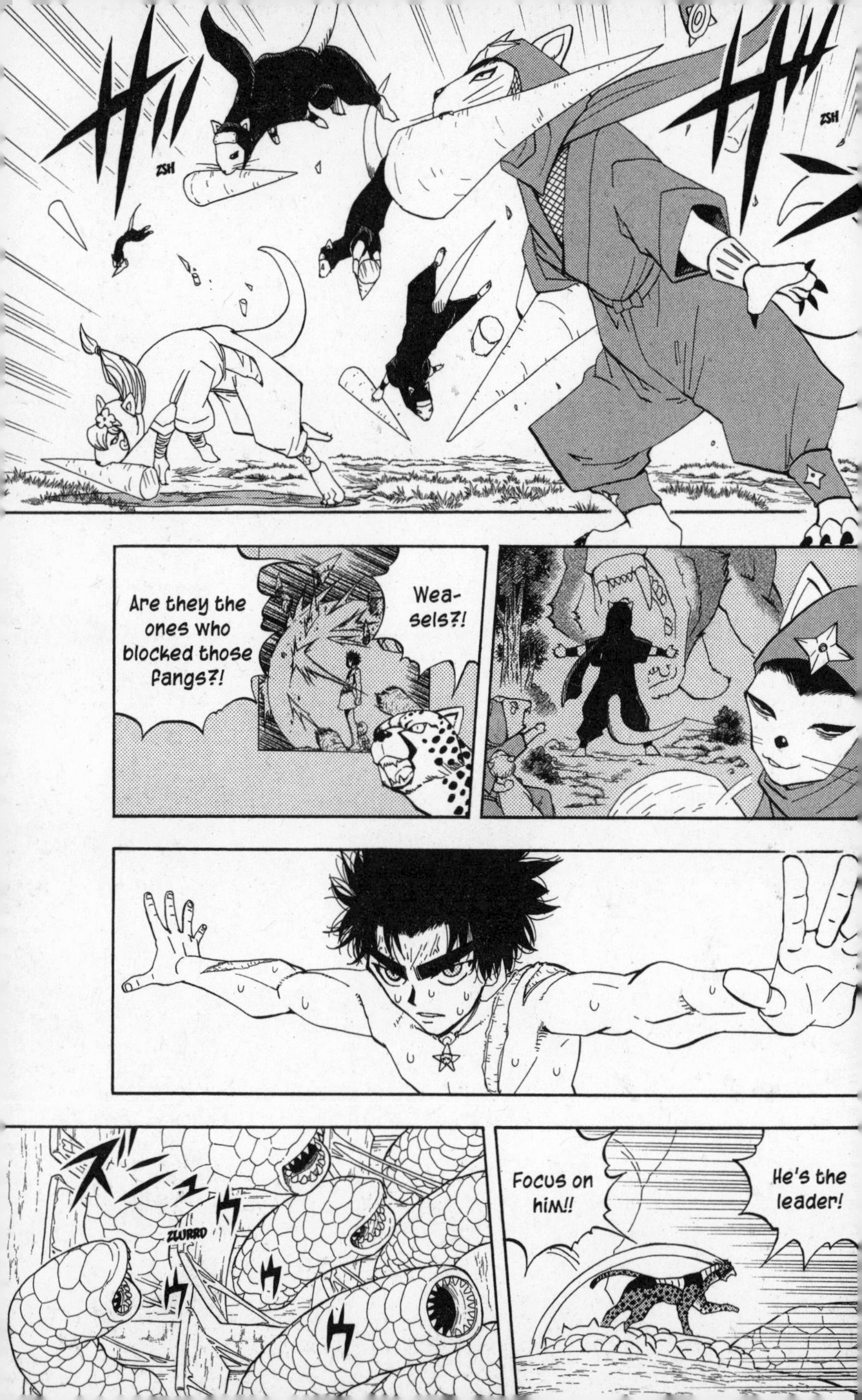
ZSH
ZSH
Wea-sels?!
Are they the ones who blocked those fangs?!
He's the leader!
Focus on him!!
ZLURRD

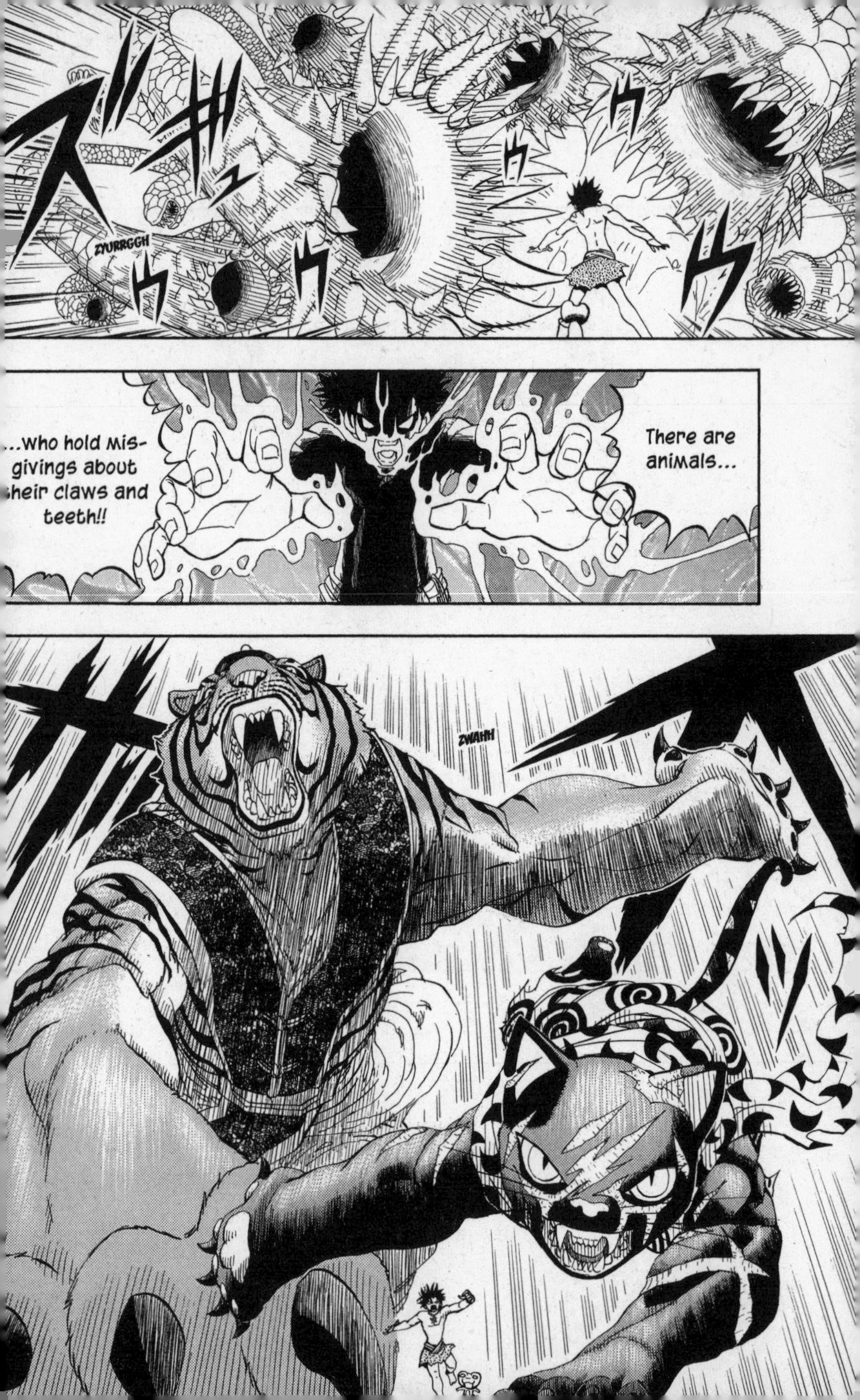
ZYURRGGH
There are animals...
...who hold mis-givings about their claws and teeth!!
ZWAHH

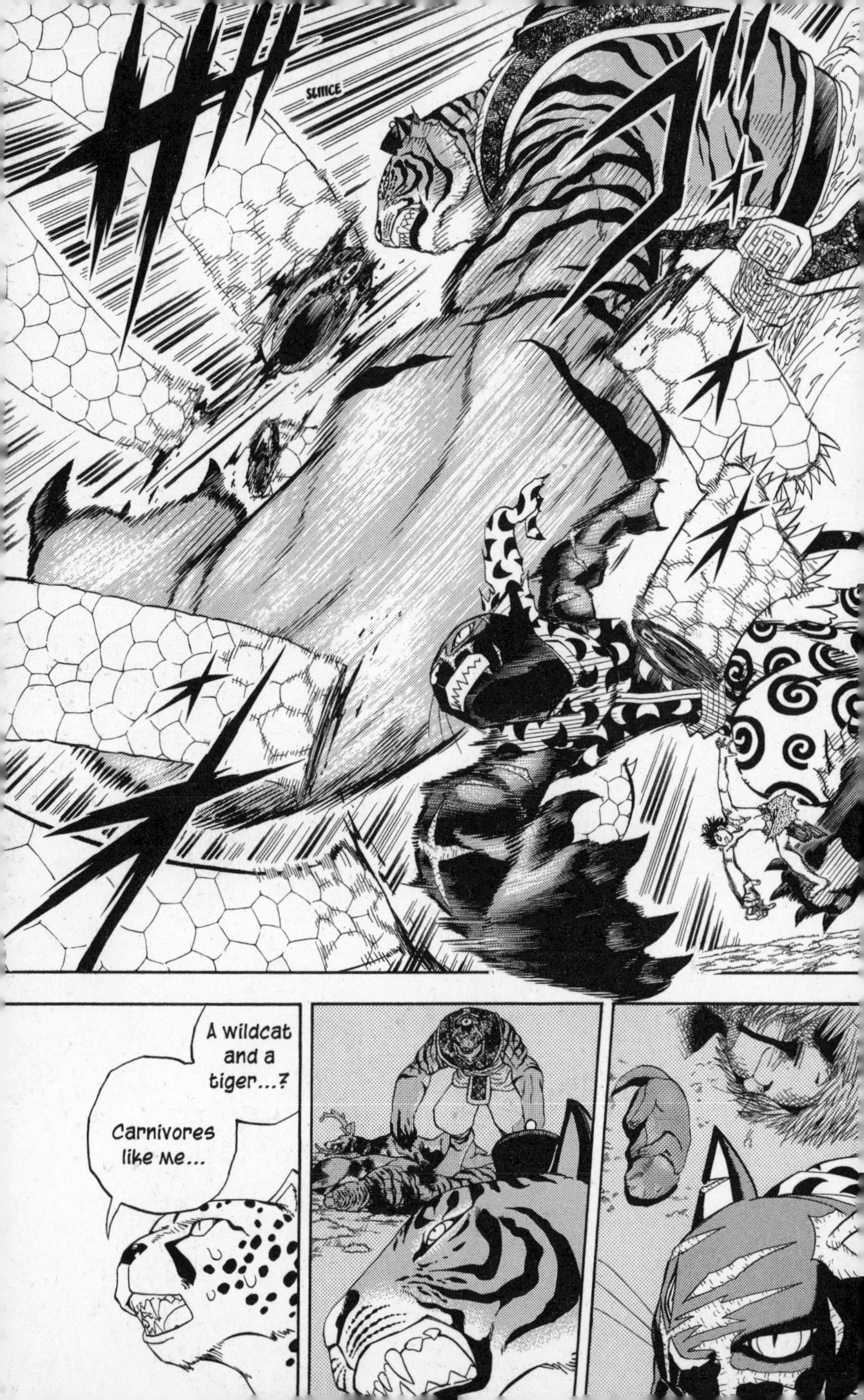
SLIIICE
A wildcat and a tiger...?
Carnivores like me...

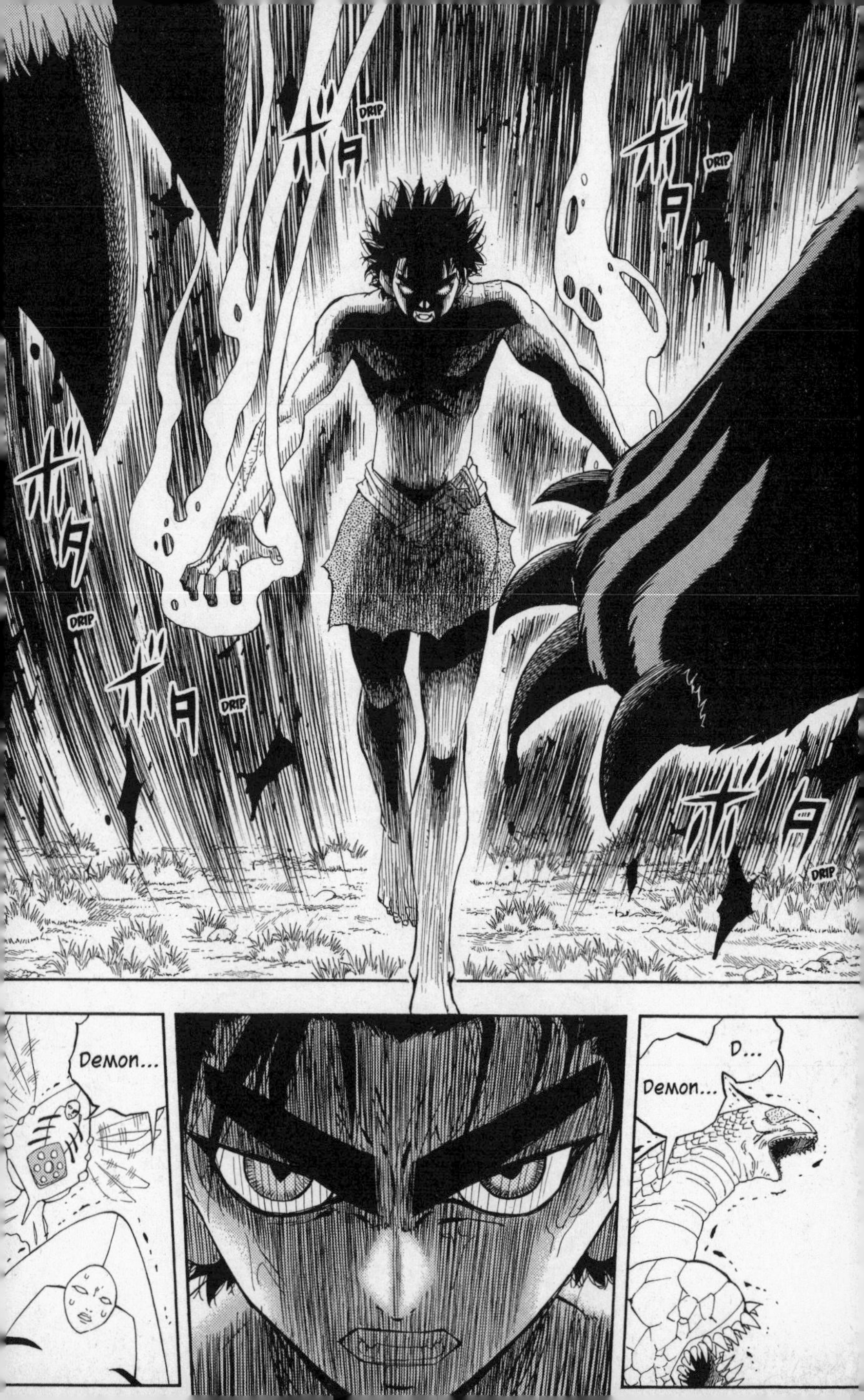
ボタ
DRIP
ボタ
DRIP
ボタ
DRIP
ボタ
DRIP
ボタ
DRIP
D...
Demon...
Demon...

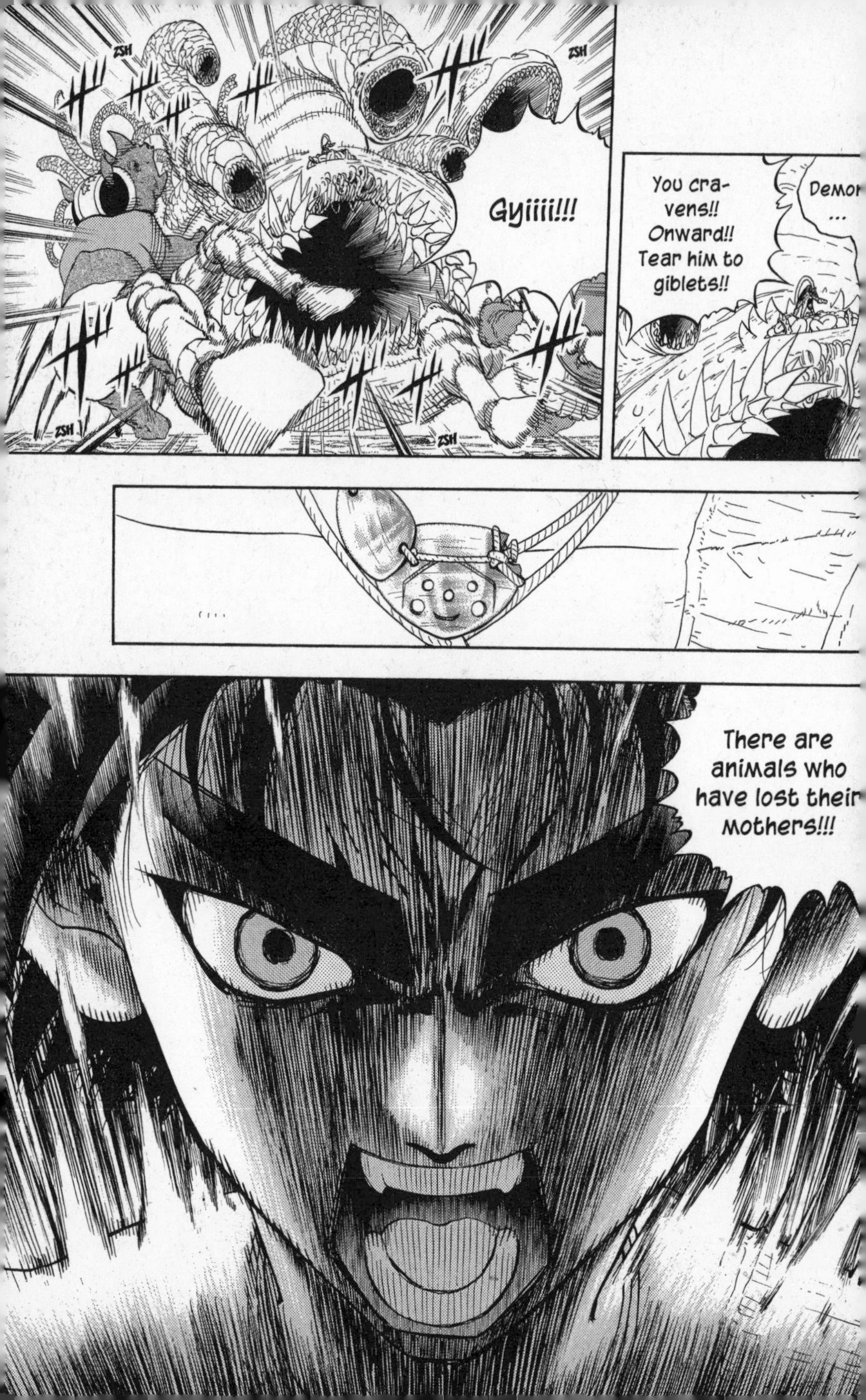
Demon
...
You cra-
vens!!
Onward!!
Tear him to
giblets!!
ZSH
ZSH
Gyiiii!!!
ZSH
ZSH
...
There are
animals who
have lost their
mothers!!!

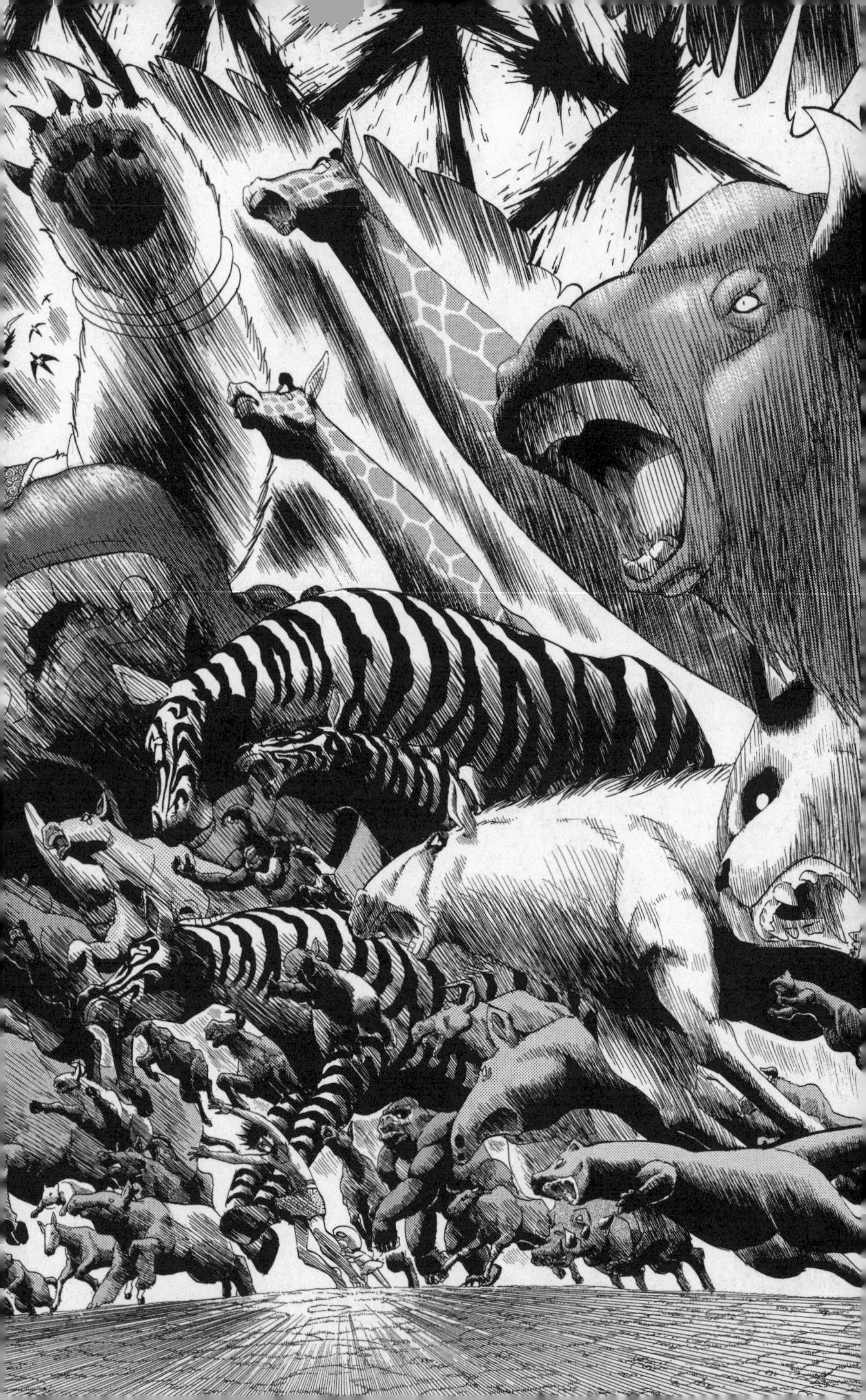

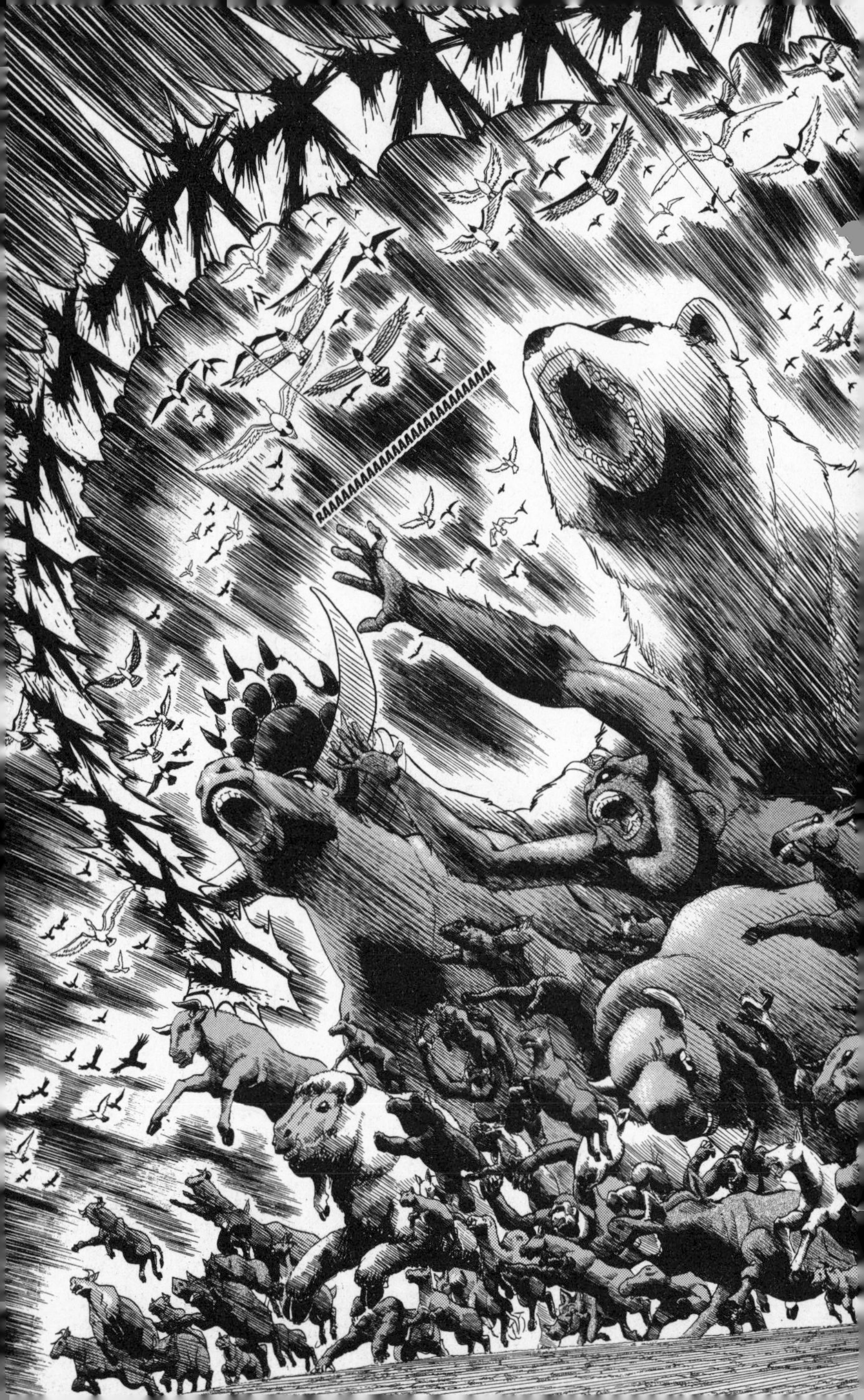
RAAAAAAAAAAAAAAAAAAAAAAAA

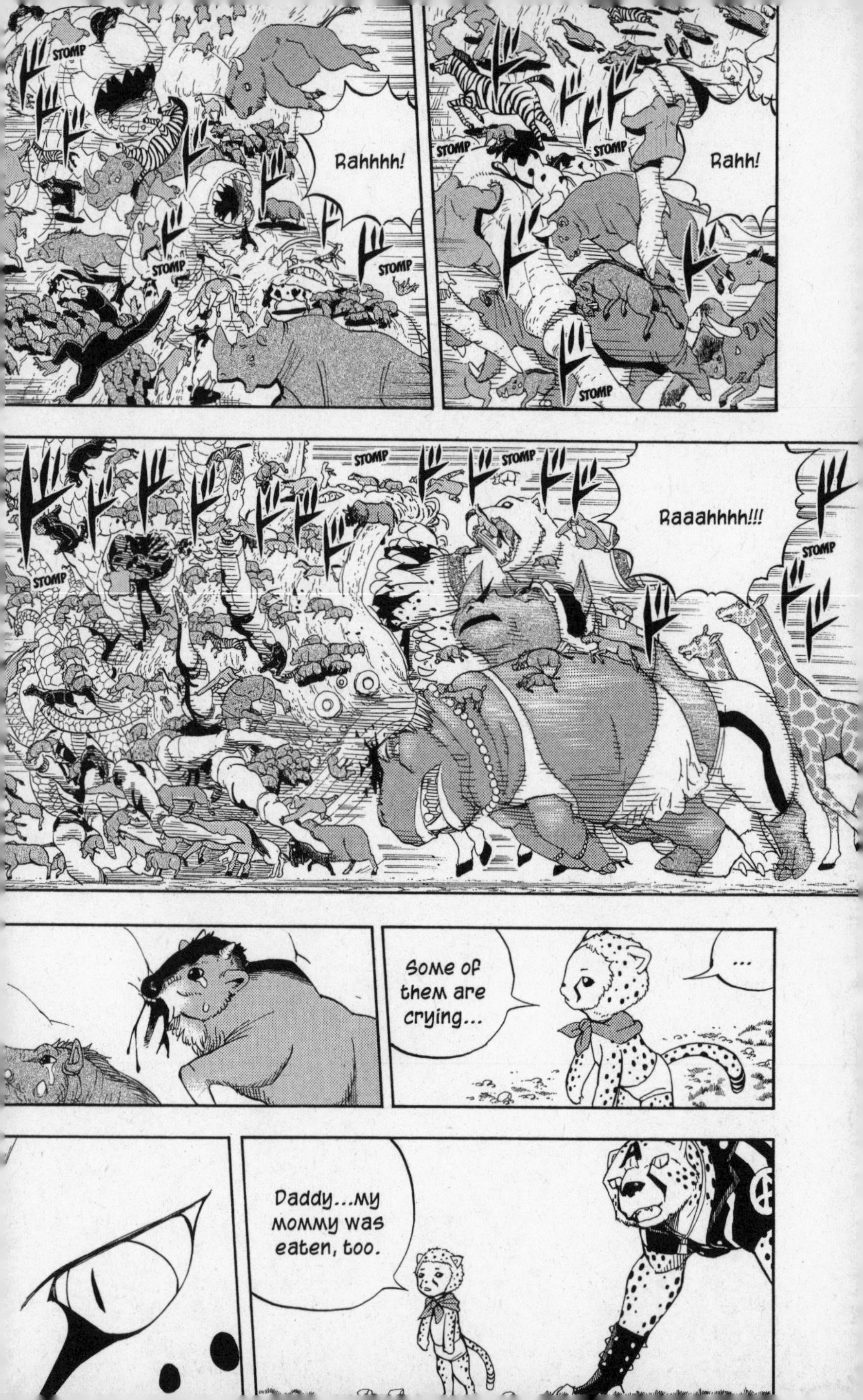
STOMP
STOMP
Rahh!
STOMP
STOMP
Rahhhh!
STOMP
STOMP
STOMP
Raaahhhh!!!
STOMP
STOMP
STOMP
STOMP
...
Some of them are crying...
Daddy...my mommy was eaten, too.

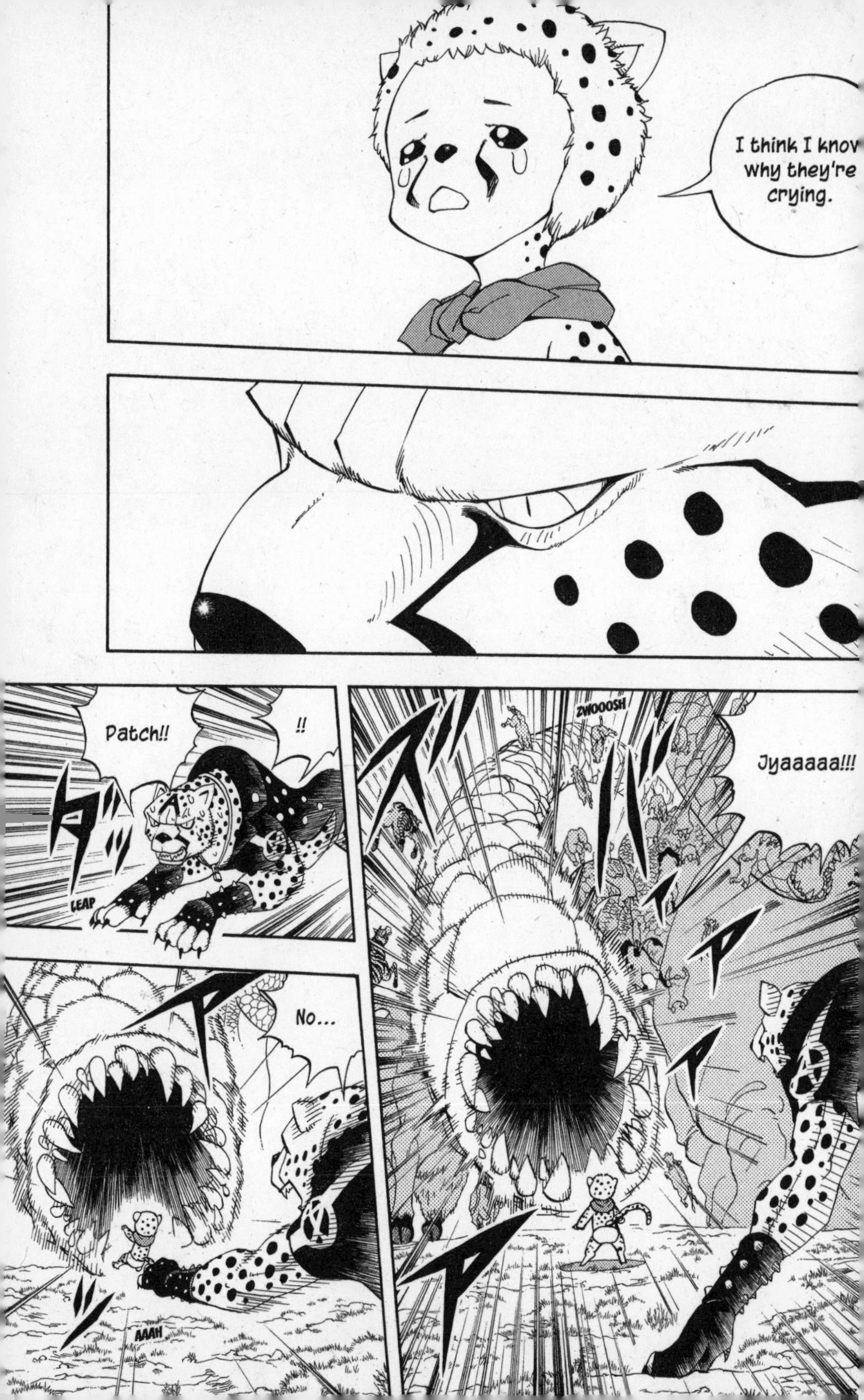
I think I know why they're crying.
ZWOOOSH
Jyaaaaa!!!
Patch!!
!!
LEAP
No...
AAAH

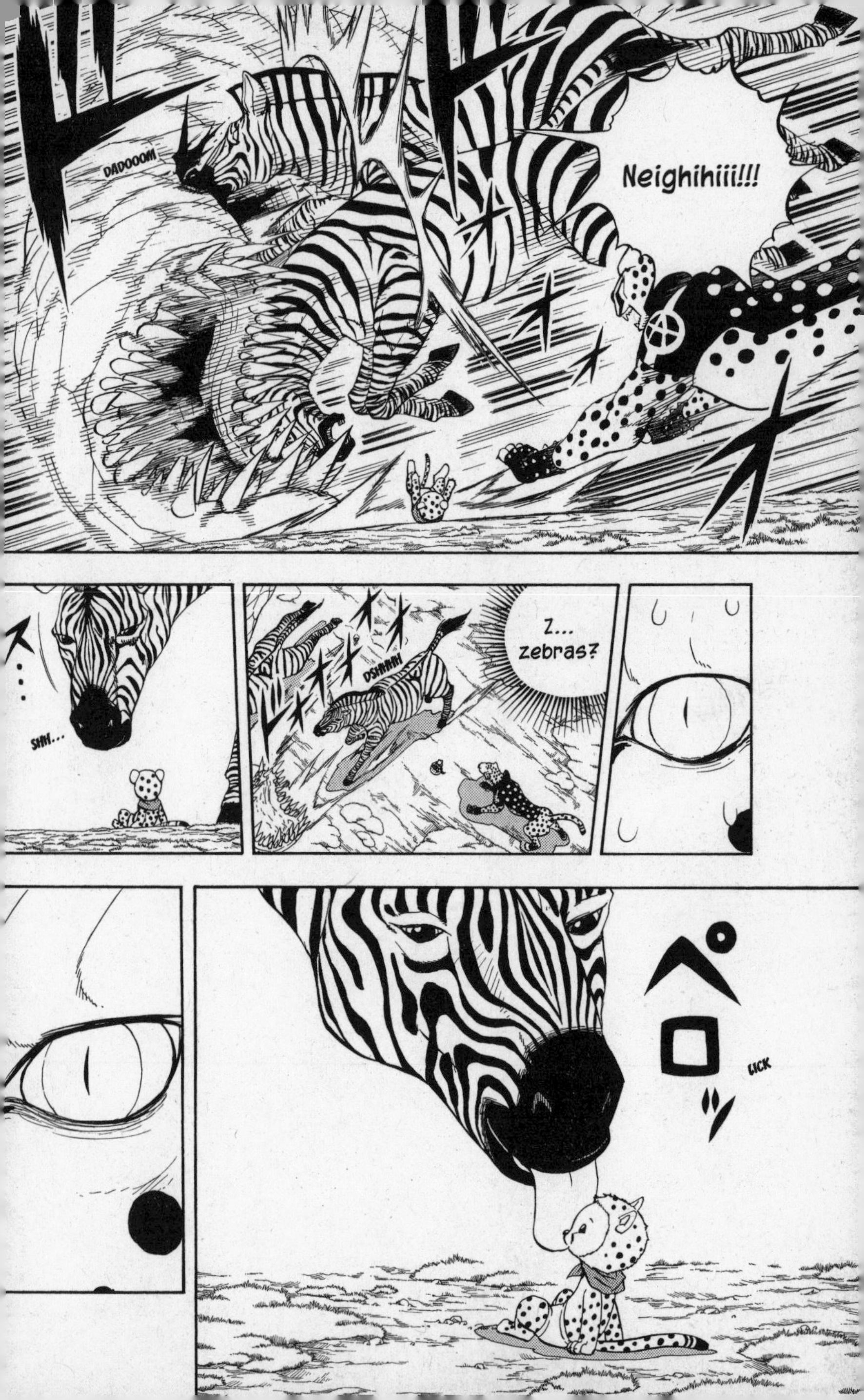
Neighihiii!!!
DADOOOM
Z... zebras?
DSHHHH
ス…
SHH...
ペロッ
LICK

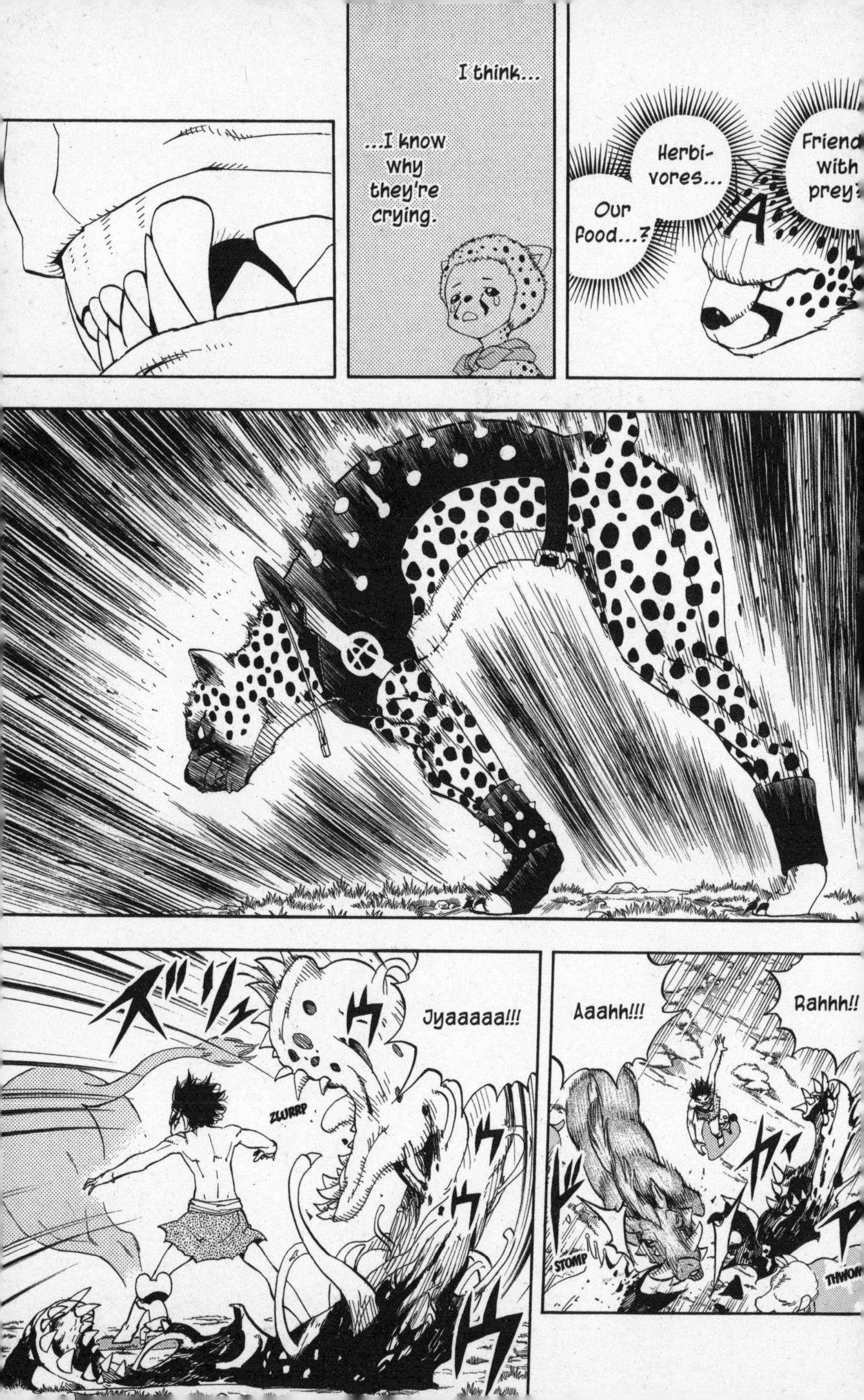
Friend with prey?
Herbi-vores...
Our food...?
I think...
...I know why they're crying.
Rahhh!!
Aaahh!!!
STOMP
THWOM
Jyaaaaa!!!
ZLURRP

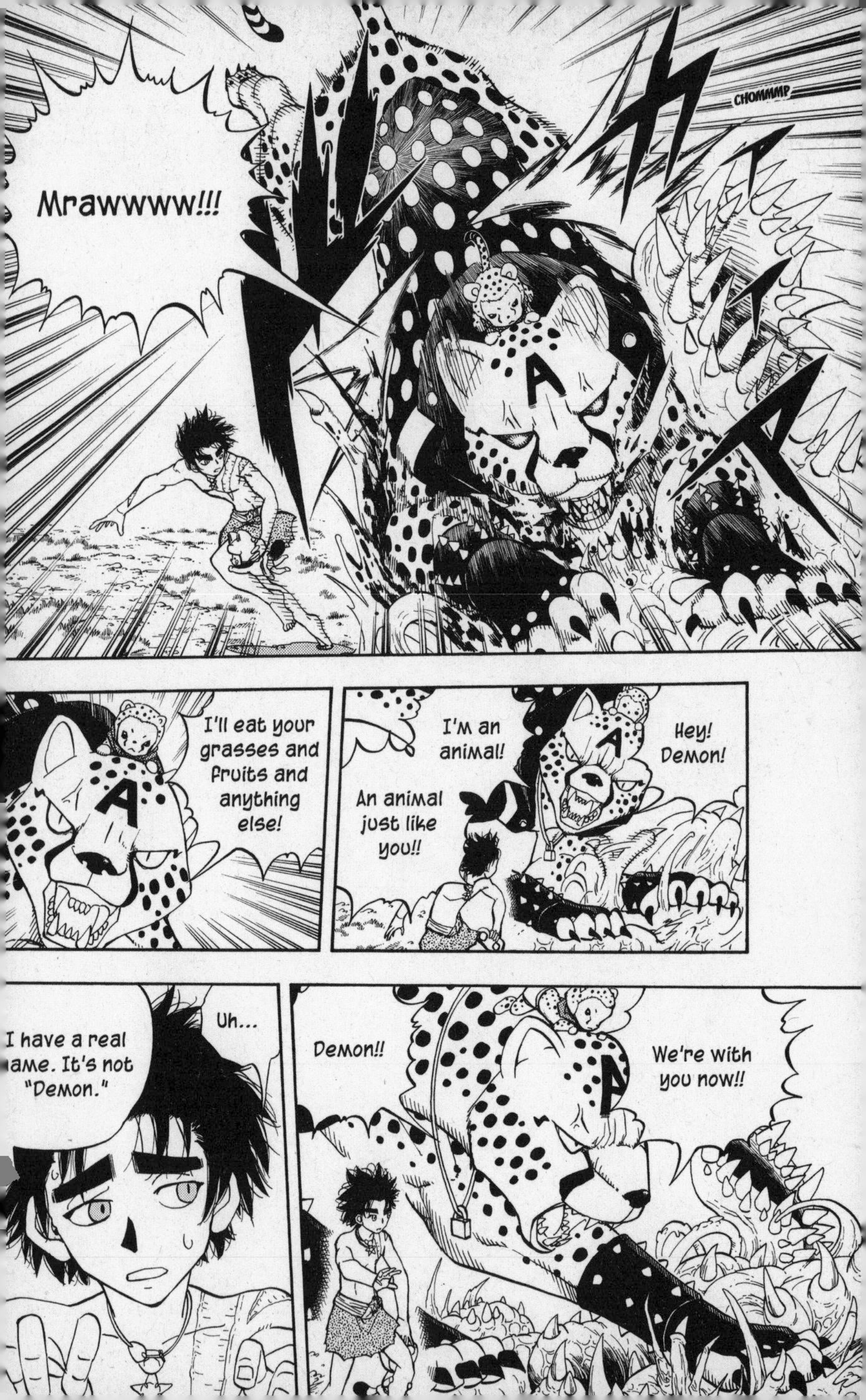
CHOMMMP
Mrawwww!!!
Hey! Demon!
I'm an animal!
An animal just like you!!
I'll eat your grasses and fruits and anything else!
We're with you now!!
Demon!!
Uh...
I have a real ame. It's not "Demon."

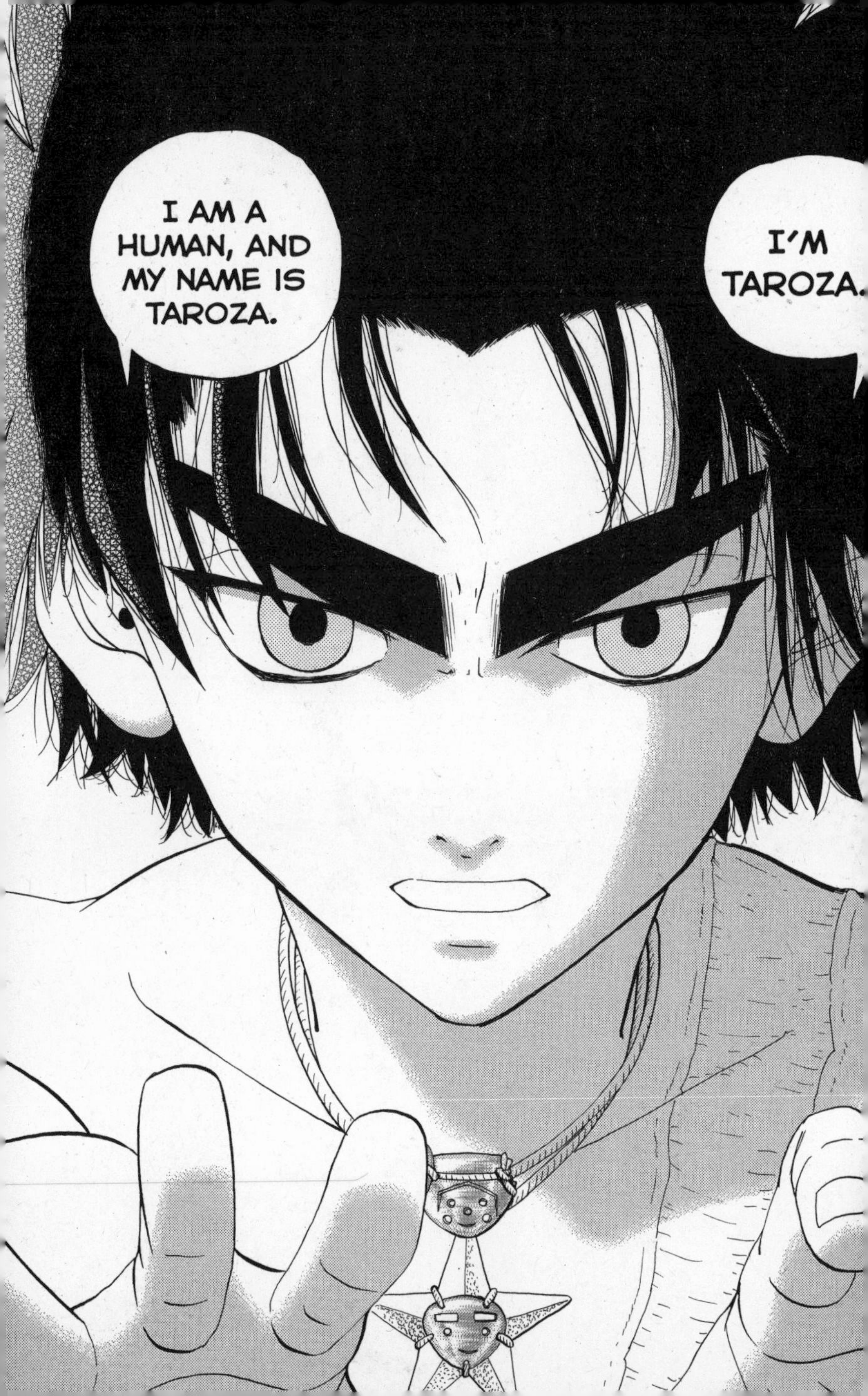
I'M TAROZA.
I AM A HUMAN, AND MY NAME IS TAROZA.

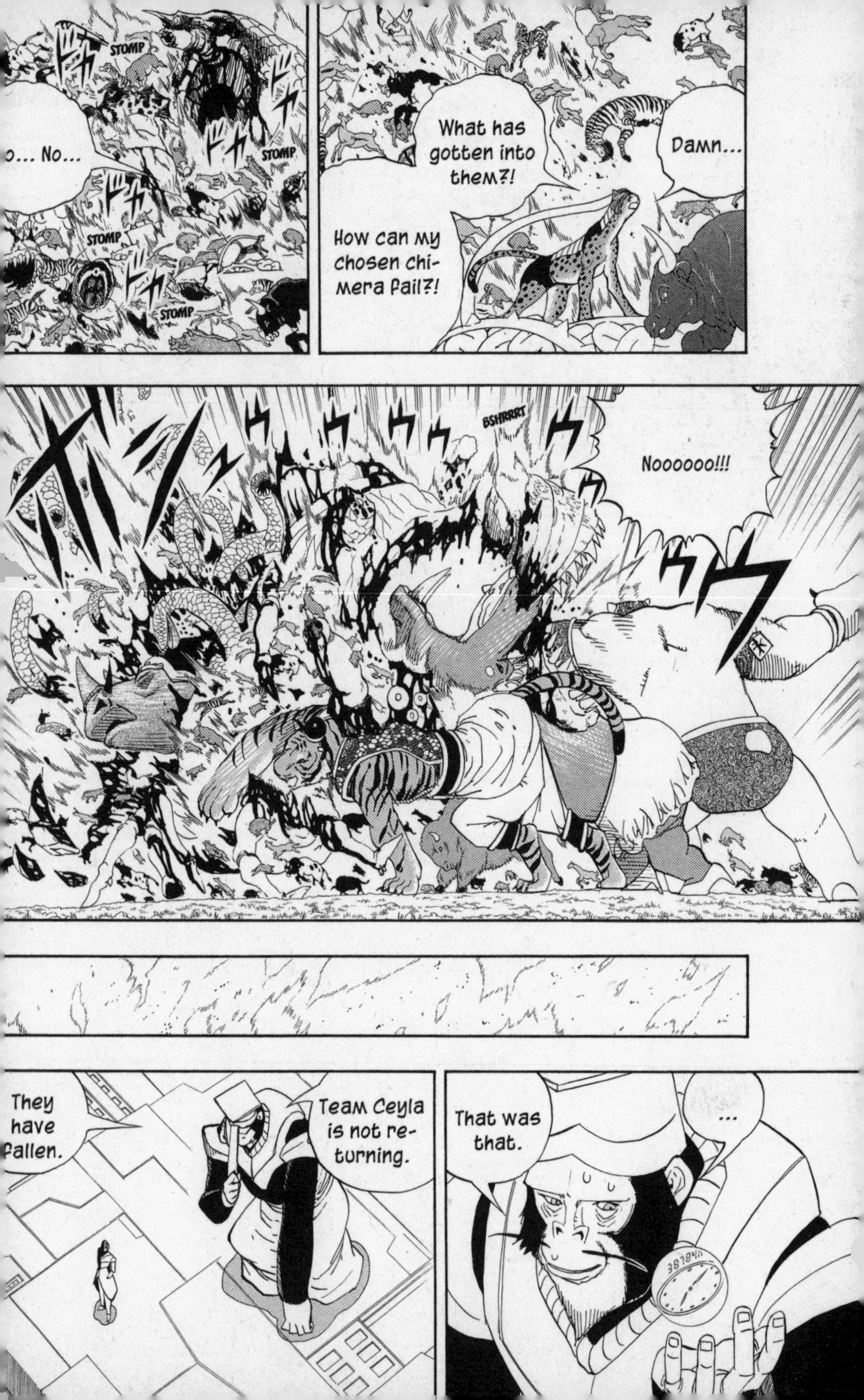
Damn...
What has gotten into them?!
How can my chosen chi-mera fail?!
STOMP
STOMP
o... No... No...
STOMP
STOMP
BSHRRRT
Noooooo!!!
...
That was that.
Team Ceyla is not re-turning.
They have fallen.

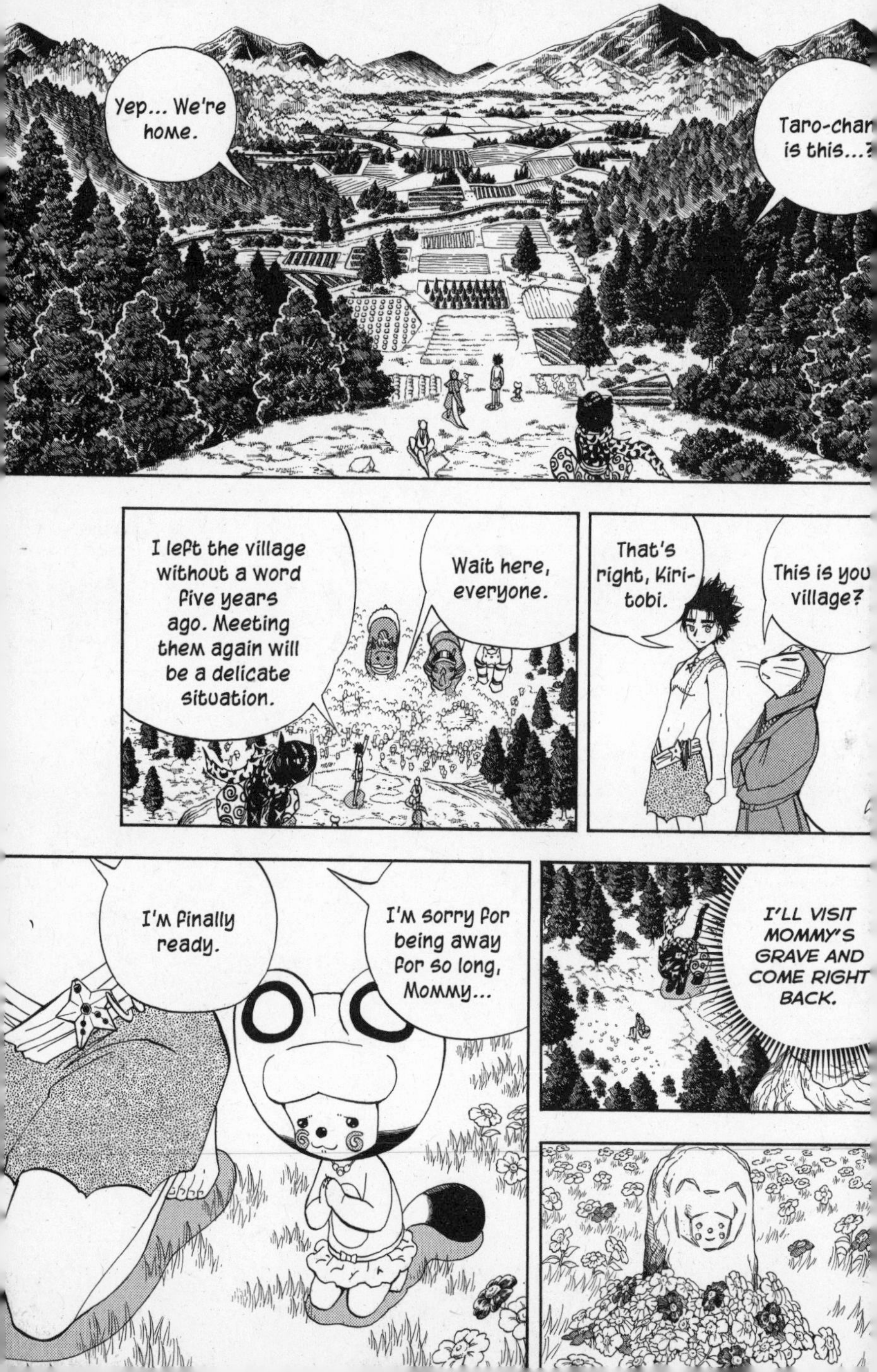

Taro-chan is this...?
Yep... We're home.
This is you village?
That's right, Kiri-tobi.
Wait here, everyone.
I left the village without a word five years ago. Meeting them again will be a delicate situation.
I'LL VISIT MOMMY'S GRAVE AND COME RIGHT BACK.
I'm sorry for being away for so long, Mommy...
I'm finally ready.

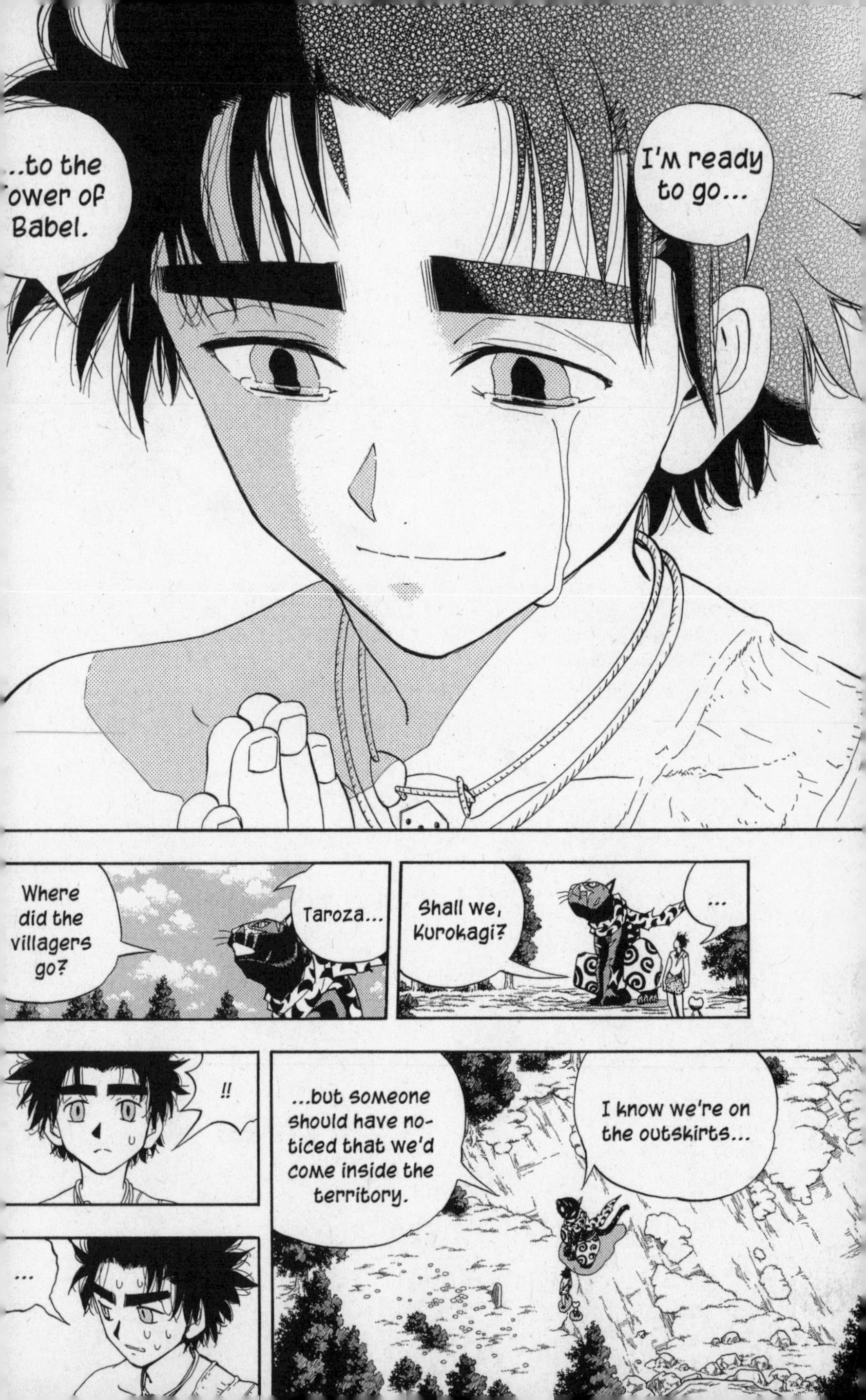
I'm ready to go...
...to the
ower of
Babel.
...
Shall we, Kurokagi?
Taroza...
Where did the villagers go?
I know we're on the outskirts...
...but someone should have noticed that we'd come inside the territory.
!!
...

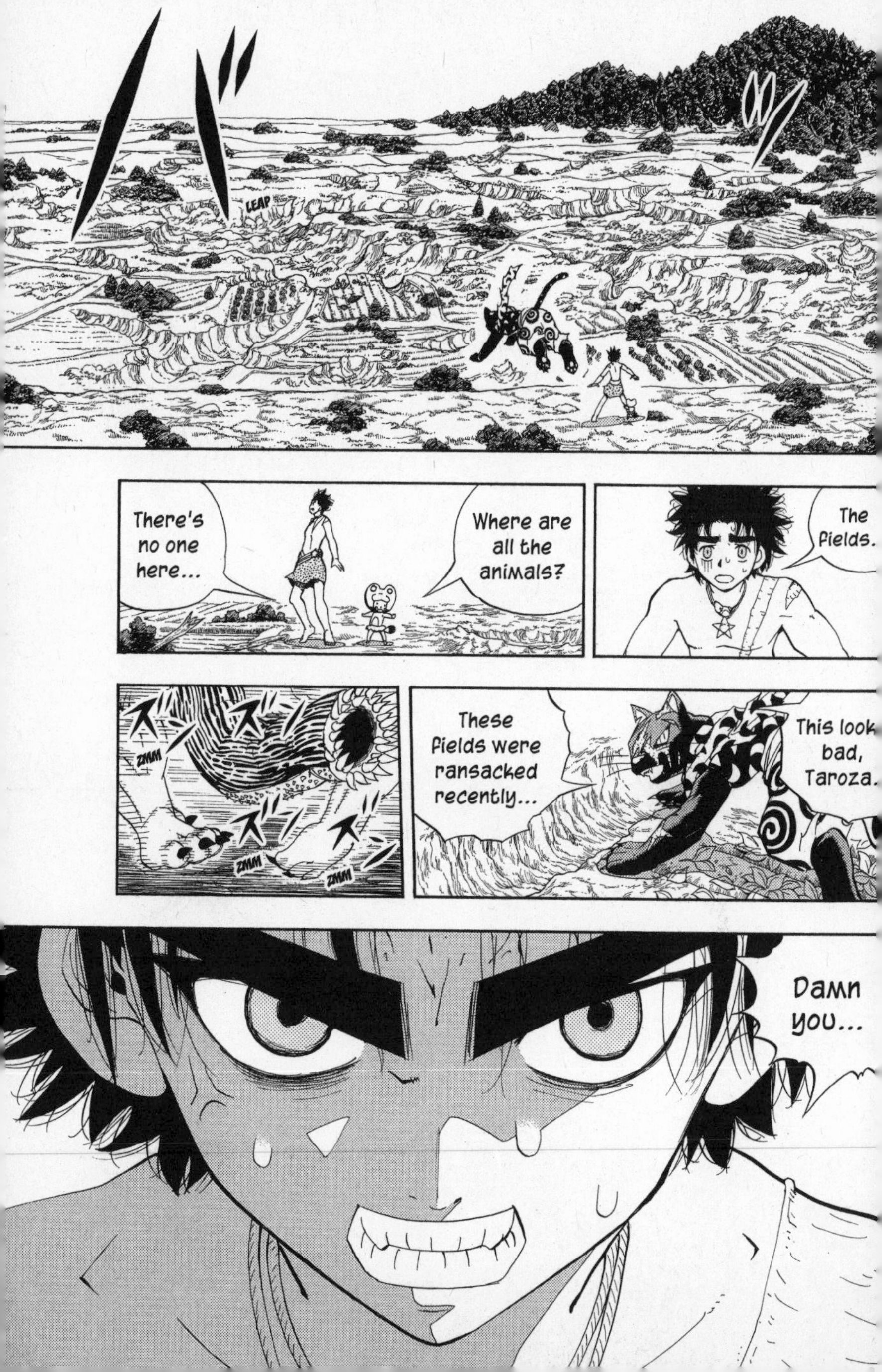
LEAP
The fields.
Where are all the animals?
There's no one here...
This look bad, Taroza.
These fields were ransacked recently...
ZMM
ZMM
ZMM
Damn you...

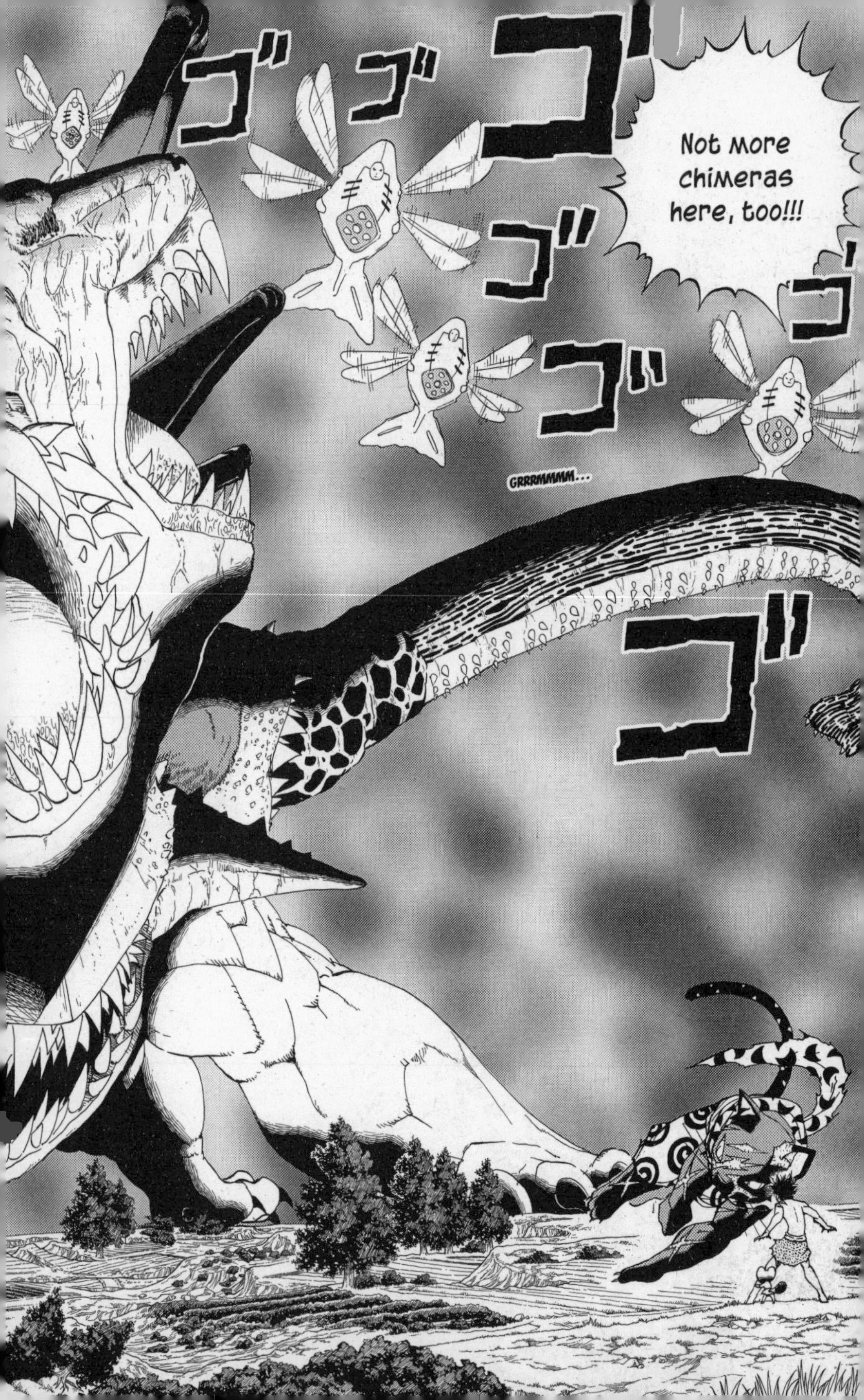
ゴ ゴ ゴ ゴ ゴ ゴ ゴ ゴ
Not more chimeras here, too!!!
GRRRMMMM...

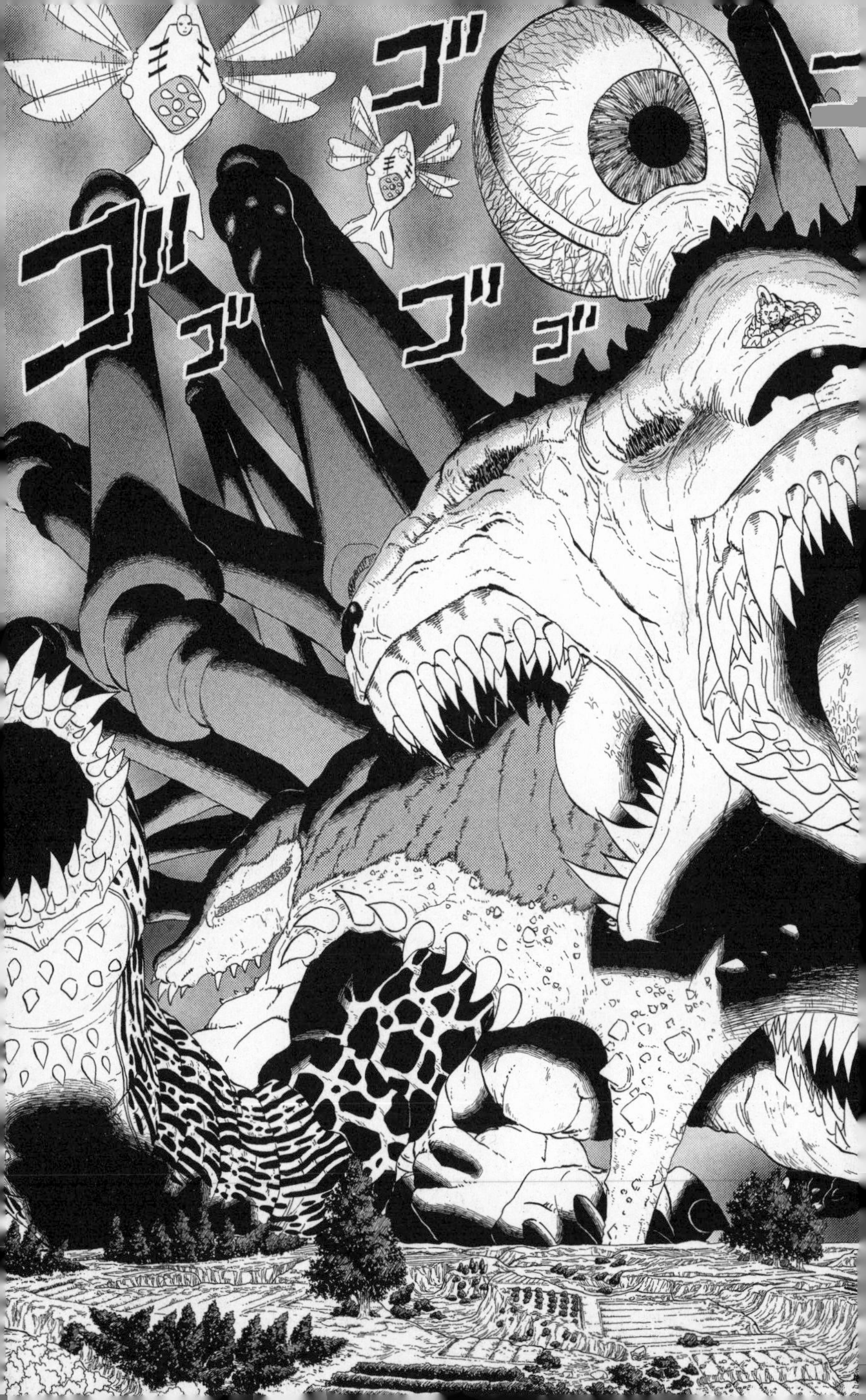
ゴ
ゴ
ゴ
ゴ
ゴ

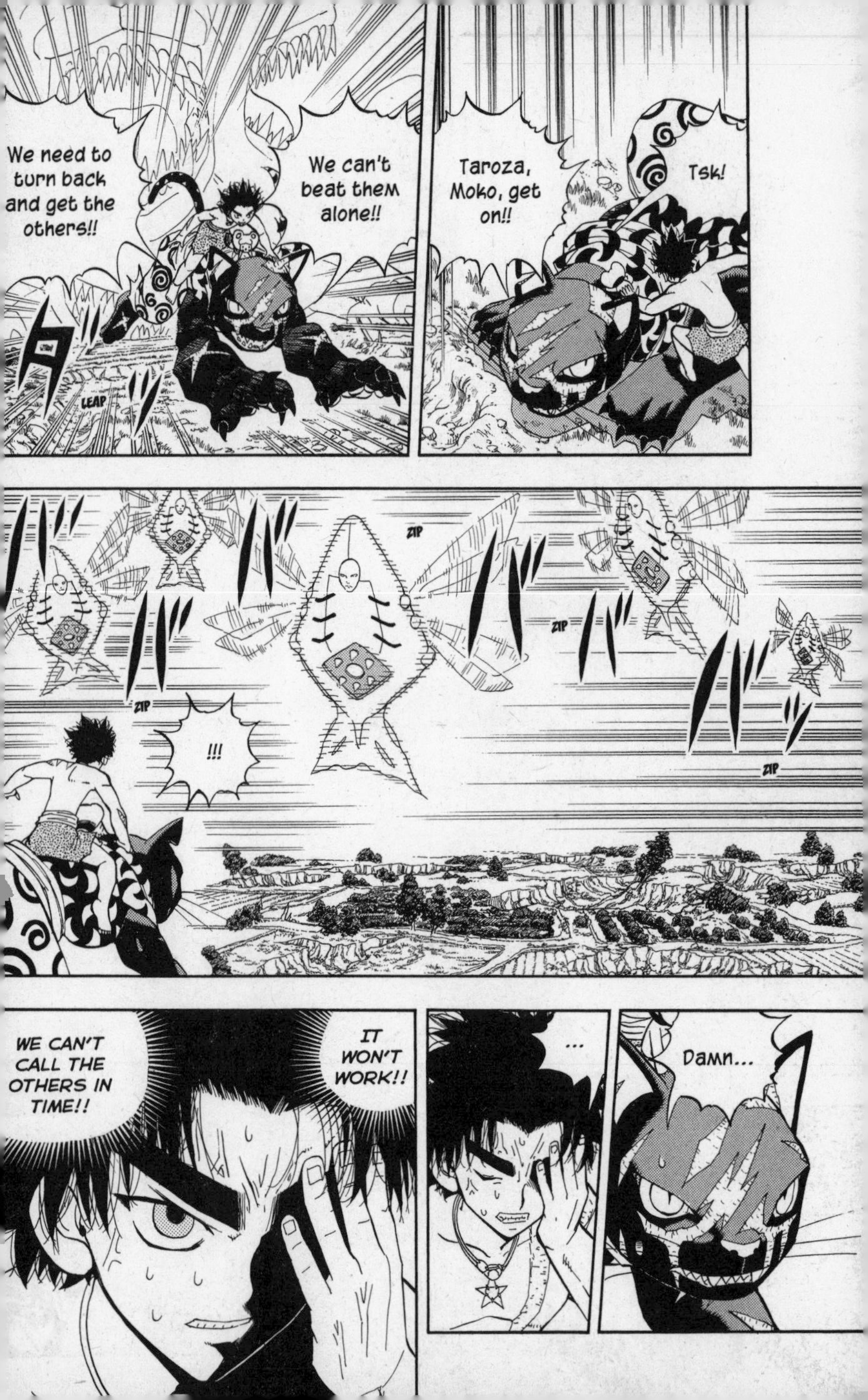
Tsk!
Taroza, Moko, get on!!
We can't beat them alone!!
We need to turn back and get the others!!
LEAP
ZIP
ZIP
ZIP
ZIP
!!!
Damn...
...
IT WON'T WORK!!
WE CAN'T CALL THE OTHERS IN TIME!!

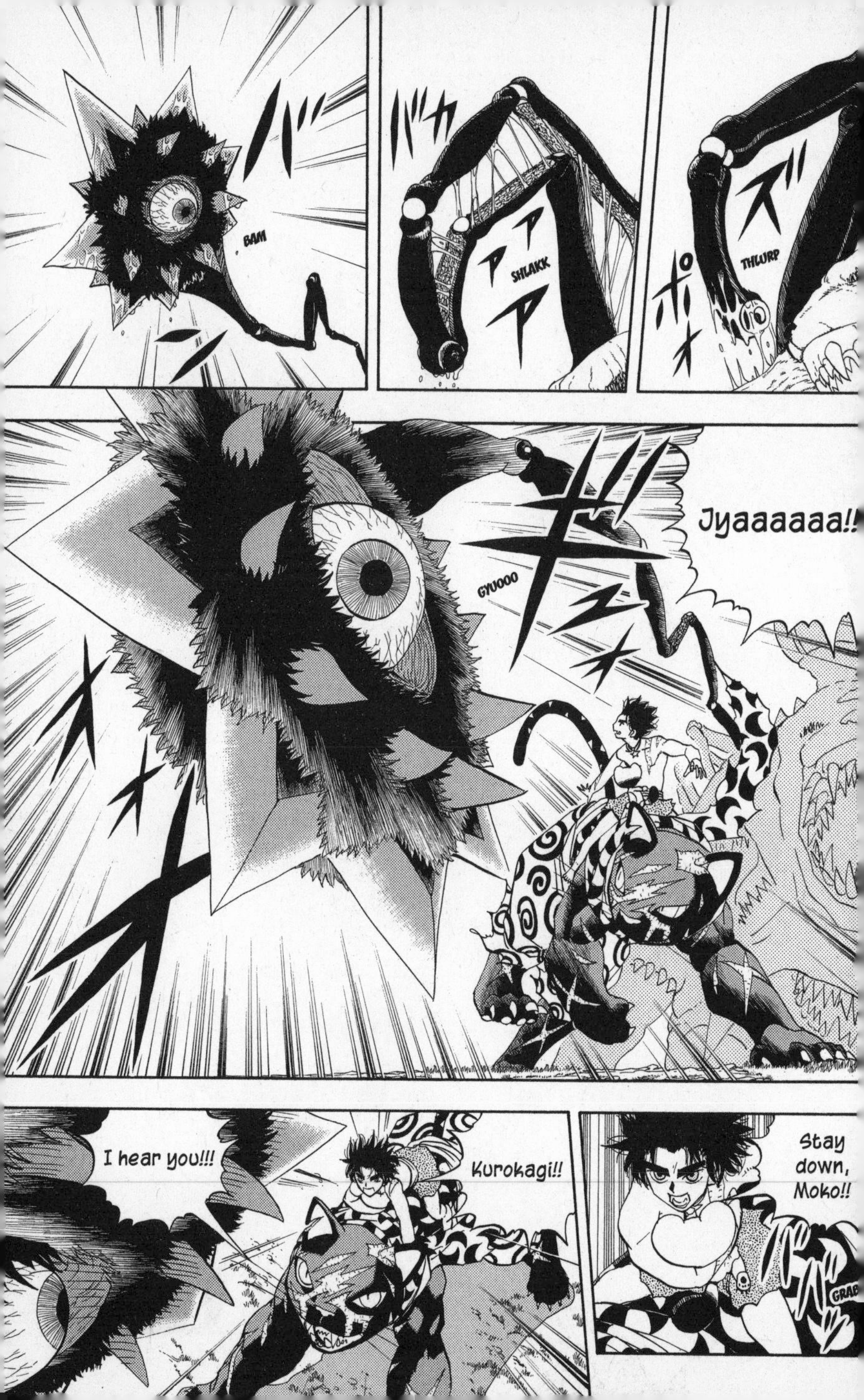
THLURP
SHLAKK
BAM
Jyaaaaaa!!
GYUOOO
Stay down, Moko!!
GRAB
Kurokagi!!
I hear you!!!

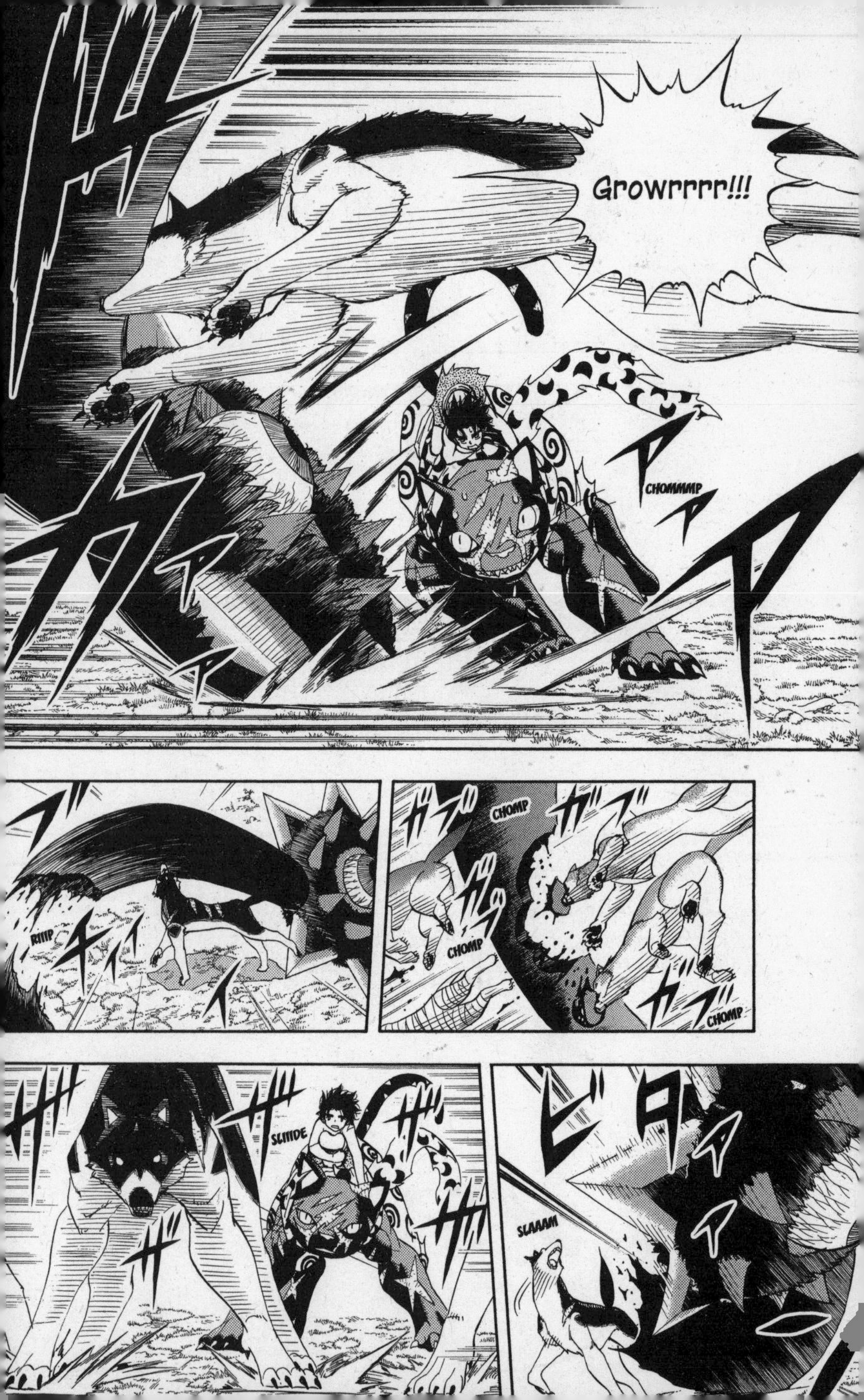
Growrrrr!!!
CHOMMMP
CHOMP
CHOMP
CHOMP
RIIIP
SLAAAM
SLIIIDE

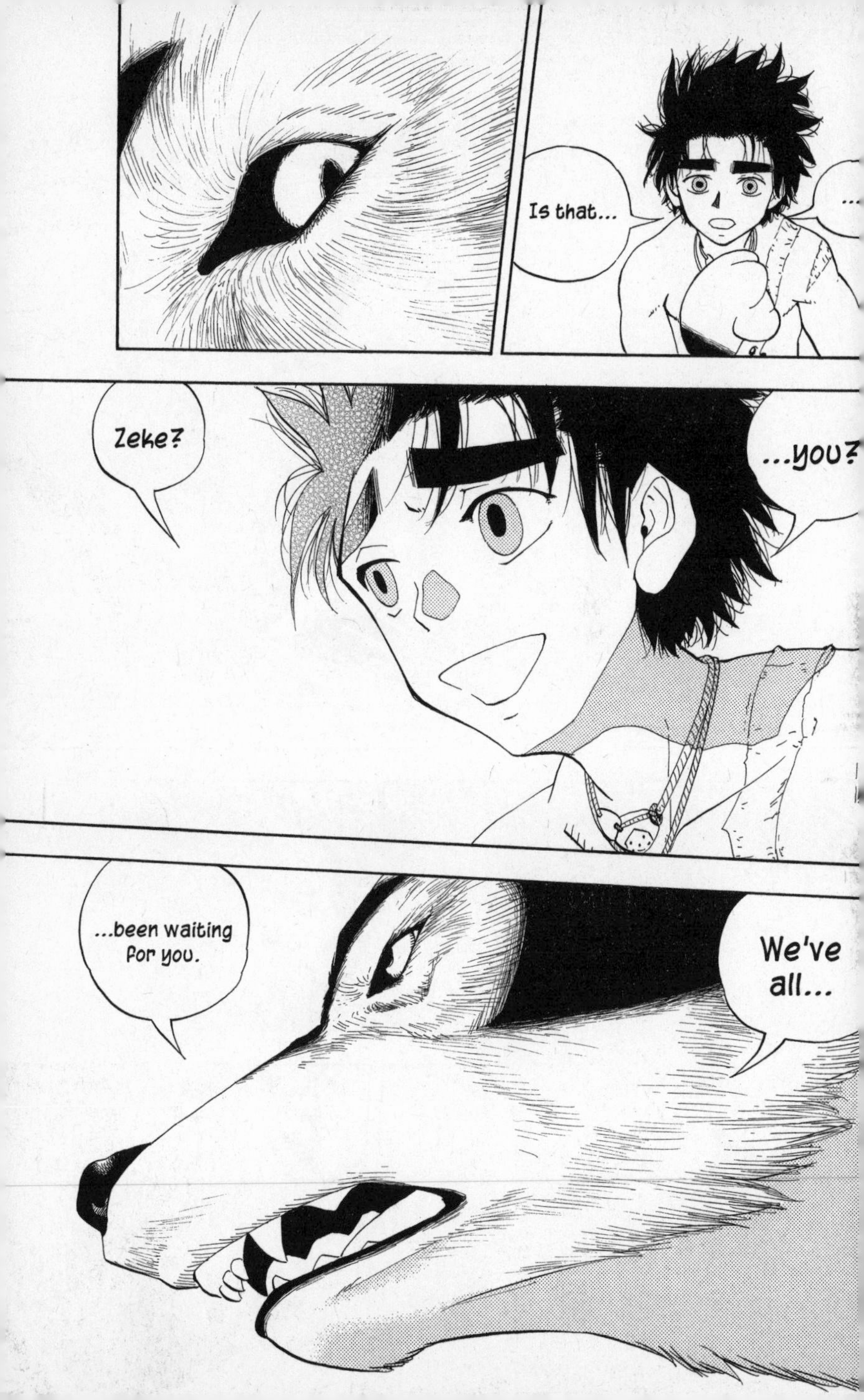
...
Is that...
...you?
Zeke?
We've all...
...been waiting for you.

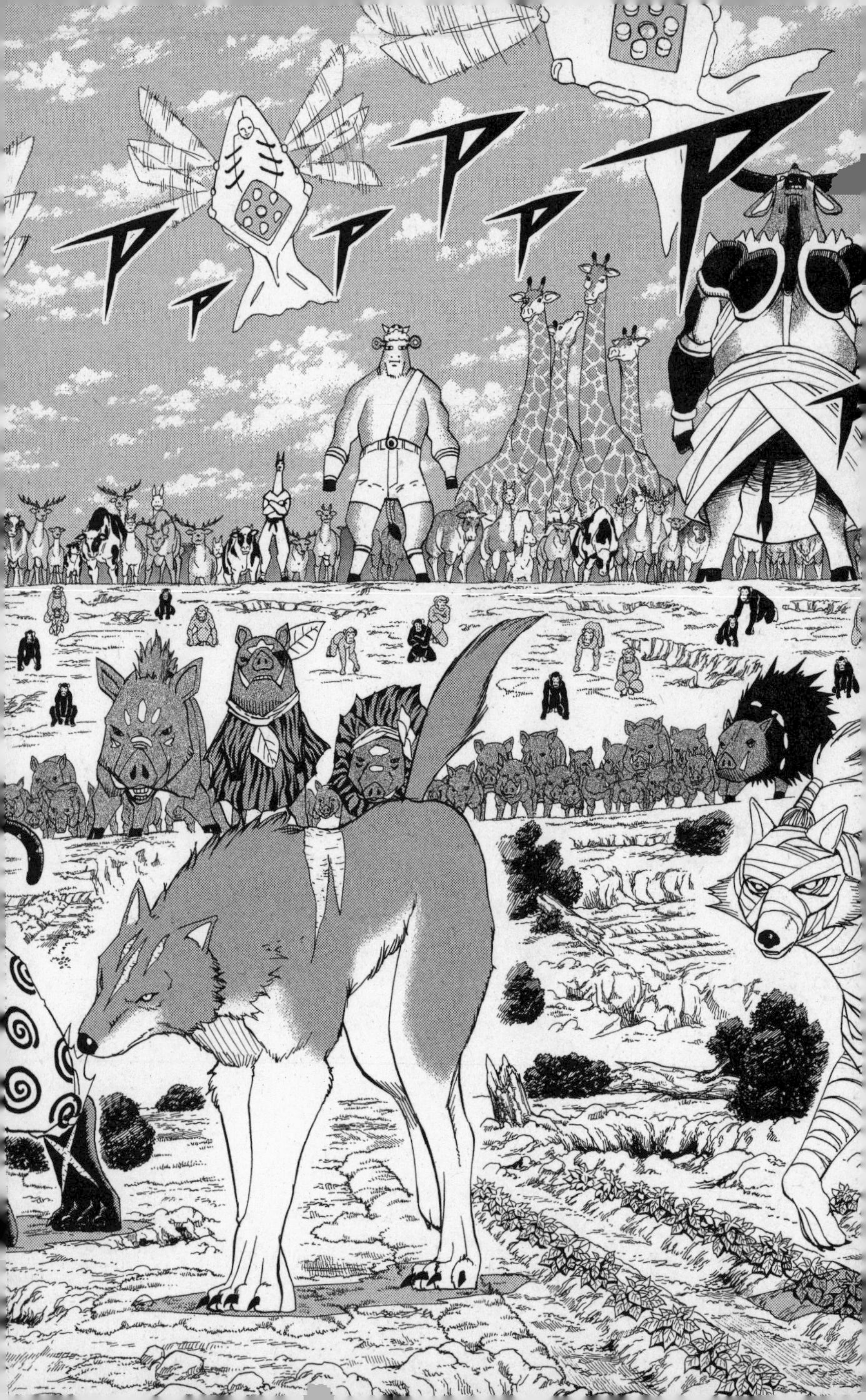

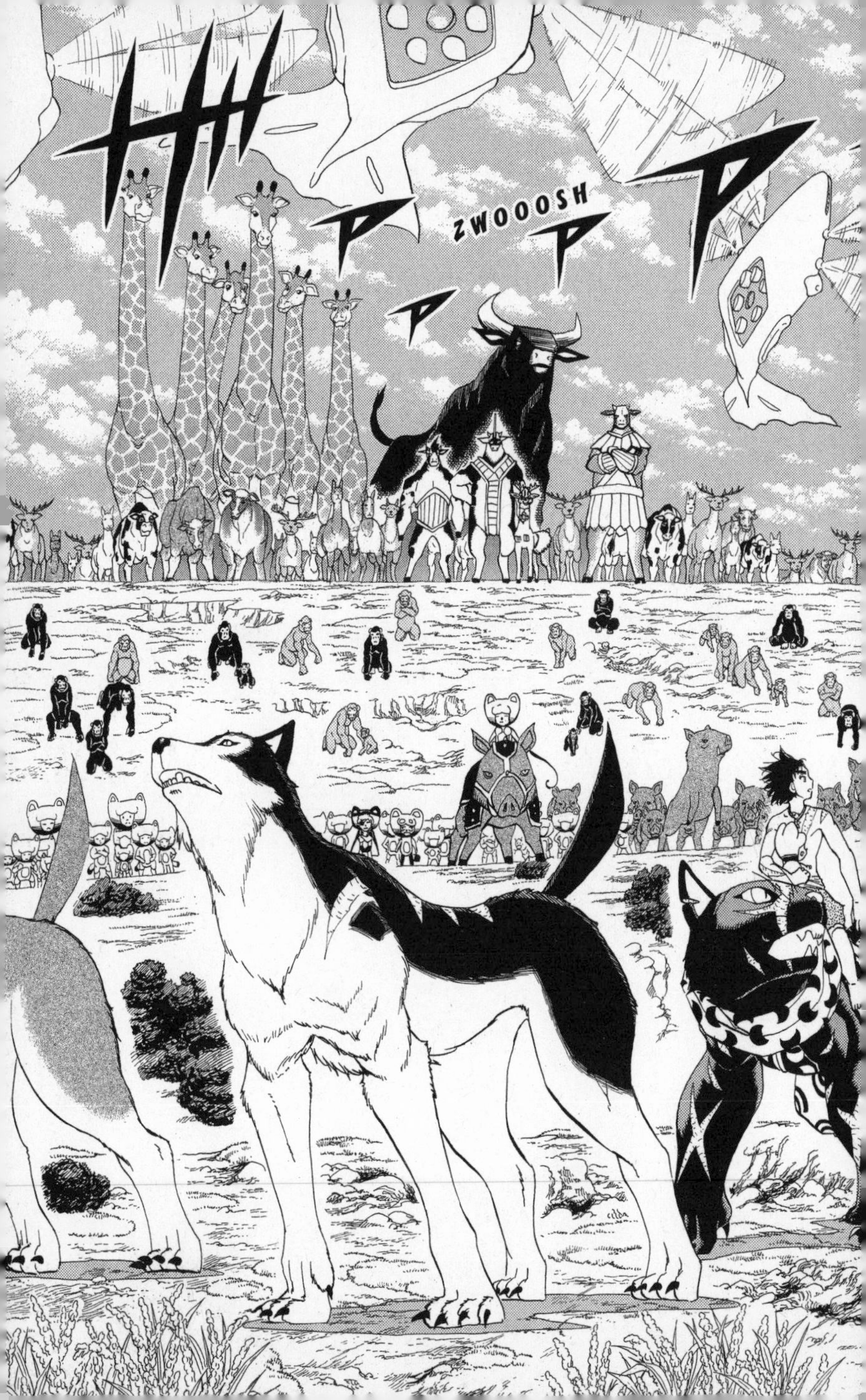
ZWOOOSH

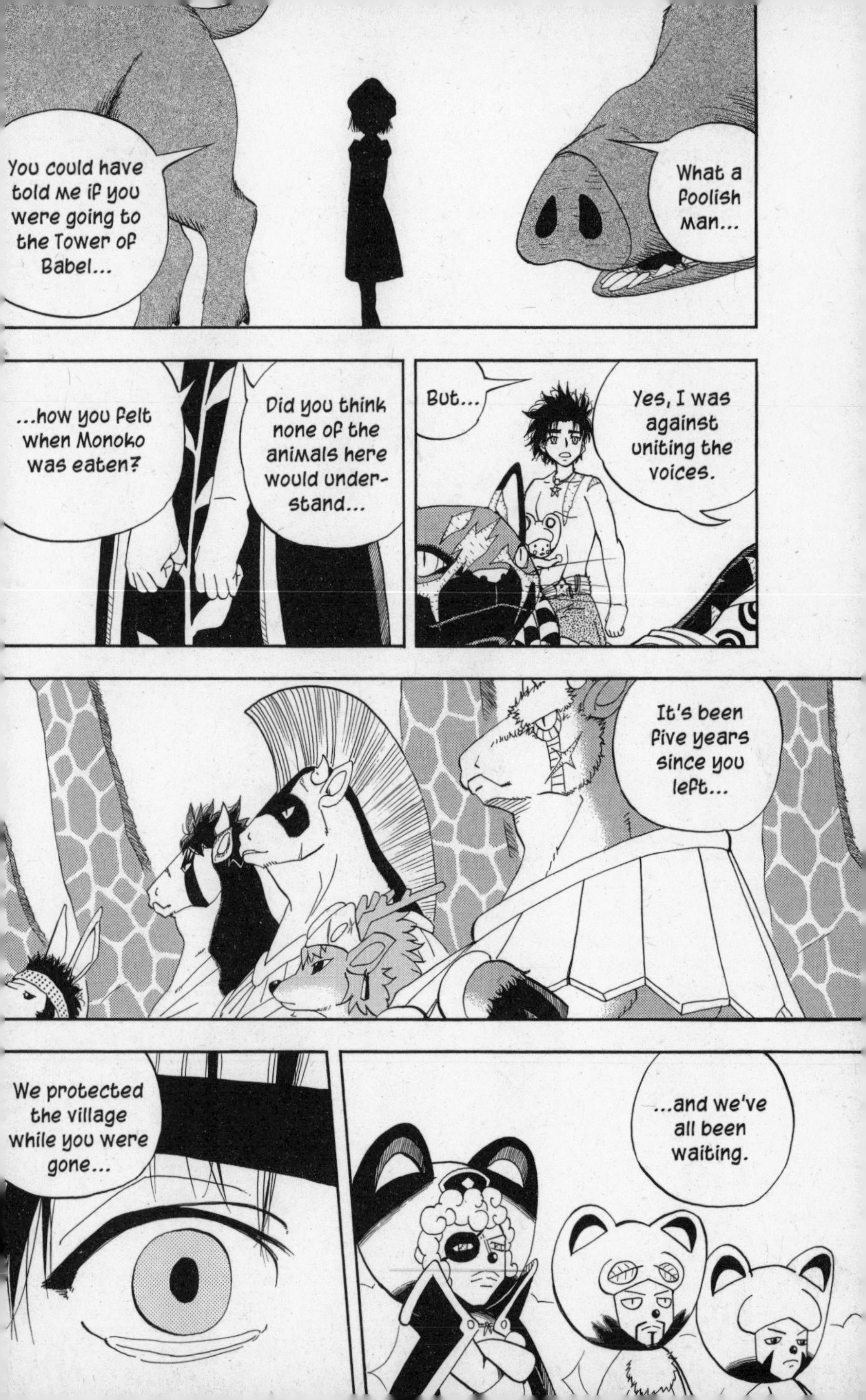
What a foolish man...
You could have told me if you were going to the Tower of Babel...
Yes, I was against uniting the voices.
But...
Did you think none of the animals here would under-stand...
...how you felt when Monoko was eaten?
It's been five years since you left...
...and we've all been waiting.
We protected the village while you were gone...

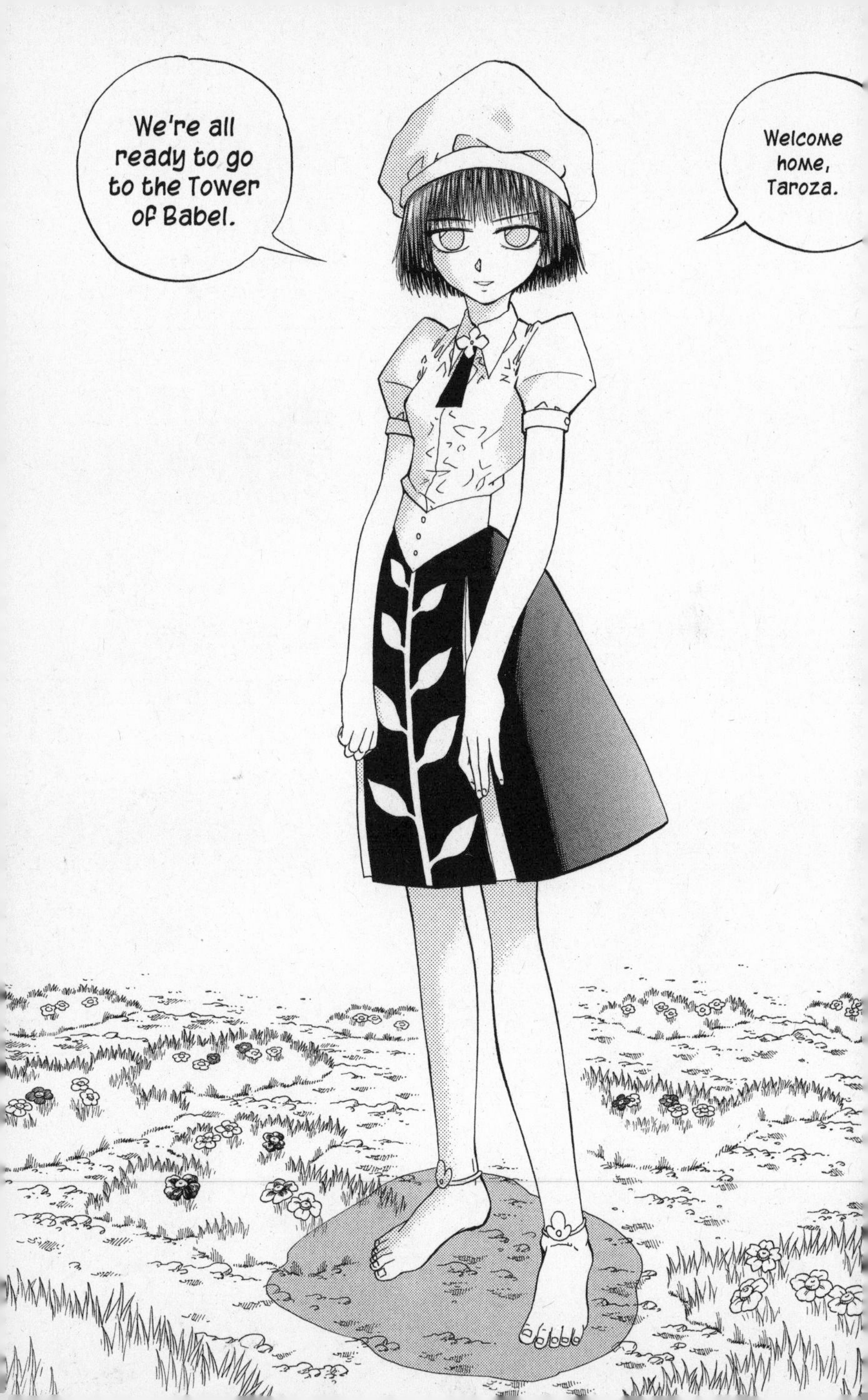
Welcome home, Taroza.
We're all ready to go to the Tower of Babel.

Bonus Page 1: The Akiko Llama Show

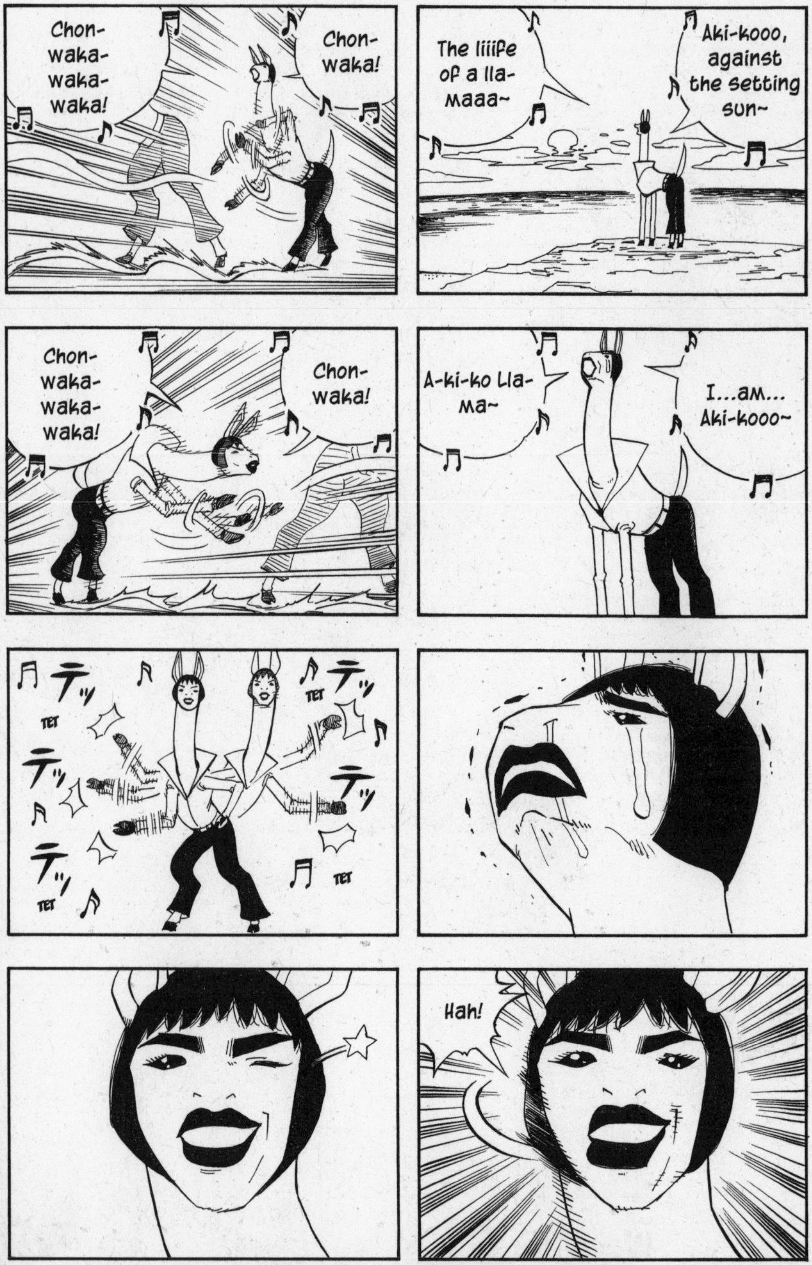

Aki-kooo, against the setting sun~
The liiife of a lla-maaa~
Chon-waka!
Chon-waka-waka-waka!
I...am... Aki-kooo~
A-ki-ko Lla-ma~
Chon-waka!
Chon-waka-waka-waka!
テッ TET
テッ TET
テッ
テッ
テッ TET
テッ TET
Hah!

Next Volume: Crabbyko Llama!

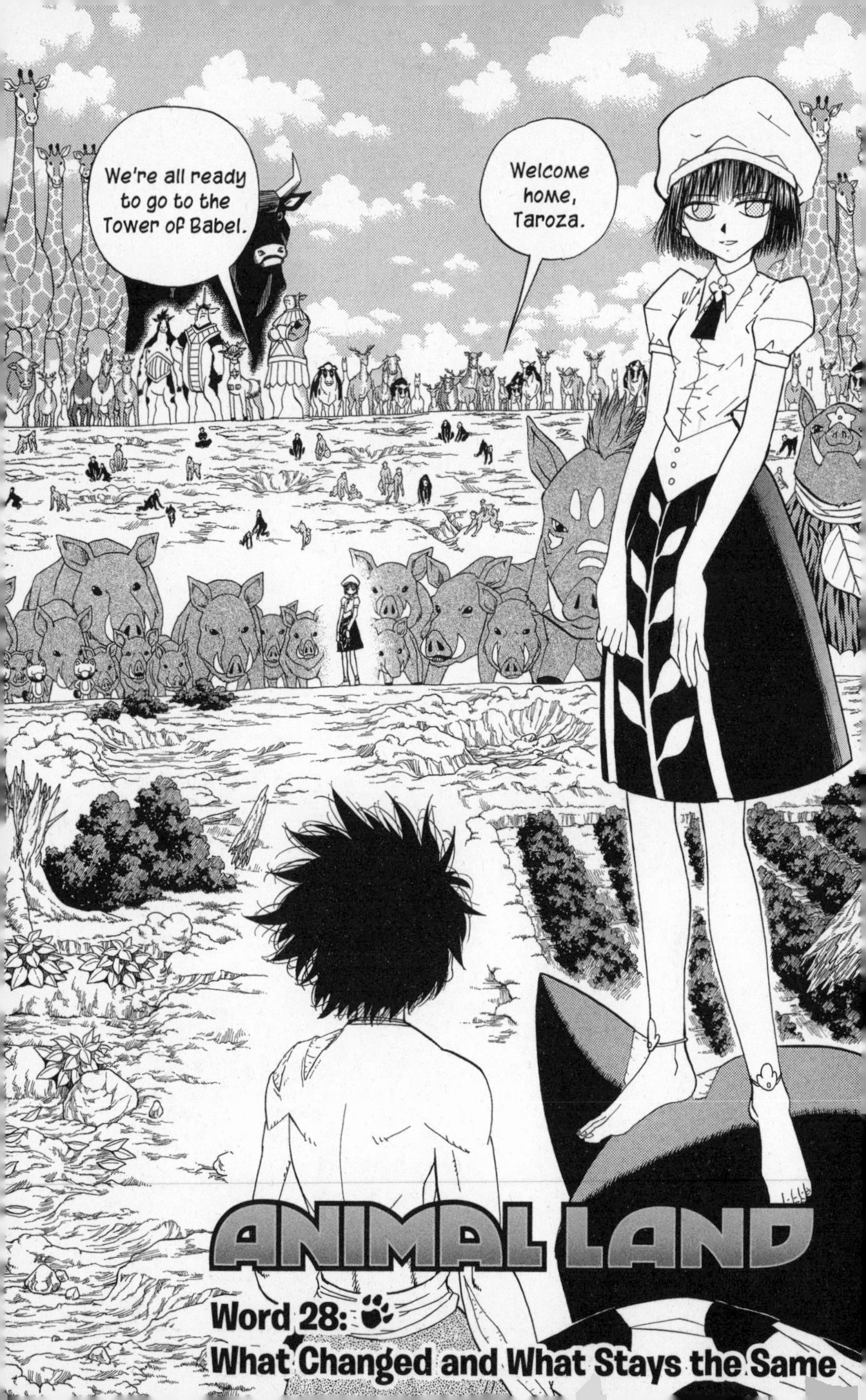
Welcome home, Taroza.
We're all ready to go to the Tower of Babel.
ANIMAL LAND
Word 28:
What Changed and What Stays the Same

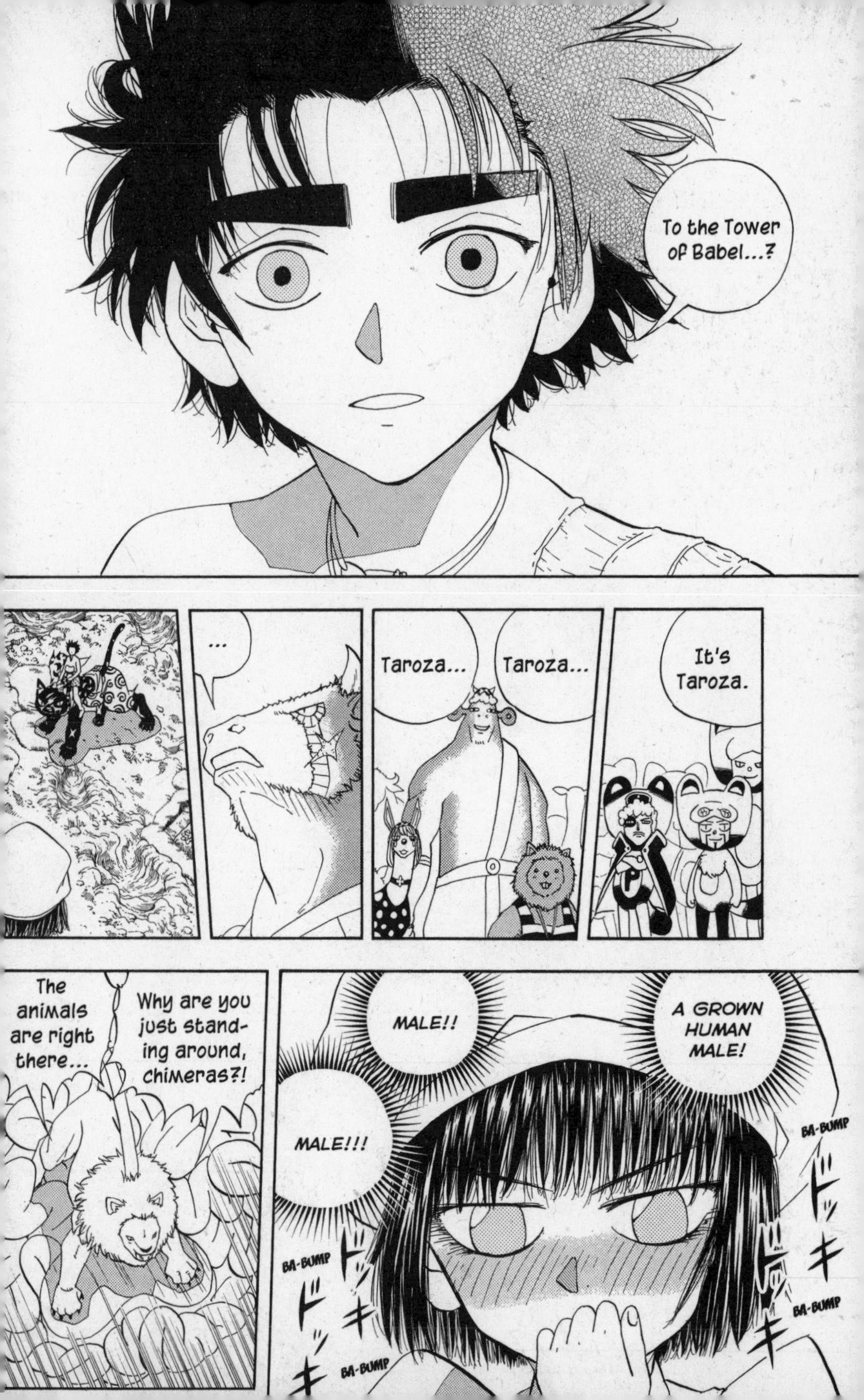
To the Tower of Babel...?
It's Taroza.
Taroza...
Taroza...
...
A GROWN HUMAN MALE!
MALE!!
MALE!!!
BA-BUMP
BA-BUMP
BA-BUMP
BA-BUMP
Why are you just standing around, chimeras?!
The animals are right there...

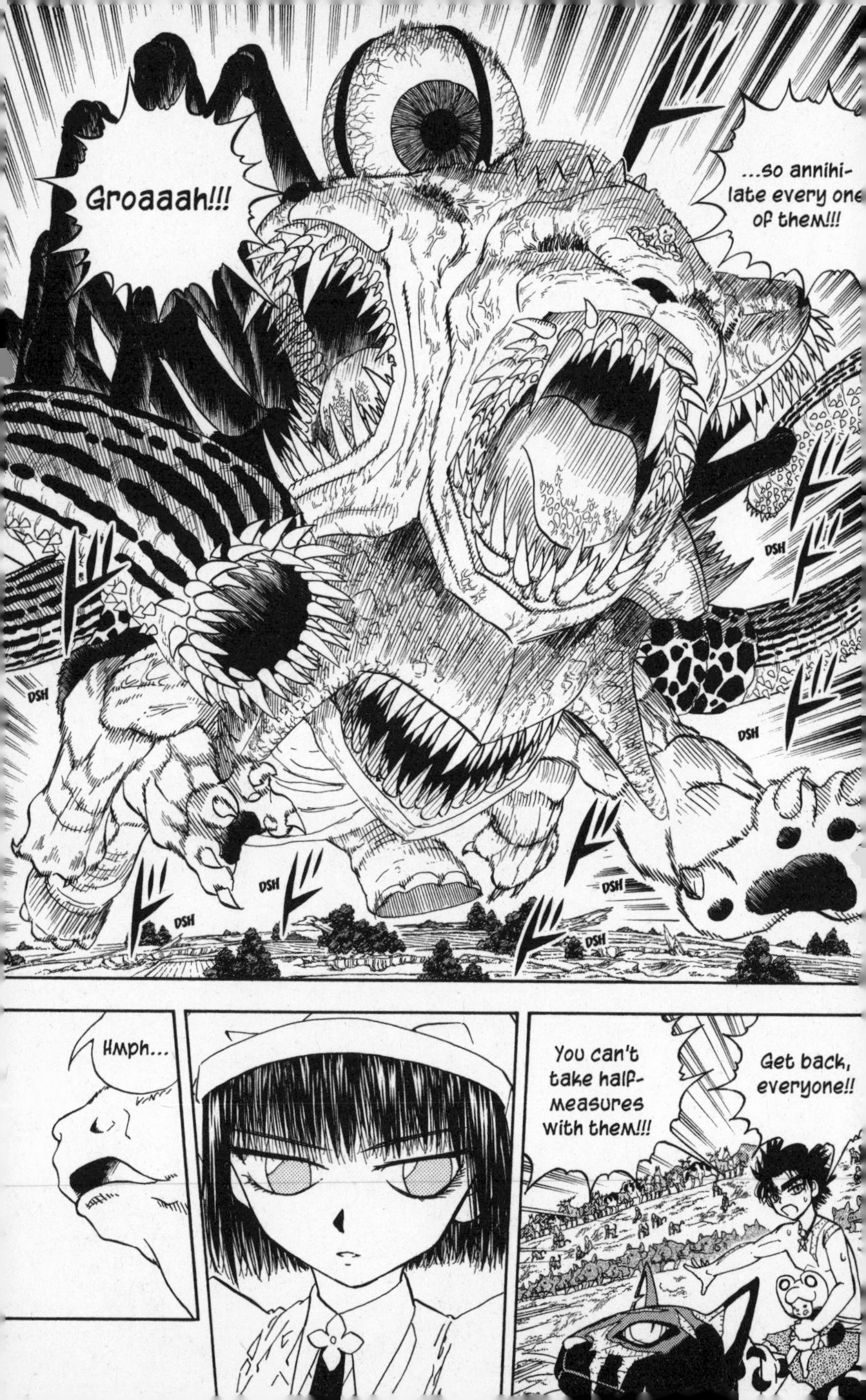
...so annihilate every one of them!!!
Groaaah!!!
DSH
DSH
DSH
DSH
DSH
DSH
DSH
Get back, everyone!!
You can't take half-measures with them!!!
Hmph...

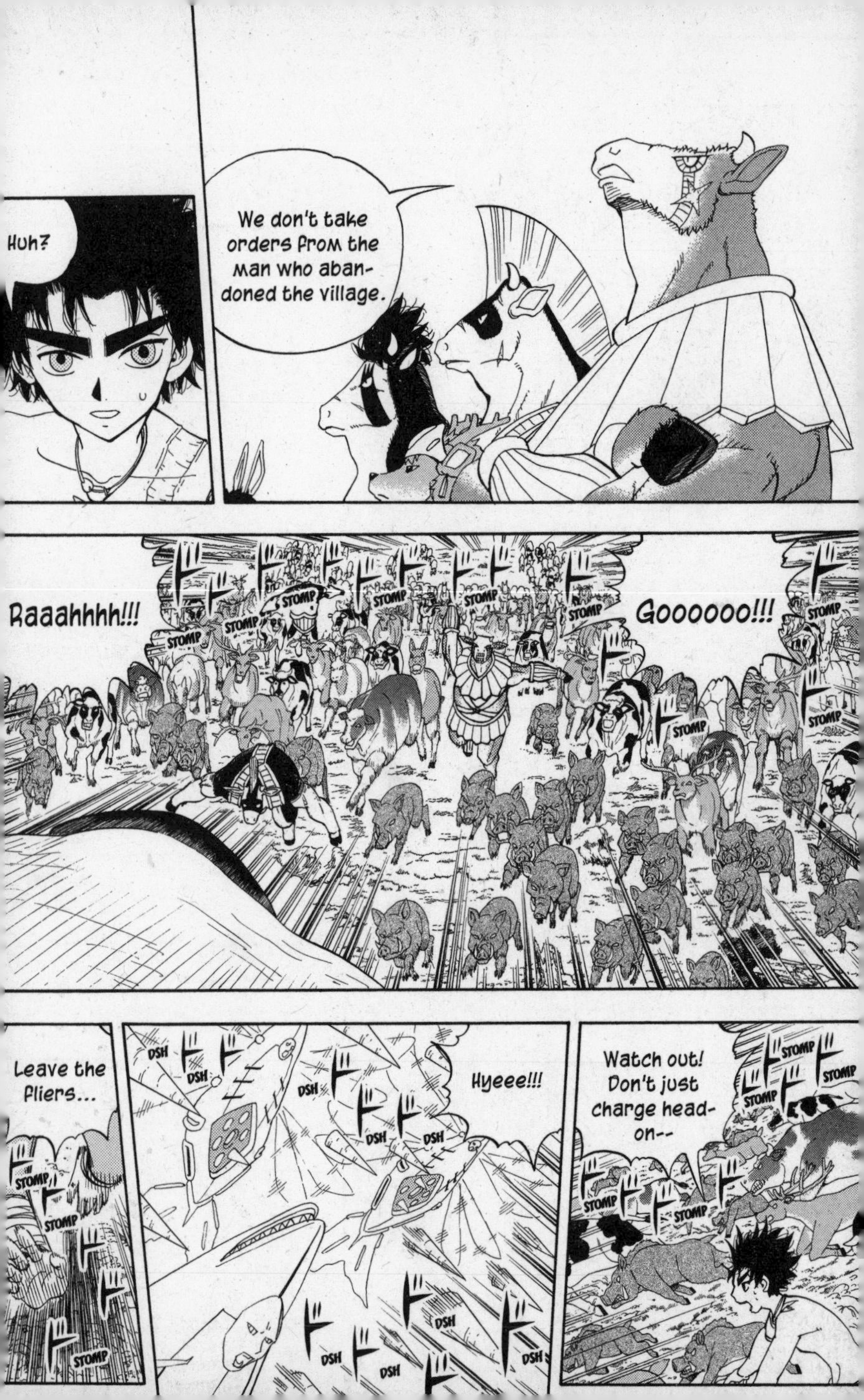
We don't take orders from the man who abandoned the village.
Huh?
Goooooo!!!
STOMP
STOMP
STOMP
STOMP
Raaahhhh!!!
STOMP
STOMP
STOMP
Watch out! Don't just charge head-on--
STOMP
STOMP
STOMP
STOMP
Hyeee!!!
DSH
DSH
DSH
DSH
Leave the fliers...
STOMP
STOMP
STOMP

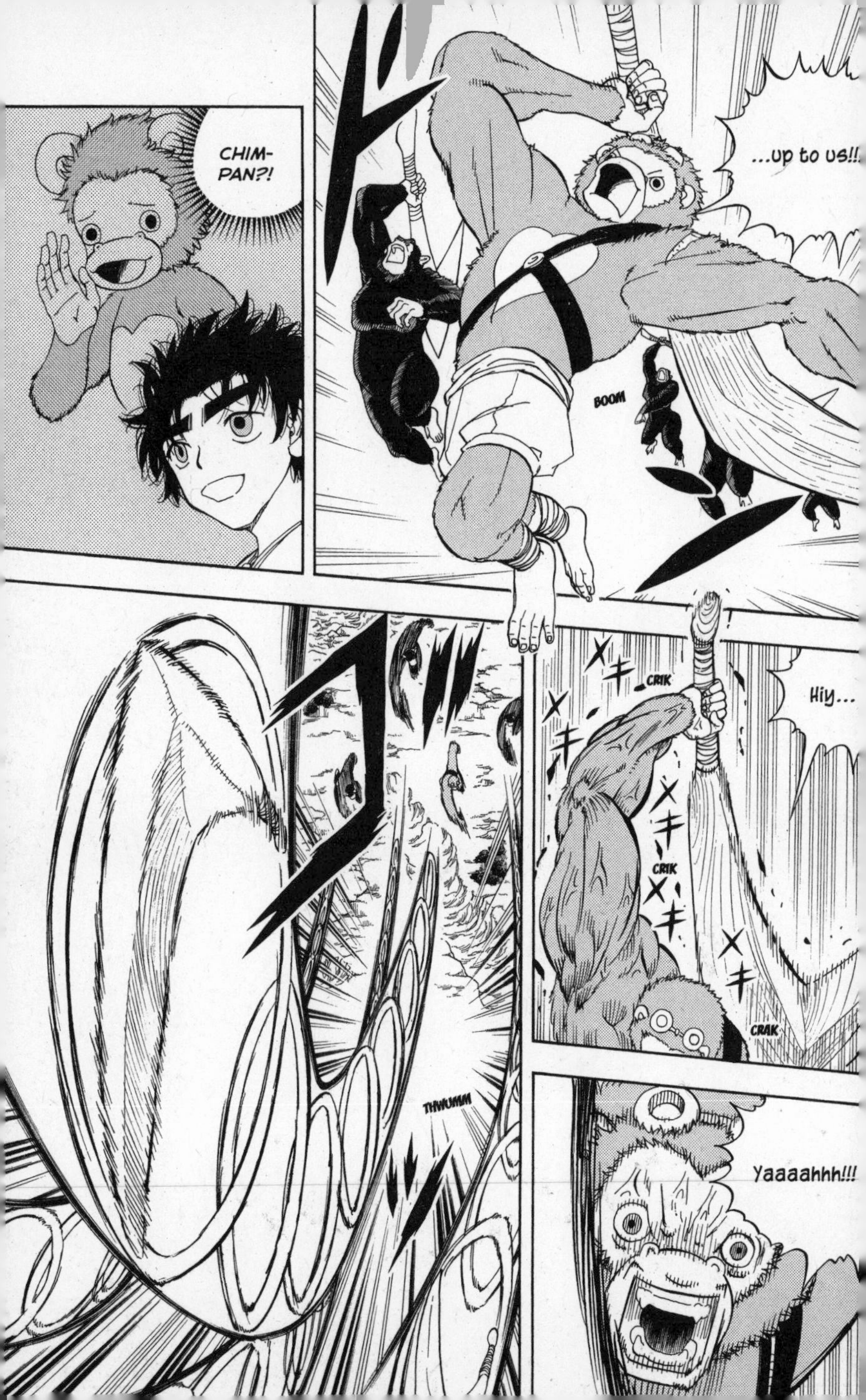
...up to us!!
BOOM
CHIM-PAN?!
Hiy...
CRIK
CRIK
CRAK
Yaaaahhh!!!
THWUMM

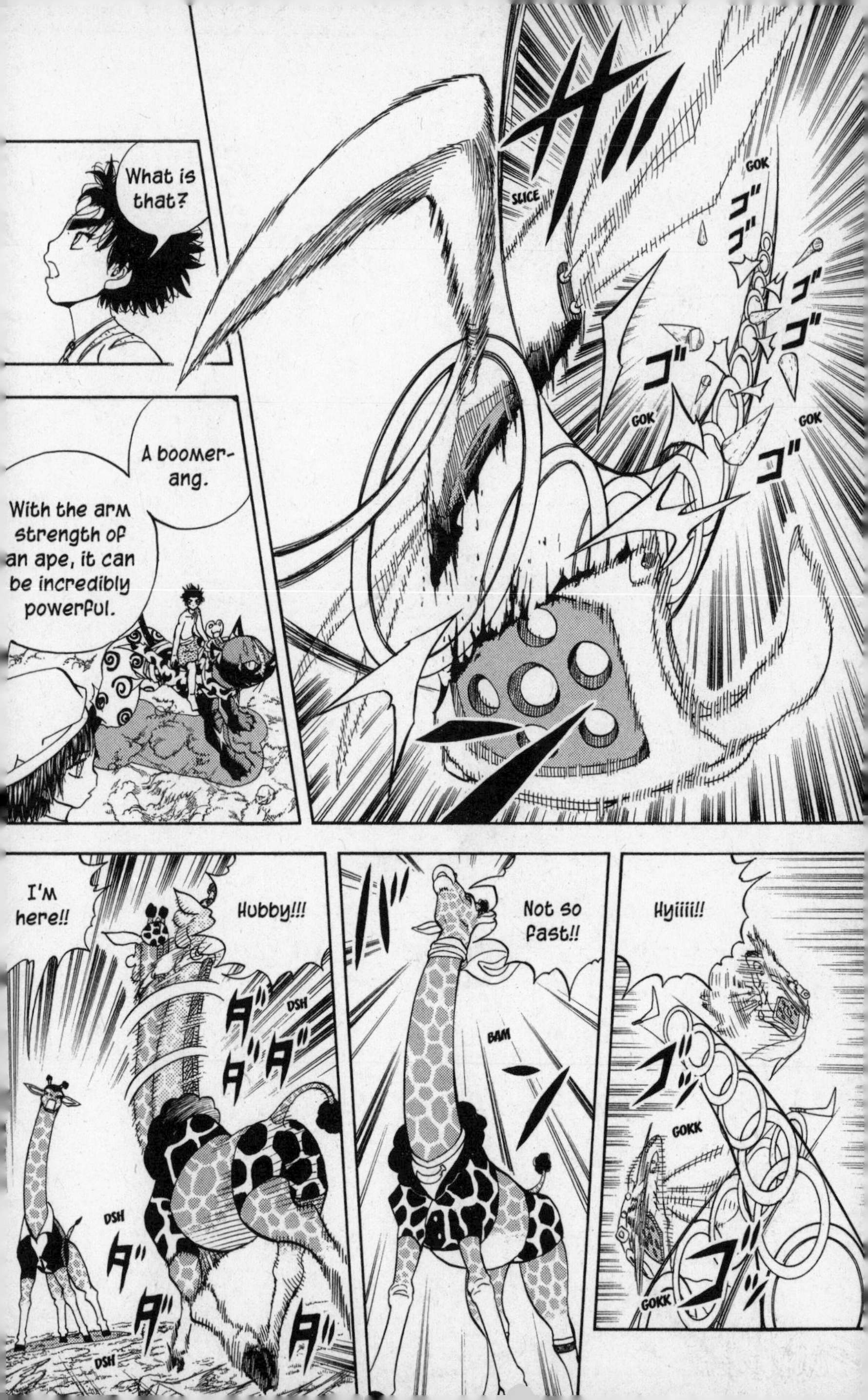
SLICE
GOK
GOK
GOK
What is that?
A boomer-ang.
With the arm strength of an ape, it can be incredibly powerful.
Hyiiii!!
GOKK
GOKK
Not so fast!!
BAM
Hubby!!!
I'm here!!
DSH
DSH
DSH

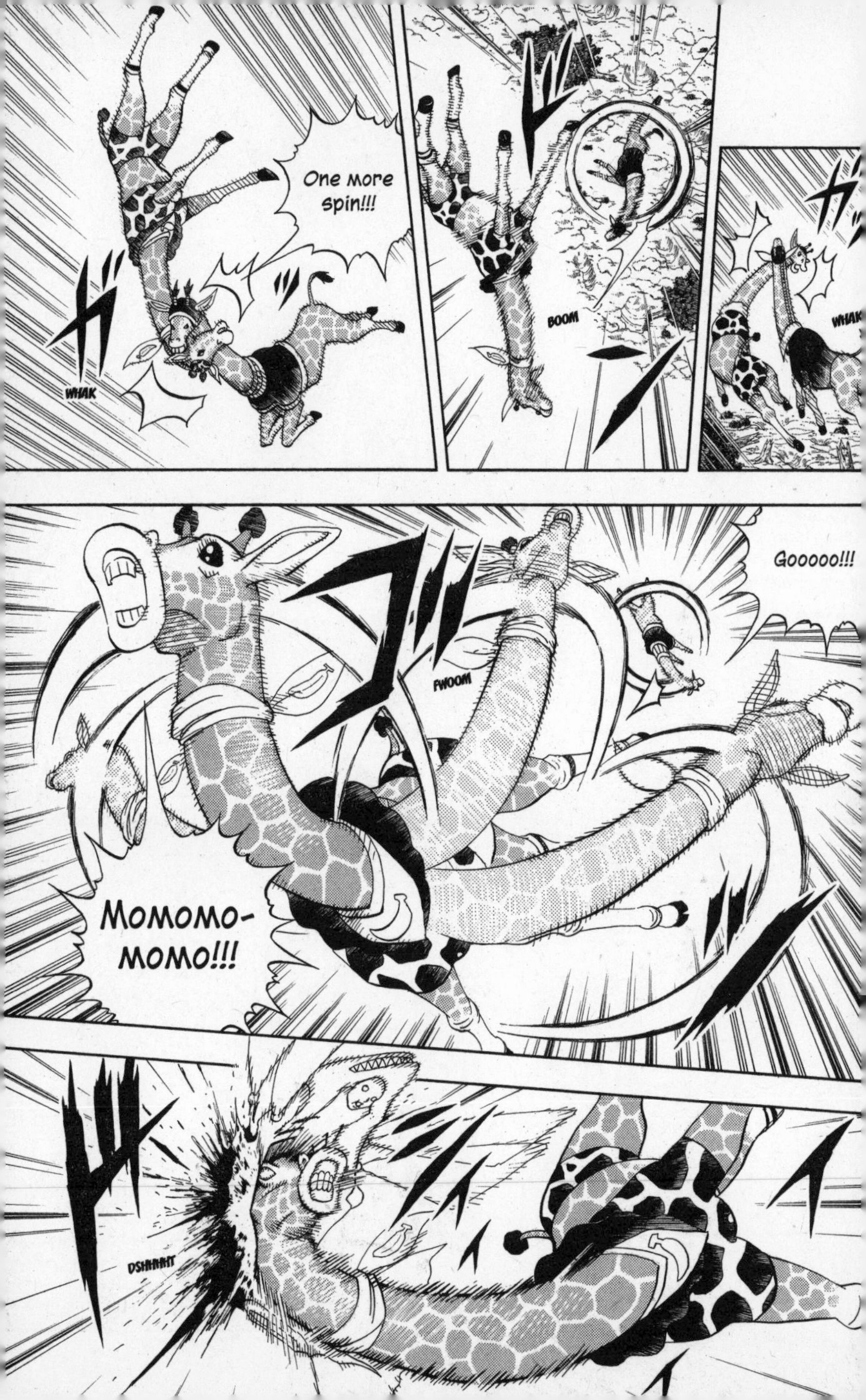
WHAK
BOOM
One more spin!!!
WHAK
Gooooo!!!
FWOOM
MOMOMO-MOMO!!!
DSHHHHT

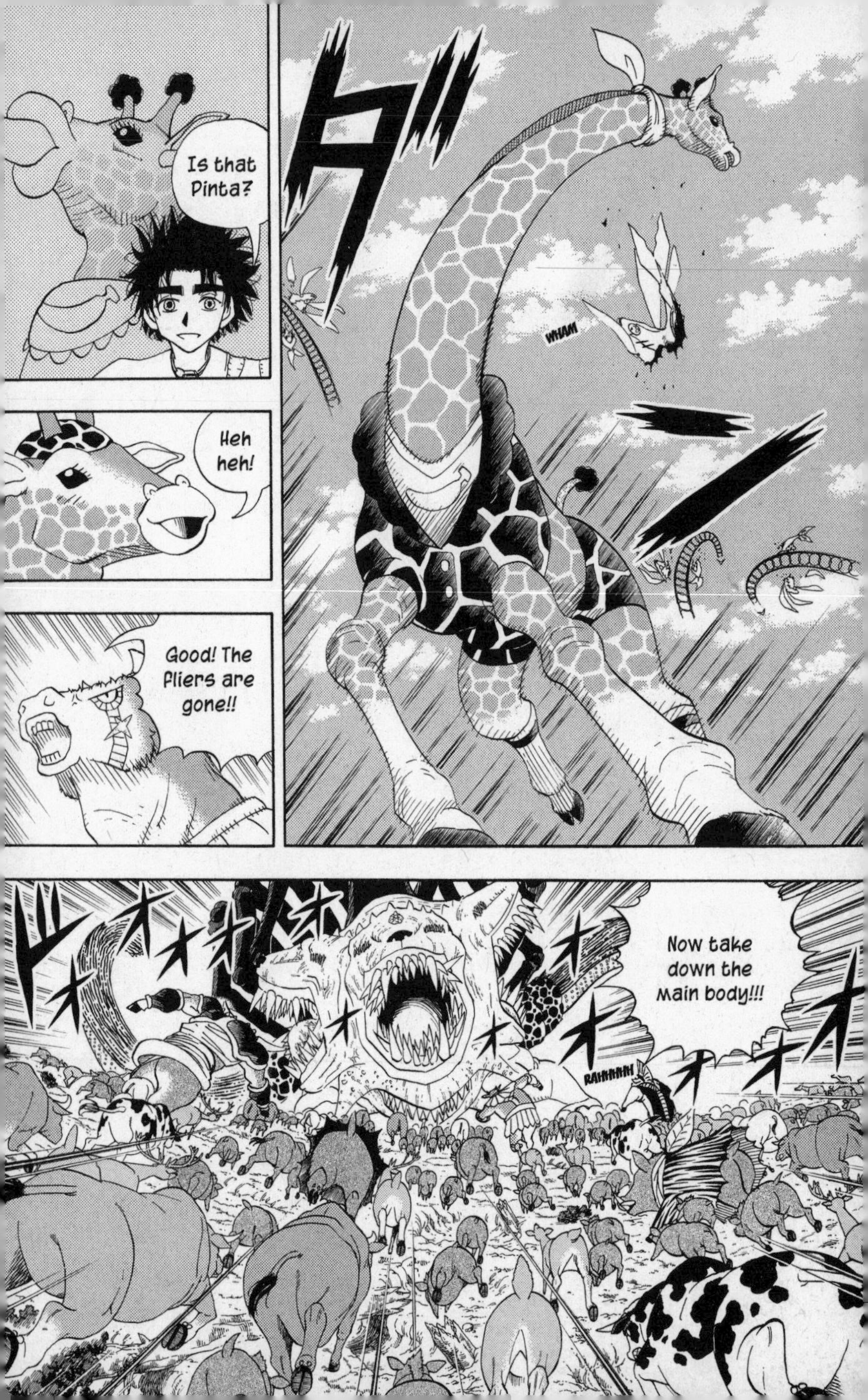
WHAM
Is that Pinta?
Heh heh!
Good! The fliers are gone!!
Now take down the main body!!!
RAHHHHH

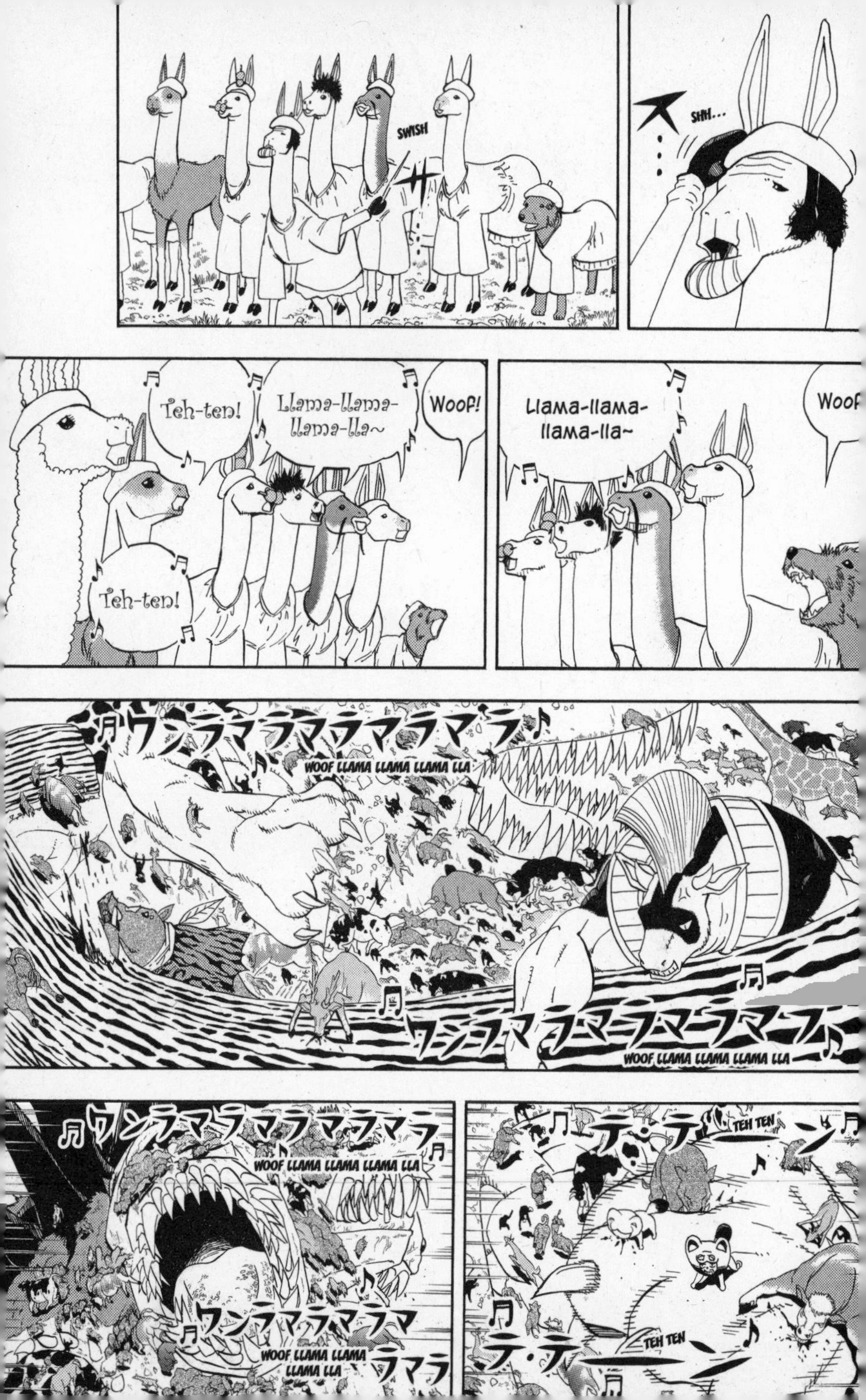
SHH...
SWISH
Woof
Llama-llama-llama-lla~
Woof!
Llama-llama-llama-lla~
Teh-ten!
Teh-ten!
ワンラマラマラマラマラ
WOOF LLAMA LLAMA LLAMA LLA
ワンラマラーマーラマーラマーラ
WOOF LLAMA LLAMA LLAMA LLA
テ・テーン
TEH TEN
テ・テーン
TEH TEN
ワンラマラマラマラマラ
WOOF LLAMA LLAMA LLAMA LLA
ワンラマラマラマ
ラマラ
WOOF LLAMA LLAMA LLAMA LLA

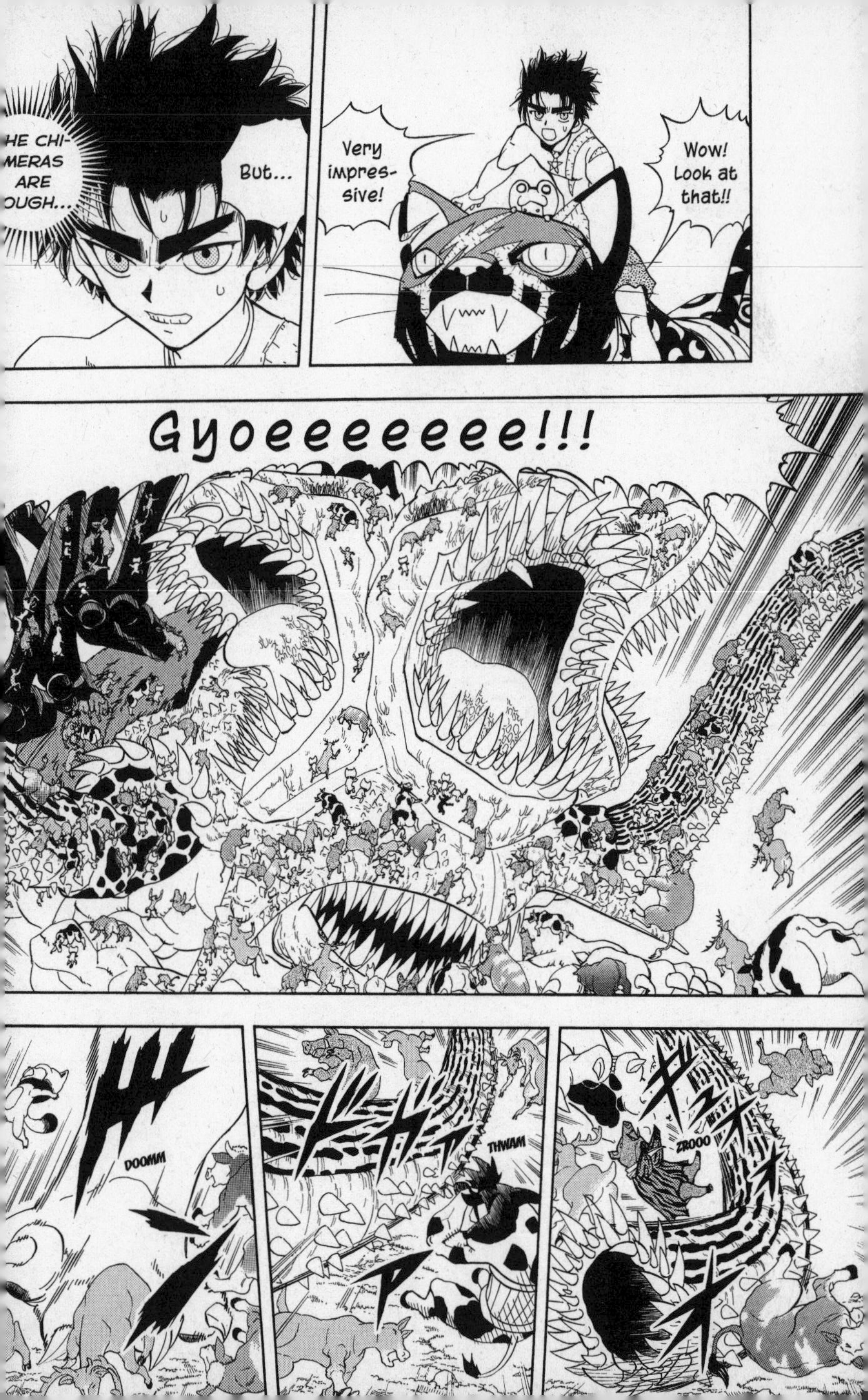
Wow! Look at that!!
Very impres- sive!
But...
HE CHI- MERAS ARE OUGH...
Gyoeeeeeeee!!!
ZROOO
THWAM
DOOMM

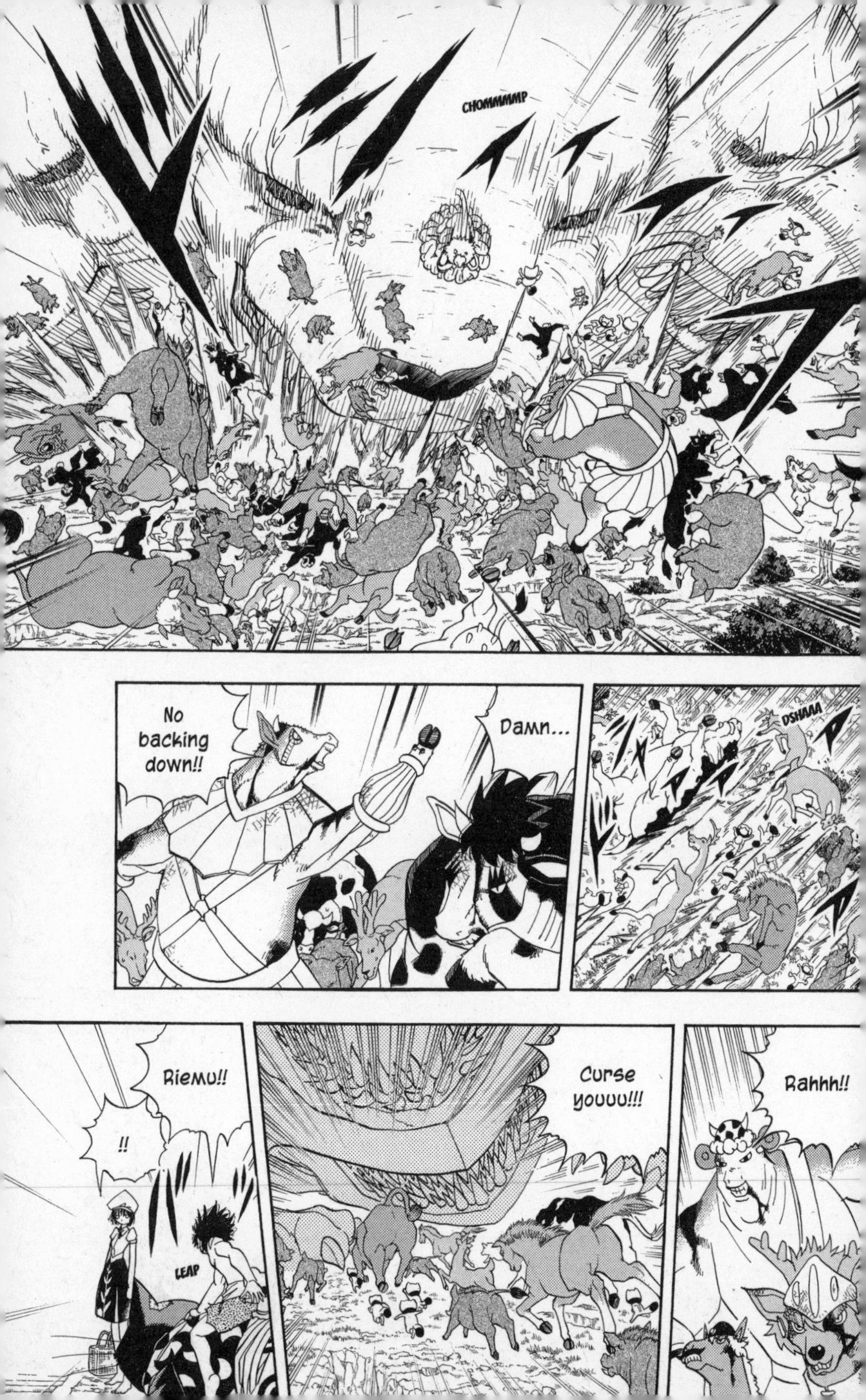
CHOMMMMP
DSHAAA
Damn...
No backing down!!
Rahhh!!
Curse youuu!!!
Riemu!!
!!
LEAP

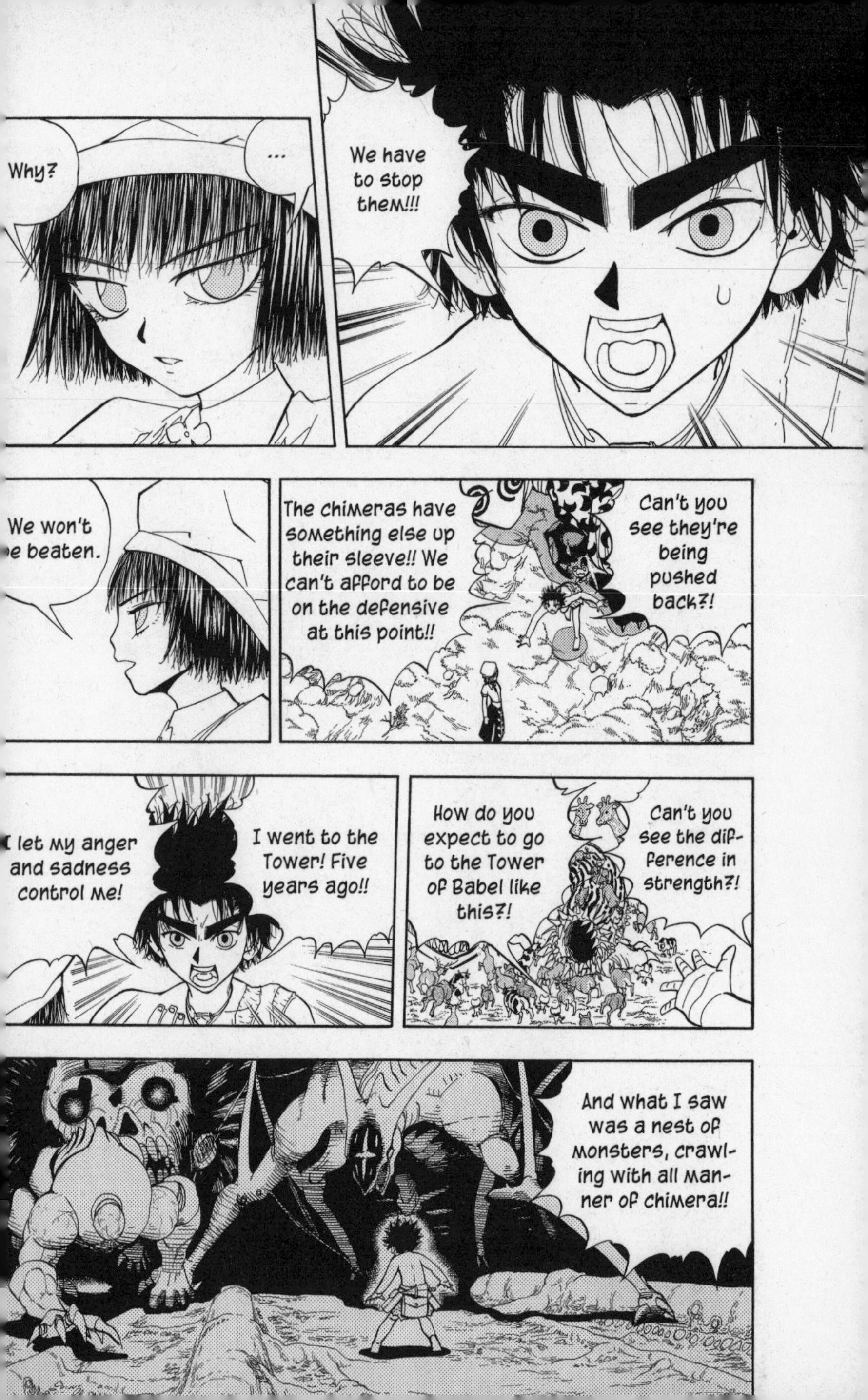

We have to stop them!!!
...
Why?
Can't you see they're being pushed back?!
The chimeras have something else up their sleeve!! We can't afford to be on the defensive at this point!!
We won't e beaten.
Can't you see the dif- ference in strength?!
How do you expect to go to the Tower of Babel like this?!
I went to the Tower! Five years ago!!
I let my anger and sadness control me!
And what I saw was a nest of monsters, crawl- ing with all man- ner of chimera!!

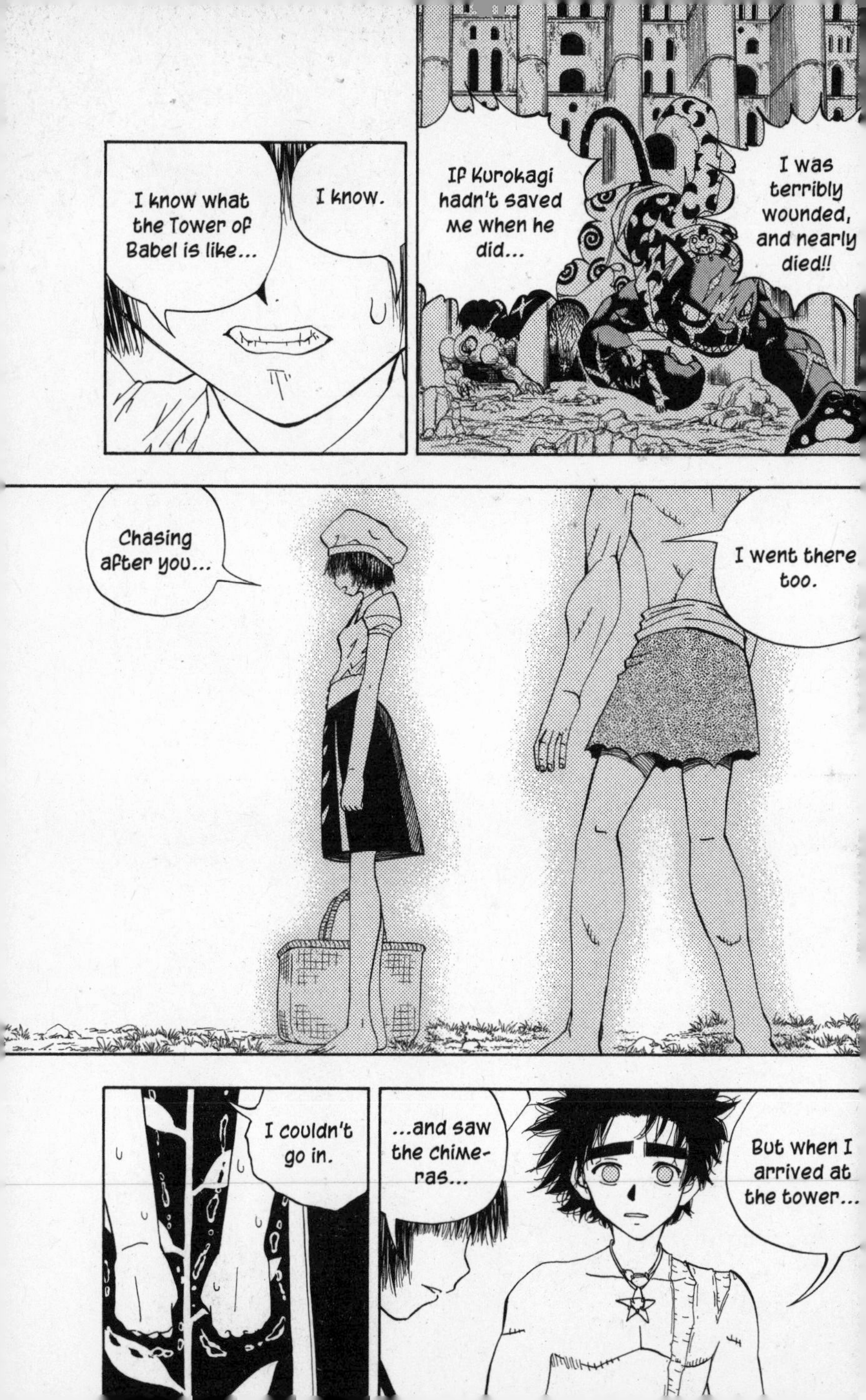
I was terribly wounded, and nearly died!!
If Kurokagi hadn't saved me when he did...
I know.
I know what the Tower of Babel is like...
I went there too.
Chasing after you...
But when I arrived at the tower...
...and saw the chime-ras...
I couldn't go in.

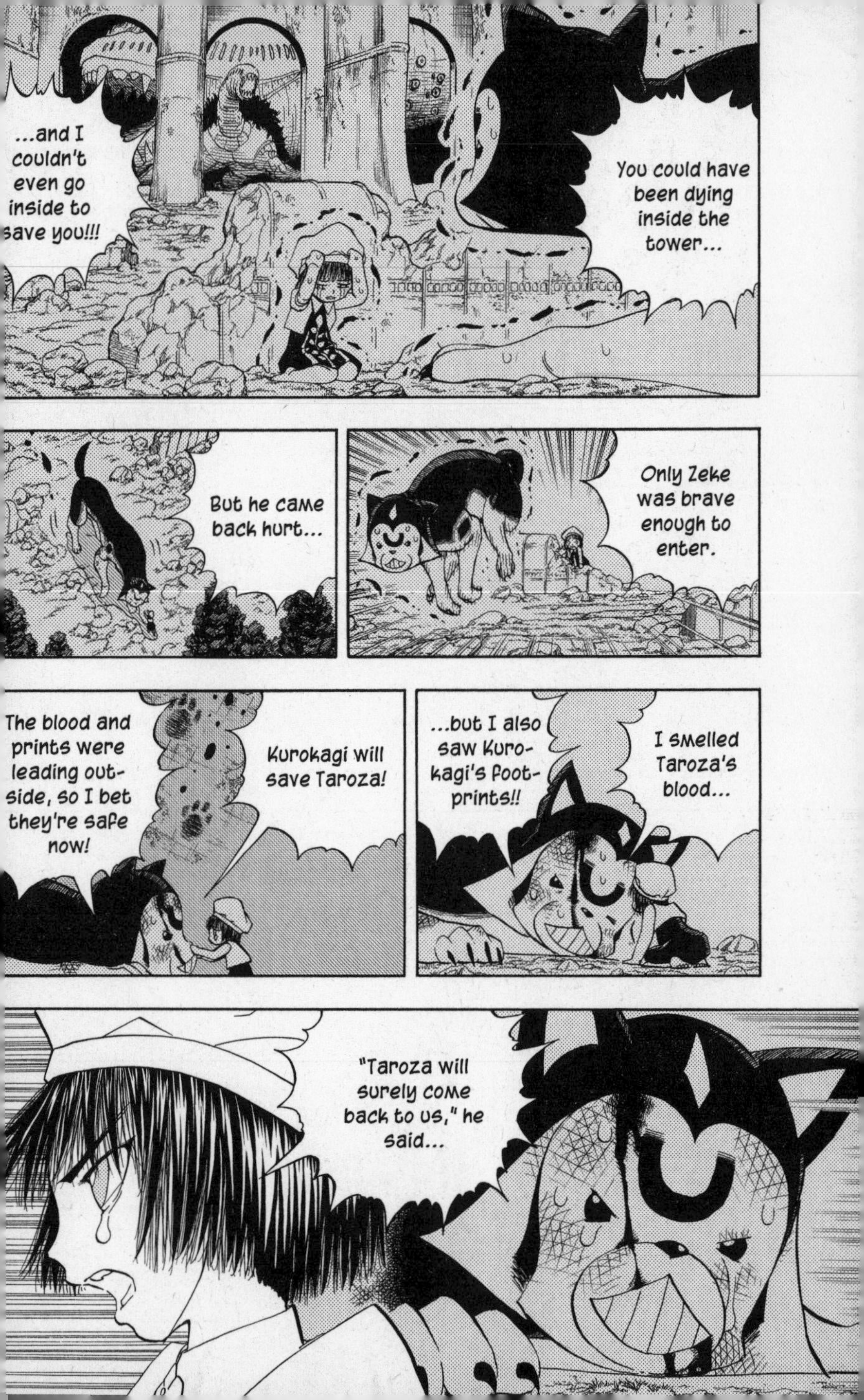
You could have been dying inside the tower...
...and I couldn't even go inside to save you!!!
Only Zeke was brave enough to enter.
But he came back hurt...
I smelled Taroza's blood...
...but I also saw Kurokagi's foot-prints!!
Kurokagi will save Taroza!
The blood and prints were leading out-side, so I bet they're safe now!
"Taroza will surely come back to us," he said...

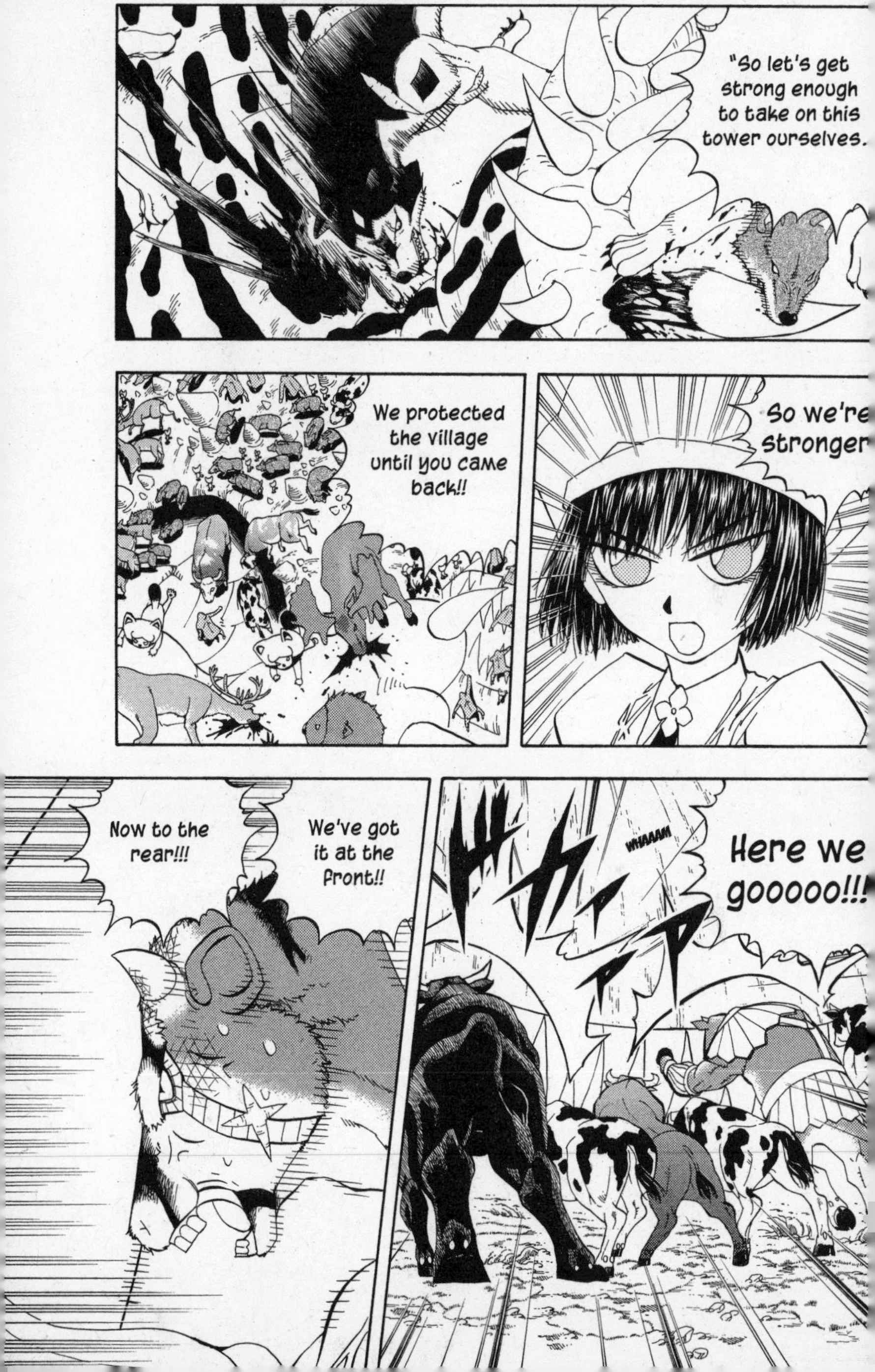
"So let's get strong enough to take on this tower ourselves.
So we're stronger
We protected the village until you came back!!
Here we gooooo!!!
WHAAAM
We've got it at the front!!
Now to the rear!!!

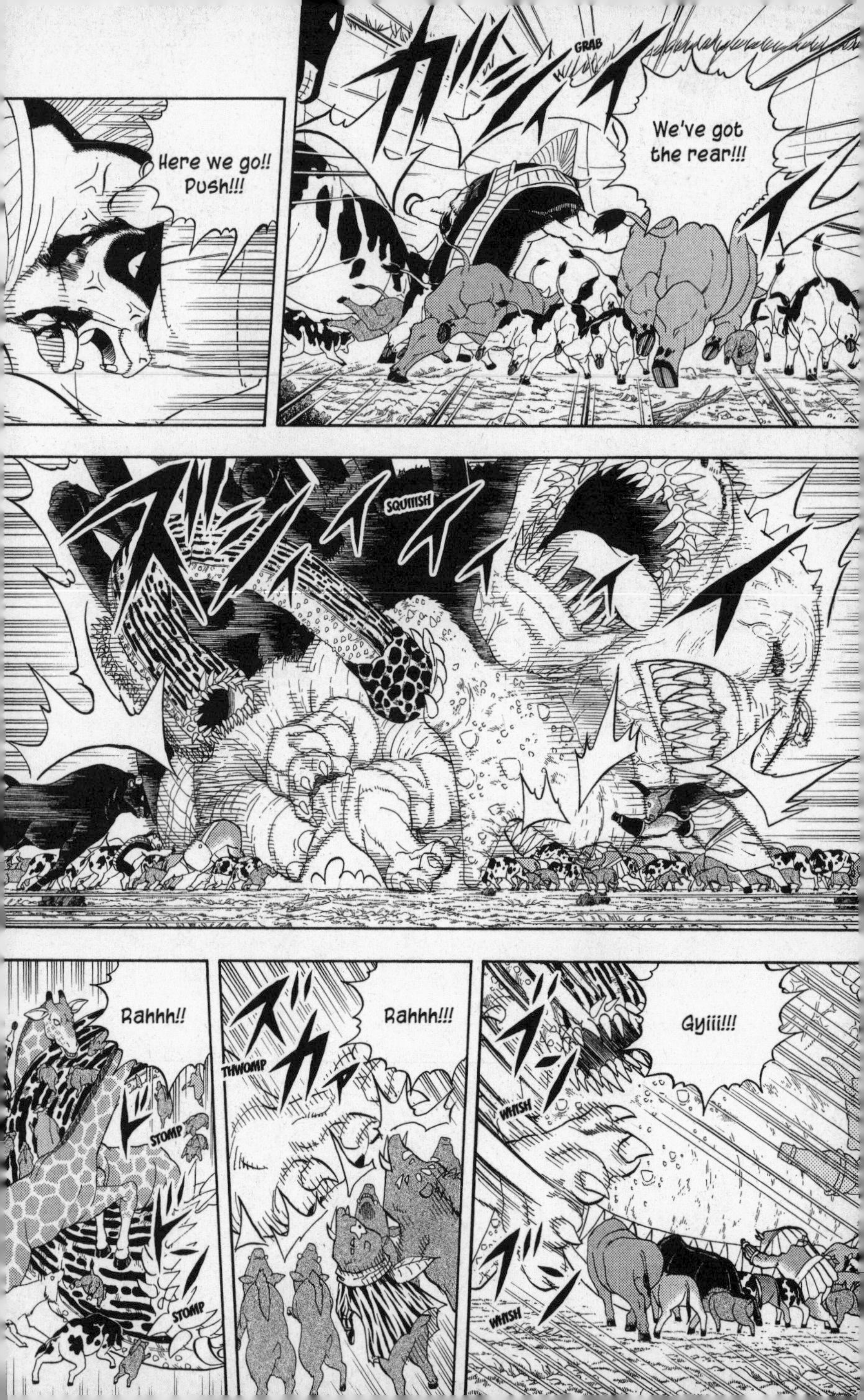
GRAB
We've got the rear!!!
Here we go!! Push!!!
SQUIIISH
Gyiii!!!
WHISH
WHISH
Rahhh!!!
THWOMP
Rahhh!!
STOMP
STOMP

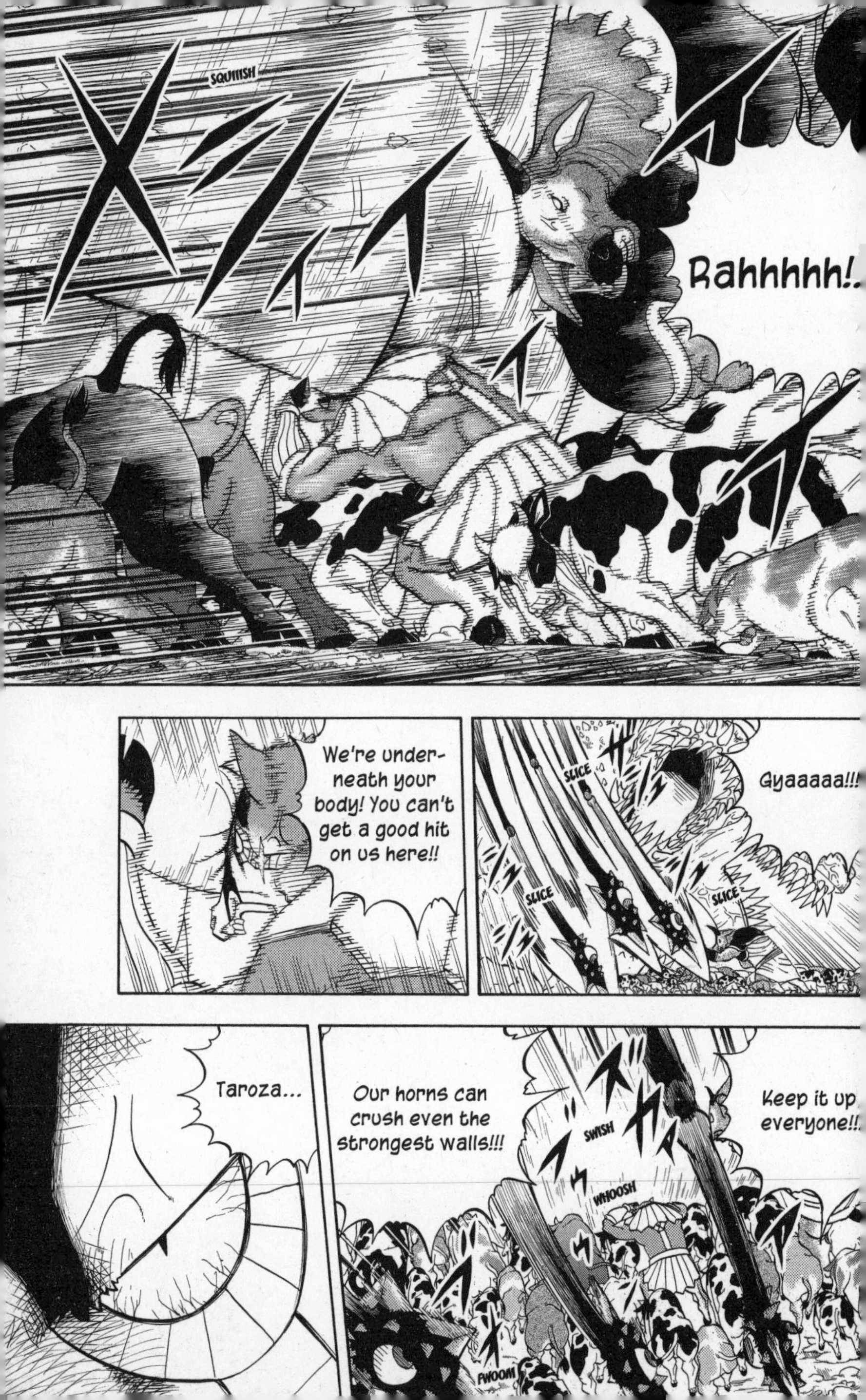
Rahhhhh!!
SQUIIISH
Gyaaaaa!!!
SLICE
SLICE
SLICE
We're under-neath your body! You can't get a good hit on us here!!
Keep it up everyone!!
Our horns can crush even the strongest walls!!!
SWISH
WHOOSH
FWOOM
Taroza...

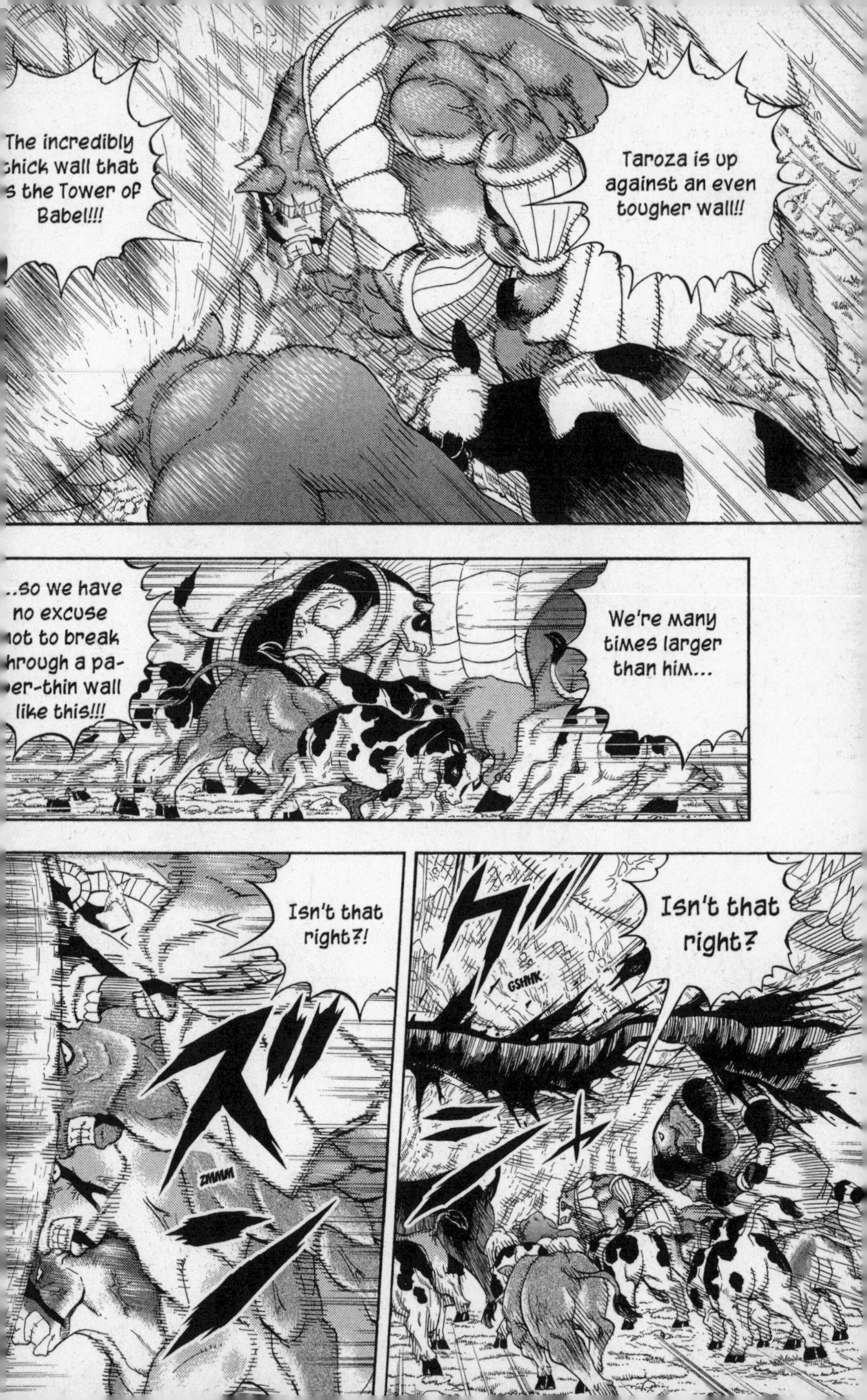
Taroza is up against an even tougher wall!!
The incredibly hick wall that s the Tower of Babel!!!
We're many times larger than him...
..so we have no excuse ot to break hrough a pa- er-thin wall like this!!!
Isn't that right?
GSHWK
Isn't that right?!
ZMMM

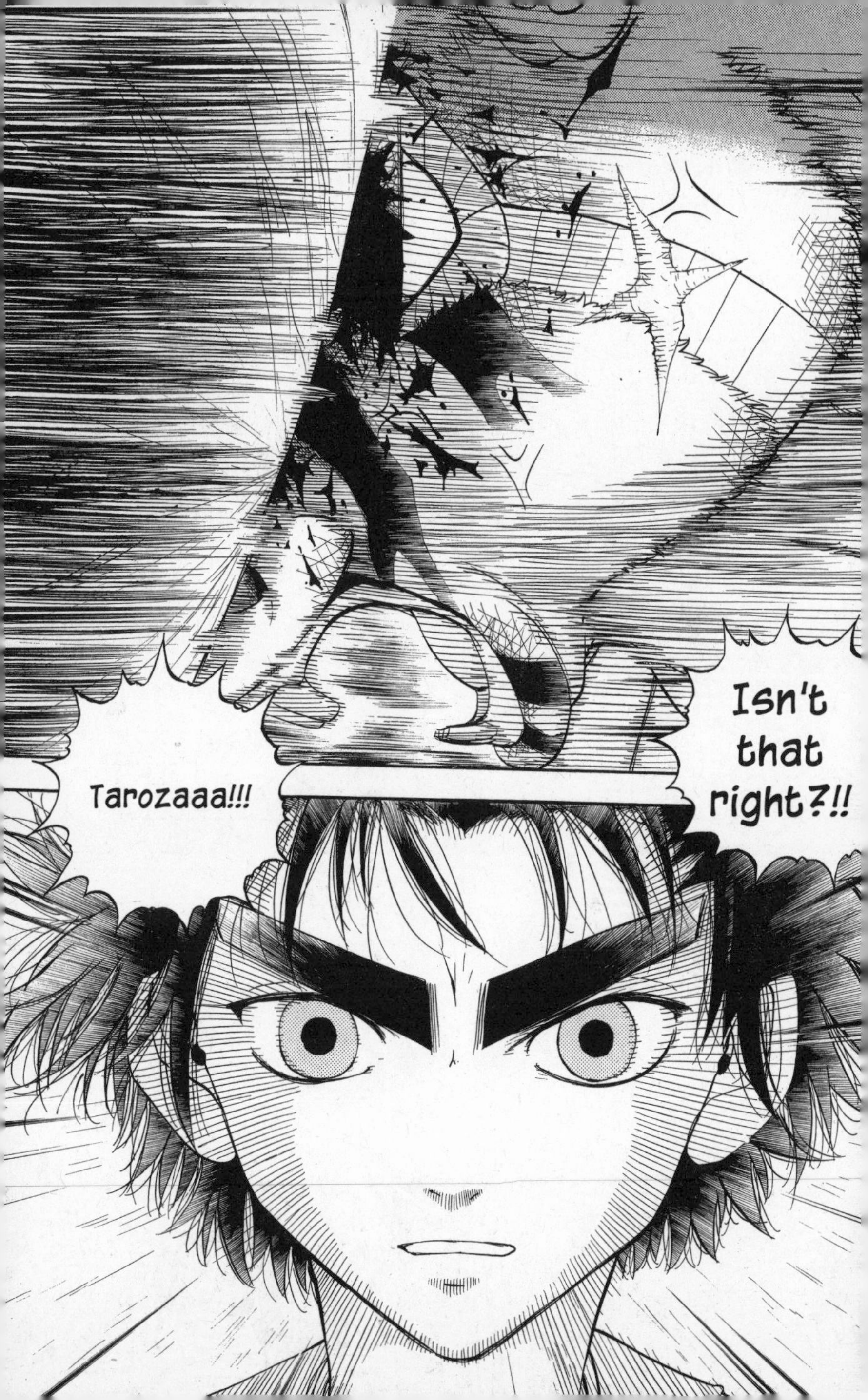
Isn't that right?!!
Tarozaaa!!!

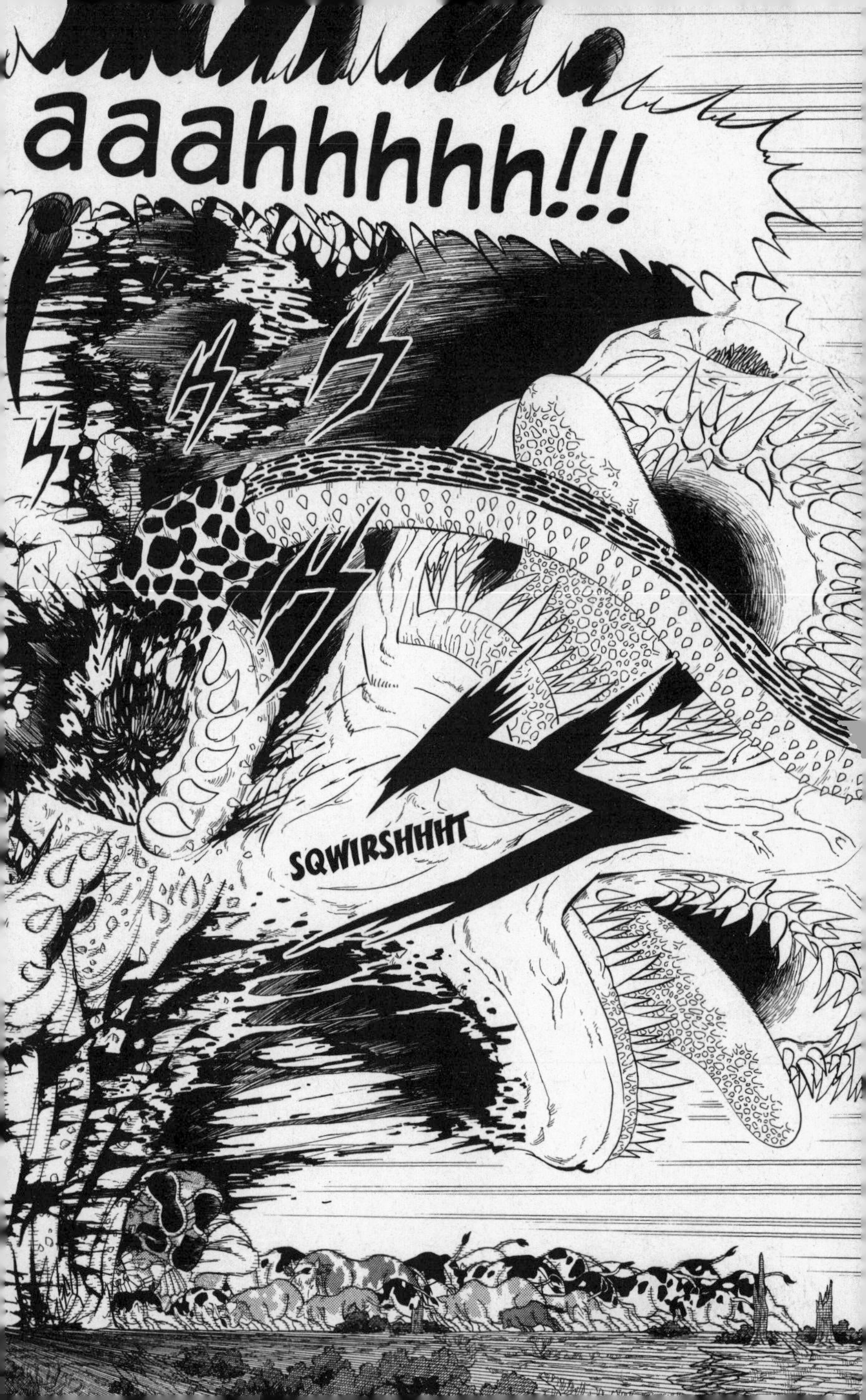
aaahhhhhh!!!
SQWIRSHHHT

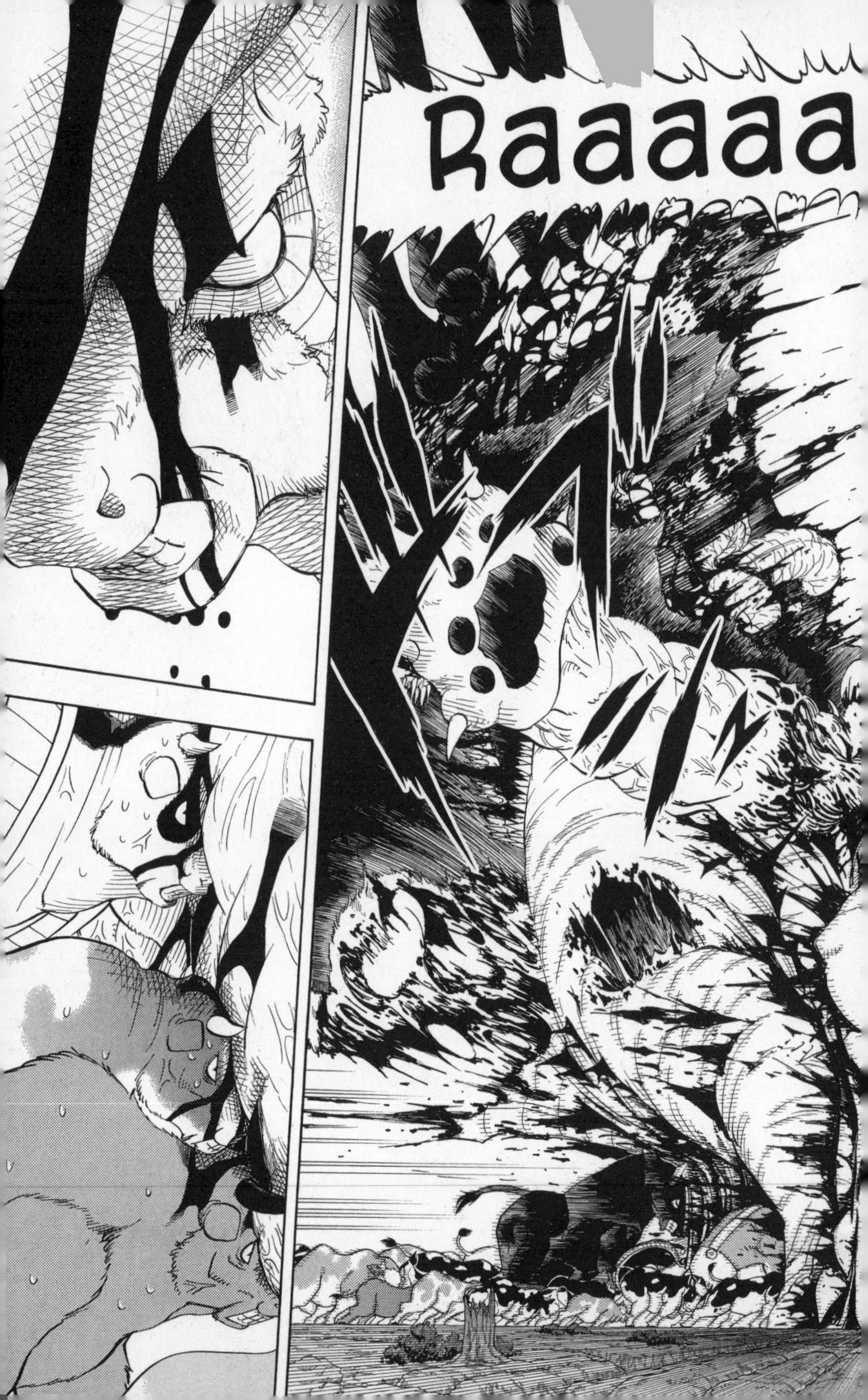
Raaaaaa

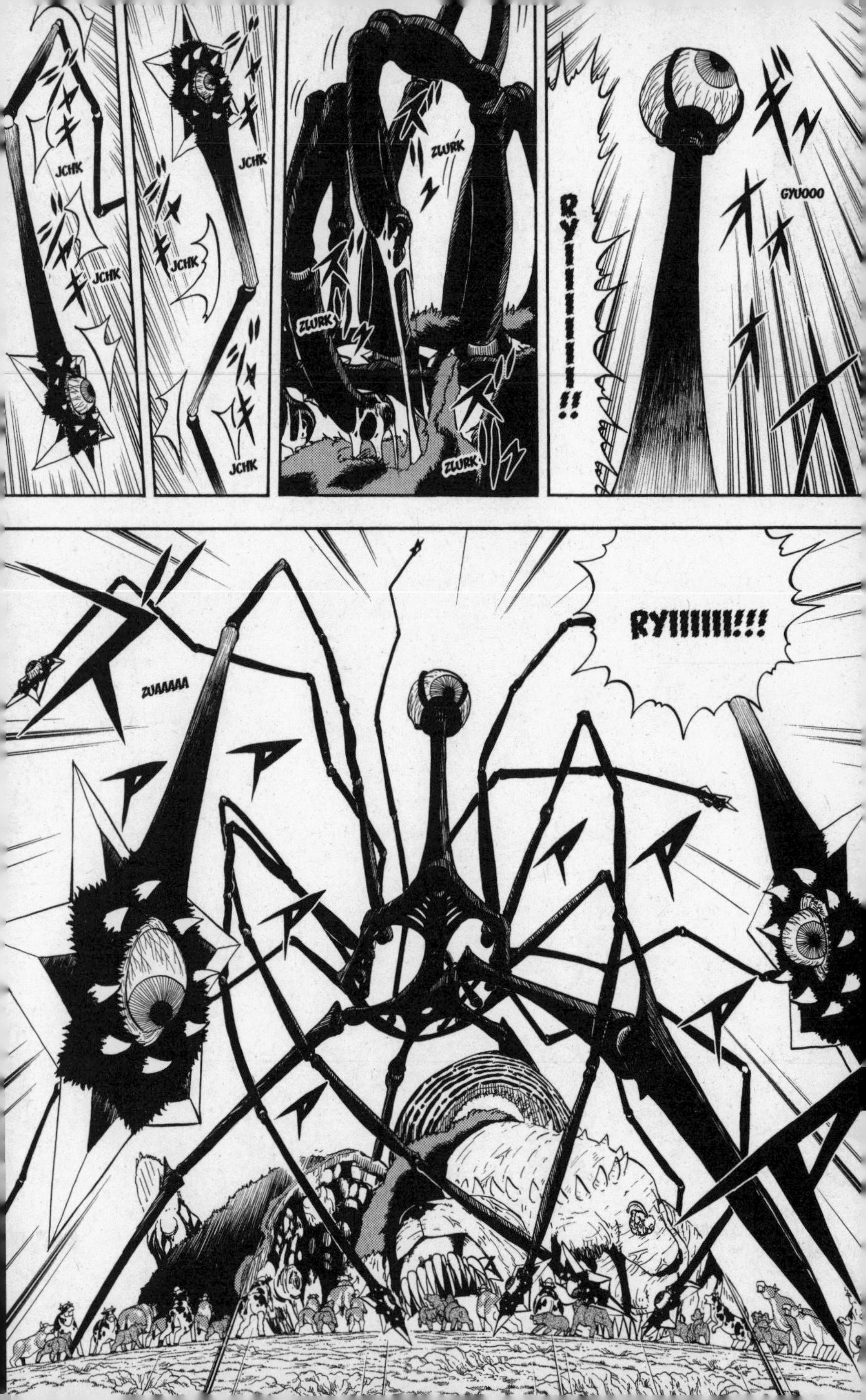
GYUOOO
RYIIIIIIII!!
ZURK
ZURK
ZURK
JCHK
JCHK
JCHK
JCHK
JCHK
RYIIIIIII!!!
ZUAAAAA

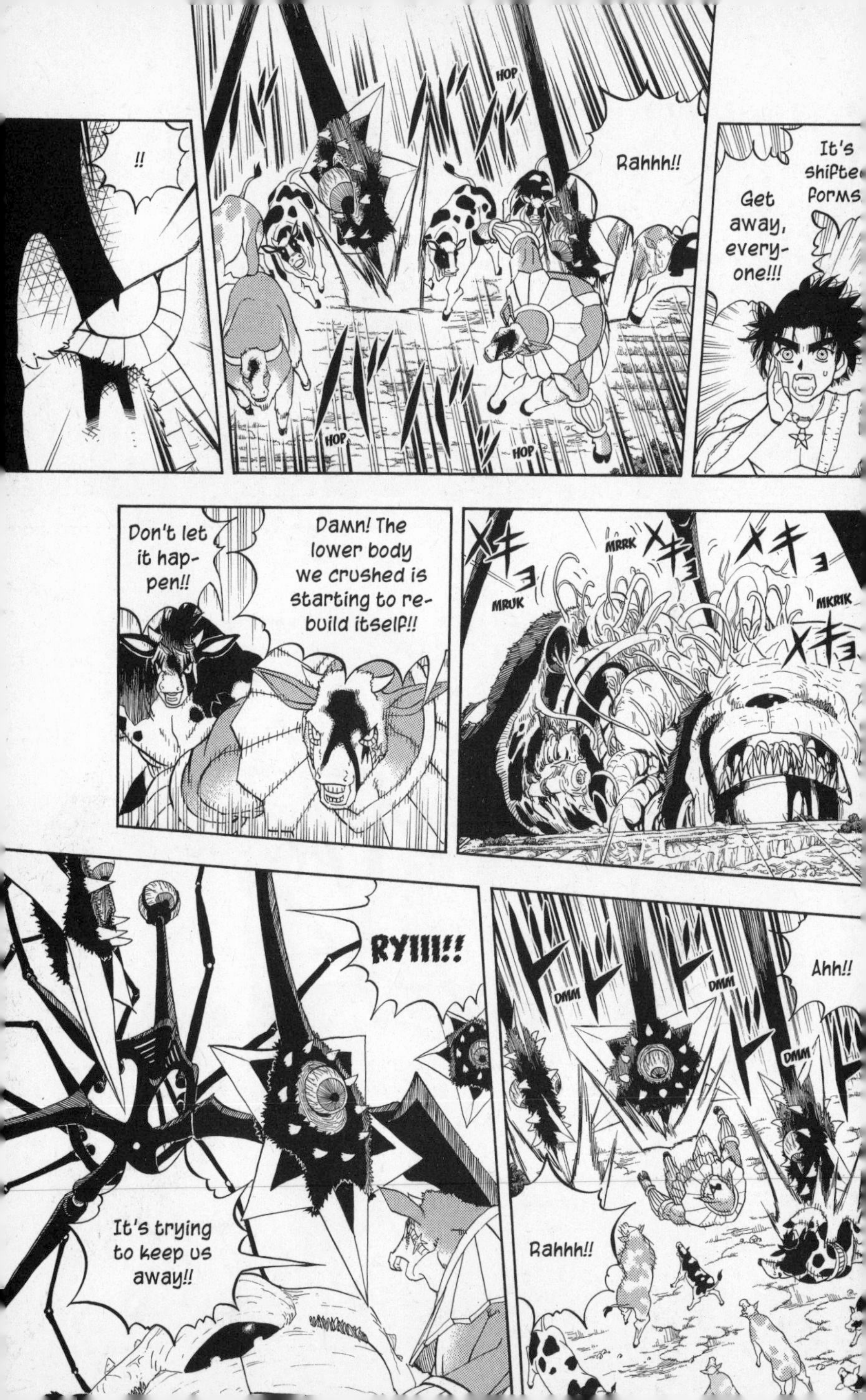
It's shifte forms
Get away, everyone!!!
Rahhh!!
HOP
HOP
HOP
!!
MKRIK
MRRK
MRUK
Damn! The lower body we crushed is starting to rebuild itself!!
Don't let it happen!!
Ahh!!
DMM
DMM
DMM
Rahhh!!
RYIII!!
It's trying to keep us away!!

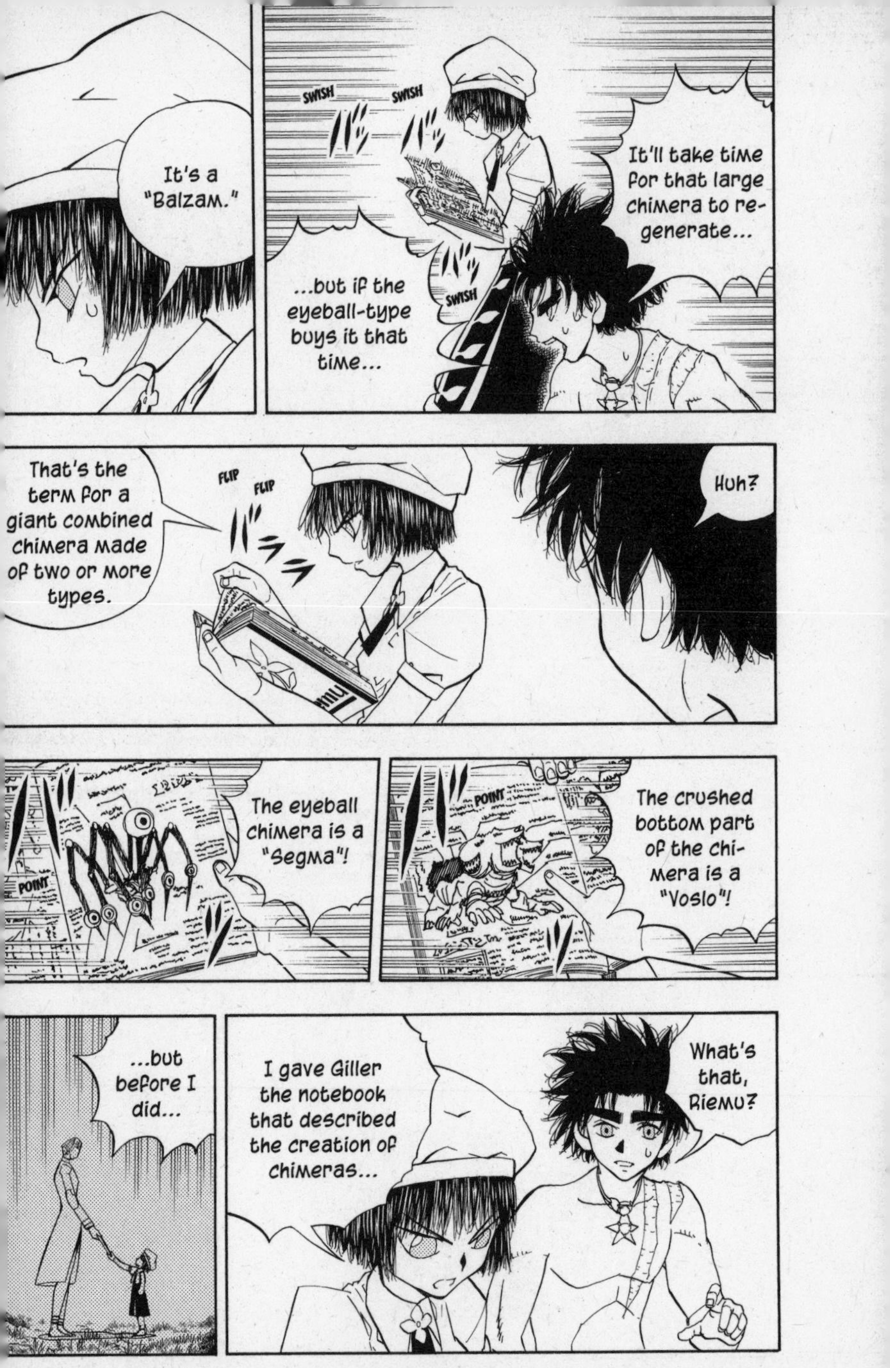
SWISH
SWISH
It'll take time for that large chimera to regenerate...
SWISH
...but if the eyeball-type buys it that time...
It's a "Balzam."
Huh?
FLIP
FLIP
That's the term for a giant combined chimera made of two or more types.
POINT
The crushed bottom part of the chimera is a "Voslo"!
POINT
The eyeball chimera is a "Segma"!
What's that, Riemu?
I gave Giller the notebook that described the creation of chimeras...
...but before I did...

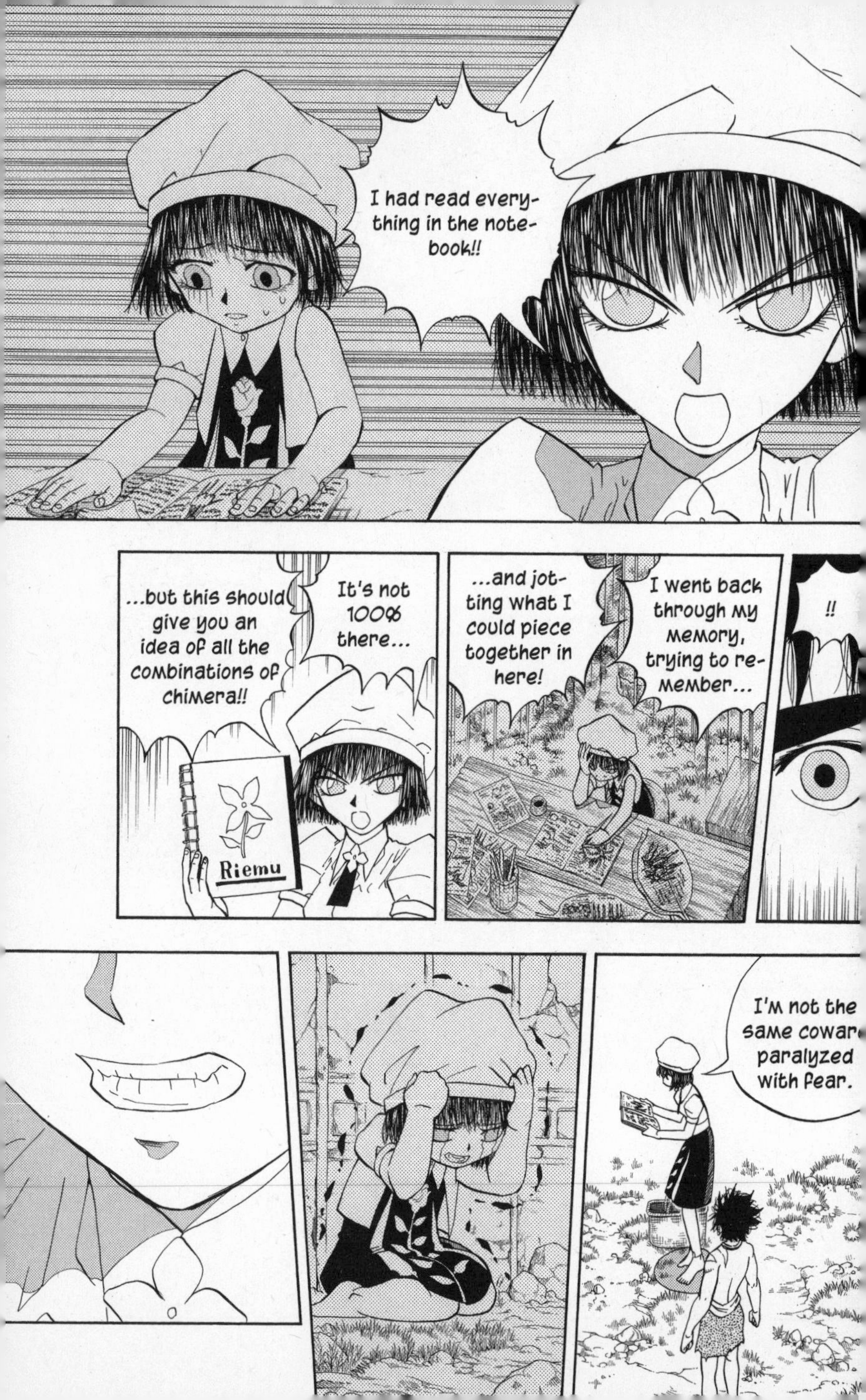
I had read everything in the notebook!!
!!
I went back through my memory, trying to remember...
...and jotting what I could piece together in here!
It's not 100% there...
...but this should give you an idea of all the combinations of chimera!!
Riemu
I'm not the same cowar paralyzed with fear.

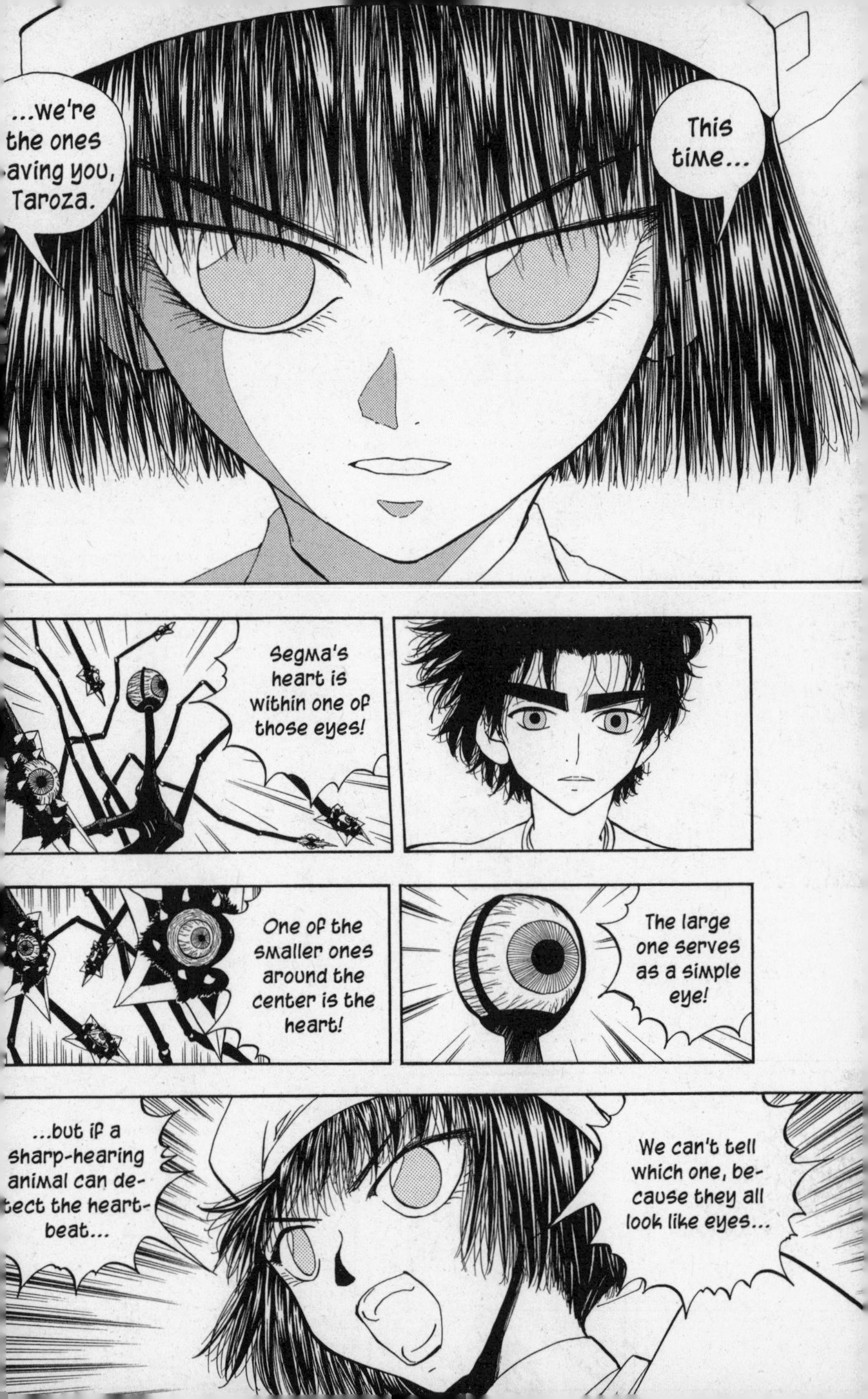

This time...
...we're the ones aving you, Taroza.
Segma's heart is within one of those eyes!
The large one serves as a simple eye!
One of the smaller ones around the center is the heart!
We can't tell which one, because they all look like eyes...
...but if a sharp-hearing animal can detect the heartbeat...

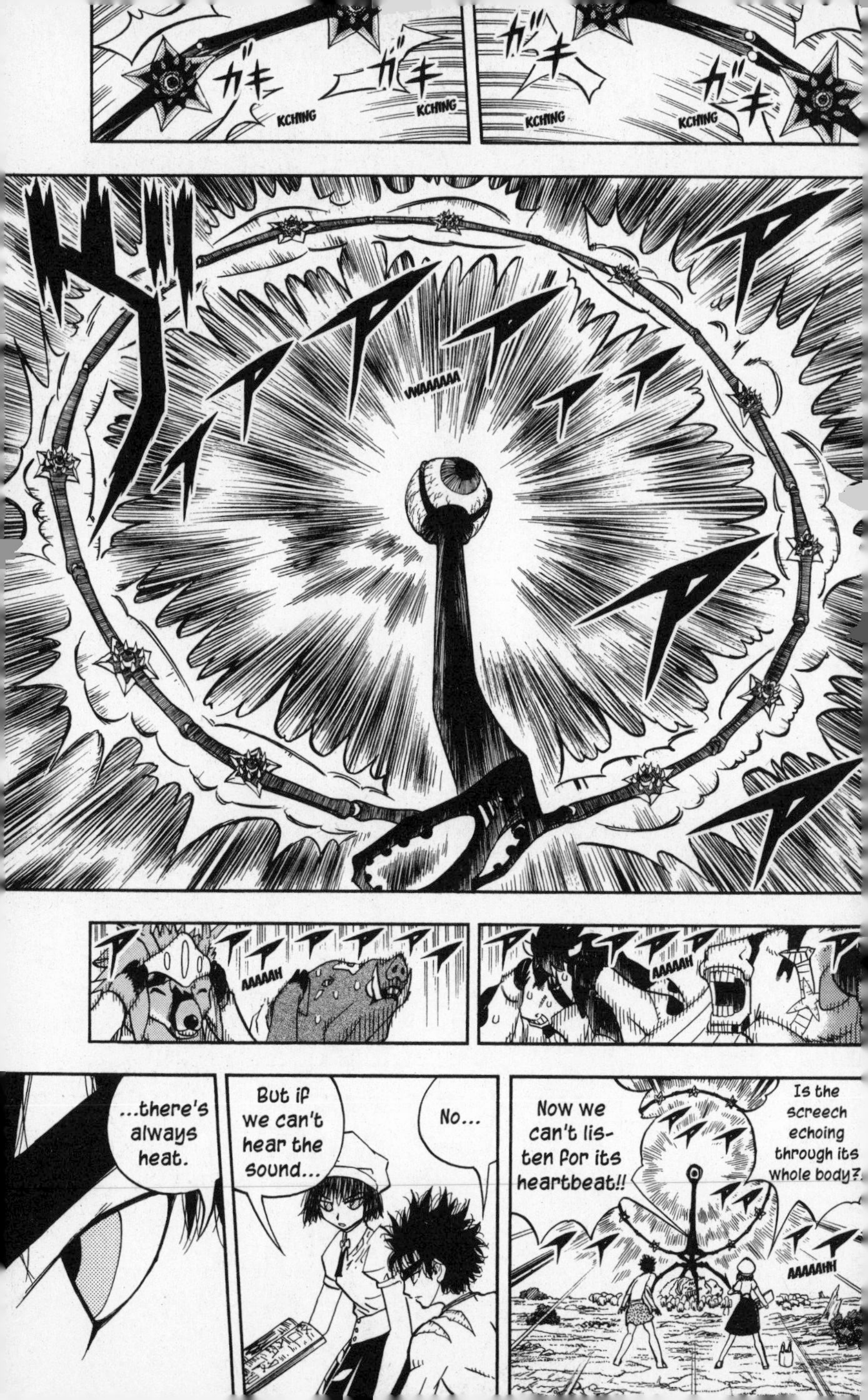
KCHING
KCHING
KCHING
KCHING
VWAAAAAA
AAAAAH
AAAAAH
Is the screech echoing through its whole body?!
Now we can't lis-ten for its heartbeat!!
AAAAAHH
No...
But if we can't hear the sound...
...there's always heat.

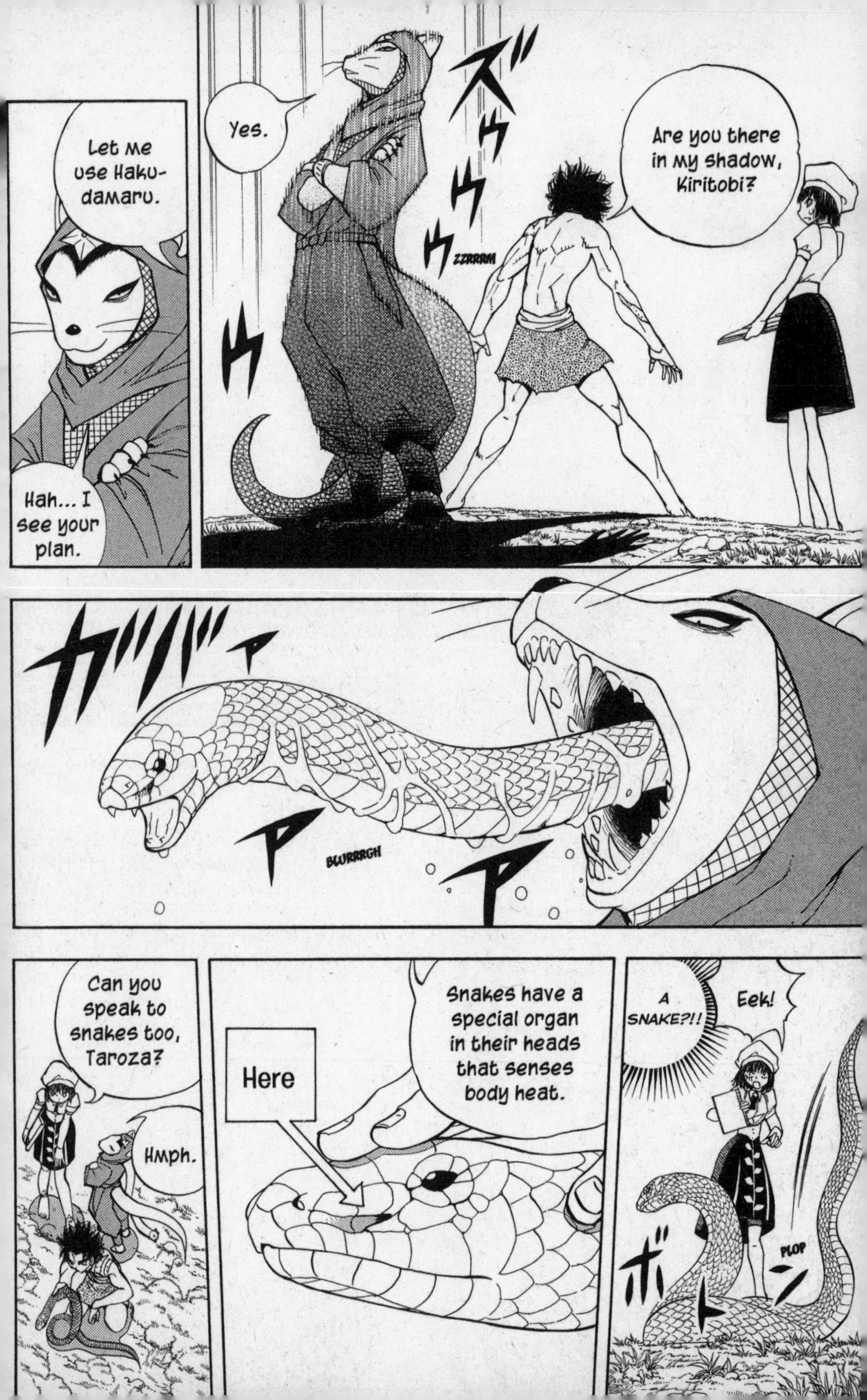
Are you there in my shadow, Kiritobi?
Yes.
ZZRRRM
Let me use Haku-damaru.
Hah... I see your plan.
BLURRRGH
Eek!
A SNAKE?!!
PLOP
Snakes have a special organ in their heads that senses body heat.
Here
Can you speak to snakes too, Taroza?
Hmph.

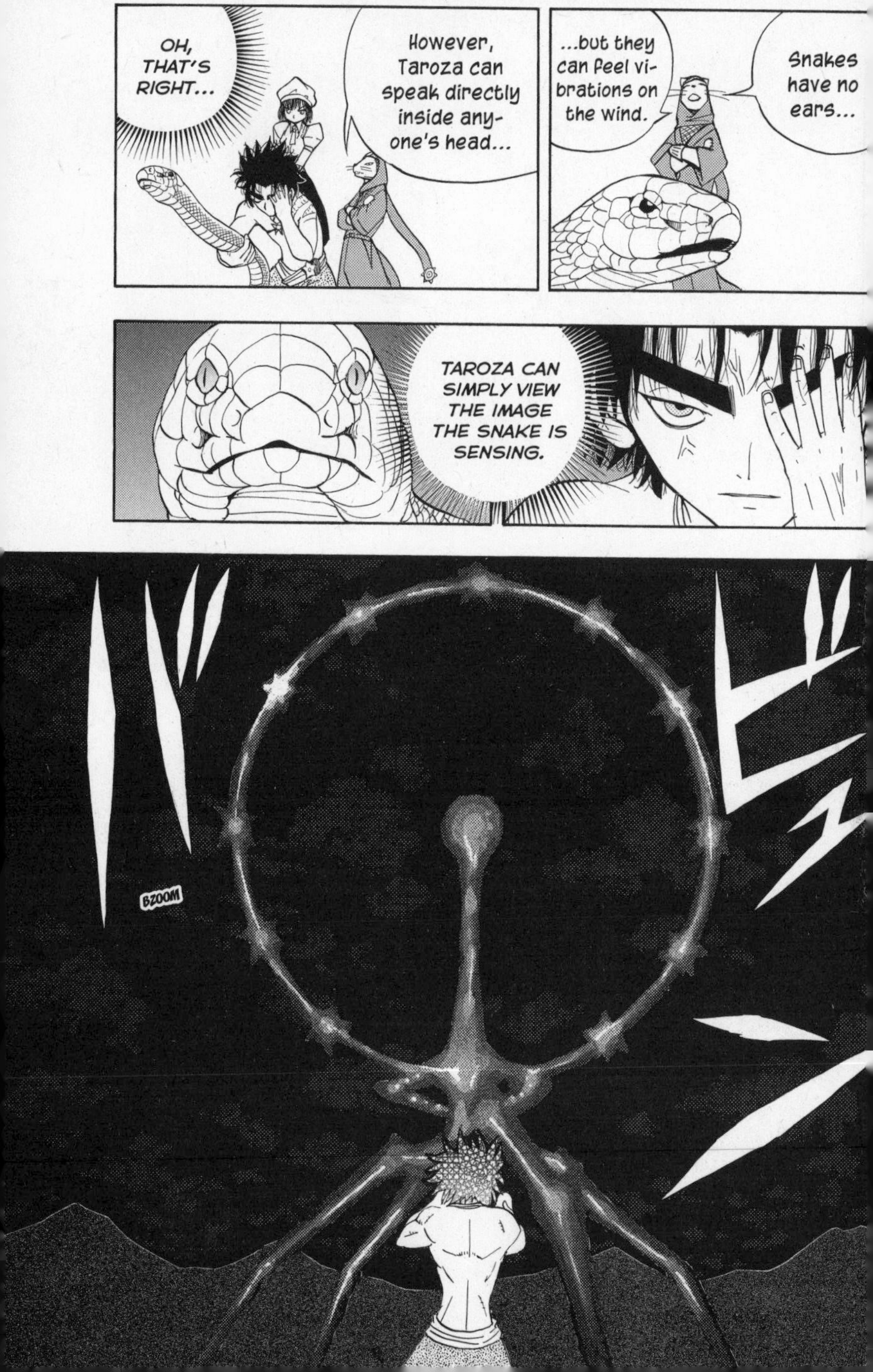
Snakes have no ears...
...but they can feel vibrations on the wind.
However, Taroza can speak directly inside anyone's head...
OH, THAT'S RIGHT...
TAROZA CAN SIMPLY VIEW THE IMAGE THE SNAKE IS SENSING.
BZOOM

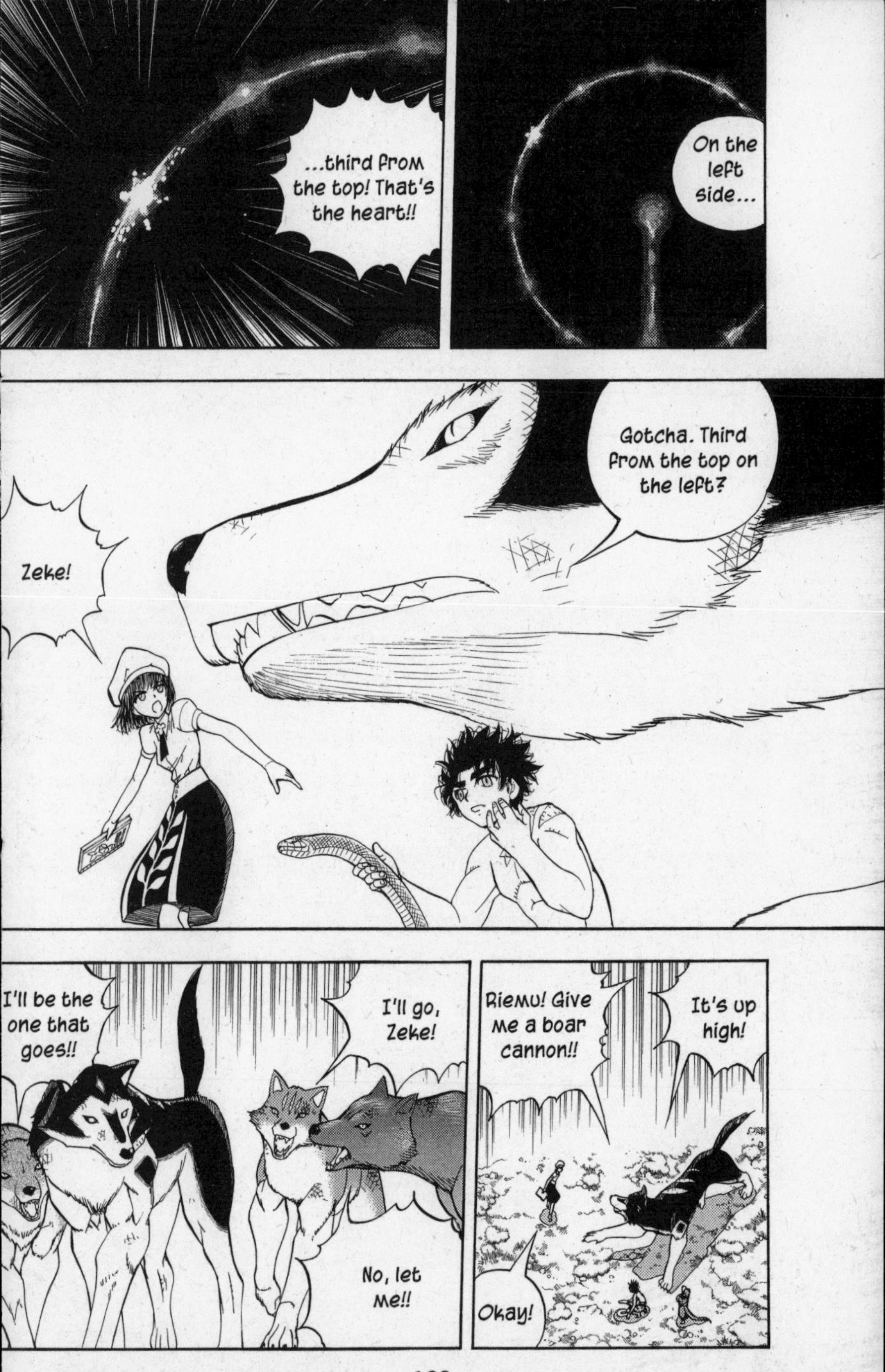
On the left side...
...third from the top! That's the heart!!
Gotcha. Third from the top on the left?
Zeke!
It's up high!
Riemu! Give me a boar cannon!!
Okay!
I'll go, Zeke!
I'll be the one that goes!!
No, let me!!

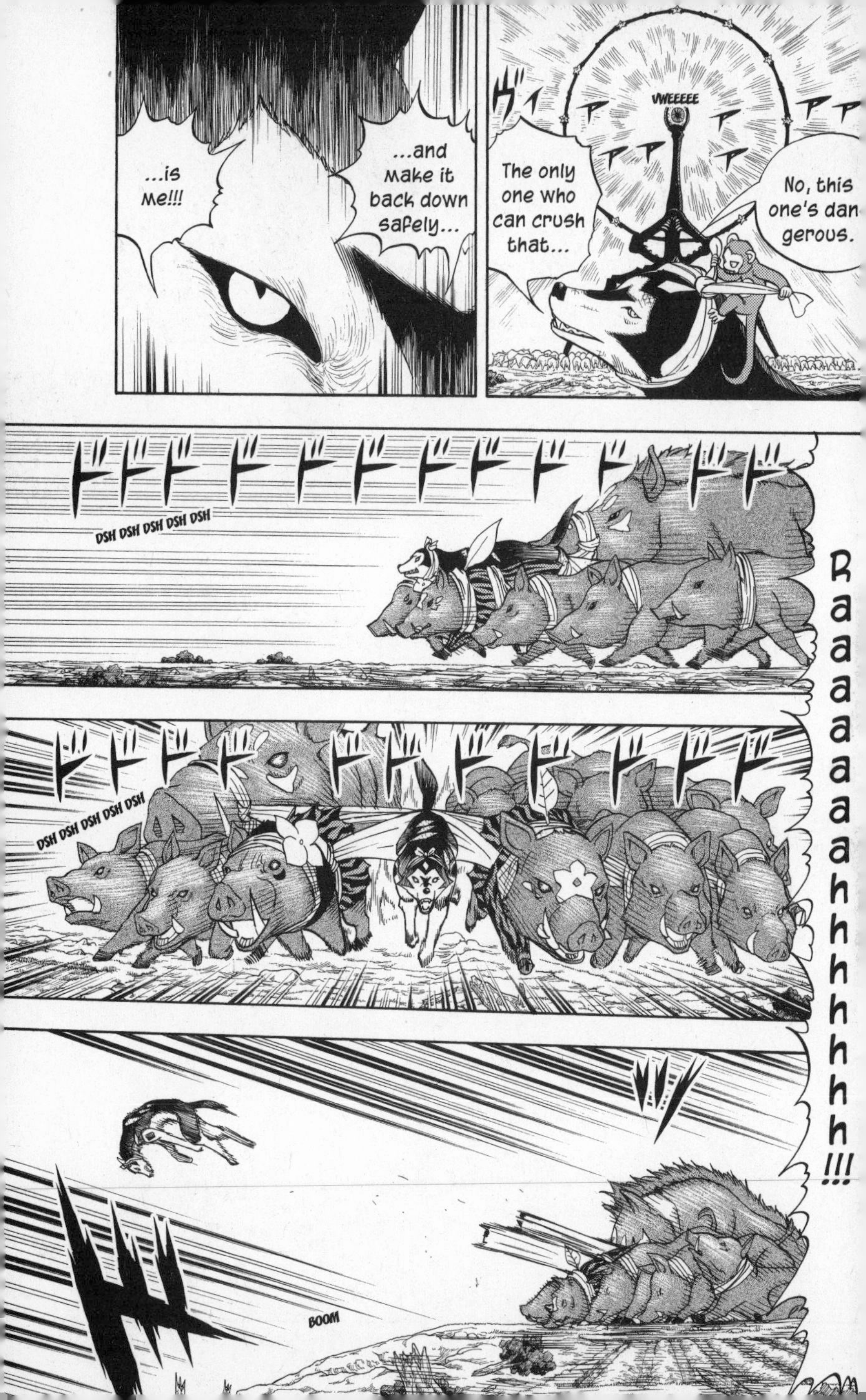

No, this one's dangerous.
VWEEEEE
The only one who can crush that...
...and make it back down safely...
...is me!!!
Raaaaaaaaaahhhhhhhhhhhh!!!
DSH DSH DSH DSH DSH
DSH DSH DSH DSH DSH
BOOM

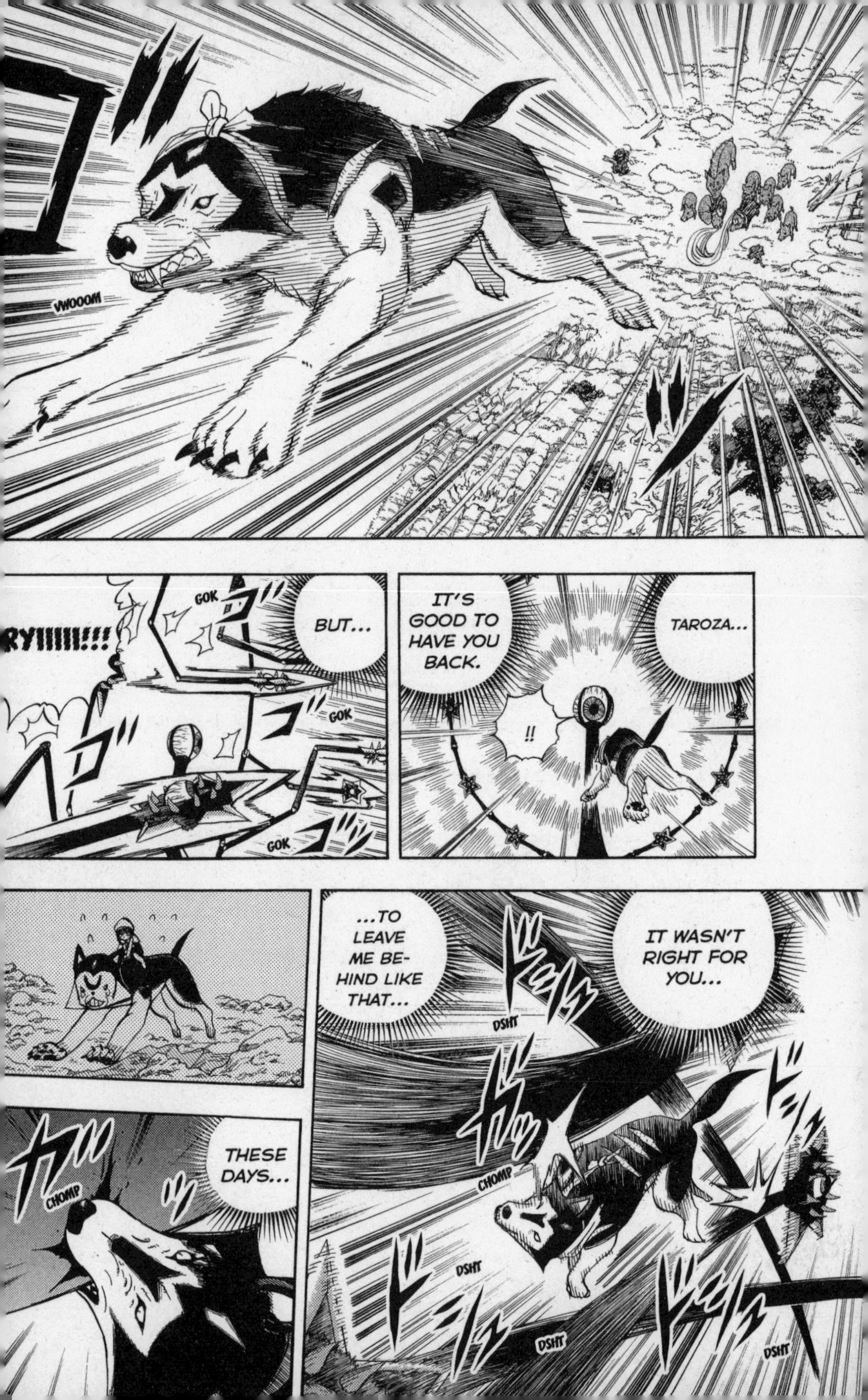
VWOOOM
TAROZA...
IT'S GOOD TO HAVE YOU BACK.
!!
BUT...
GOK
GOK
GOK
IT WASN'T RIGHT FOR YOU...
...TO LEAVE ME BE-HIND LIKE THAT...
DSHT
CHOMP
DSHT
DSHT
DSHT
THESE DAYS...
CHOMP

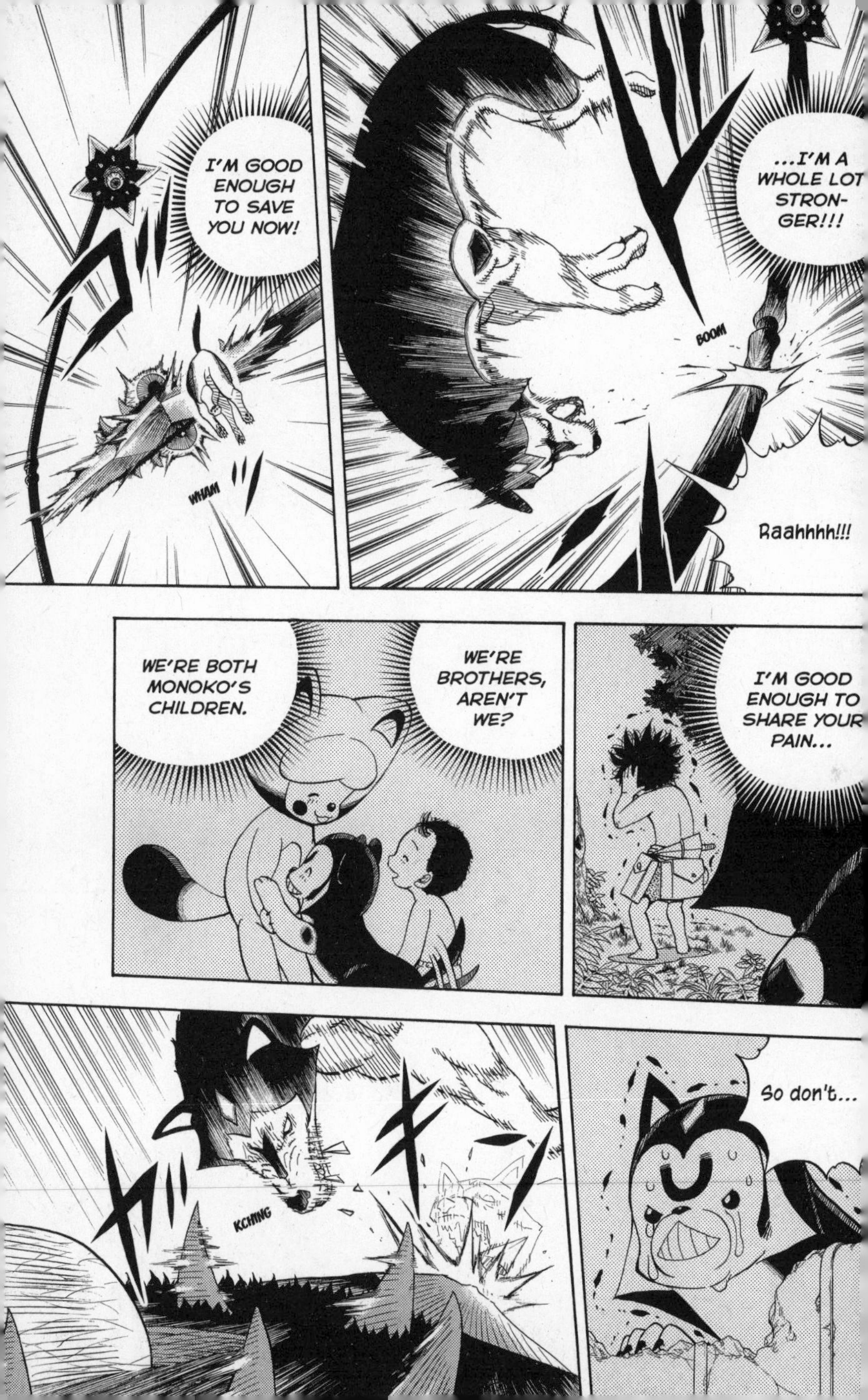
...I'M A WHOLE LOT STRON-GER!!!
BOOM
Raahhhh!!!
I'M GOOD ENOUGH TO SAVE YOU NOW!
WHAM
I'M GOOD ENOUGH TO SHARE YOUR PAIN...
WE'RE BROTHERS, AREN'T WE?
WE'RE BOTH MONOKO'S CHILDREN.
So don't...
KCHING

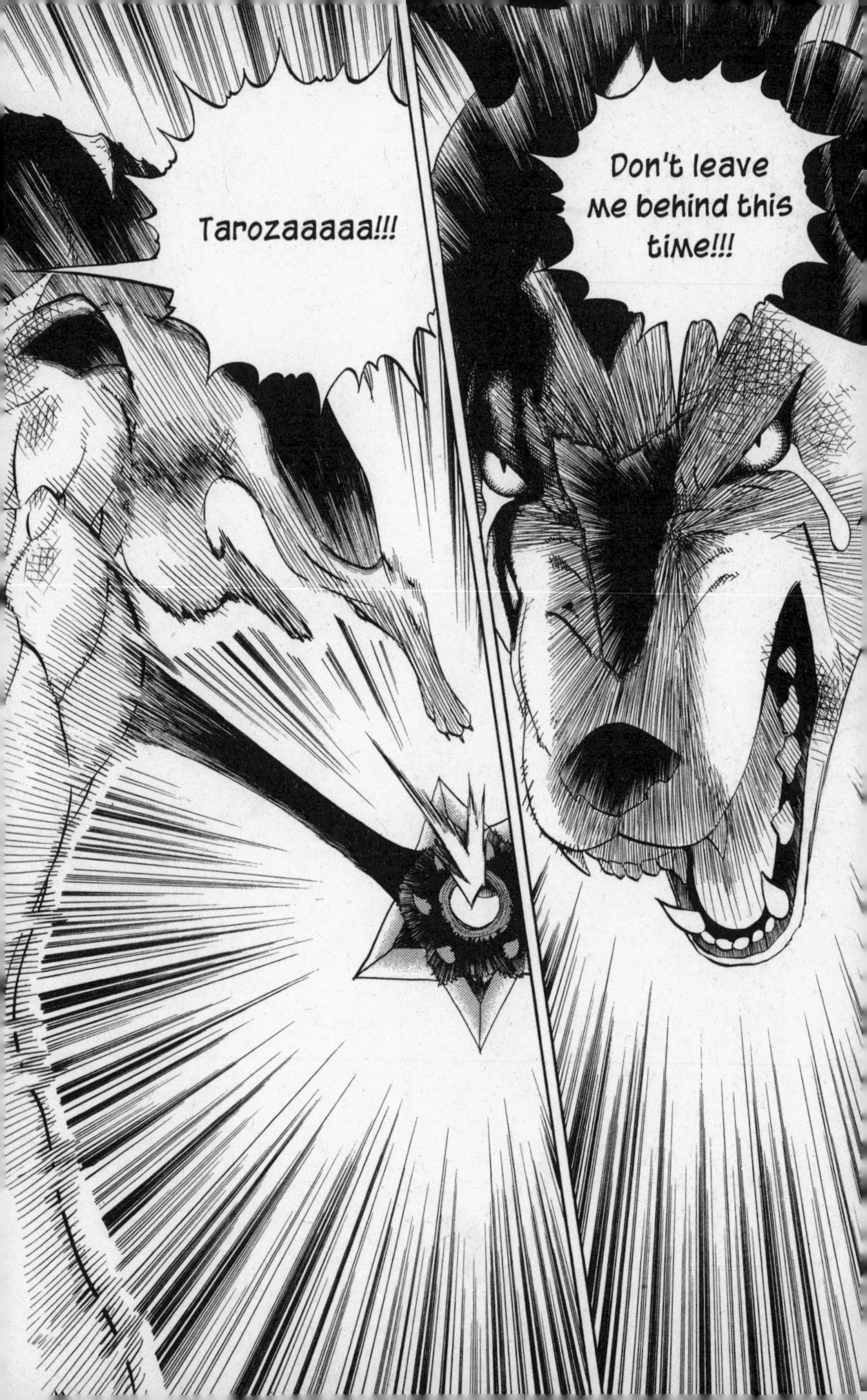
Don't leave me behind this time!!!
Tarozaaaaa!!!

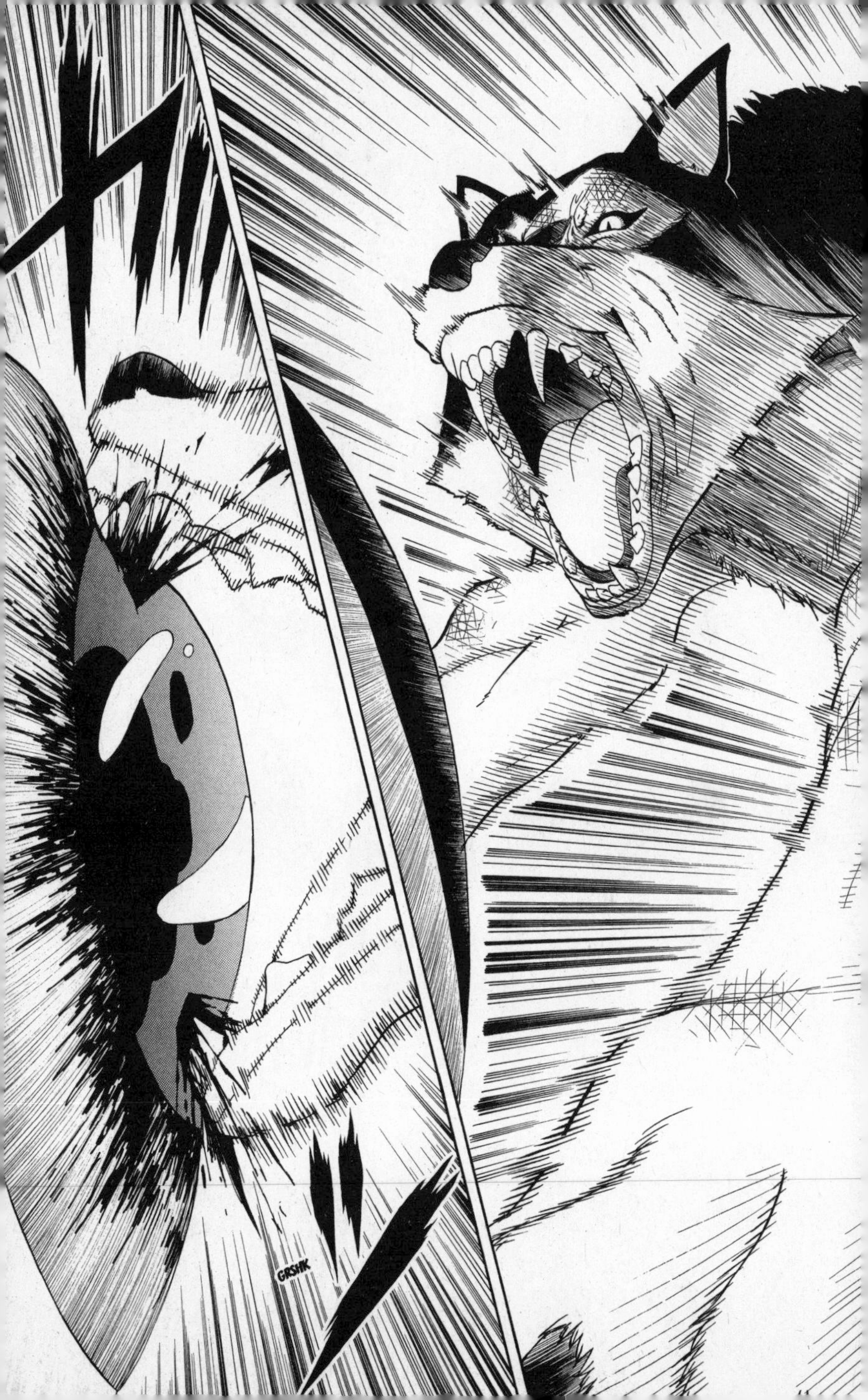
GRSHK

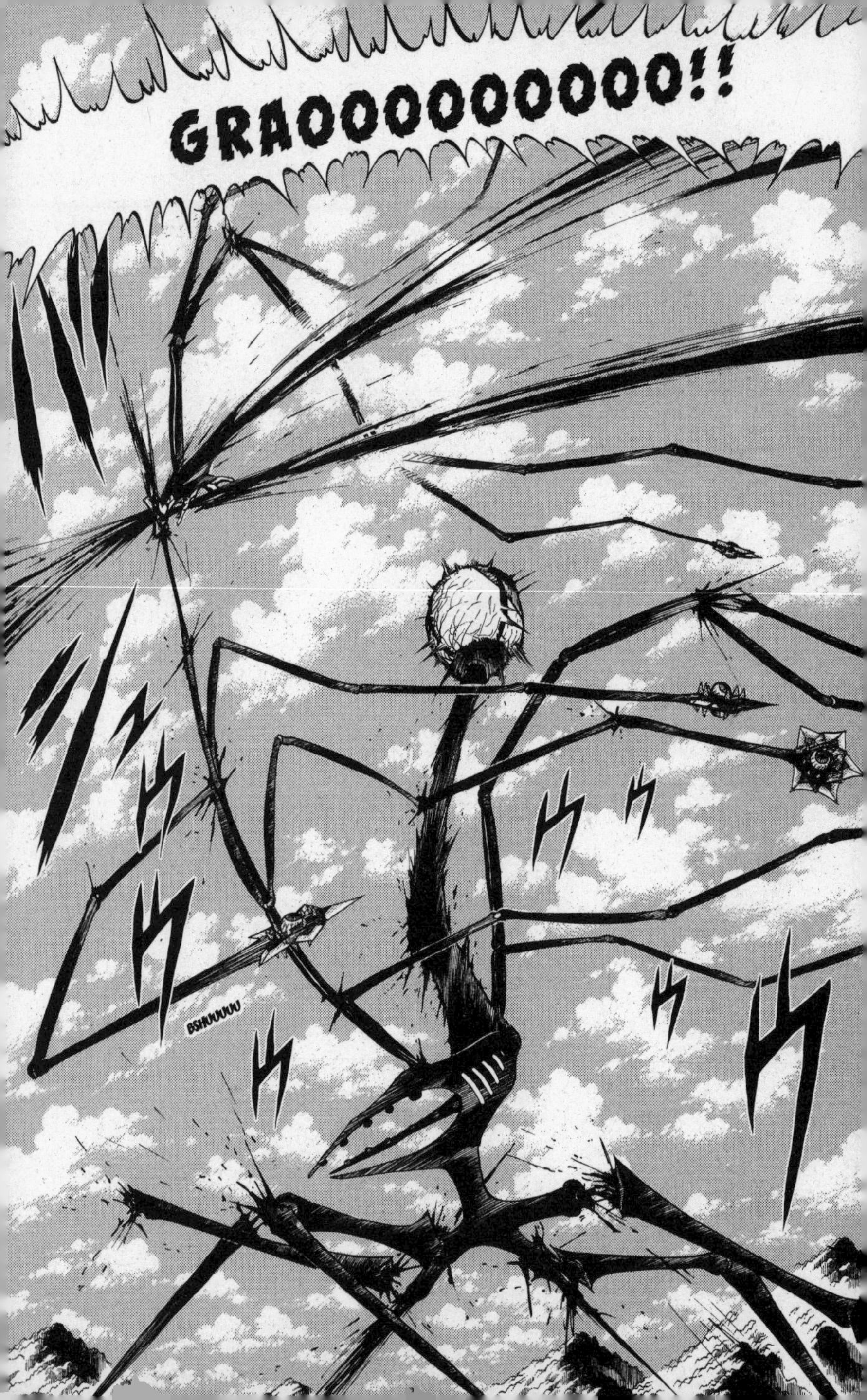
GRAOOOOOOOOOOO!!
BSHUUUUU

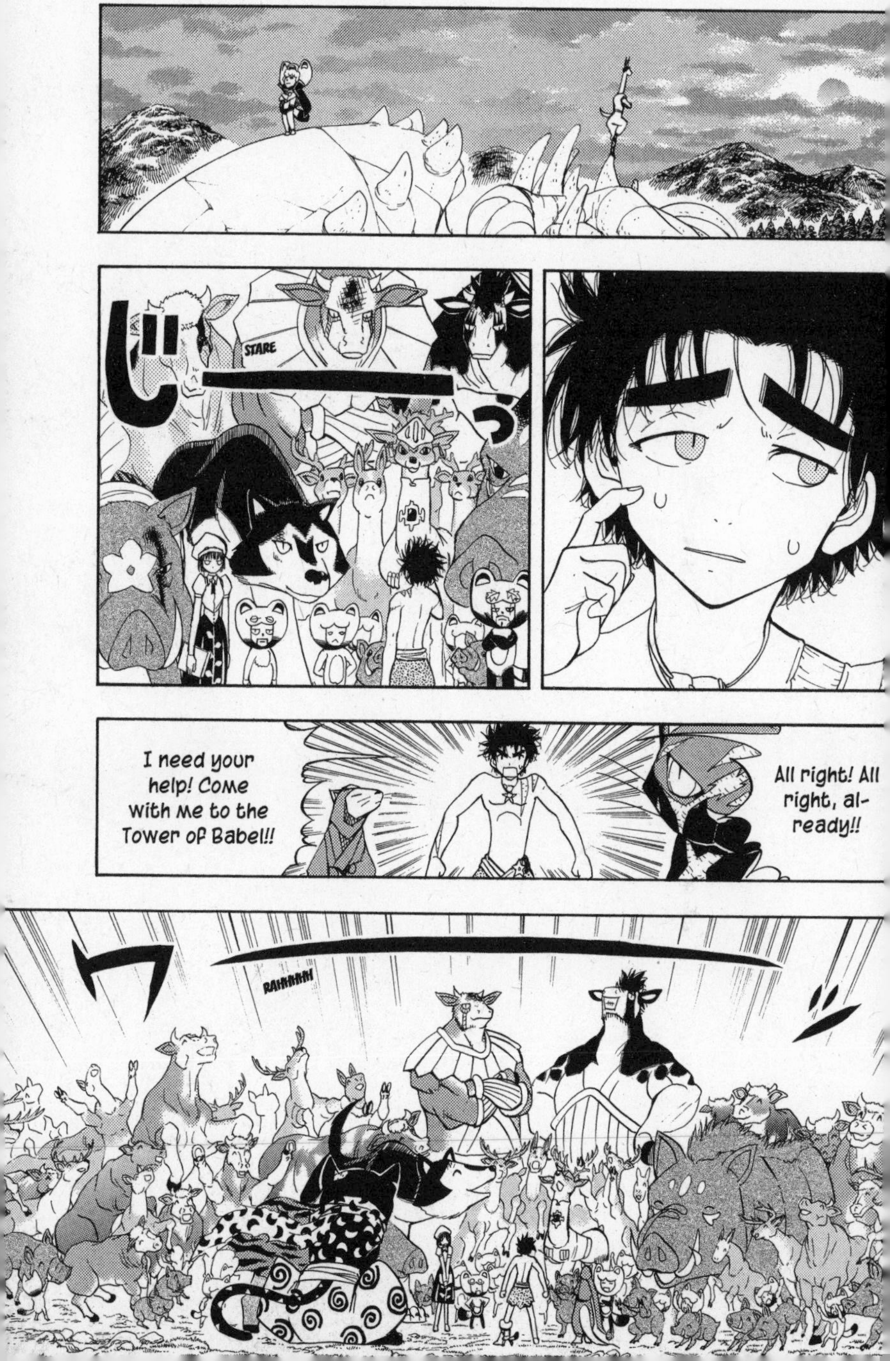
STARE
All right! All right, already!!
I need your help! Come with me to the Tower of Babel!!
RAHHHHH

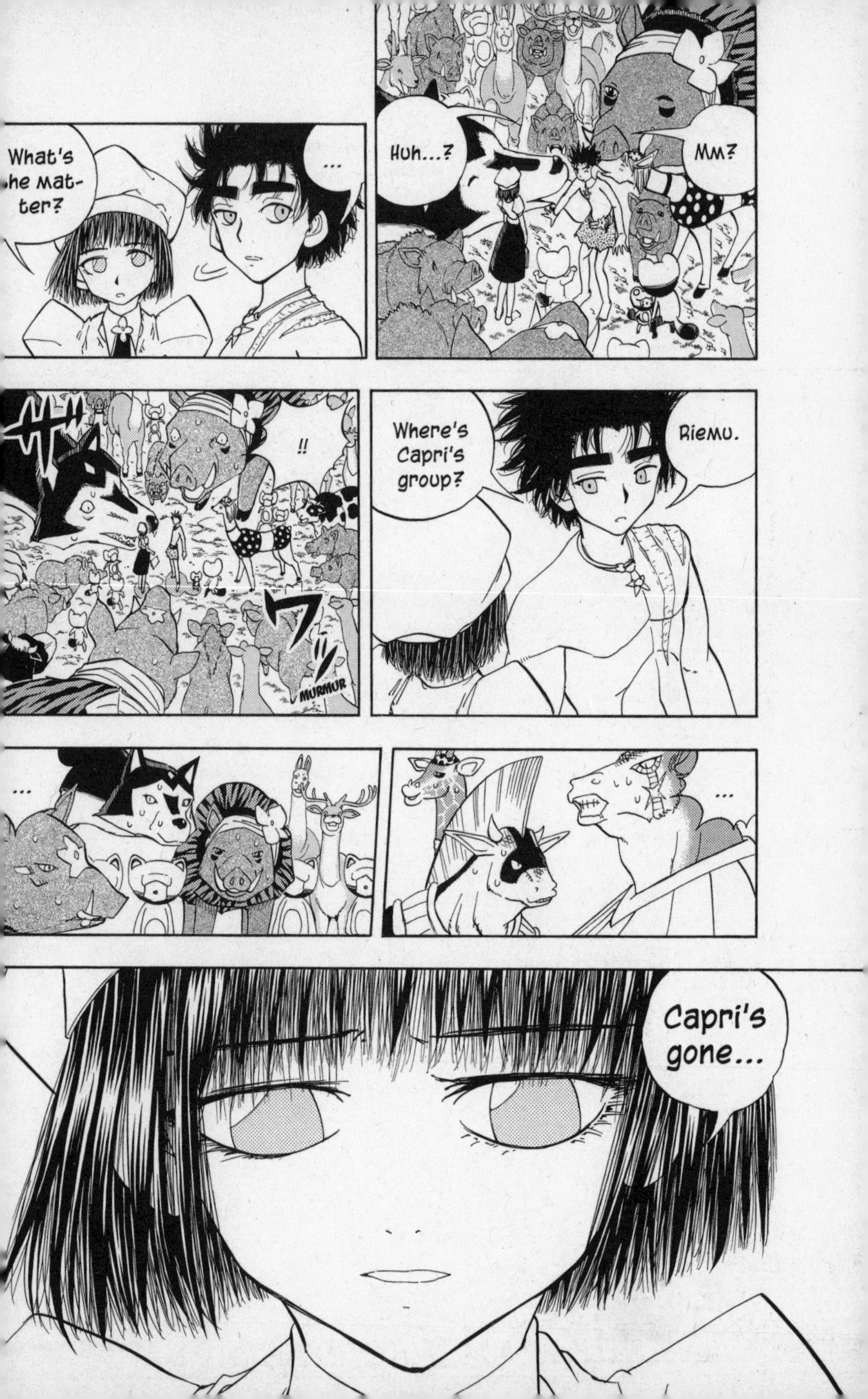
Mm?
Huh...?
...
What's he mat-ter?
Riemu.
Where's Capri's group?
!!
ザッ
ワ
MURMUR
...
...
Capri's gone...

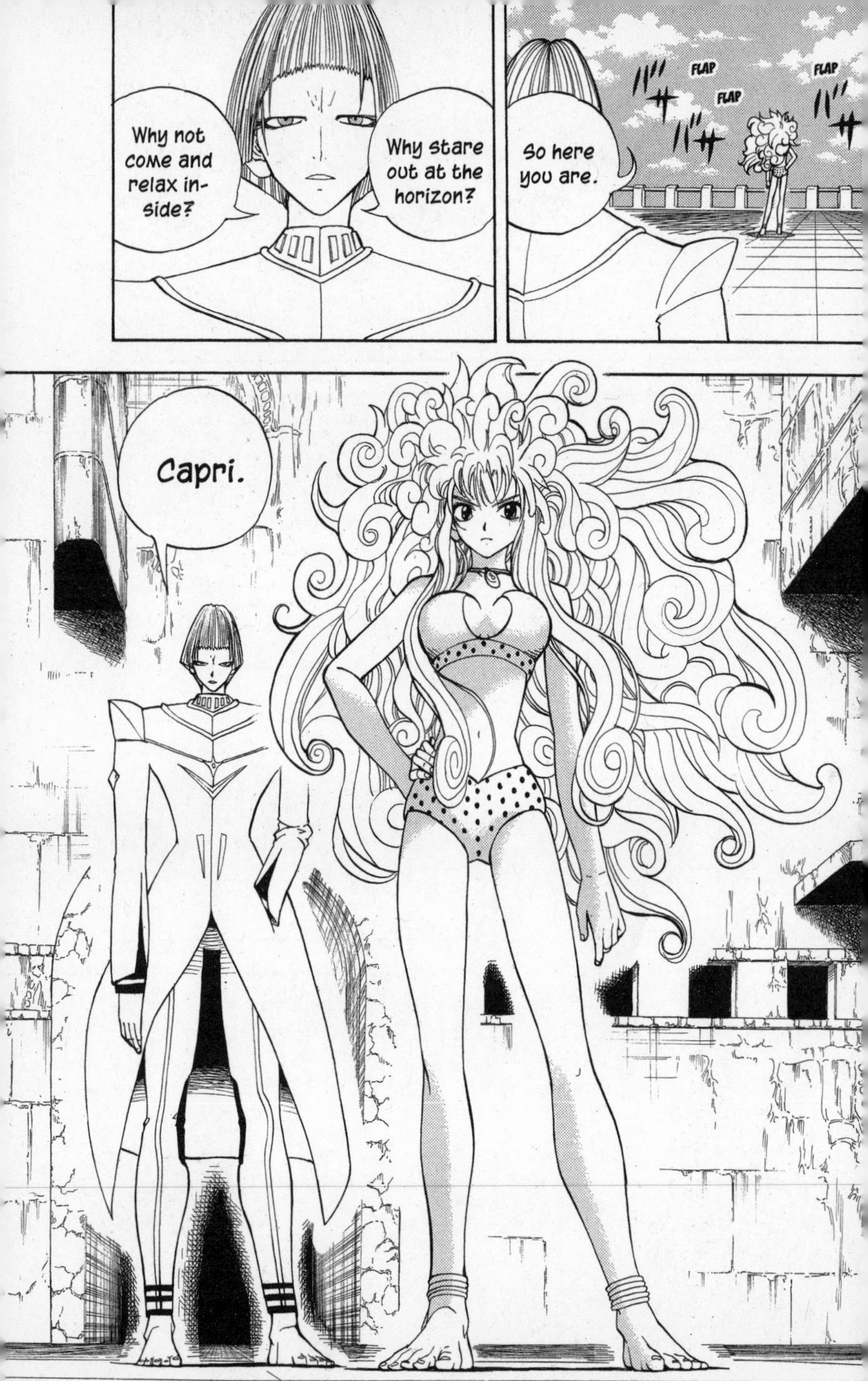
FLAP
FLAP
FLAP
So here you are.
Why stare out at the horizon?
Why not come and relax in-side?
Capri.

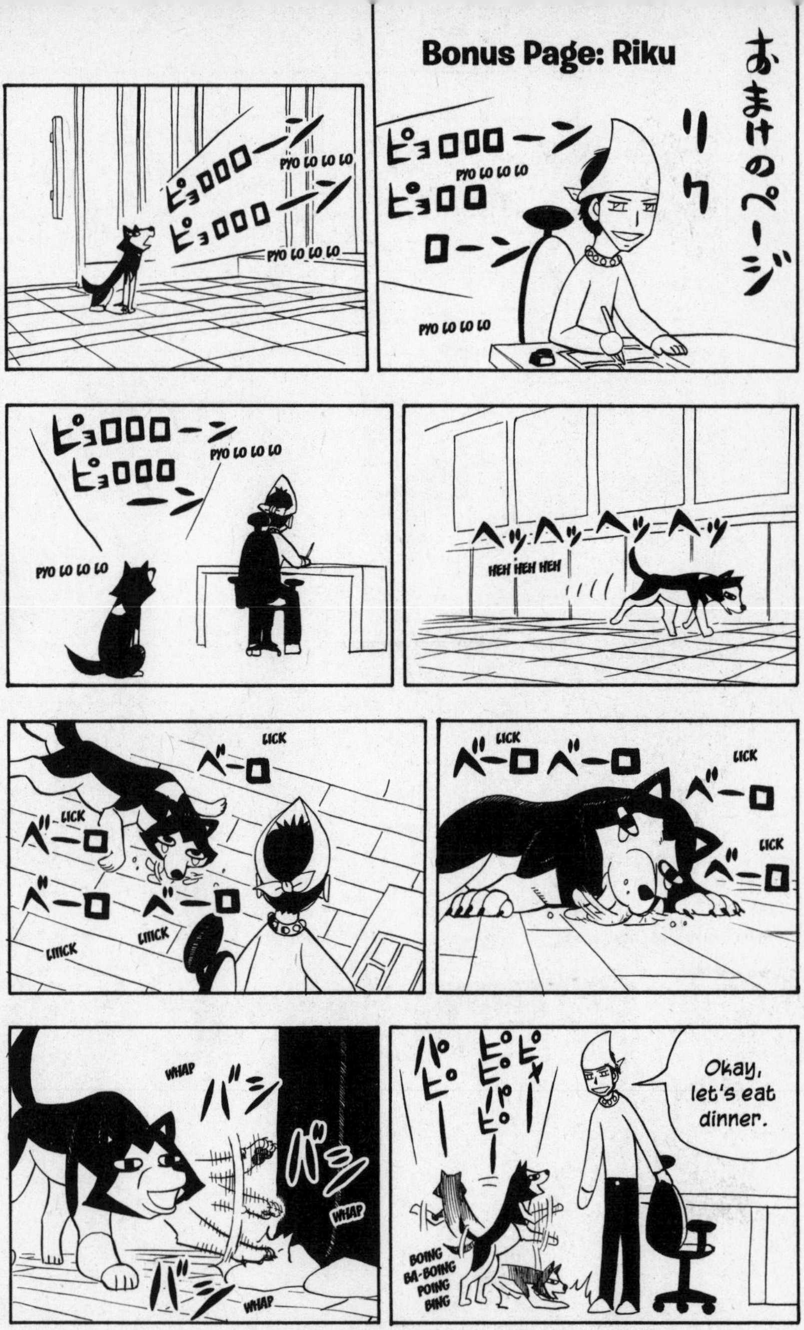

おまけのページ
リク
Bonus Page: Riku
ピョロロロローン
PYO LO LO LO
ピョロロ
ローン
PYO LO LO LO
ピョロロローン
PYO LO LO LO
ピョロロロローン
PYO LO LO LO
ヘッヘッヘッヘッ
HEH HEH HEH
ピョロロロローン
PYO LO LO LO
ピョロロロ
ーン
PYO LO LO LO
ベーロベーロ
LICK
ベーロ
LICK
ベーロ
LICK
ベーロ
LICK
ベーロ
LICK
ベーロ
LIIICK
ベーロ
LIIICK
ピャー
ピョ
ピョ
パピー
Okay, let's eat dinner.
BOING BA-BOING POING BING
バシ
WHAP
バシ
WHAP
バシ
WHAP

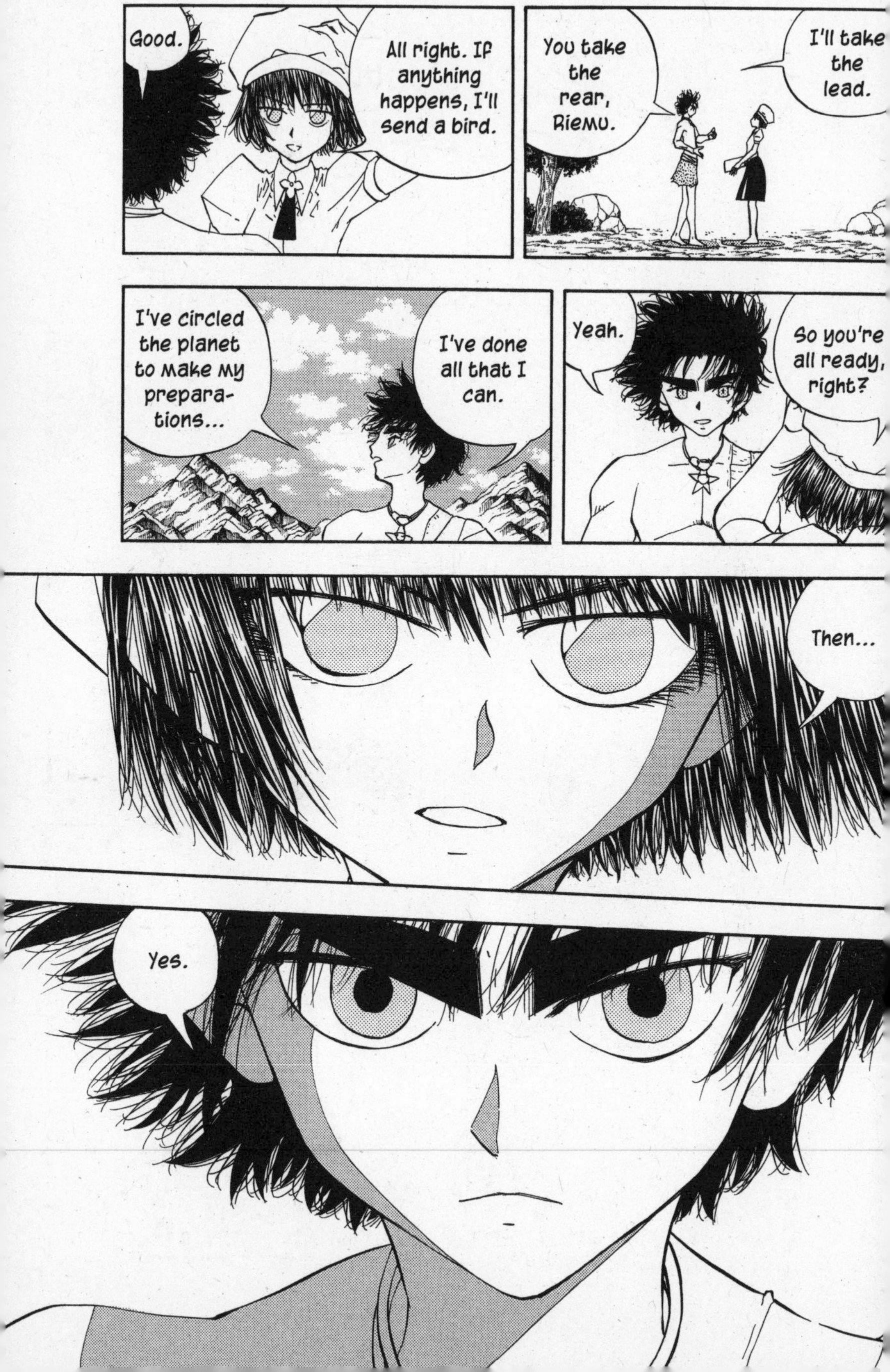
I'll take the lead.
You take the rear, Riemu.
All right. If anything happens, I'll send a bird.
Good.
So you're all ready, right?
Yeah.
I've done all that I can.
I've circled the planet to make my preparations...
Then...
Yes.

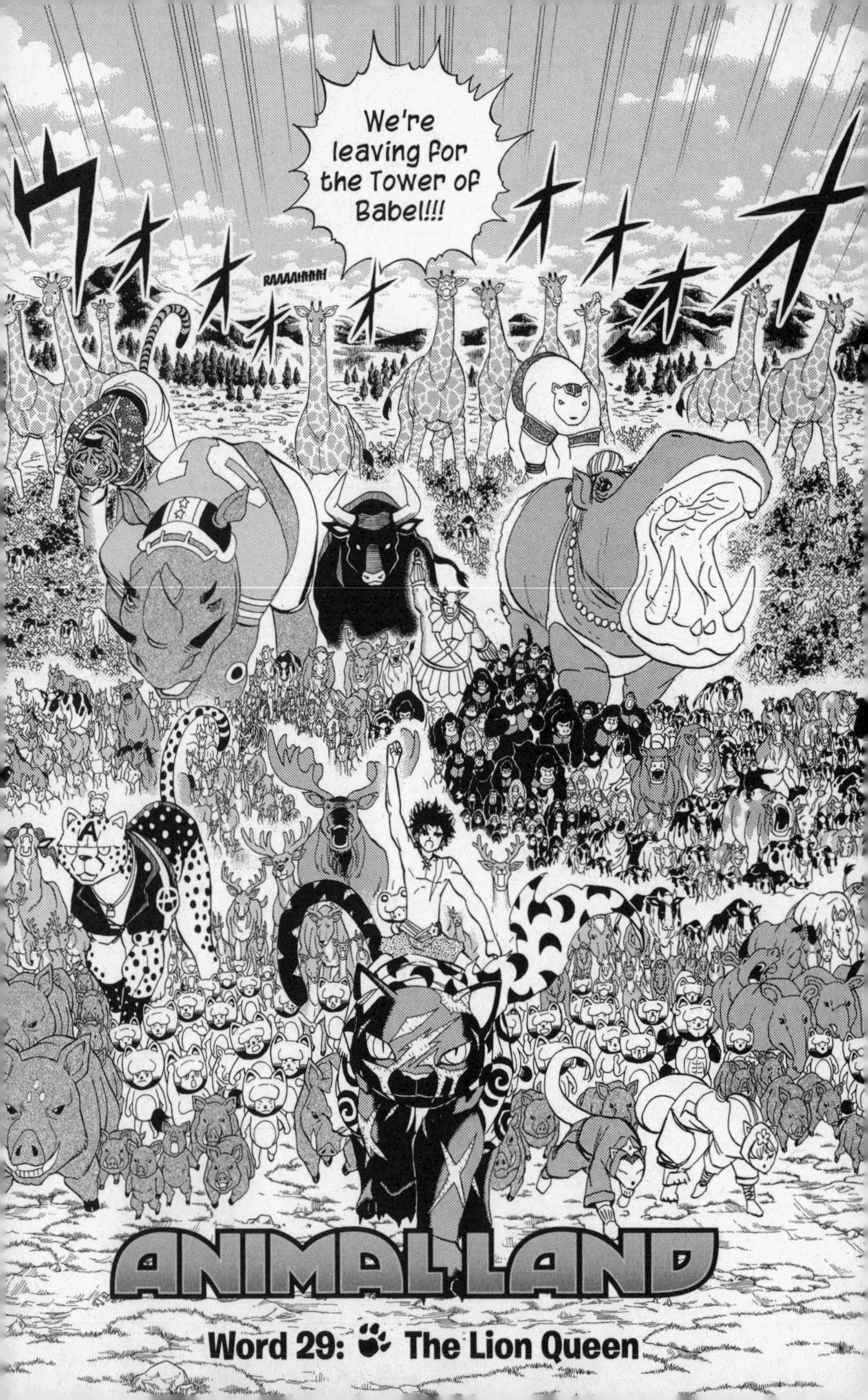
We're leaving for the Tower of Babel!!!
RAAAAHHHH
ANIMAL LAND
Word 29: The Lion Queen

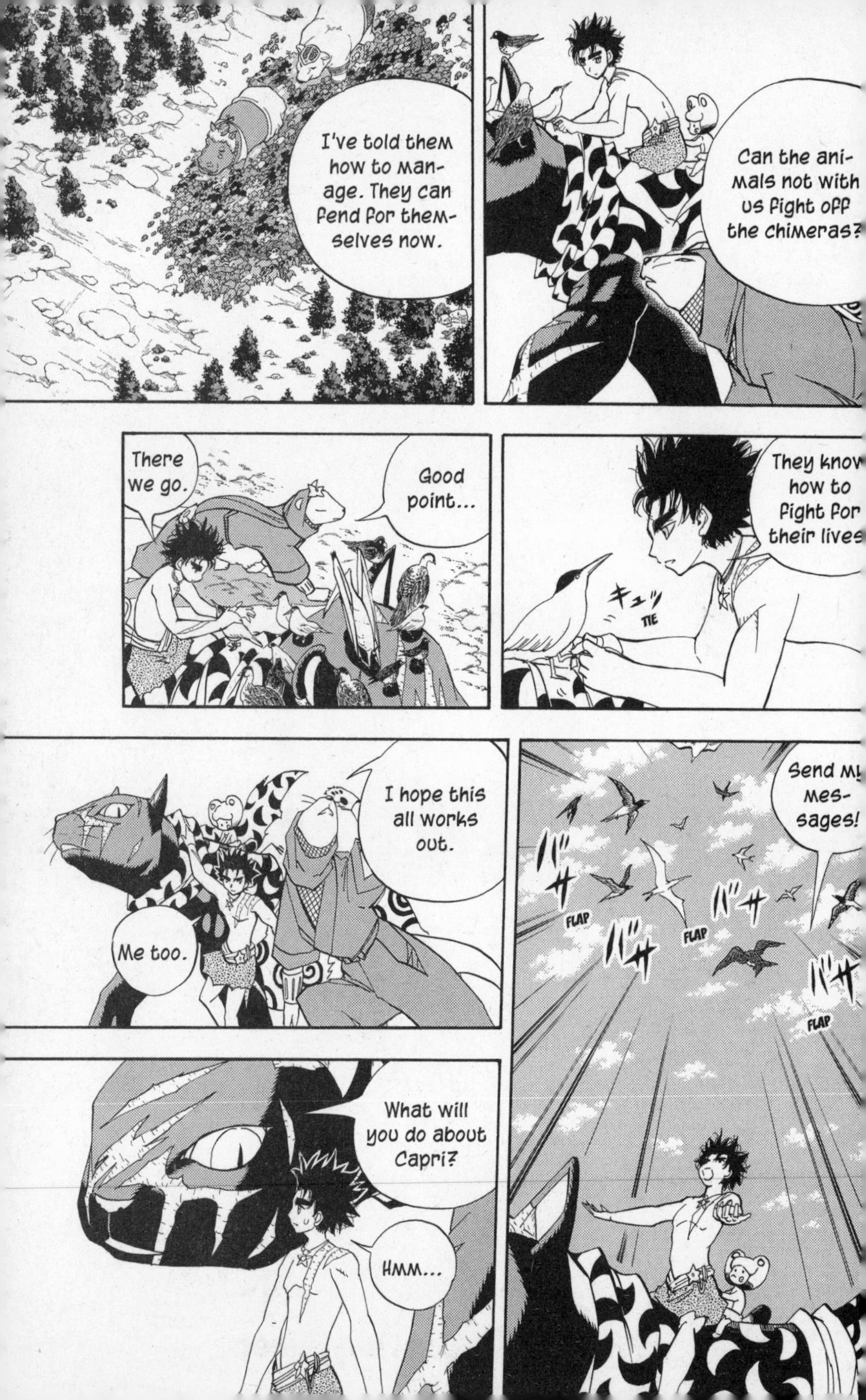
Can the animals not with us fight off the chimeras?
I've told them how to manage. They can fend for themselves now.
They know how to fight for their lives
キュッ
TIE
Good point...
There we go.
Send my messages!
バサ
FLAP
バサ
FLAP
バサ
バサ
FLAP
I hope this all works out.
Me too.
What will you do about Capri?
Hmm...

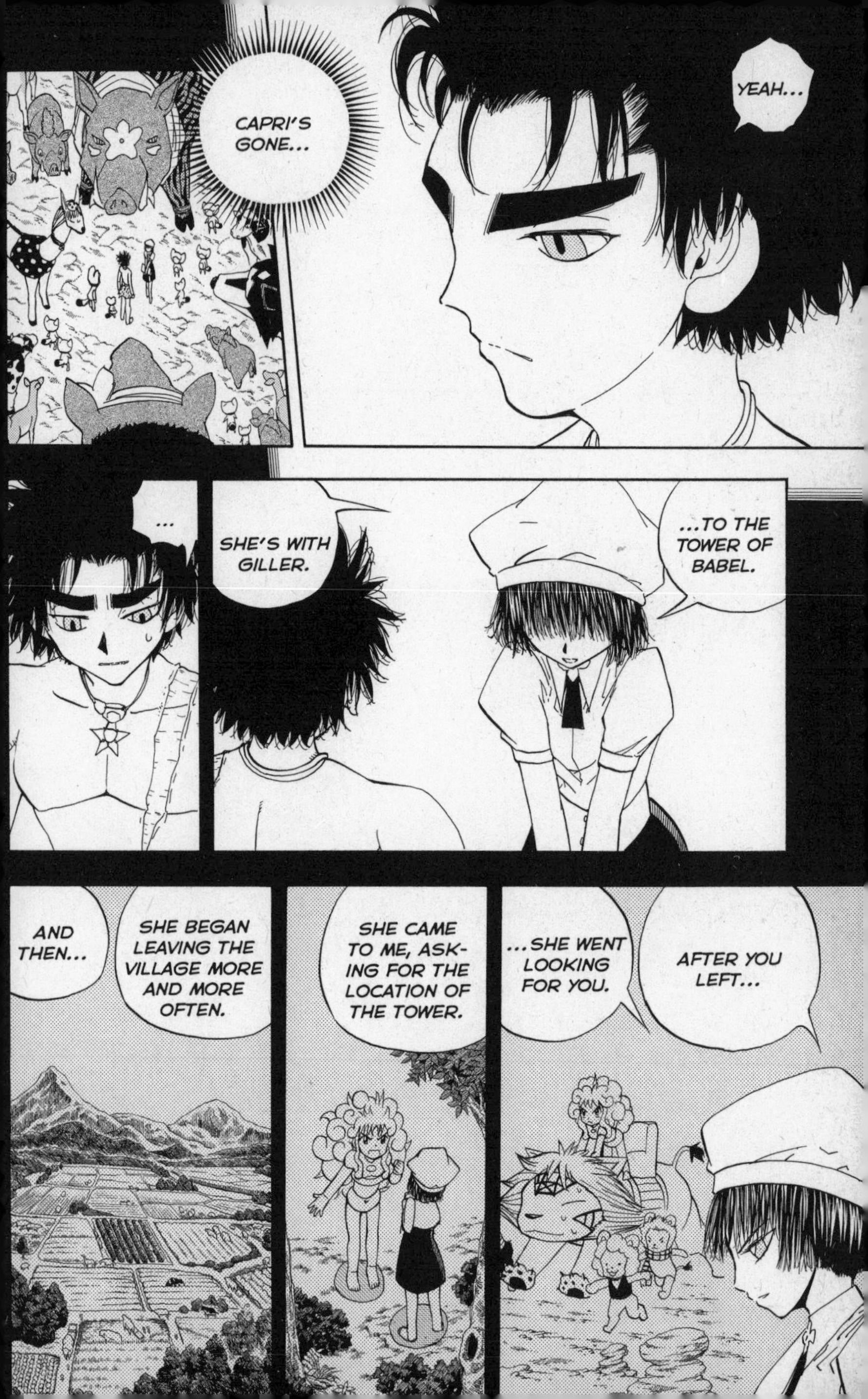
YEAH...
CAPRI'S GONE...
SHE'S WITH GILLER.
...TO THE TOWER OF BABEL.
...
AFTER YOU LEFT...
...SHE WENT LOOKING FOR YOU.
SHE CAME TO ME, ASK-ING FOR THE LOCATION OF THE TOWER.
SHE BEGAN LEAVING THE VILLAGE MORE AND MORE OFTEN.
AND THEN...

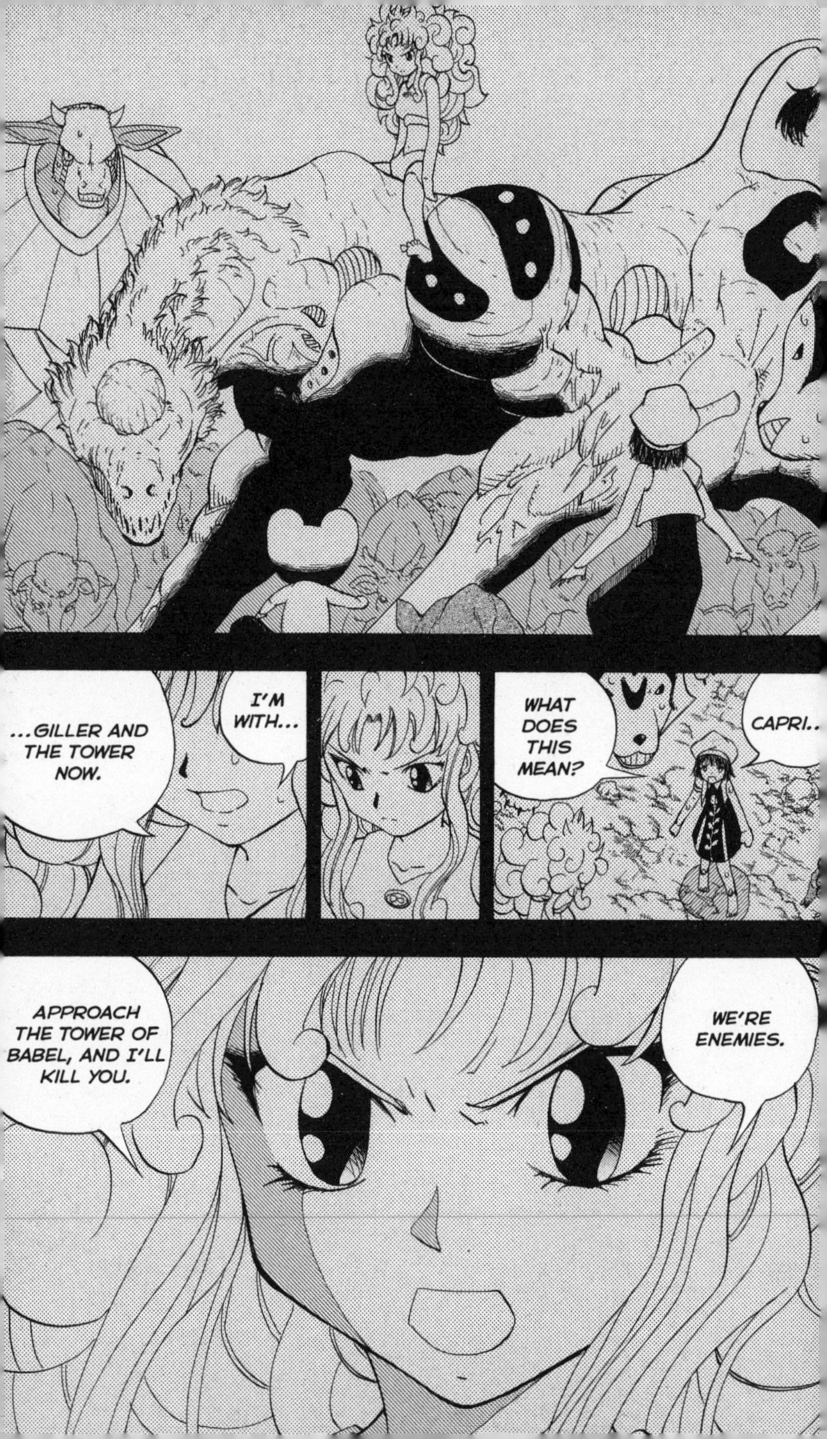
CAPRI...
WHAT DOES THIS MEAN?
I'M WITH...
...GILLER AND THE TOWER NOW.
WE'RE ENEMIES.
APPROACH THE TOWER OF BABEL, AND I'LL KILL YOU.

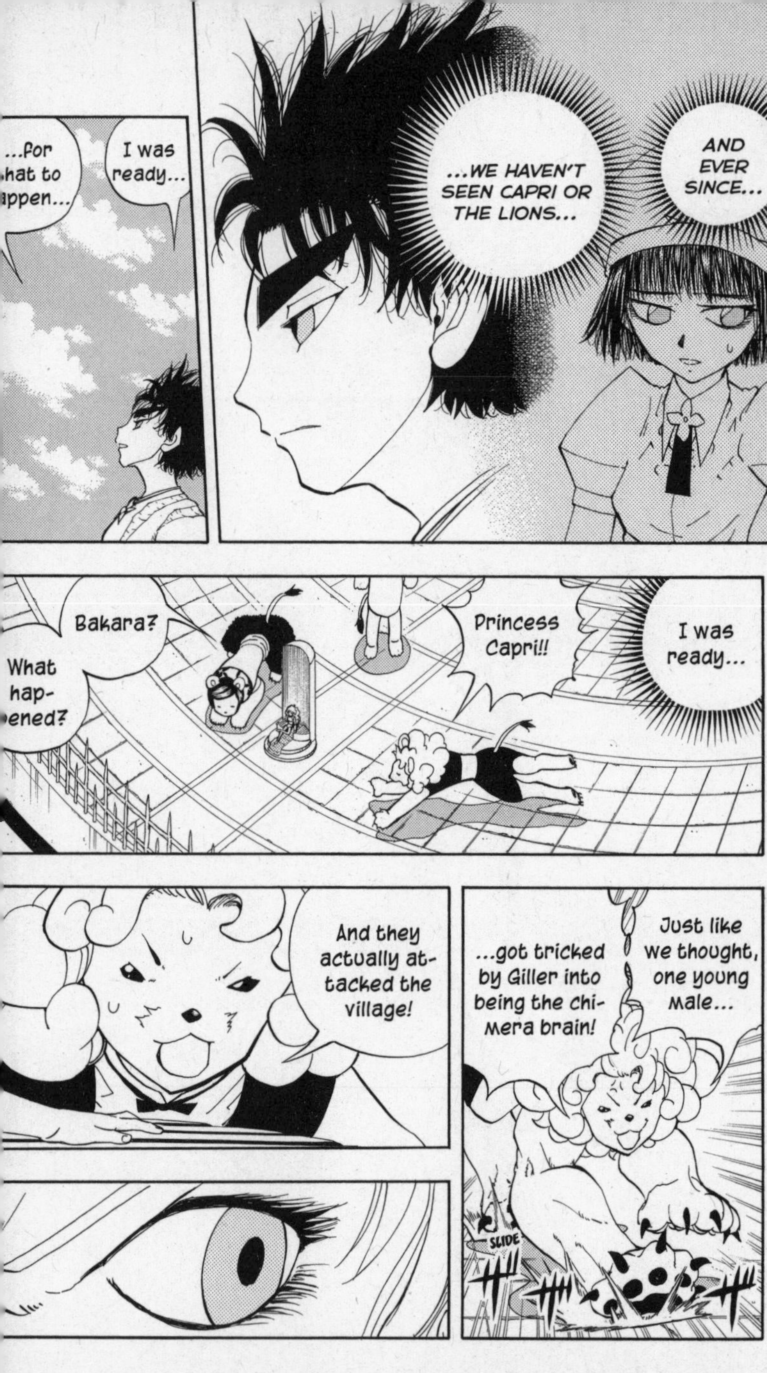
AND EVER SINCE...
...WE HAVEN'T SEEN CAPRI OR THE LIONS...
I was ready...
...for hat to appen...
I was ready...
Princess Capri!!
Bakara?
What hap-ened?
Just like we thought, one young male...
...got tricked by Giller into being the chi-mera brain!
SLIDE
And they actually at-tacked the village!

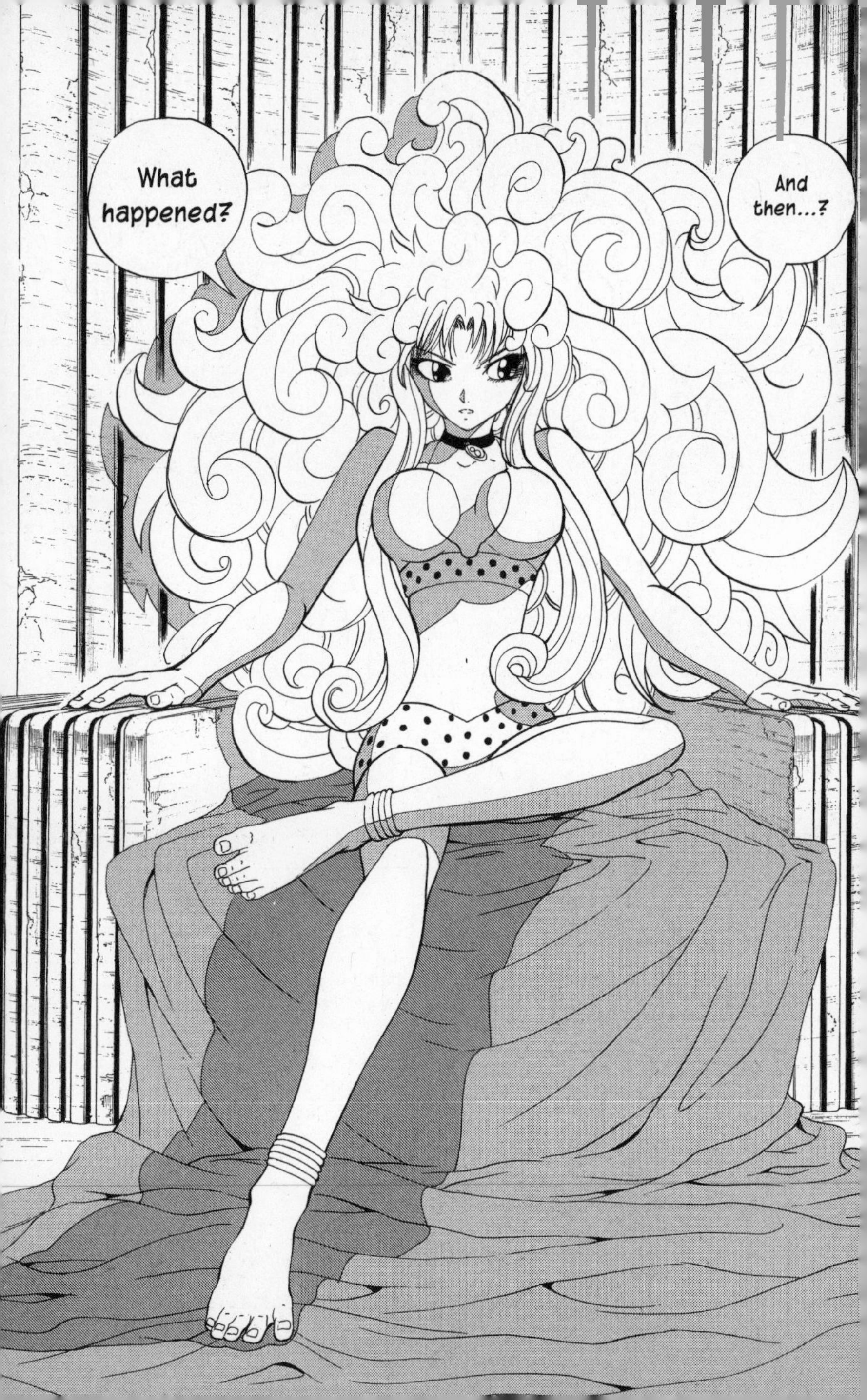
And then...?
What happened?

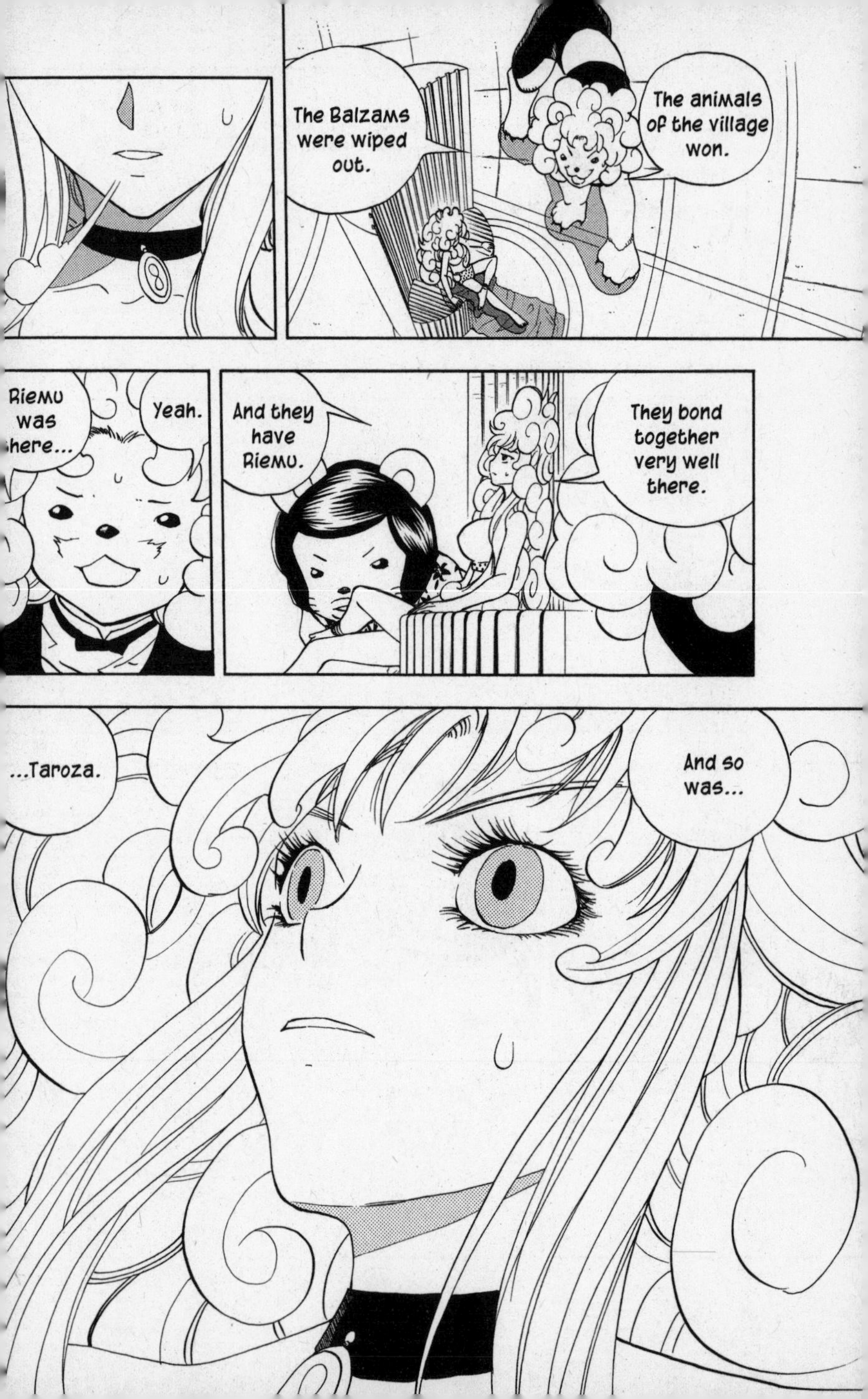
The animals of the village won.
The Balzams were wiped out.
They bond together very well there.
And they have Riemu.
Yeah.
Riemu was here...
And so was...
...Taroza.

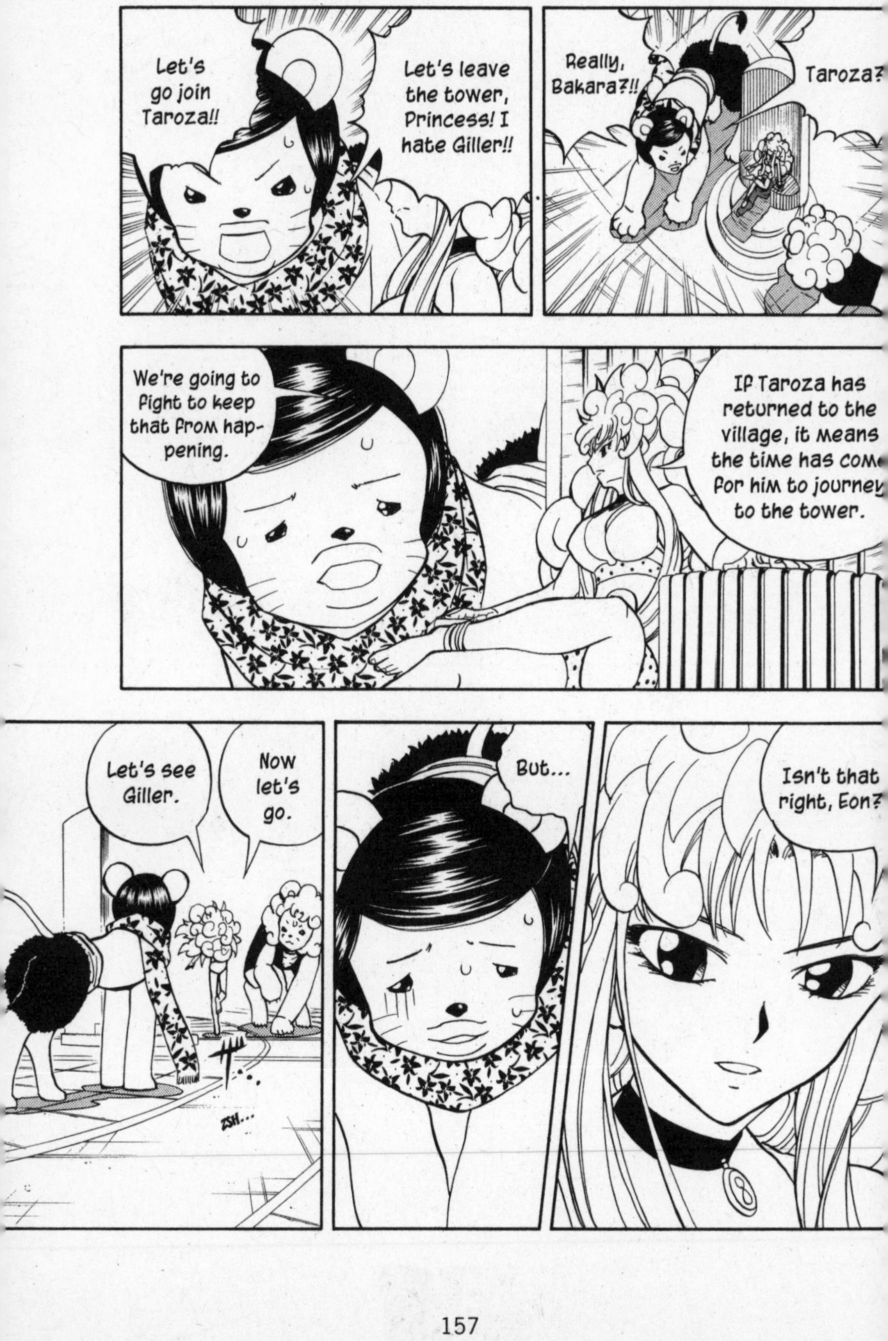

Taroza?
Really, Bakara?!!
Let's leave the tower, Princess! I hate Giller!!
Let's go join Taroza!!
If Taroza has returned to the village, it means the time has come for him to journey to the tower.
We're going to fight to keep that from happening.
Isn't that right, Eon?
But...
Now let's go.
Let's see Giller.
ZSH...

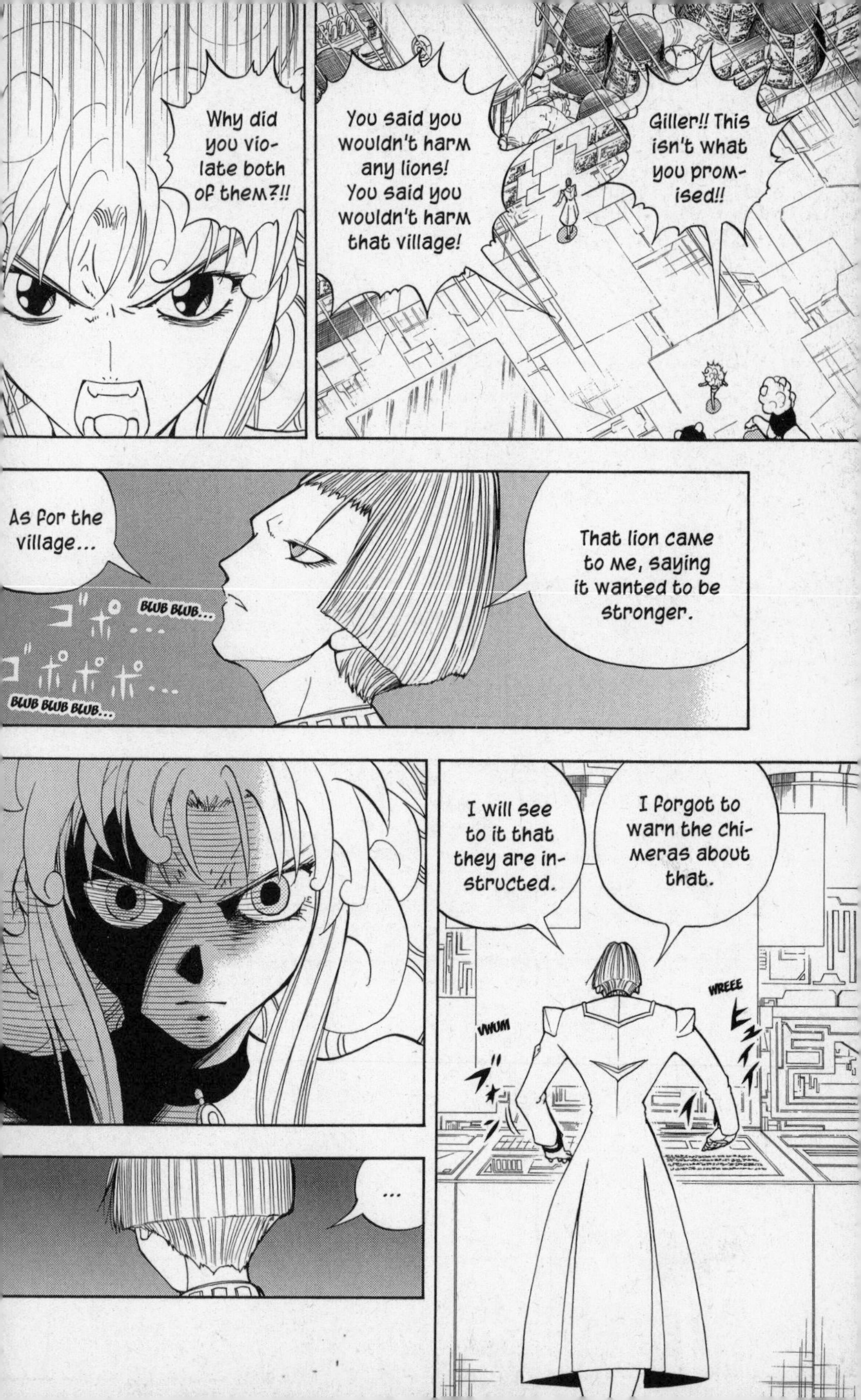
Giller!! This isn't what you promised!!
You said you wouldn't harm any lions! You said you wouldn't harm that village!
Why did you violate both of them?!!
That lion came to me, saying it wanted to be stronger.
As for the village...
ゴポ...
BLUB BLUB...
ゴポポポ...
BLUB BLUB BLUB...
I forgot to warn the chimeras about that.
I will see to it that they are instructed.
WREEE
VVUM
...

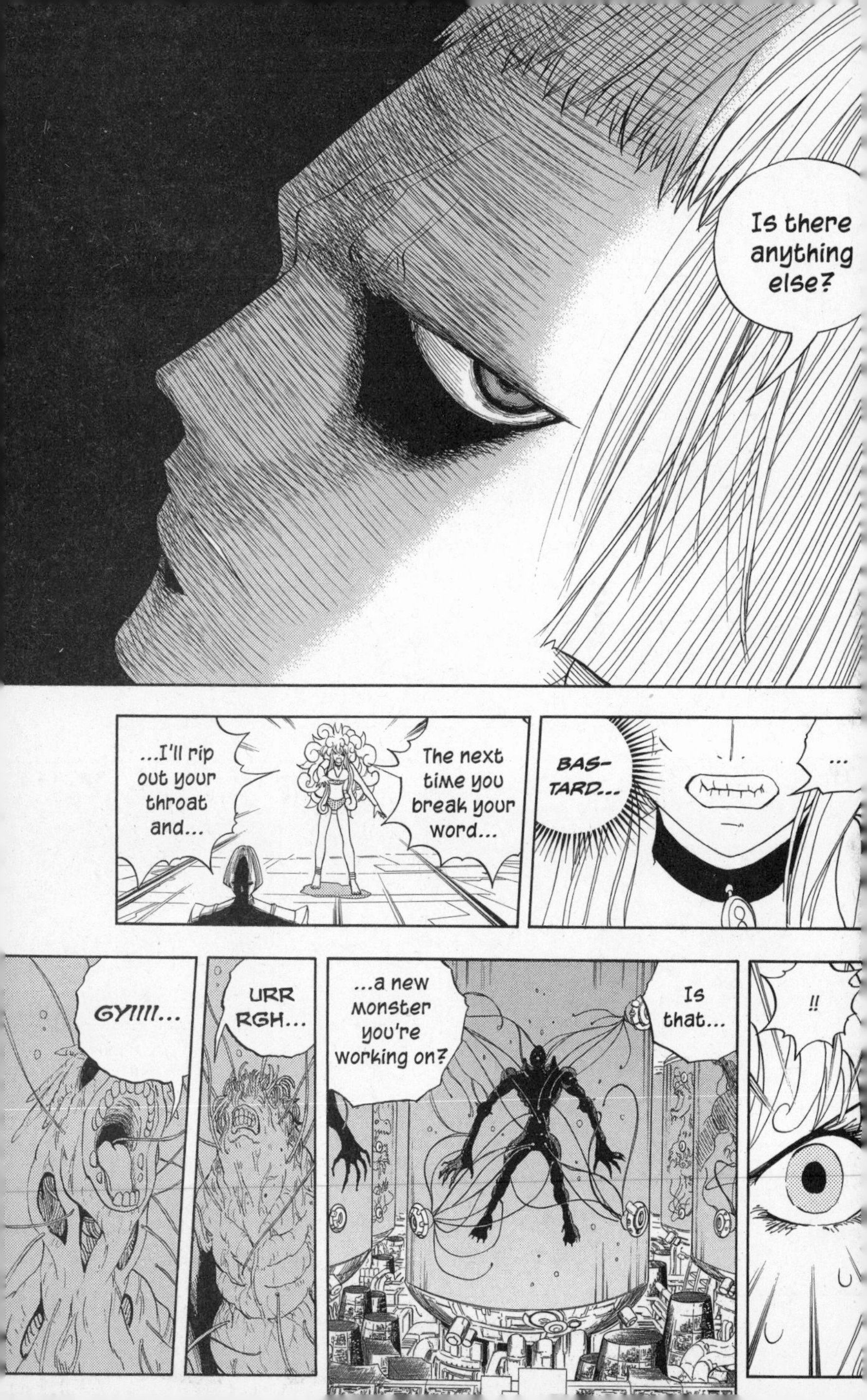
Is there anything else?
...
BAS-TARD...
The next time you break your word...
...I'll rip out your throat and...
!!
Is that...
...a new monster you're working on?
URR RGH...
GYIIII...

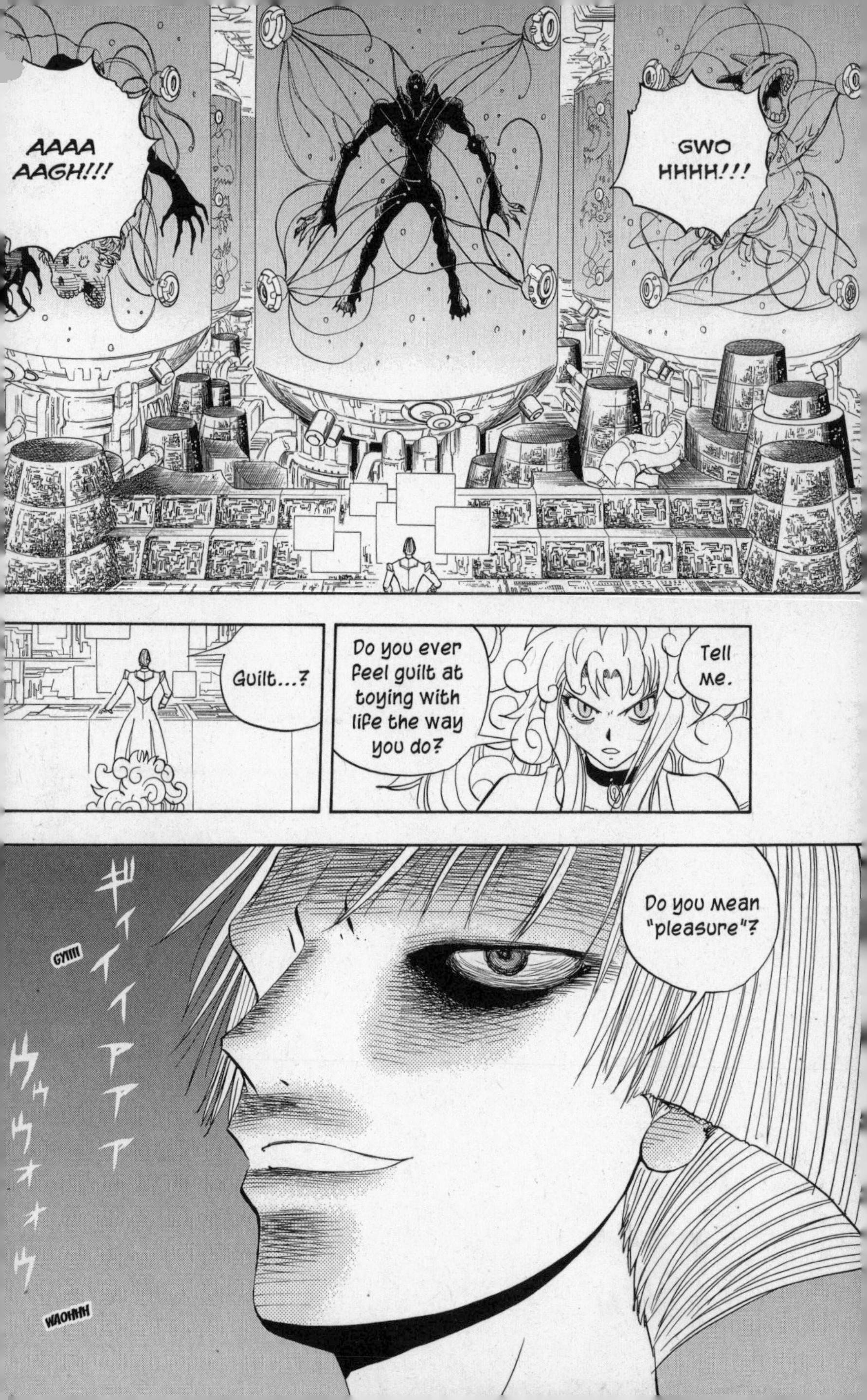
GWO HHHH!!!
AAAA AAGH!!!
Tell me.
Do you ever feel guilt at toying with life the way you do?
Guilt...?
Do you mean "pleasure"?
ギィイアアア
GYIIII
ウゥウオオウ
WAOHHH

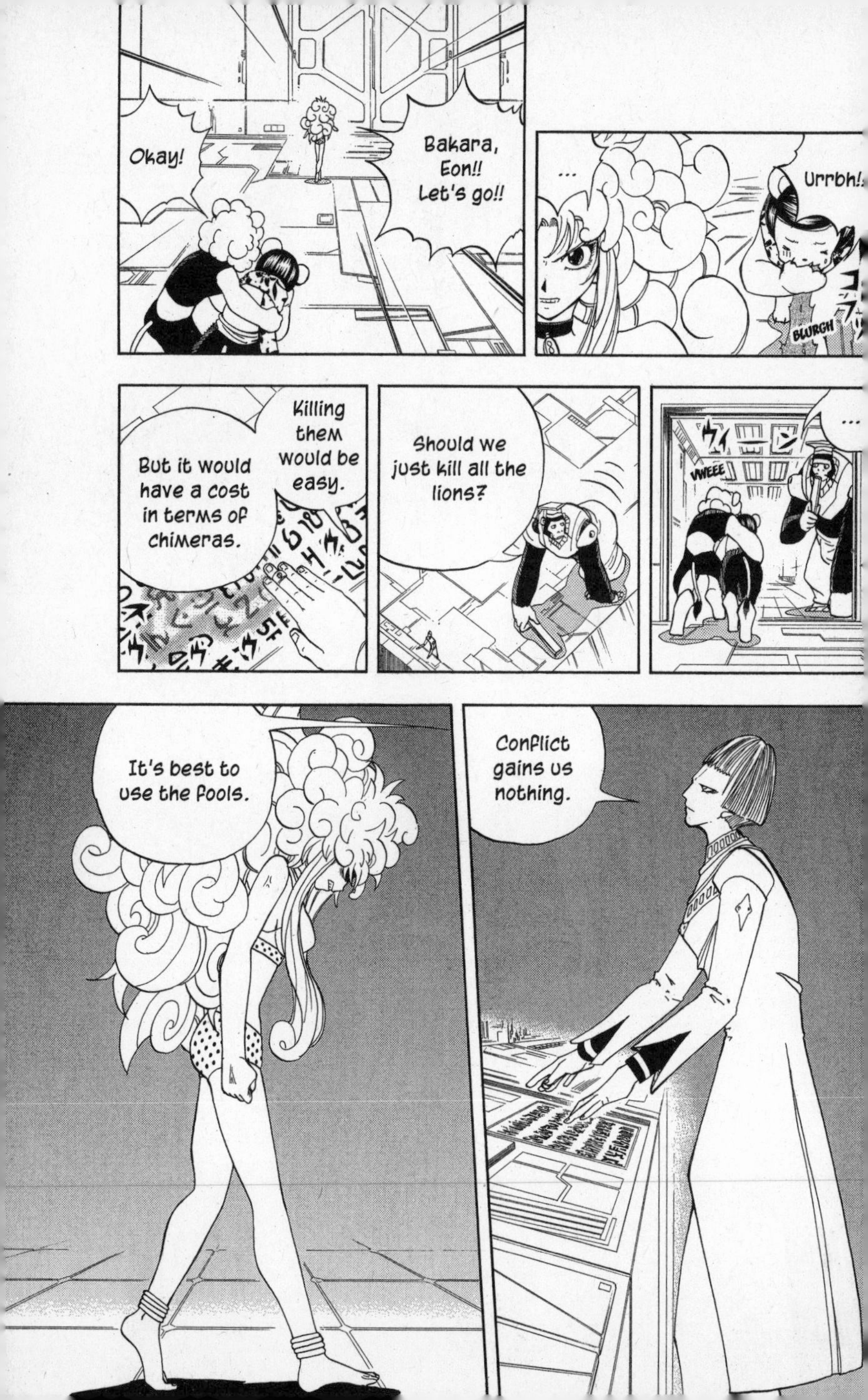
Urrbh!!
...
BLURGH
Bakara, Eon!! Let's go!!
Okay!
...
VWEEE
Should we just kill all the lions?
Killing them would be easy.
But it would have a cost in terms of chimeras.
Conflict gains us nothing.
It's best to use the fools.

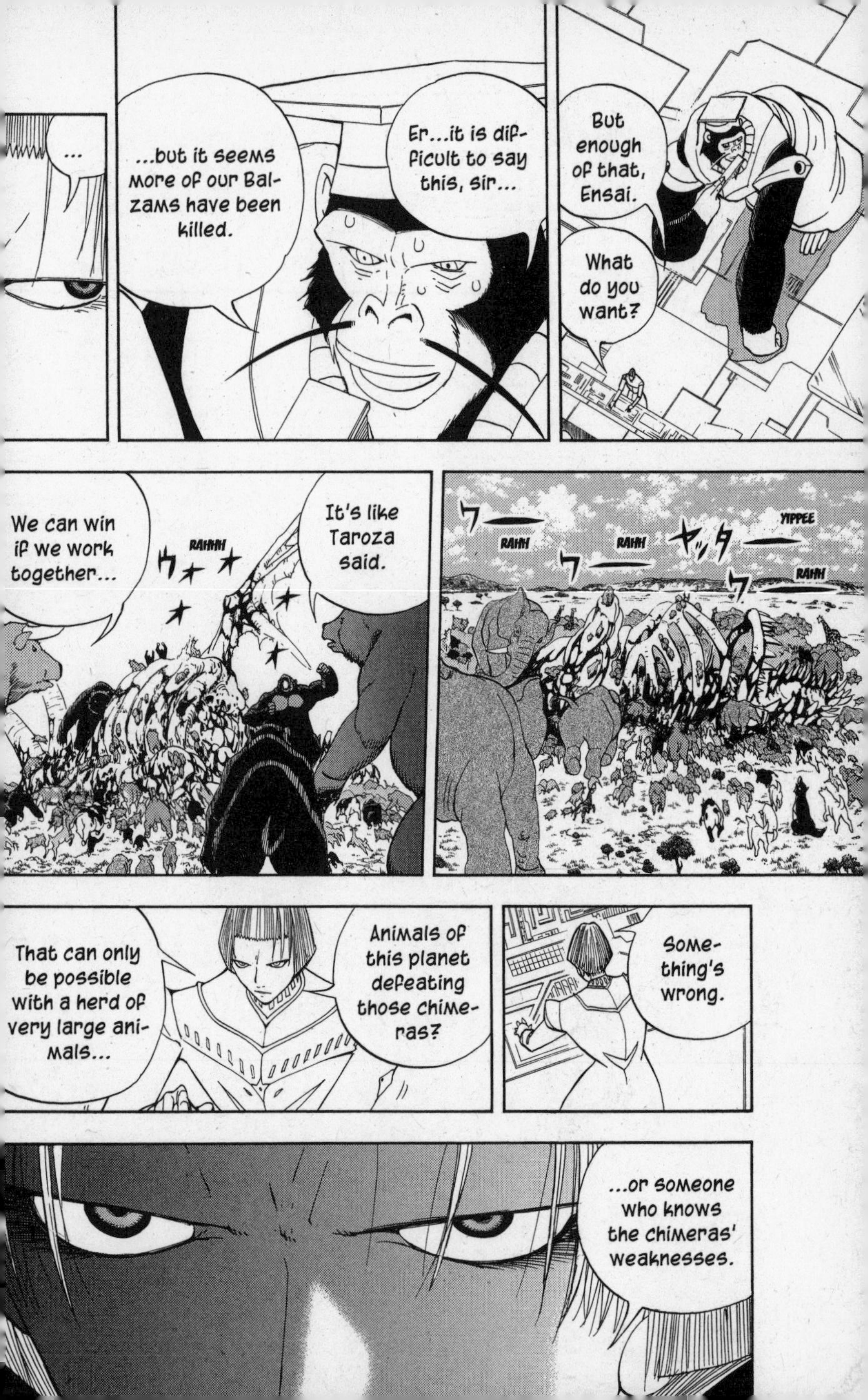

But enough of that, Ensai.
What do you want?
Er...it is difficult to say this, sir...
...but it seems more of our Balzams have been killed.
...
YIPPEE
RAHH
RAHH
RAHH
It's like Taroza said.
We can win if we work together...
RAHHH
Something's wrong.
Animals of this planet defeating those chimeras?
That can only be possible with a herd of very large animals...
...or someone who knows the chimeras' weaknesses.

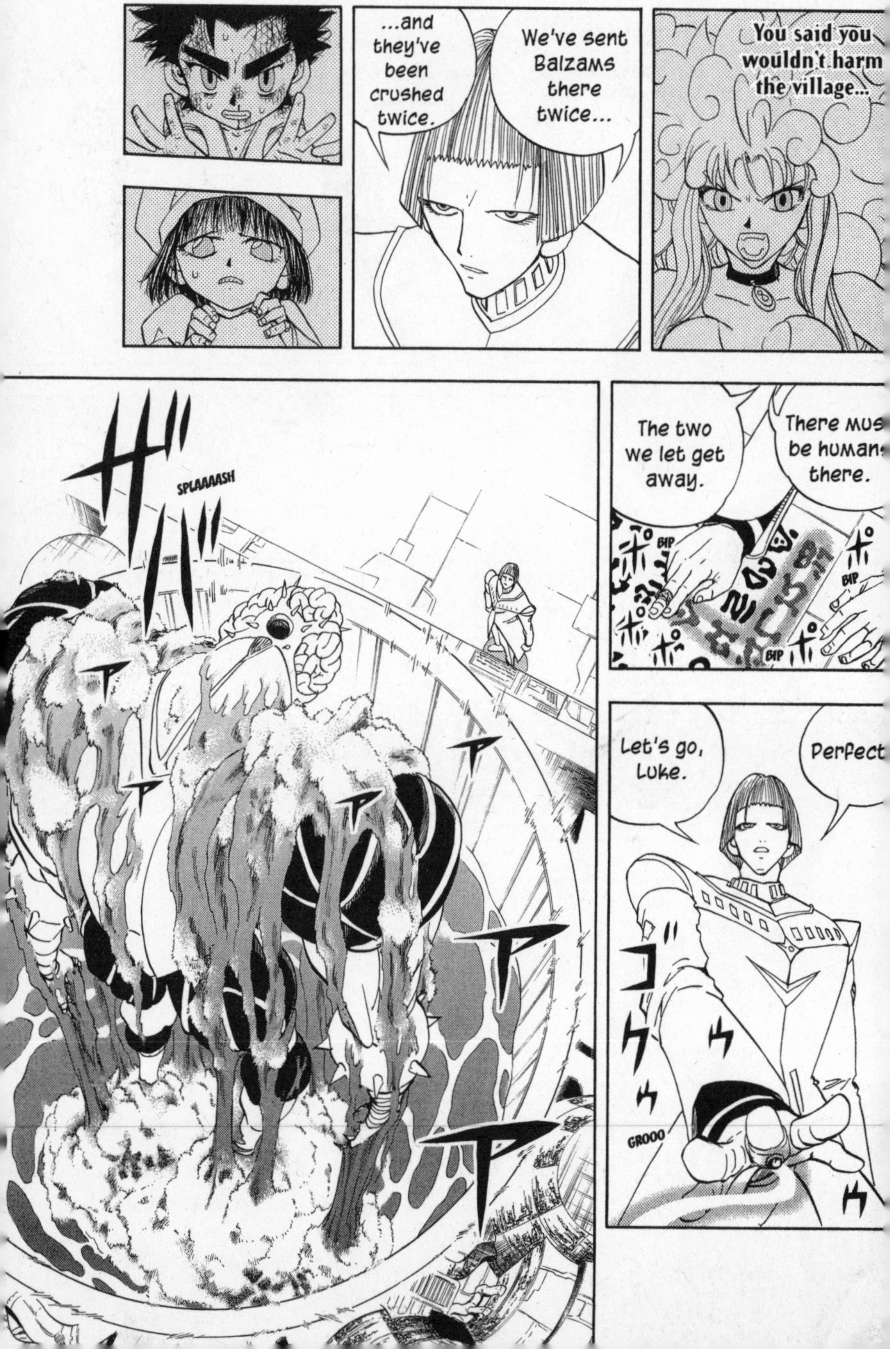

You said you wouldn't harm the village...
We've sent Balzams there twice...
...and they've been crushed twice.
There mus be humans there.
The two we let get away.
BIP
BIP
BIP
Perfect
Let's go, Luke.
GROOO
SPLAAAASH

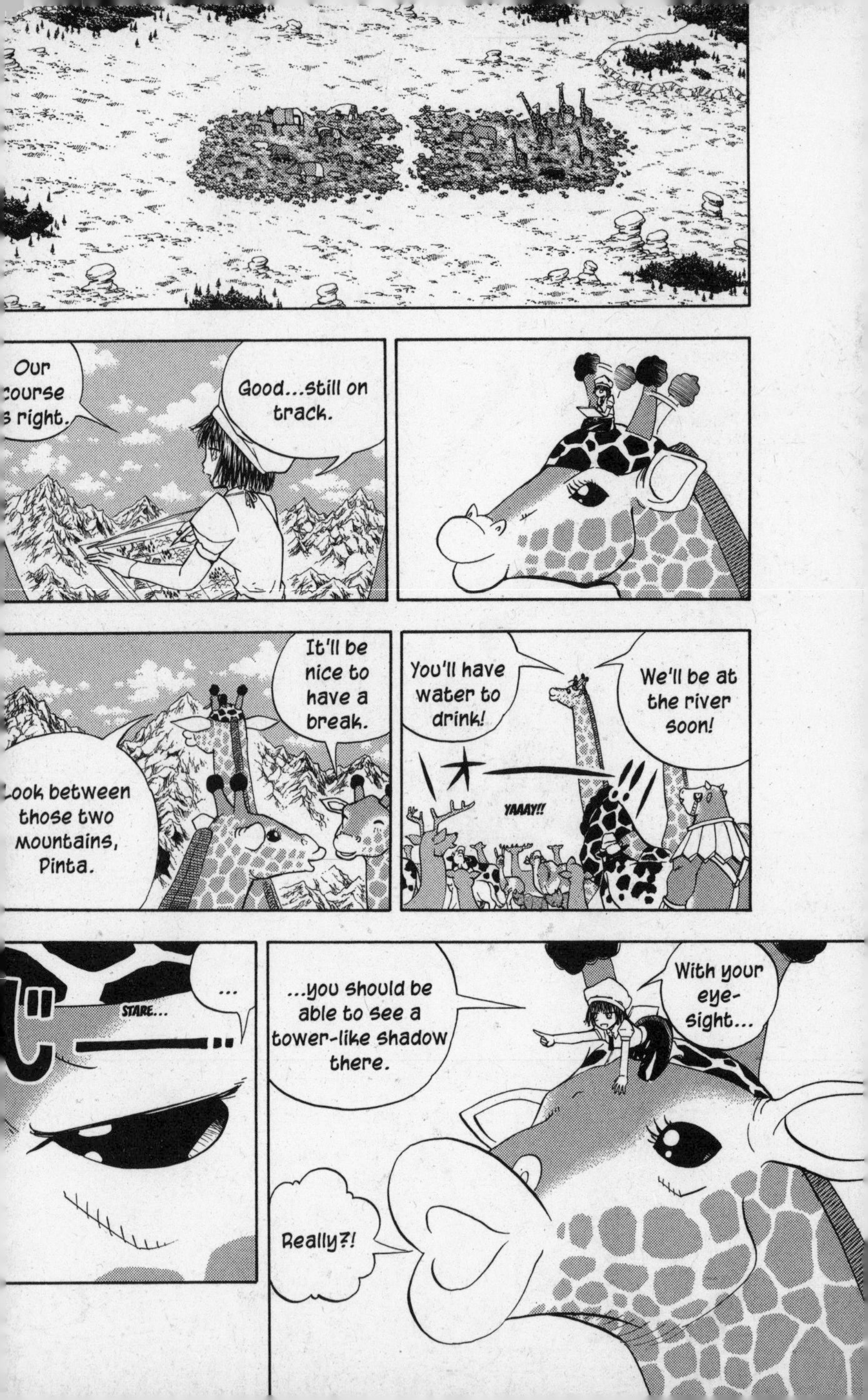
Good...still on track.
Our course is right.
We'll be at the river soon!
You'll have water to drink!
YAAAY!!
It'll be nice to have a break.
Look between those two mountains, Pinta.
With your eye-sight...
...you should be able to see a tower-like shadow there.
Really?!
...
STARE...

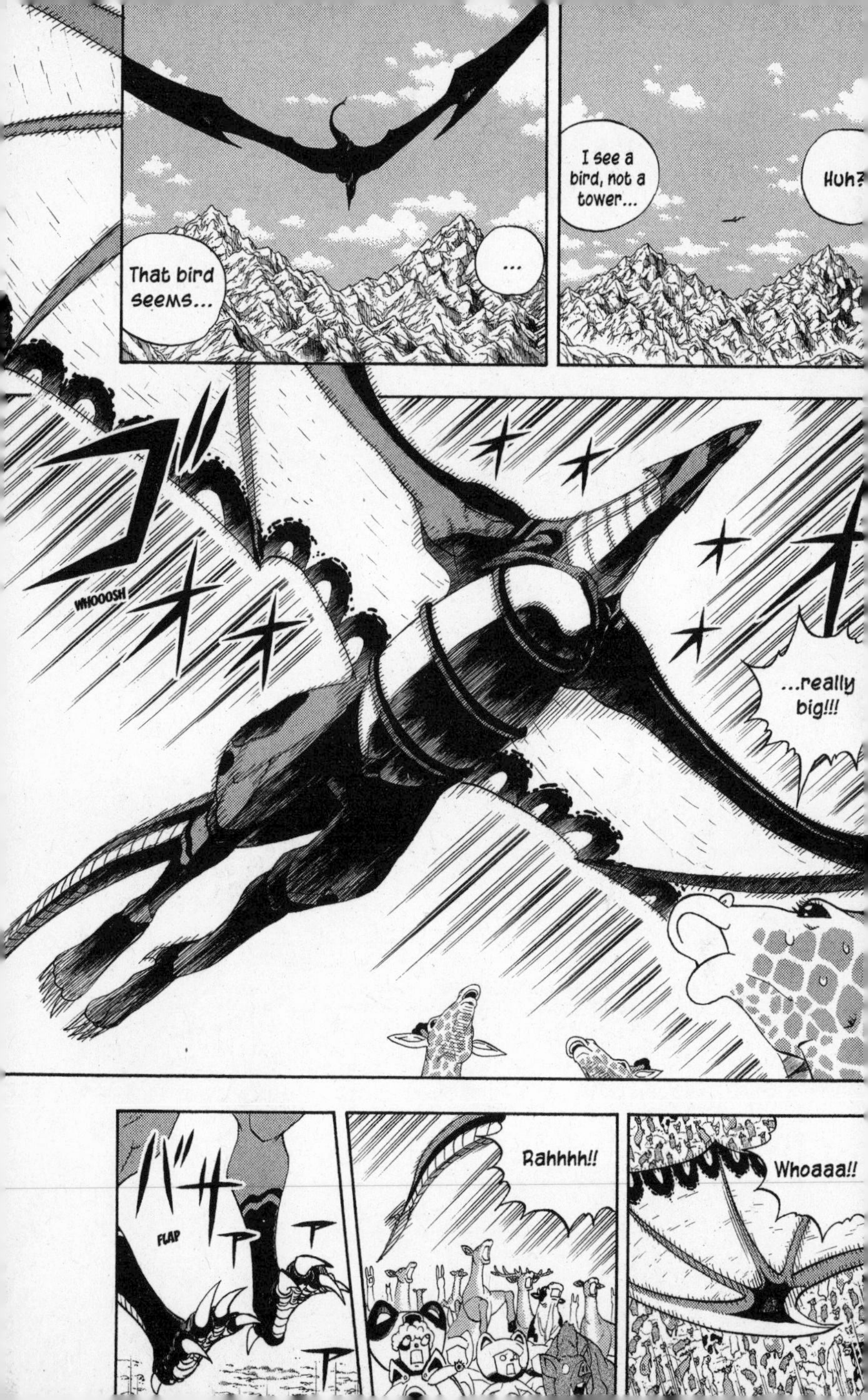
Huh?
I see a bird, not a tower...
...
That bird seems...
...really big!!!
WHOOOSH
Whoaaa!!
Rahhhh!!
FLAP

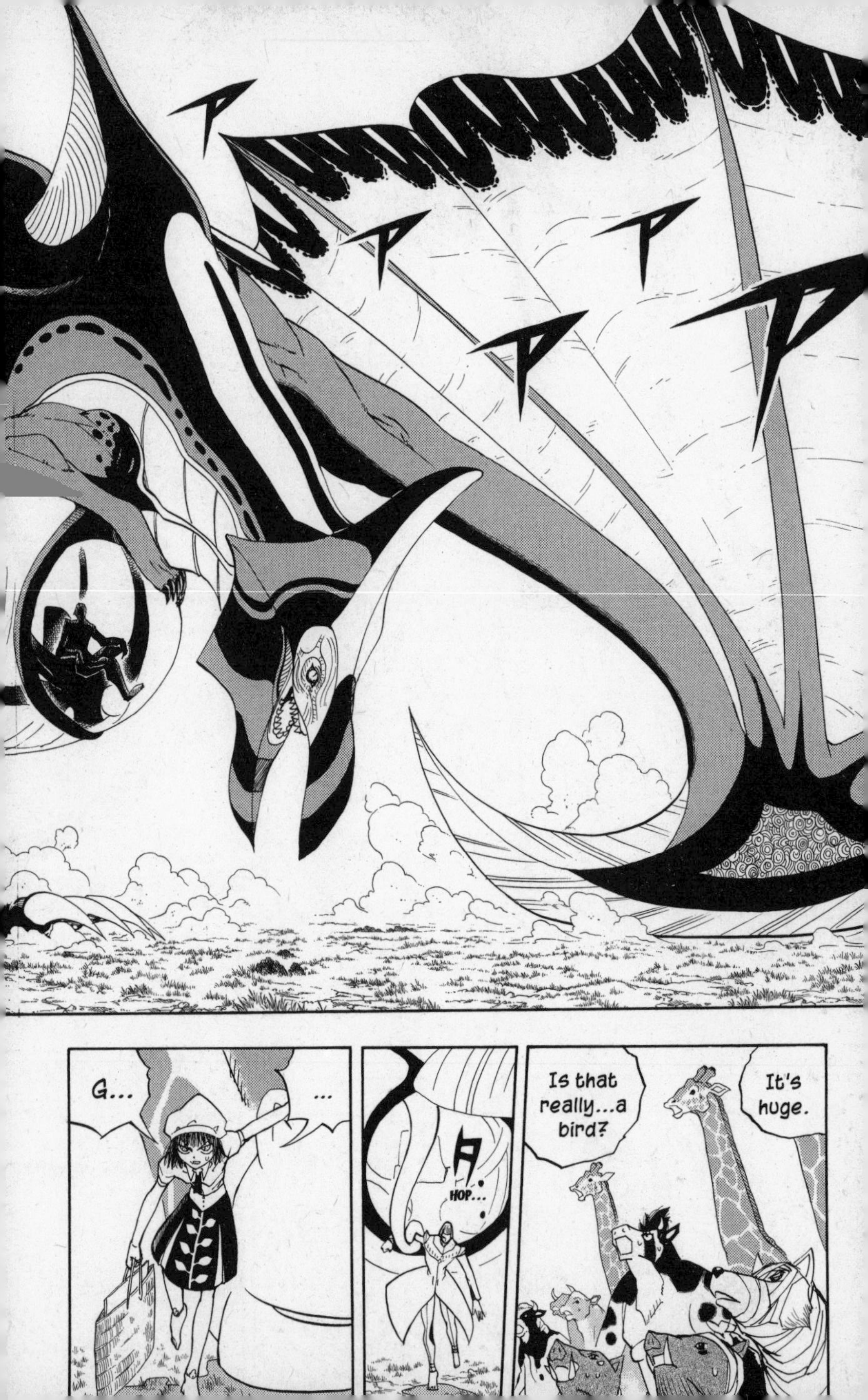
It's huge.
Is that really...a bird?
HOP...
...
G...

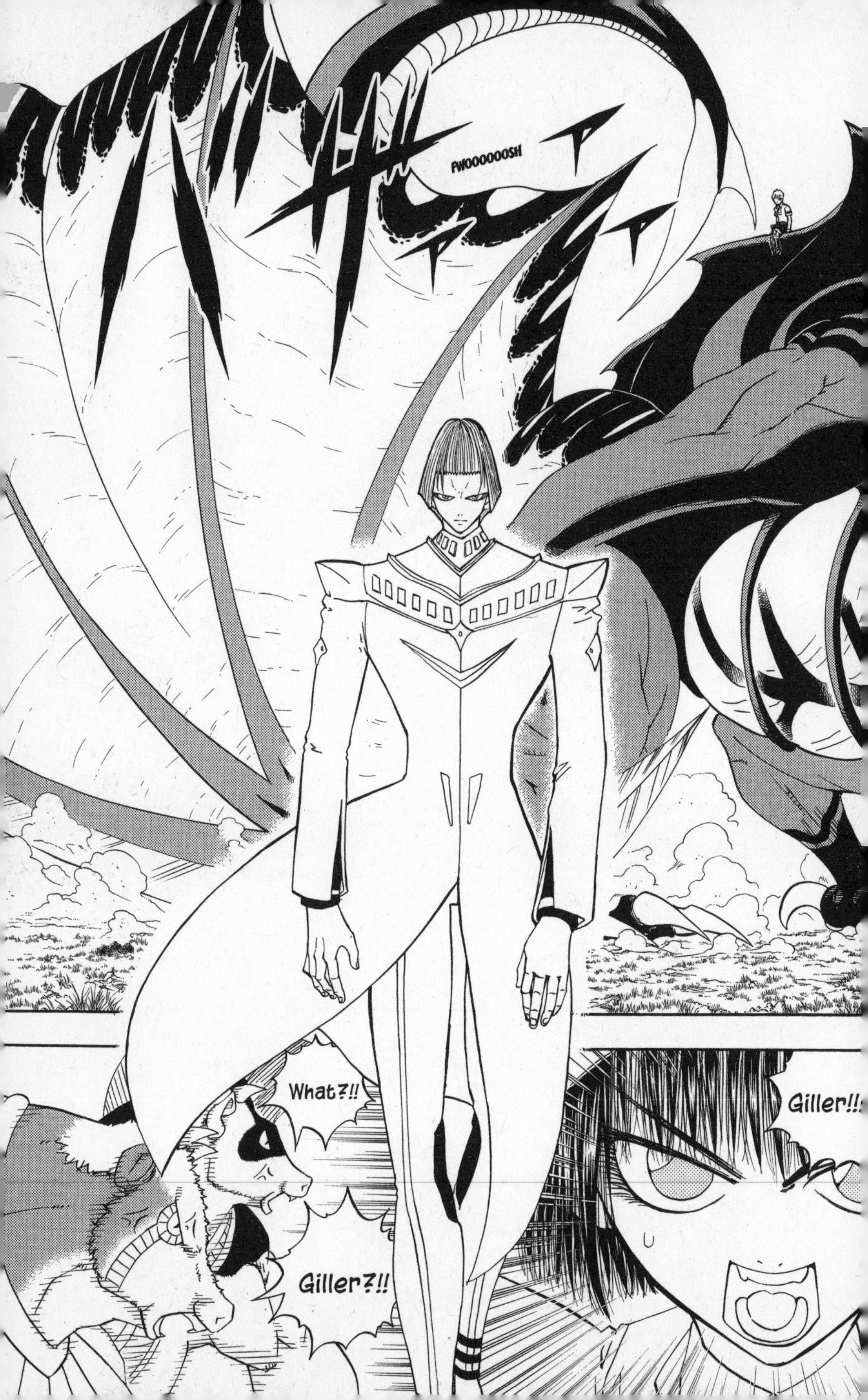
FWOOOOOOOSH
Giller!!!
What?!!
Giller?!!

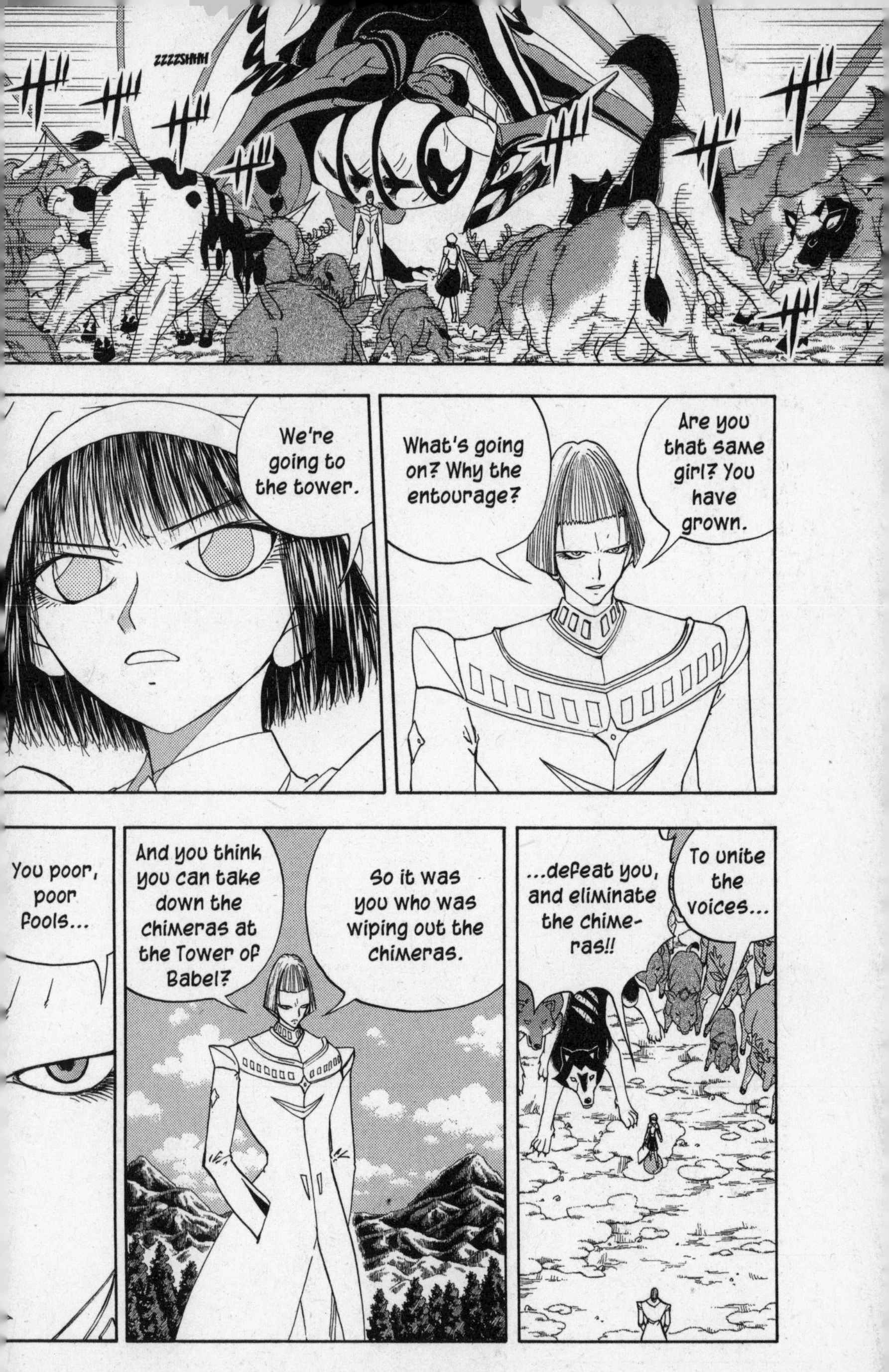
ZZZZSHHH
Are you that same girl? You have grown.
What's going on? Why the entourage?
We're going to the tower.
To unite the voices...
...defeat you, and eliminate the chime-ras!!
So it was you who was wiping out the chimeras.
And you think you can take down the chimeras at the Tower of Babel?
You poor, poor fools...

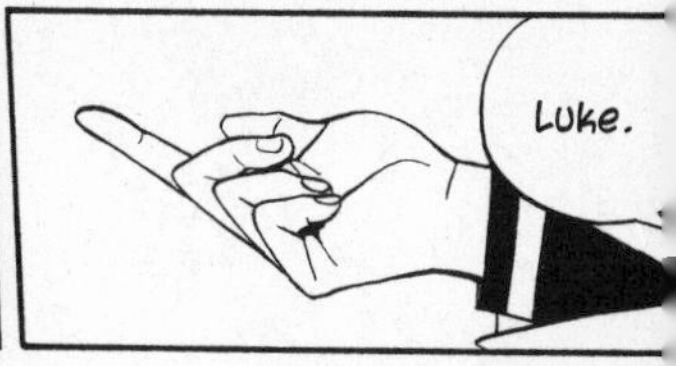
Luke.

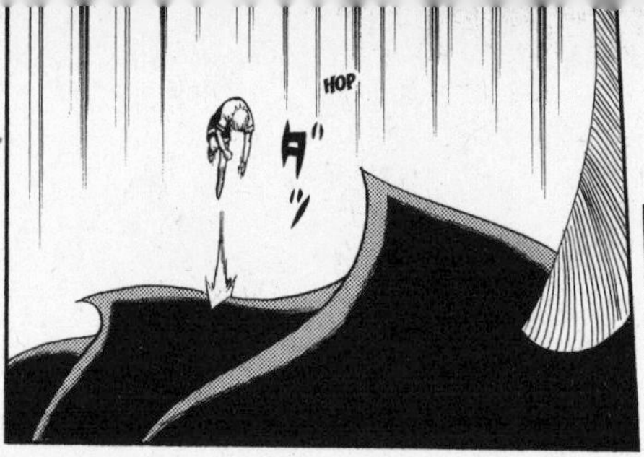
HOP
ダッ

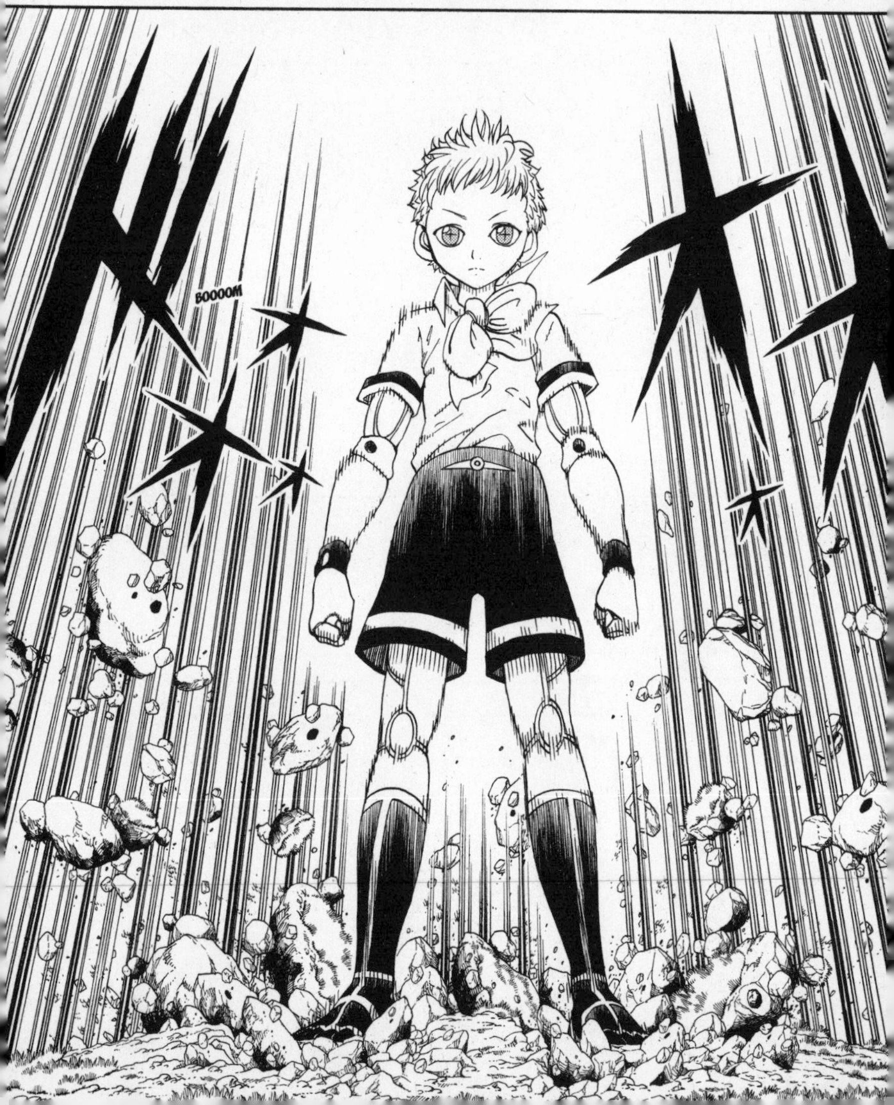
BOOOOM

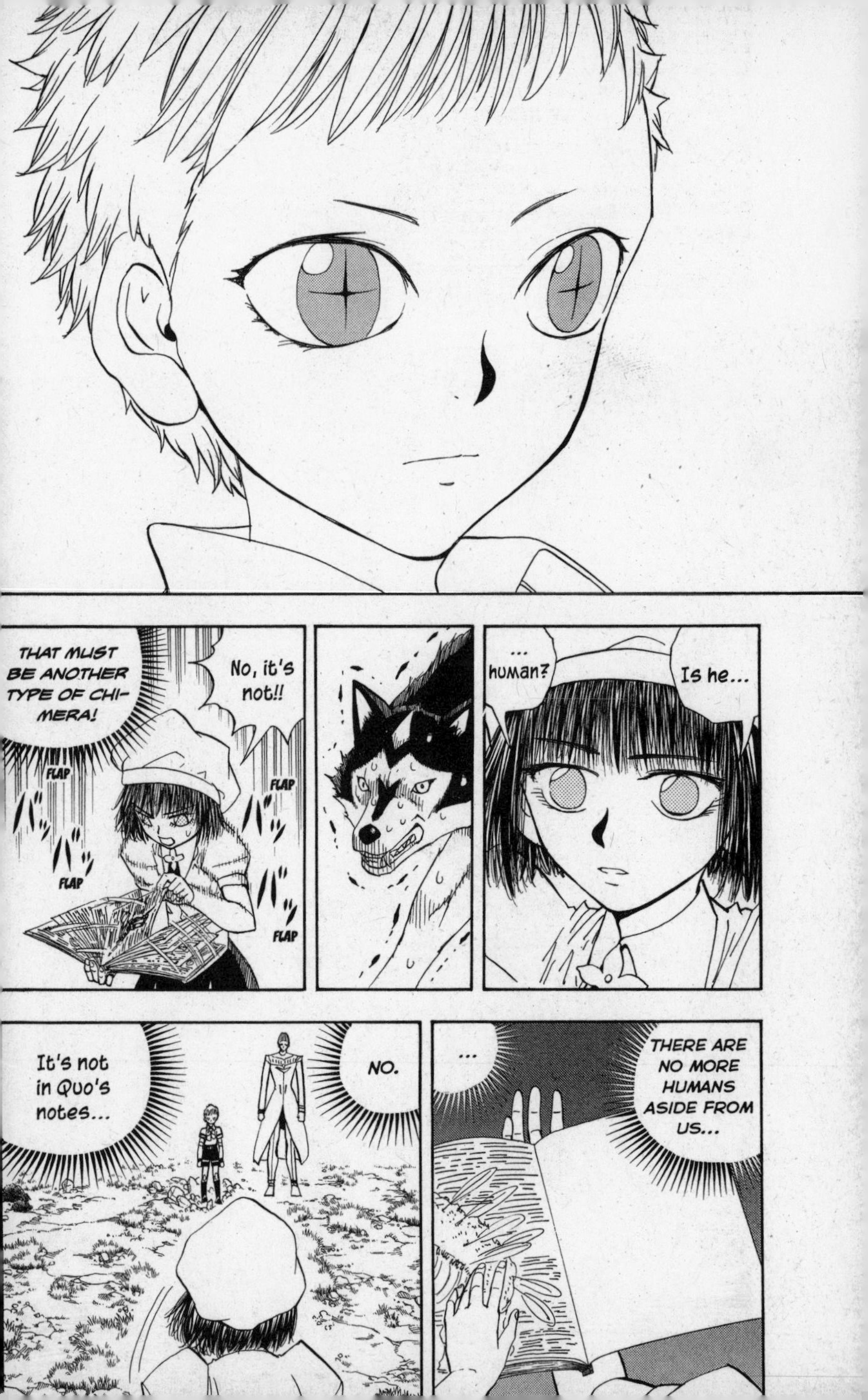
Is he...
... human?
No, it's not!!
THAT MUST BE ANOTHER TYPE OF CHI-MERA!
FLAP
FLAP
FLAP
FLAP
THERE ARE NO MORE HUMANS ASIDE FROM US...
...
NO.
It's not in Quo's notes...

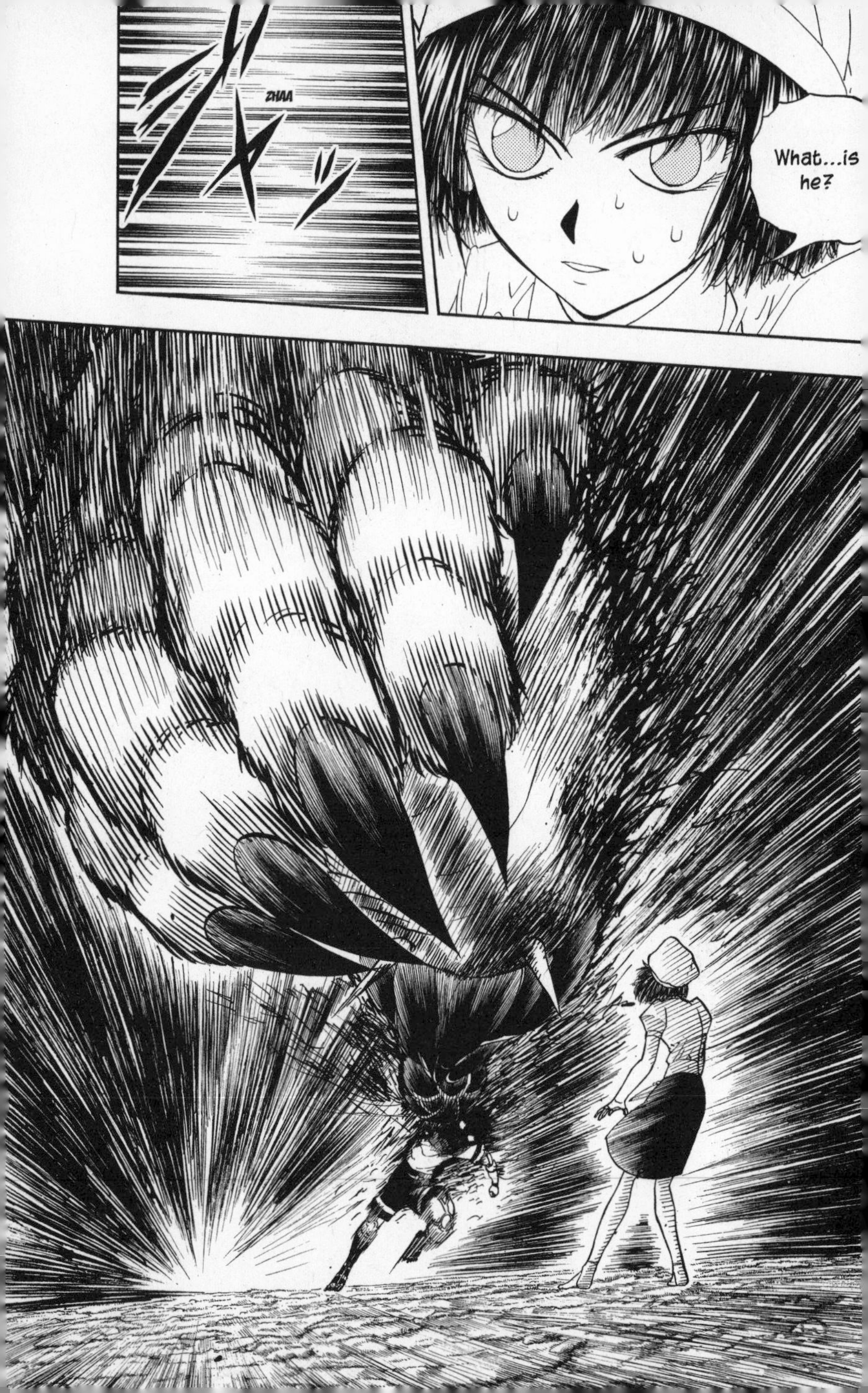
What...is he?
ZHAA

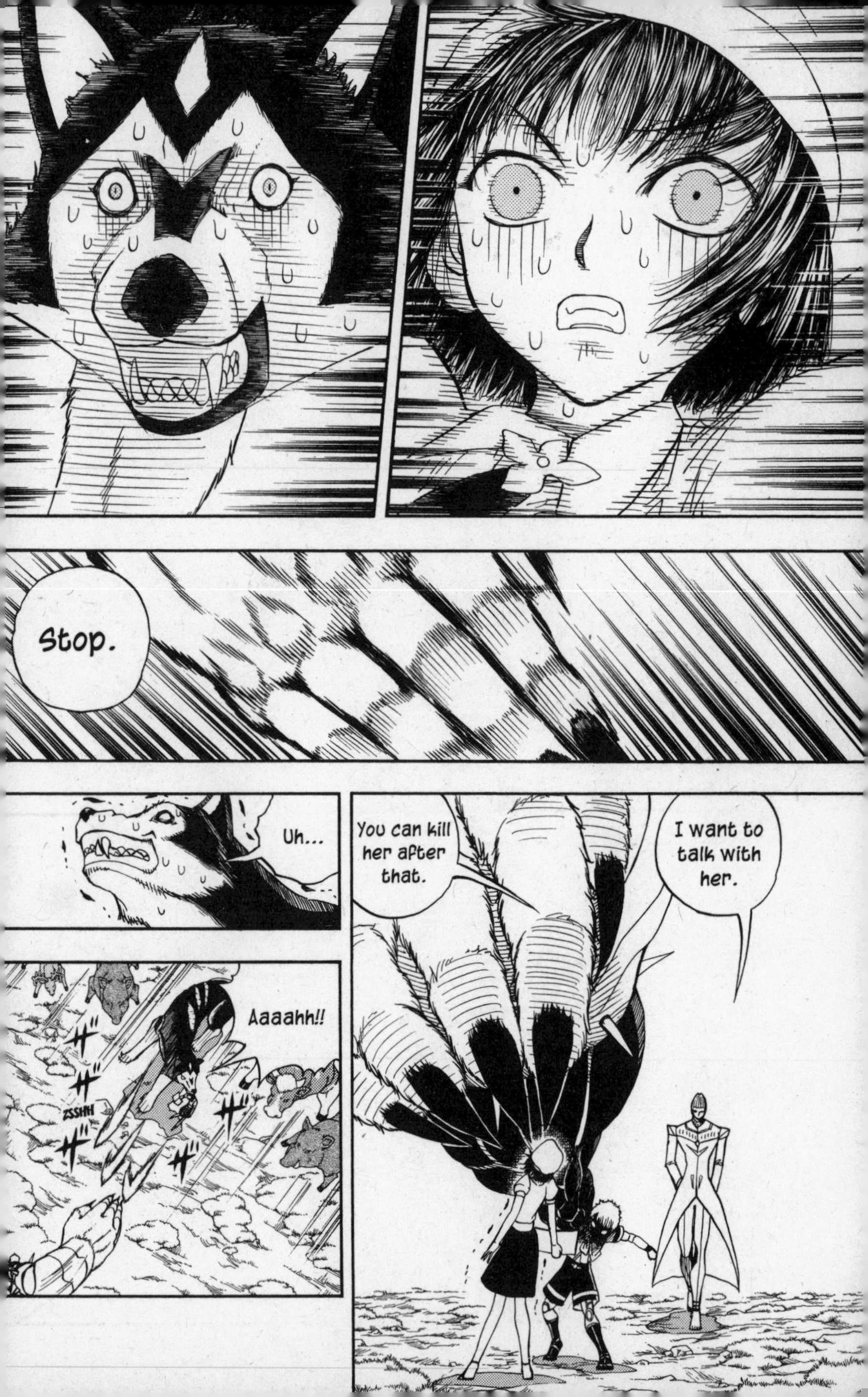
Stop.
I want to talk with her.
You can kill her after that.
Uh...
Aaaahh!!
ZSSHH

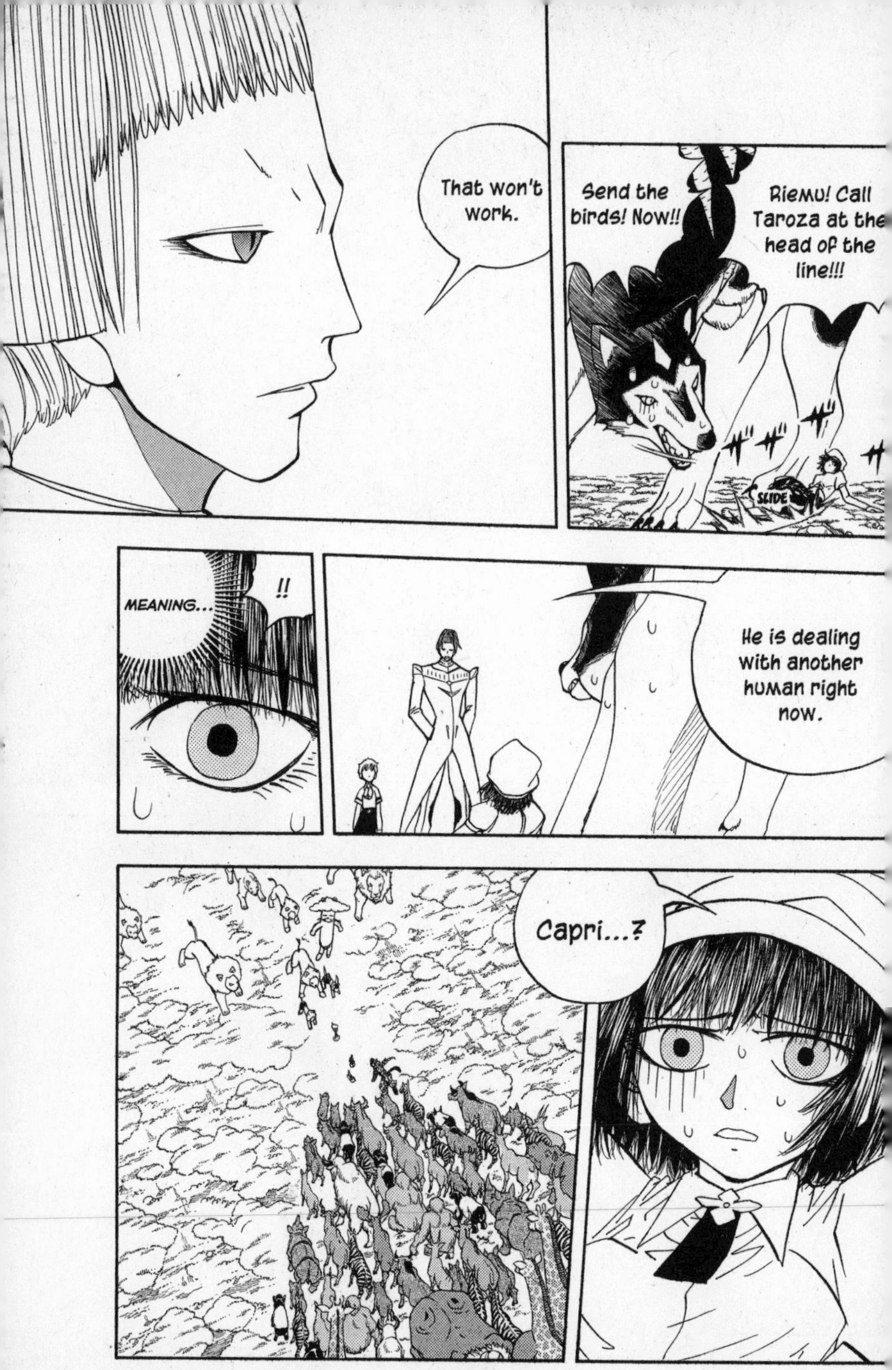
Riemu! Call Taroza at the head of the line!!!
Send the birds! Now!!
SLIDE
That won't work.
He is dealing with another human right now.
!!
MEANING...
Capri...?

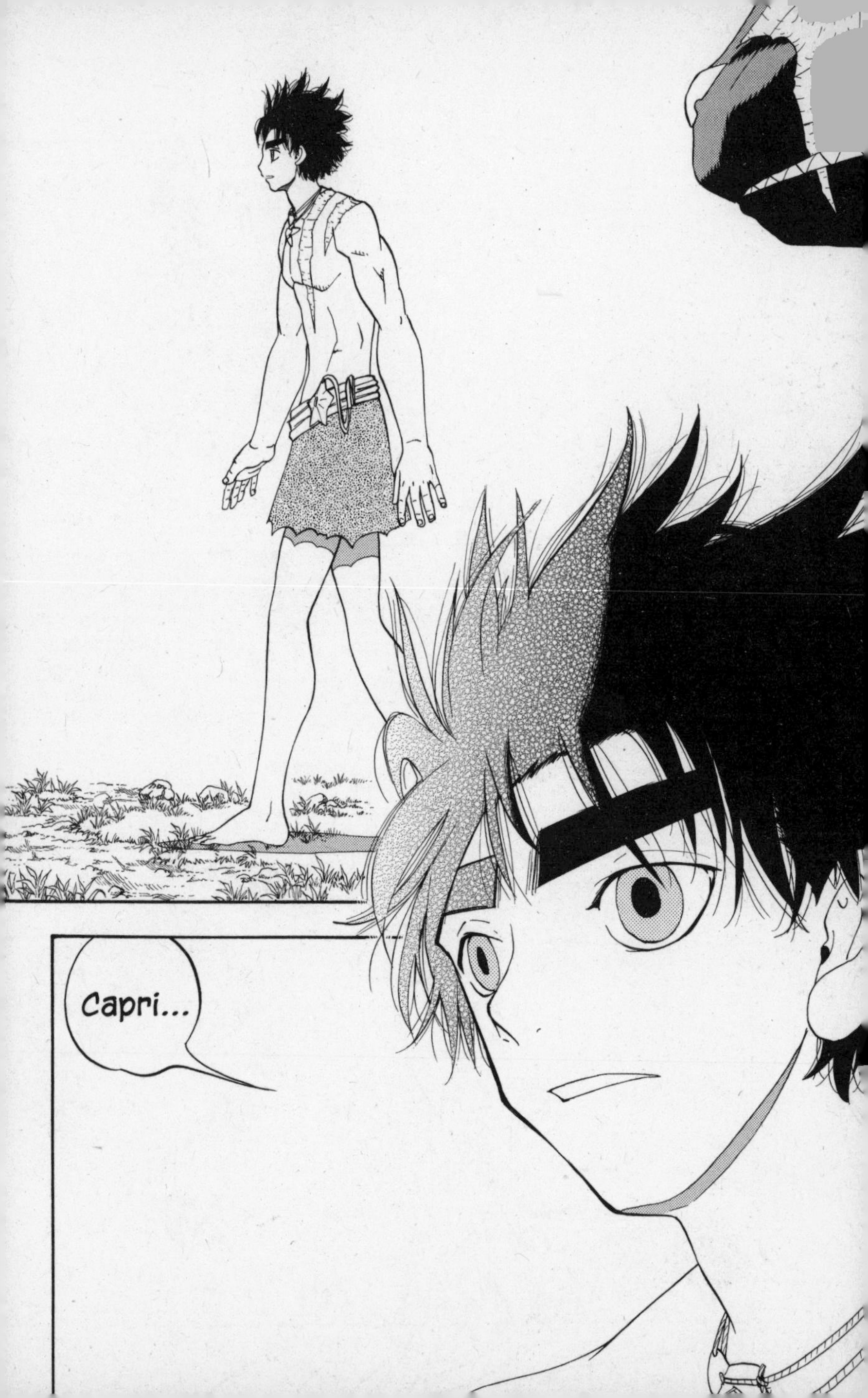
Capri...

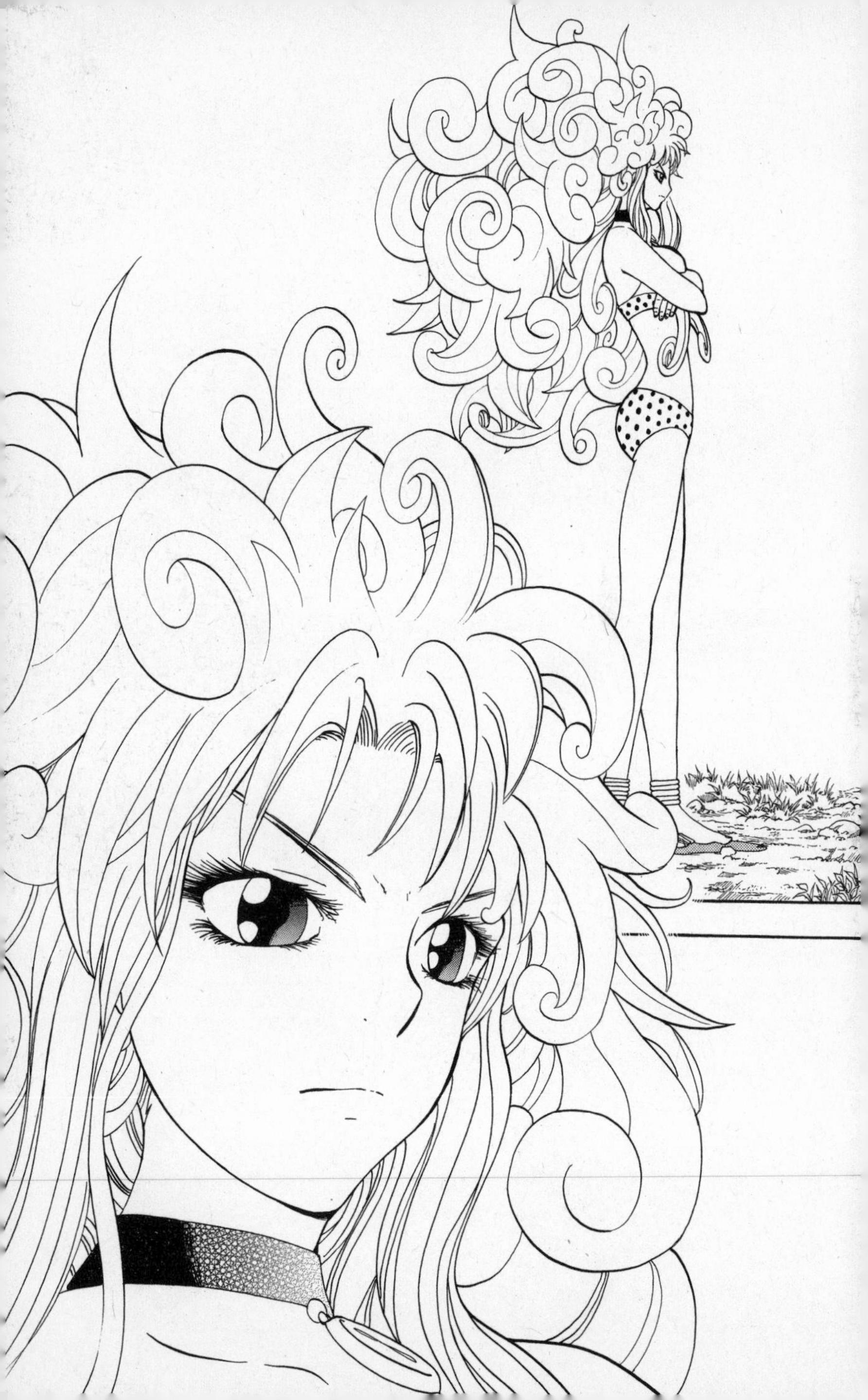

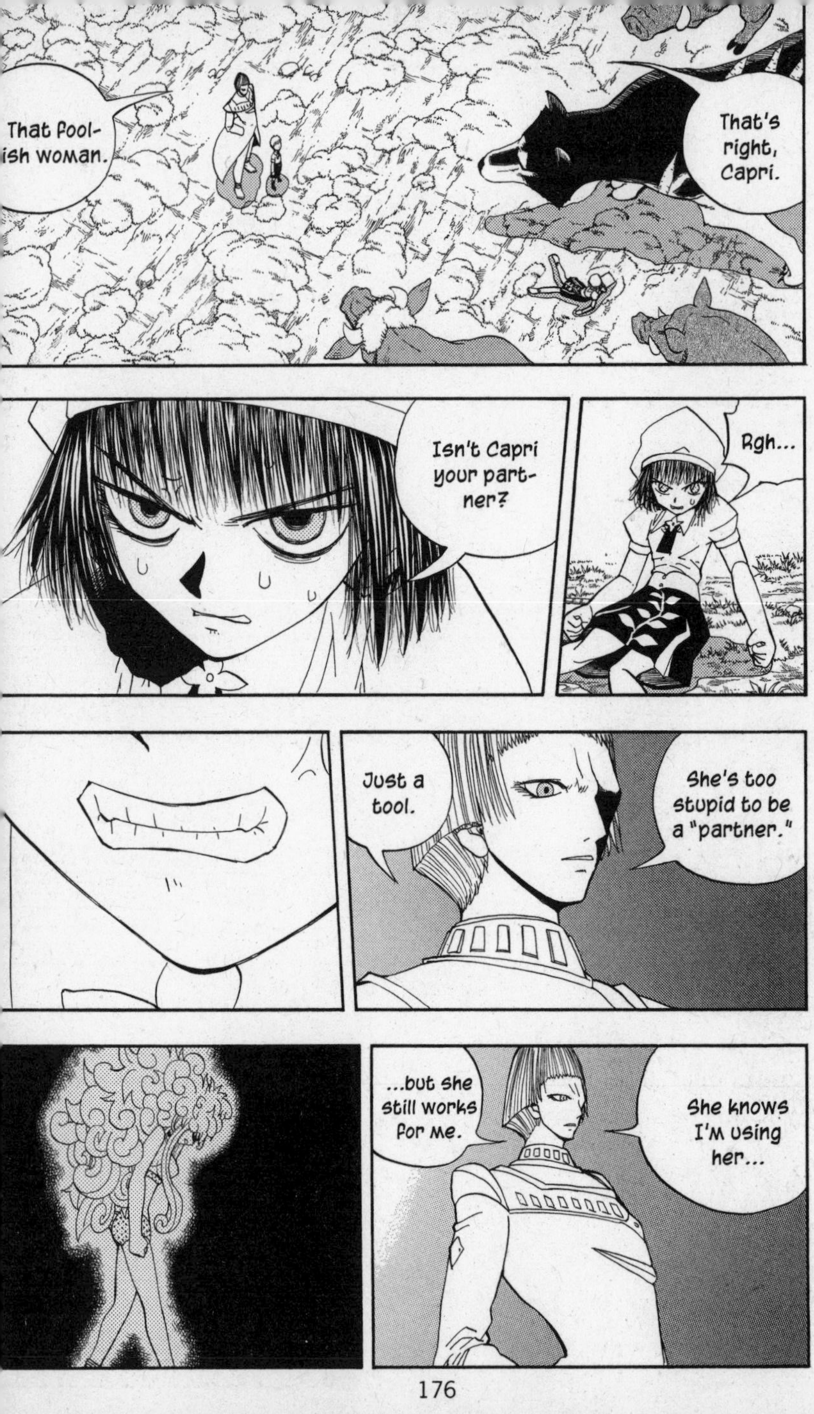
That's right, Capri.
That foolish woman.
Rgh...
Isn't Capri your partner?
She's too stupid to be a "partner."
Just a tool.
She knows I'm using her...
...but she still works for me.

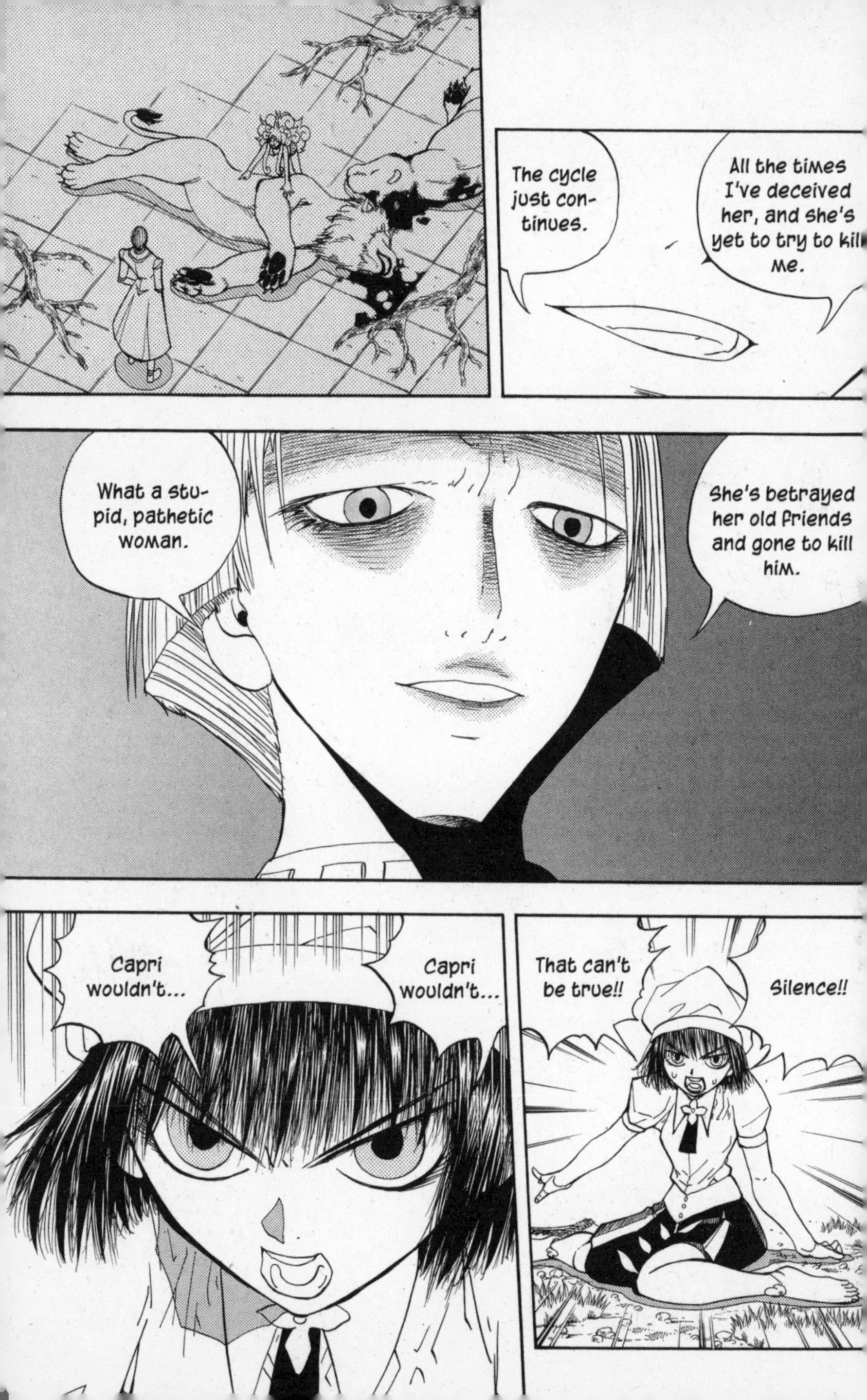
All the times I've deceived her, and she's yet to try to kil me.
The cycle just continues.
She's betrayed her old friends and gone to kill him.
What a stupid, pathetic woman.
Silence!!
That can't be true!!
Capri wouldn't...
Capri wouldn't...

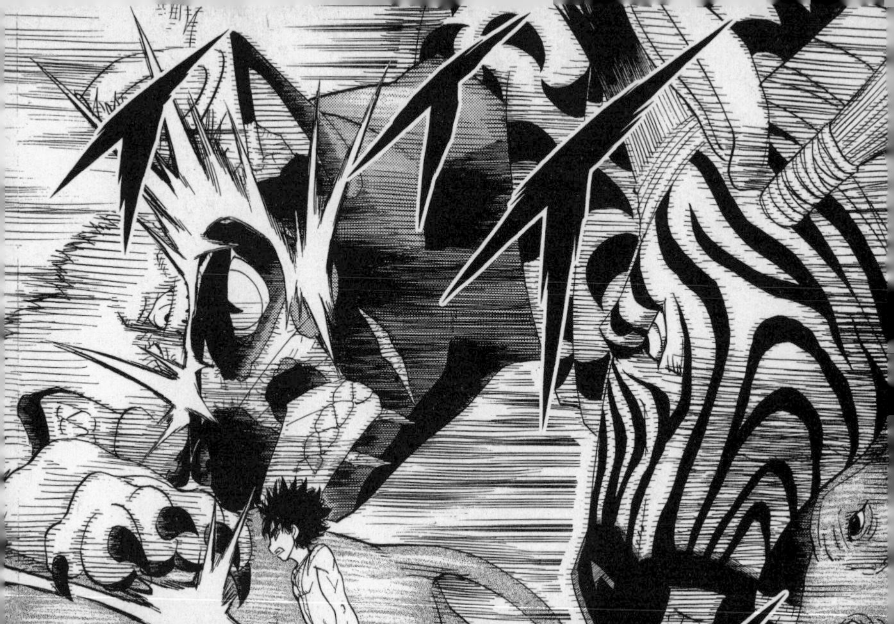

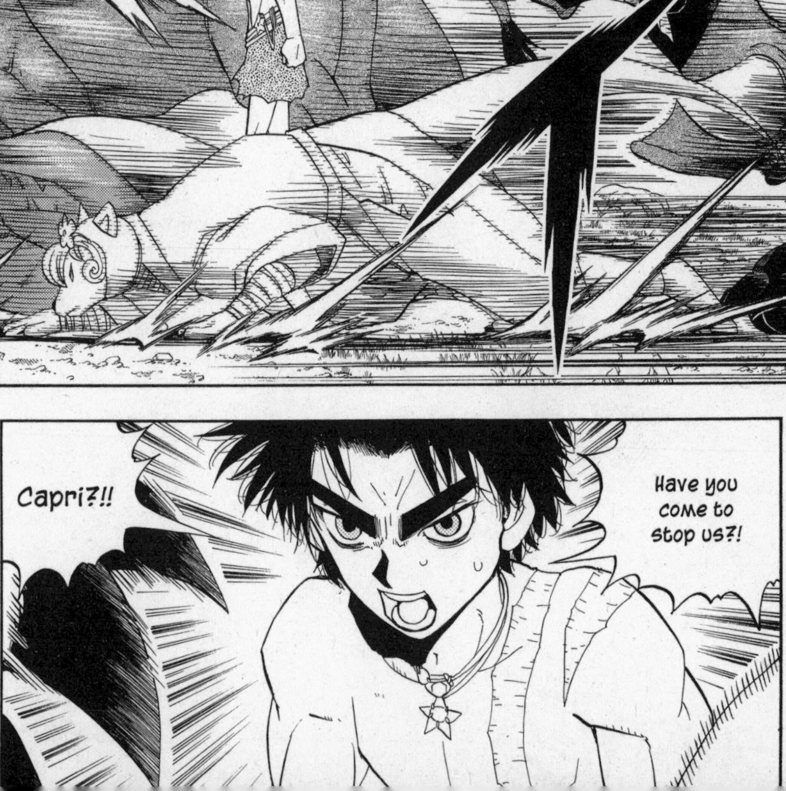
Have you come to stop us?!
Capri?!!

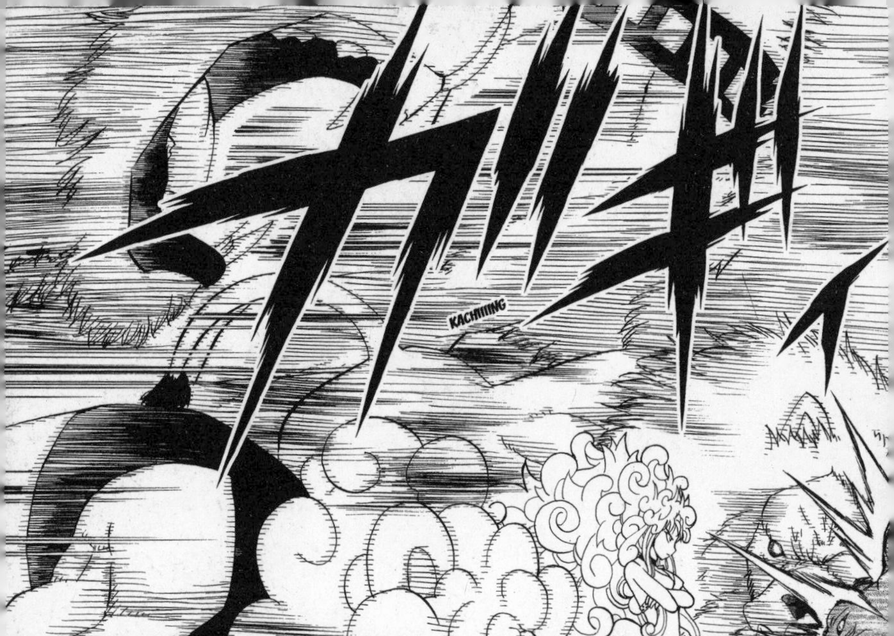
KACHIIIING
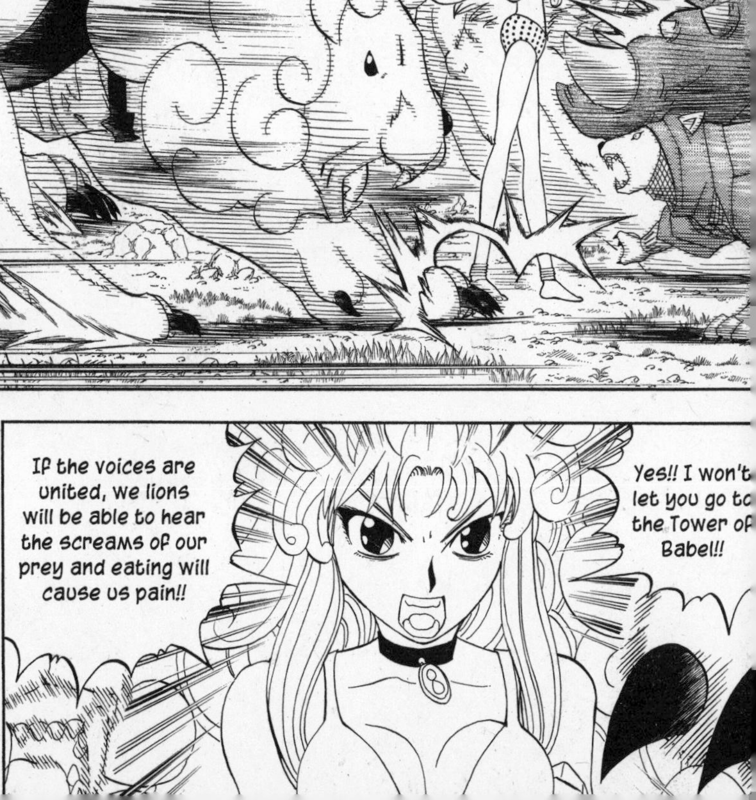
Yes!! I won't let you go to the Tower of Babel!!
If the voices are united, we lions will be able to hear the screams of our prey and eating will cause us pain!!

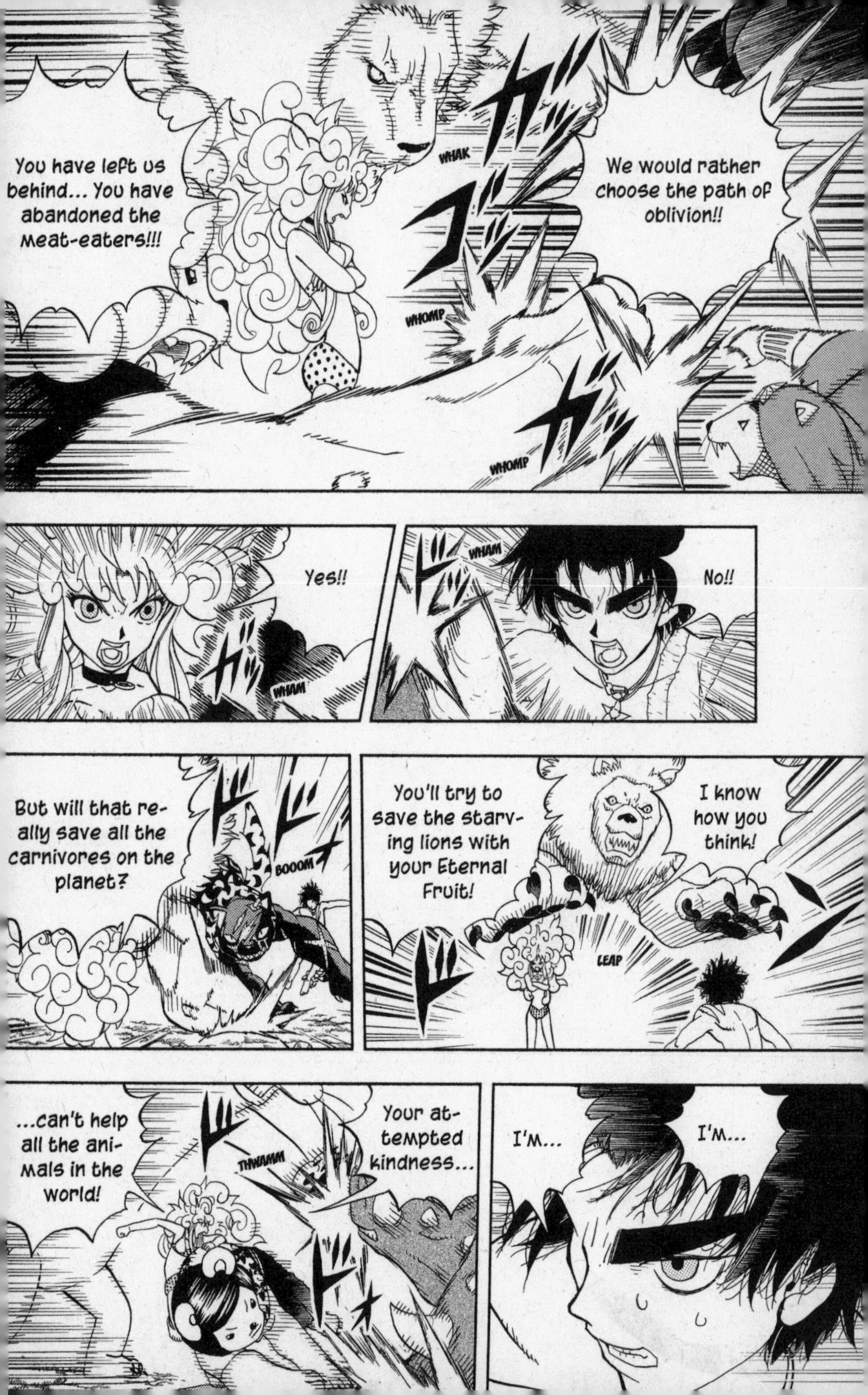
We would rather choose the path of oblivion!!
WHAK
You have left us behind... You have abandoned the Meat-eaters!!!
WHOMP
WHOMP
No!!
WHAM
Yes!!
WHAM
I know how you think!
You'll try to save the starving lions with your Eternal Fruit!
LEAP
But will that really save all the carnivores on the planet?
BOOOM
I'M...
I'M...
Your attempted kindness...
THWAMM
...can't help all the animals in the world!

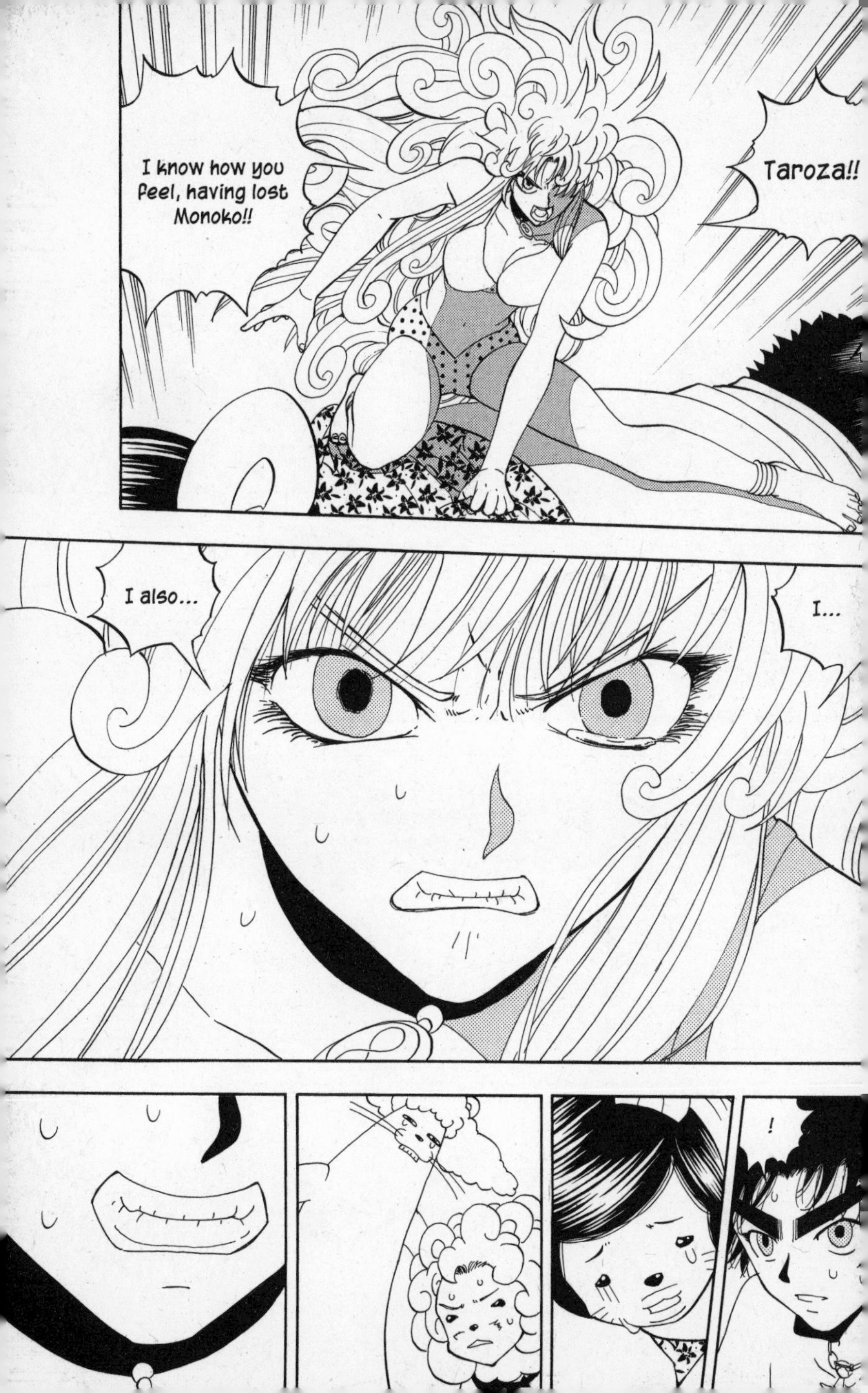
Taroza!!
I know how you feel, having lost Monoko!!
I...
I also...
!

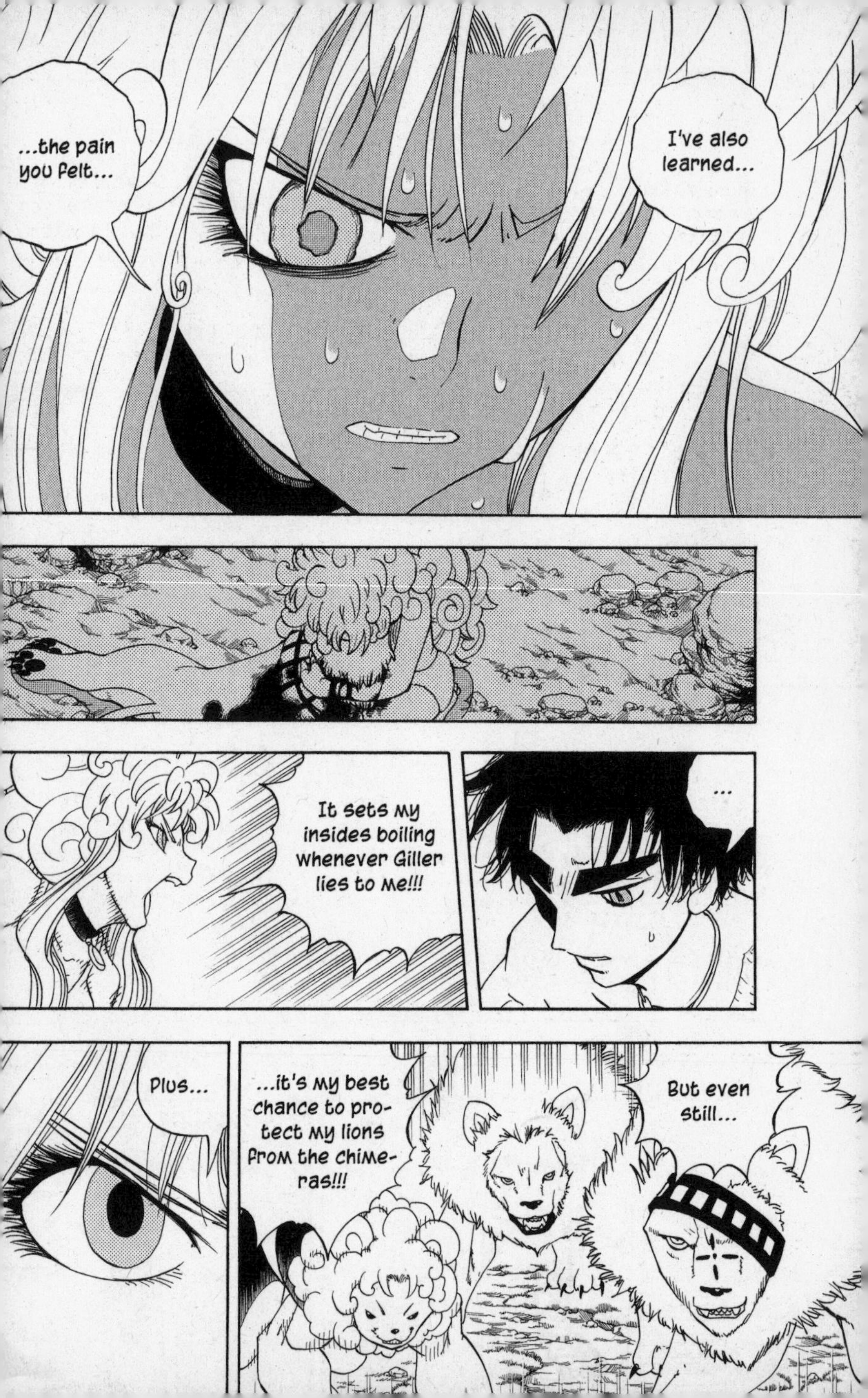
I've also learned...
...the pain you felt...
...
It sets my insides boiling whenever Giller lies to me!!!
But even still...
...it's my best chance to protect my lions from the chimeras!!!
Plus...

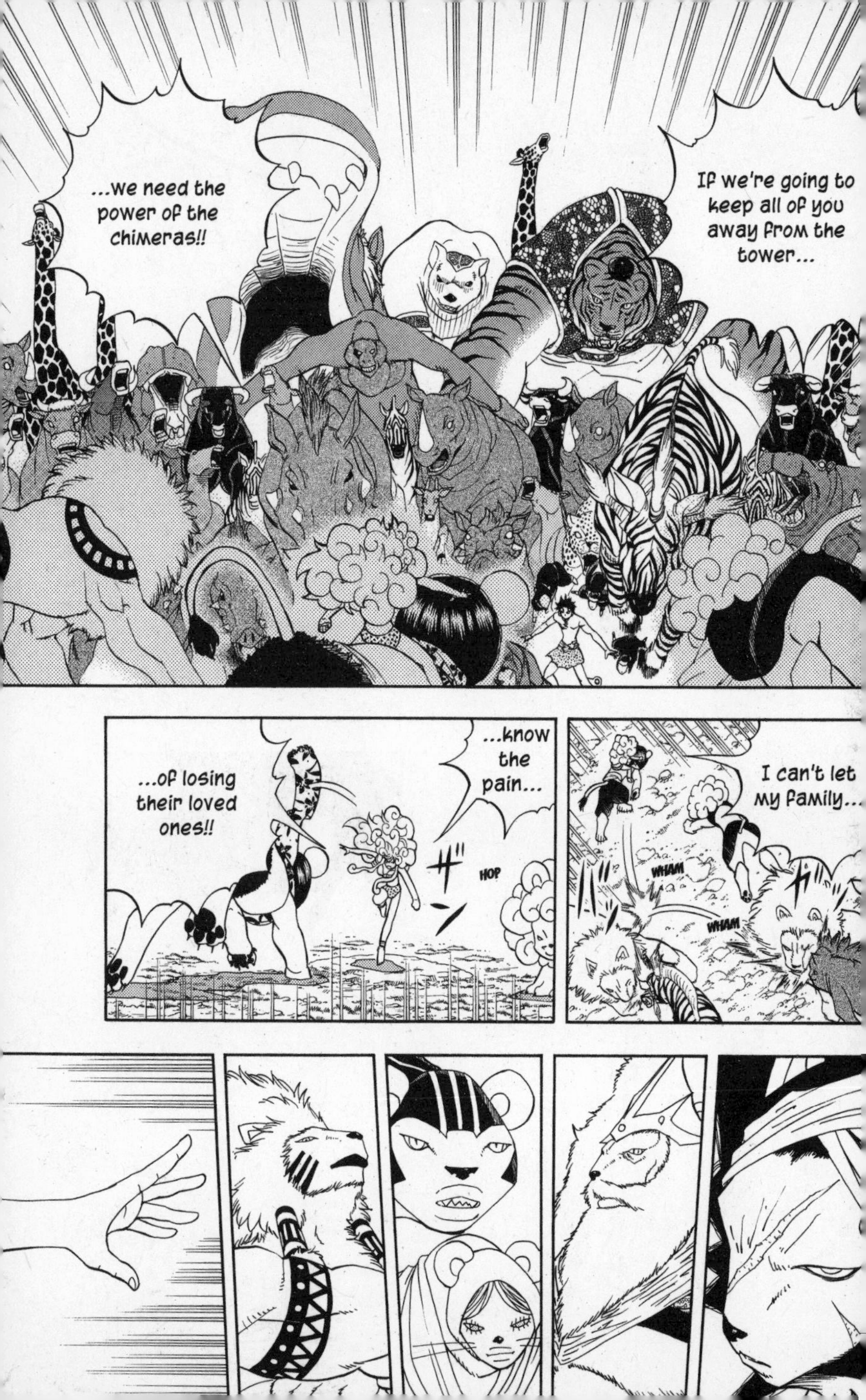

If we're going to keep all of you away from the tower...
...we need the power of the chimeras!!
I can't let my family...
WHAM
WHAM
...know the pain...
HOP
...of losing their loved ones!!

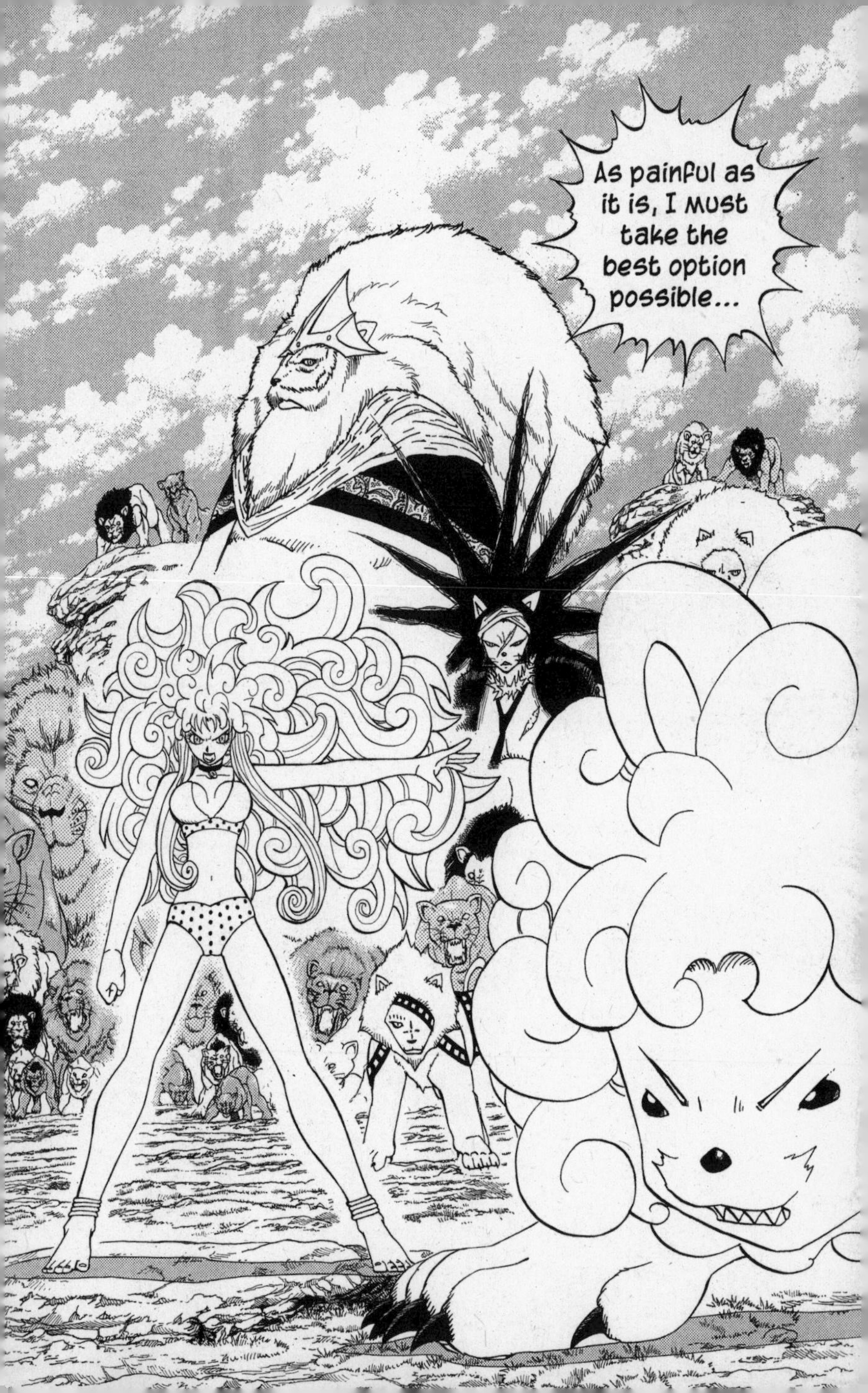
As painful as it is, I must take the best option possible...

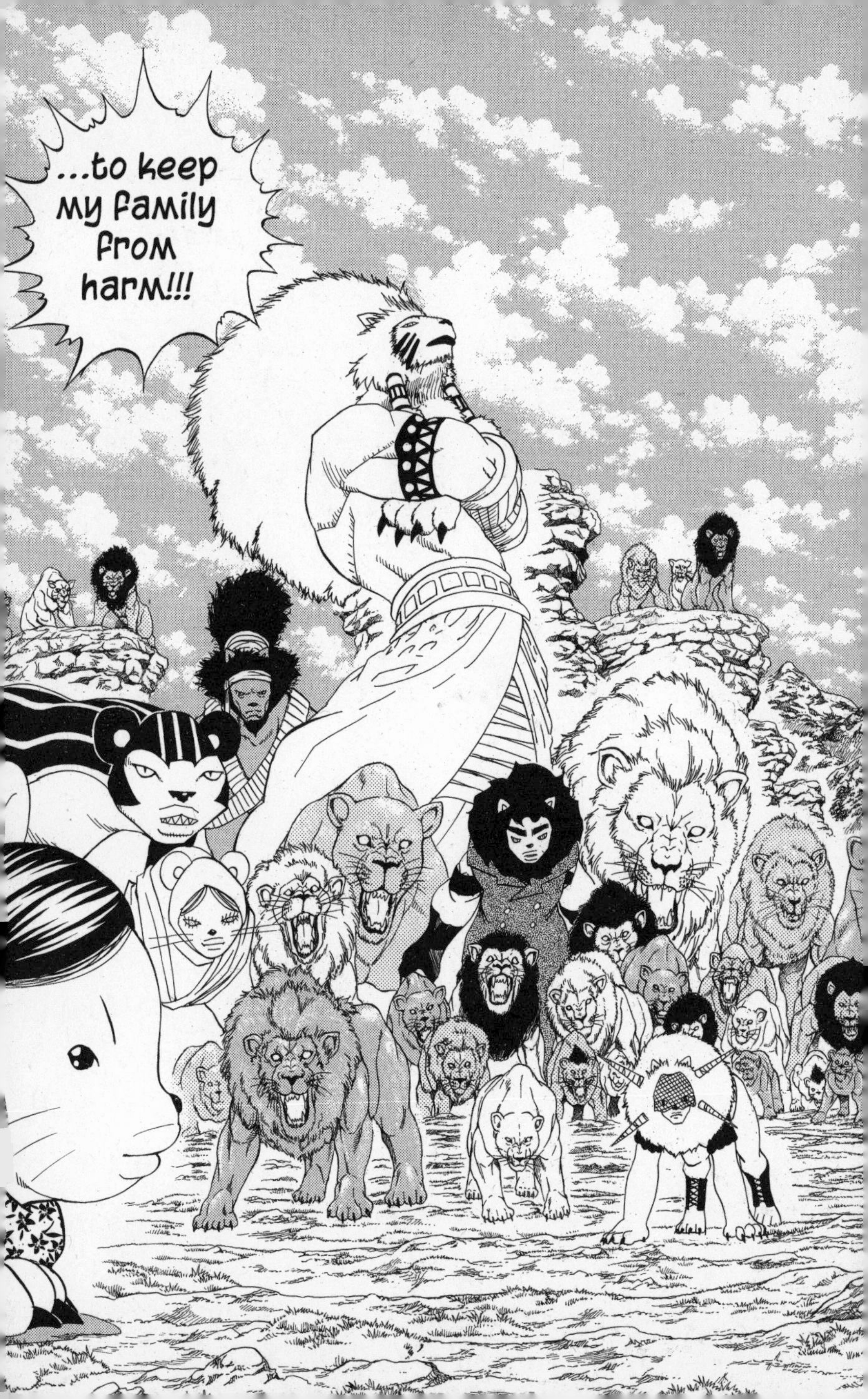
...to keep my family from harm!!!

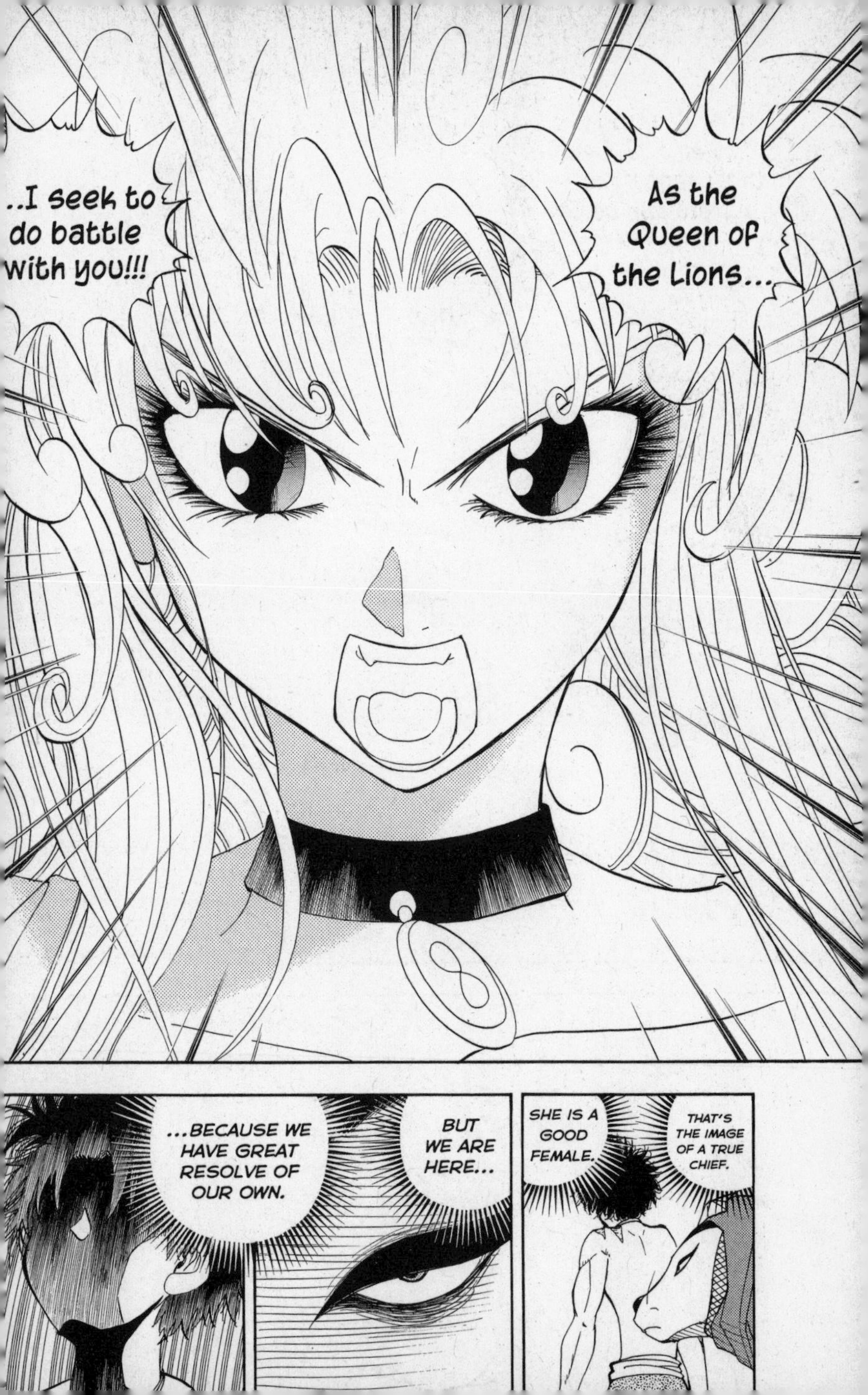
As the Queen of the Lions...
..I seek to do battle with you!!!
THAT'S THE IMAGE OF A TRUE CHIEF.
SHE IS A GOOD FEMALE.
BUT WE ARE HERE...
...BECAUSE WE HAVE GREAT RESOLVE OF OUR OWN.

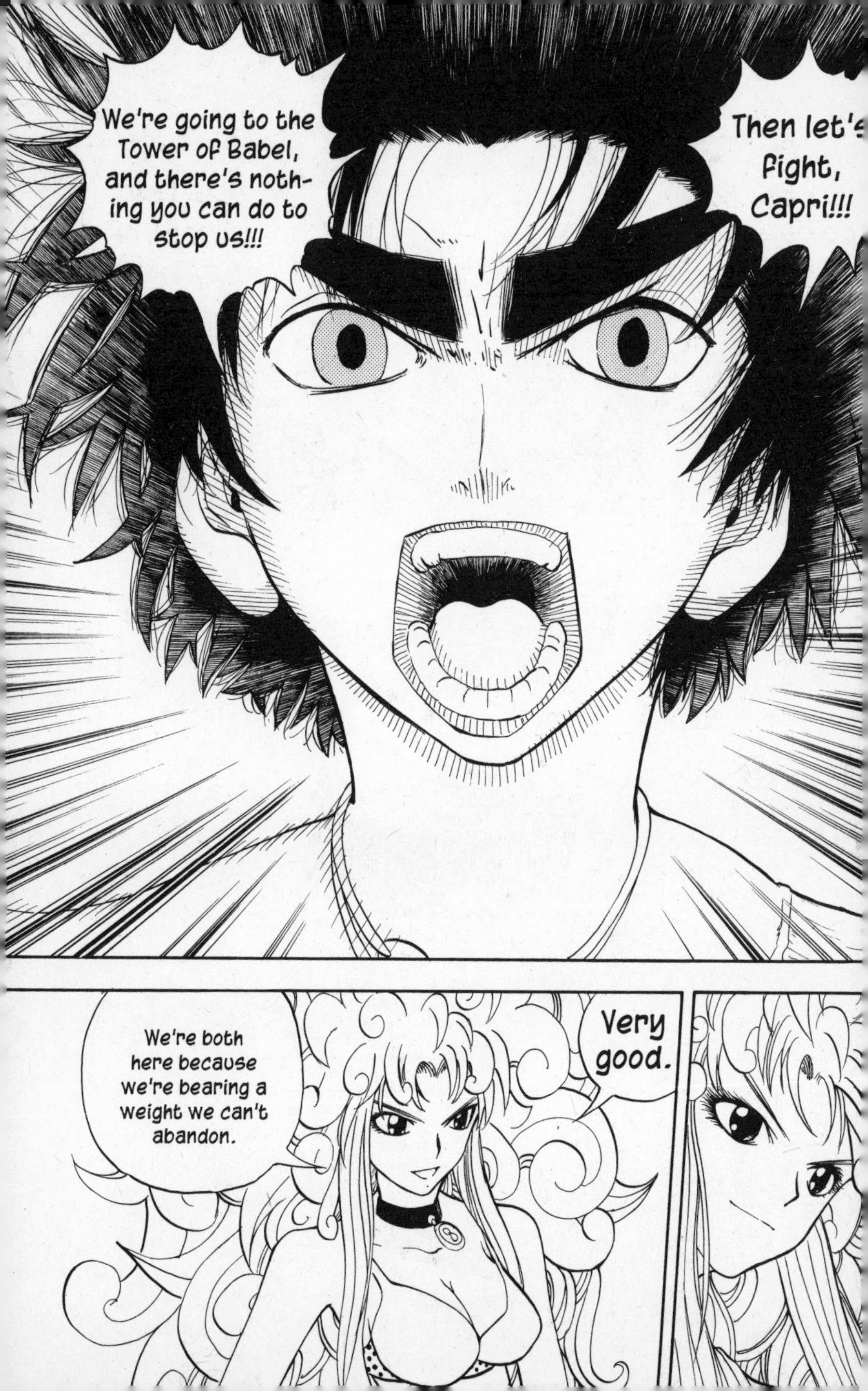
Then let's fight, Capri!!!
We're going to the Tower of Babel, and there's nothing you can do to stop us!!!
Very good.
We're both here because we're bearing a weight we can't abandon.

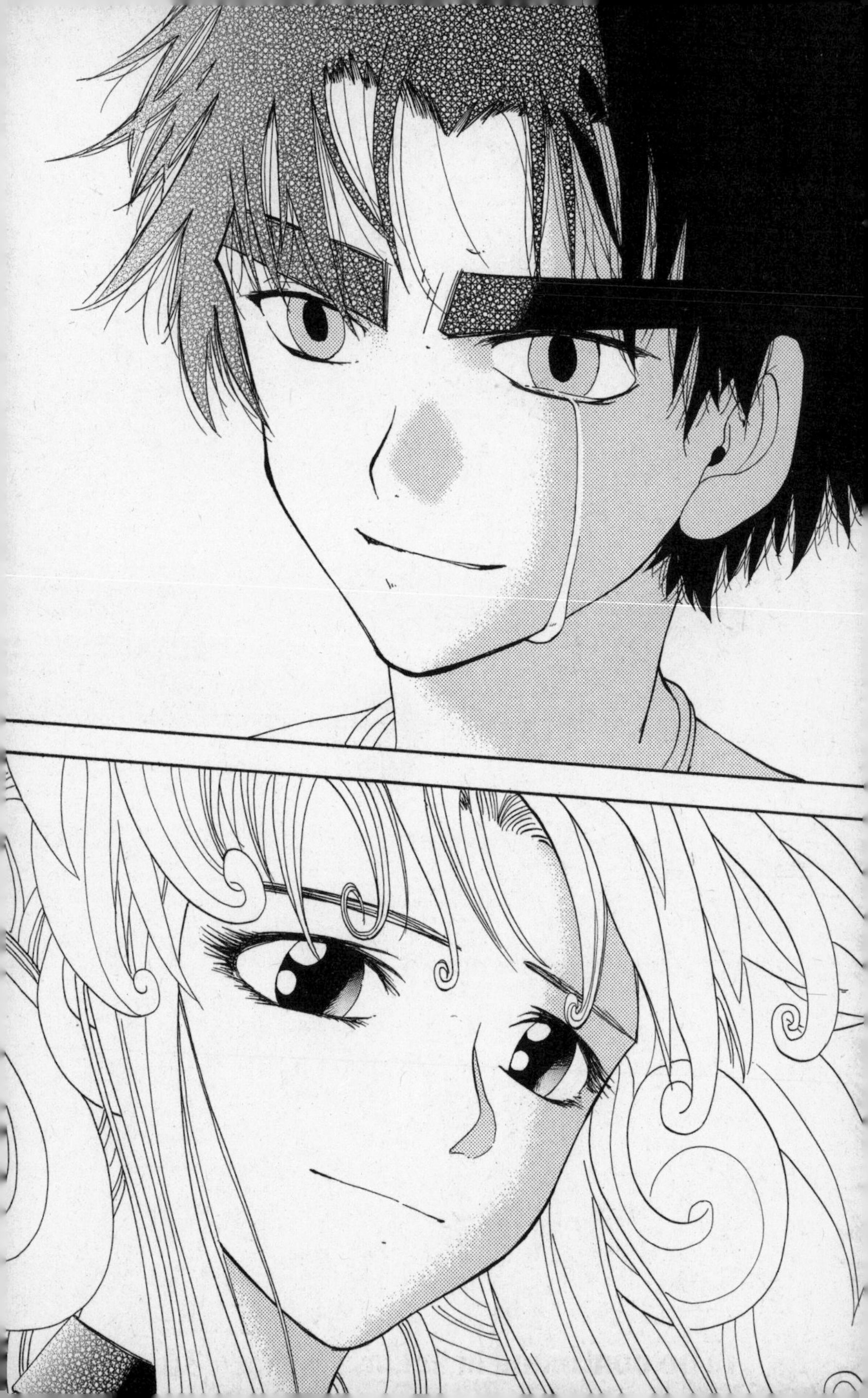

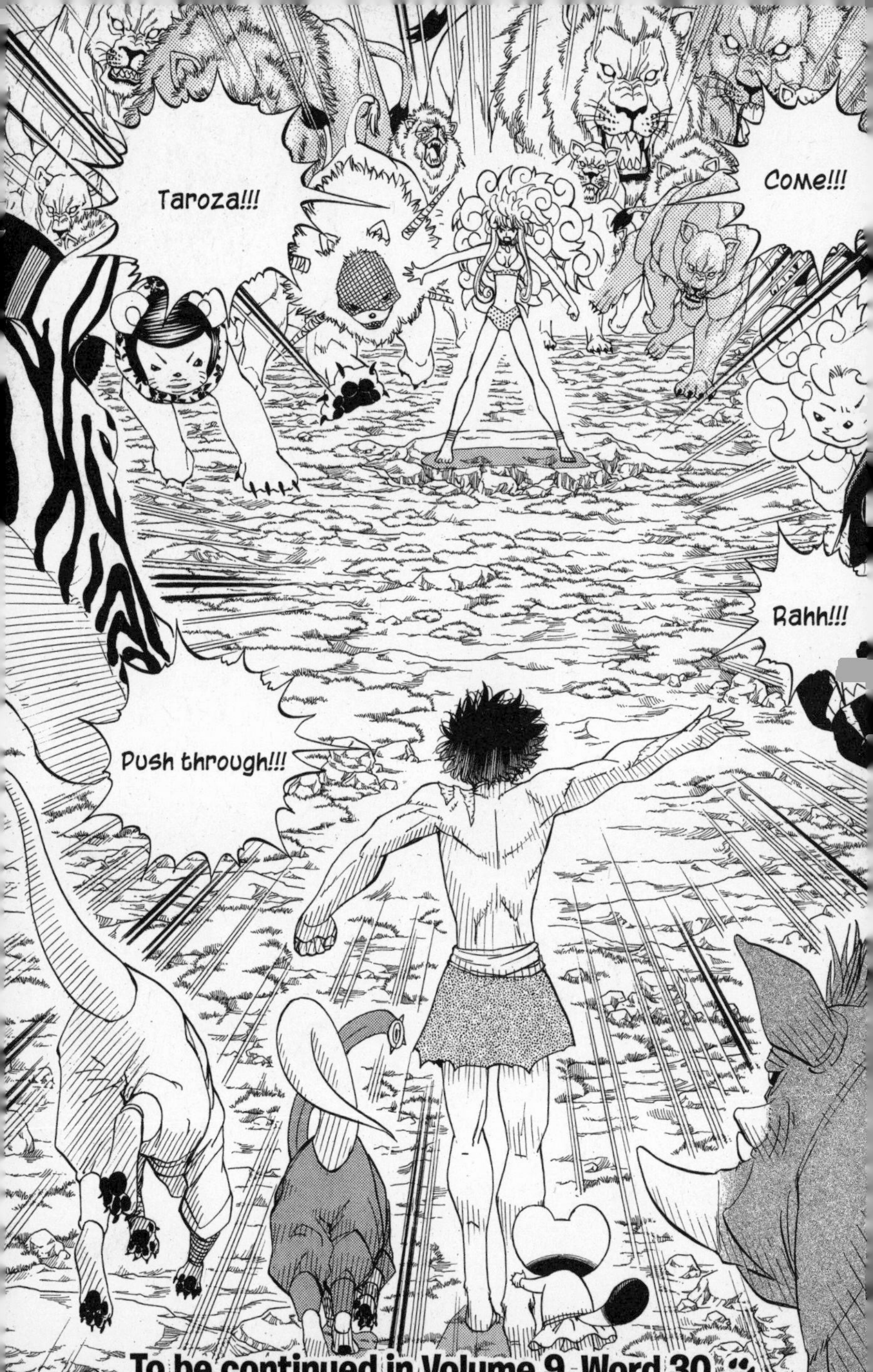
Come!!!
Taroza!!!
Rahh!!!
Push through!!!

To be continued in Volume 9, Word 30

The first chapter of this volume (Word 26) was the hardest chapter I've ever drawn in my career as a professional, including Zatch Bell!!

Makoto Raiku

A Kodansha Comics Trade Paperback Original.

Animal Land volume 8 copyright © 2012 Makoto Raiku
English translation copyright © 2013 Makoto Raiku

Published in the United States by Kodansha Comics, an imprint of Kodansha USA Publishing, LLC, New York.

Publication rights for this English edition arranged through Kodansha Ltd., Tokyo.

First published in Japan in 2012 by Kodansha Ltd., Tokyo, as *Doubutsu no Kuni*, volume 8.

ISBN 978-1-61262-250-7

Printed in the United States of America.

www.kodanshacomics.com

9 8 7 6 5 4 3 2 1

Translator: Stephen Paul
Lettering: Kiyoko Shiromasa

TOMARE!
STOP

You're going the wrong way!

Manga is a completely different type of reading experience.

To start at the beginning, Go to the end! DISCARDED

That's right! Authentic manga is read the traditional Japanese way—from right to left, exactly the opposite of how American books are read. It's easy to follow: Just go to the other end of the book and read each page—and each panel—from right side to left side, starting at the top right. Now you're experiencing manga as it was meant to be!